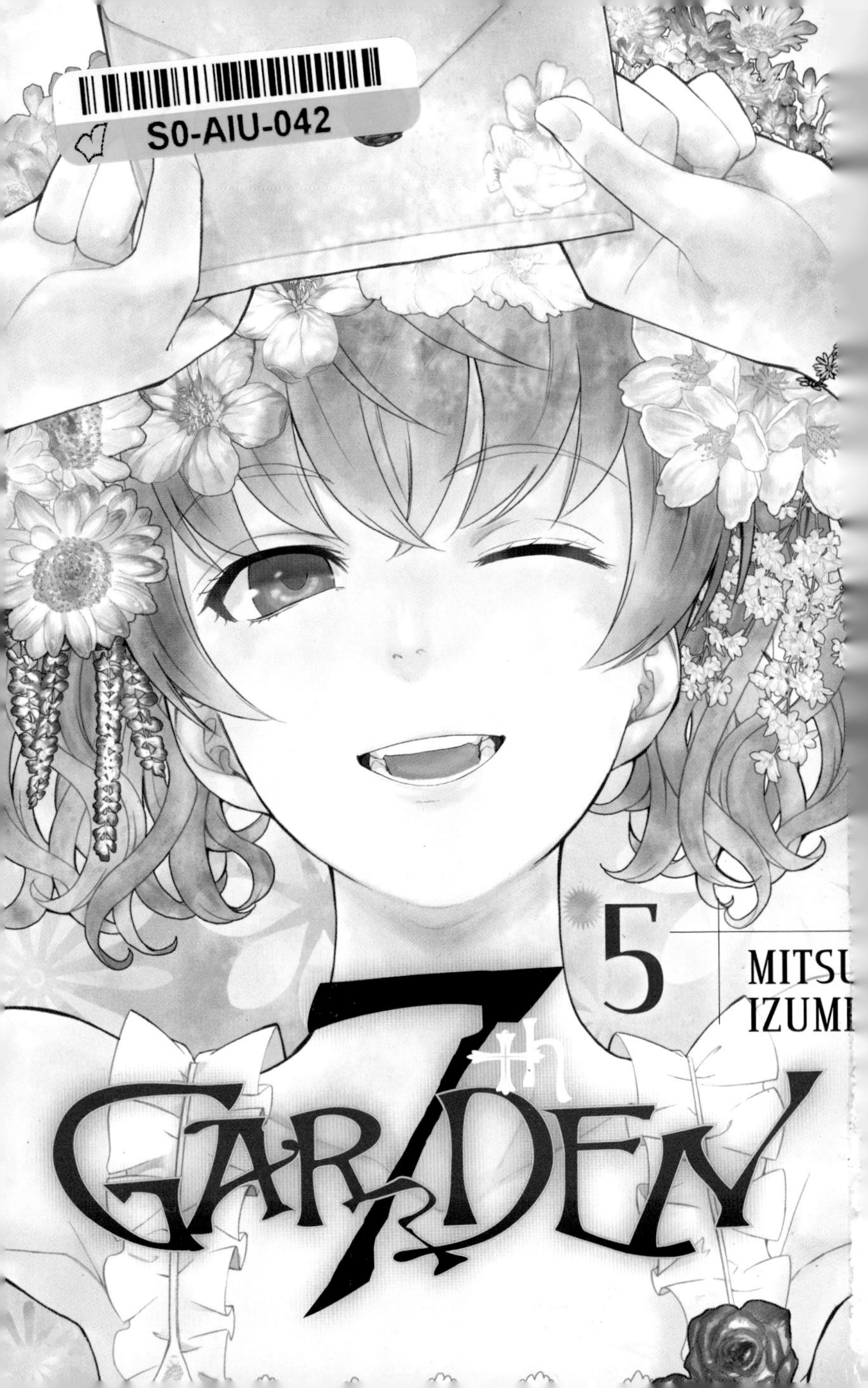
S0-AIU-042
5
MITSU
IZUMI
7th GARDEN

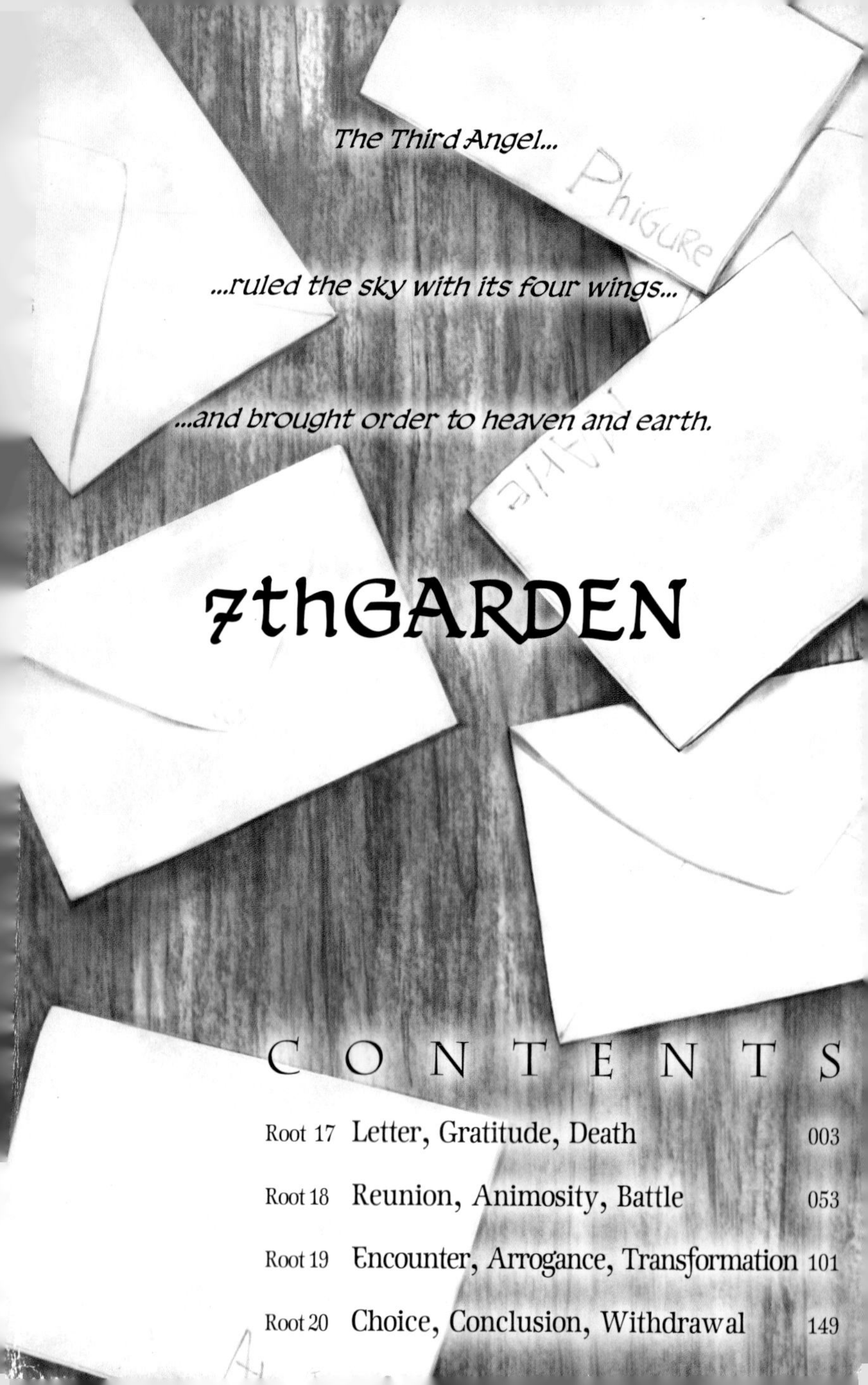
Phigure

The Third Angel...

...ruled the sky with its four wings...

...and brought order to heaven and earth.

7thGARDEN

CONTENTS

root.17

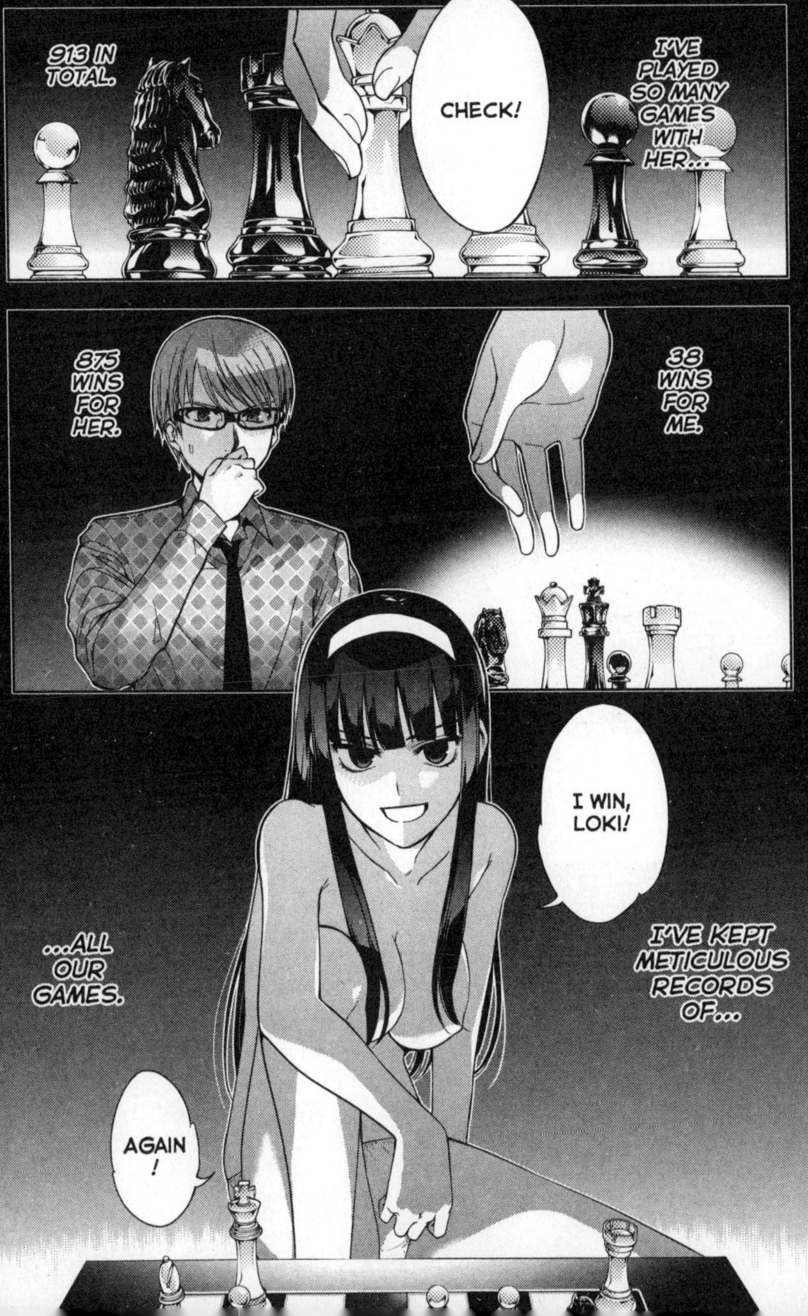
I'VE PLAYED SO MANY GAMES WITH HER...
CHECK!
913 IN TOTAL.
38 WINS FOR ME.
875 WINS FOR HER.
I WIN, LOKI!
I'VE KEPT METICULOUS RECORDS OF...
...ALL OUR GAMES.
AGAIN!

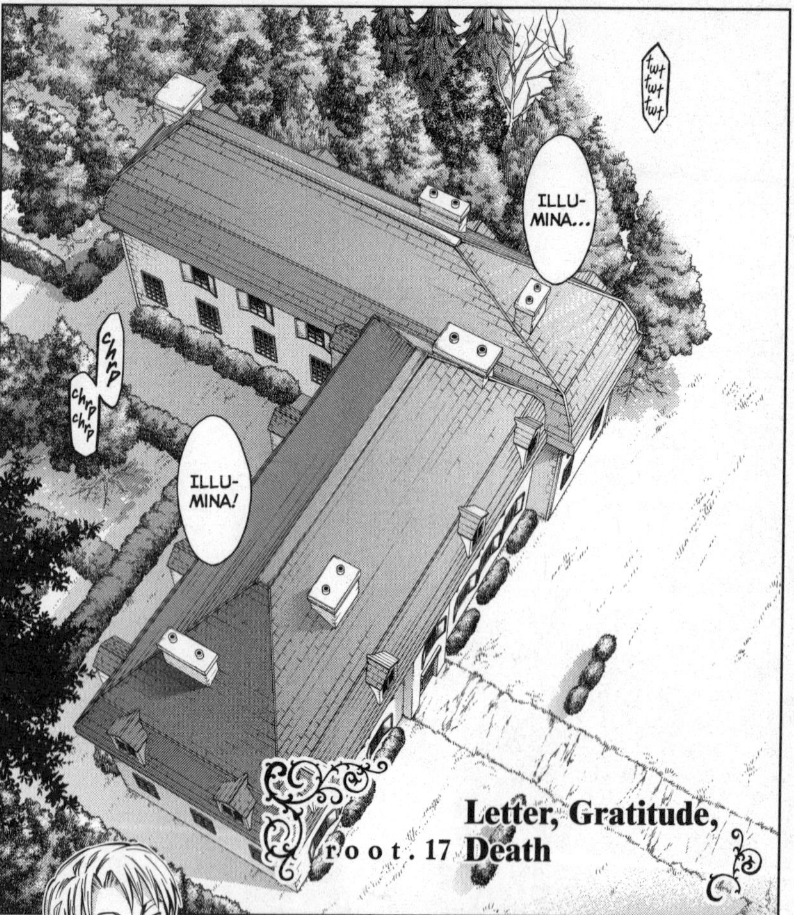
twt twt twt
ILLU-MINA...
chrp chrp chrp
ILLU-MINA!
root. 17 Letter, Gratitude, Death

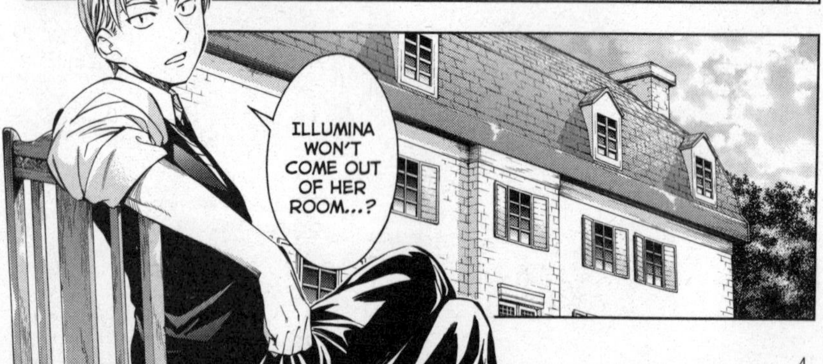
ILLUMINA WON'T COME OUT OF HER ROOM...?

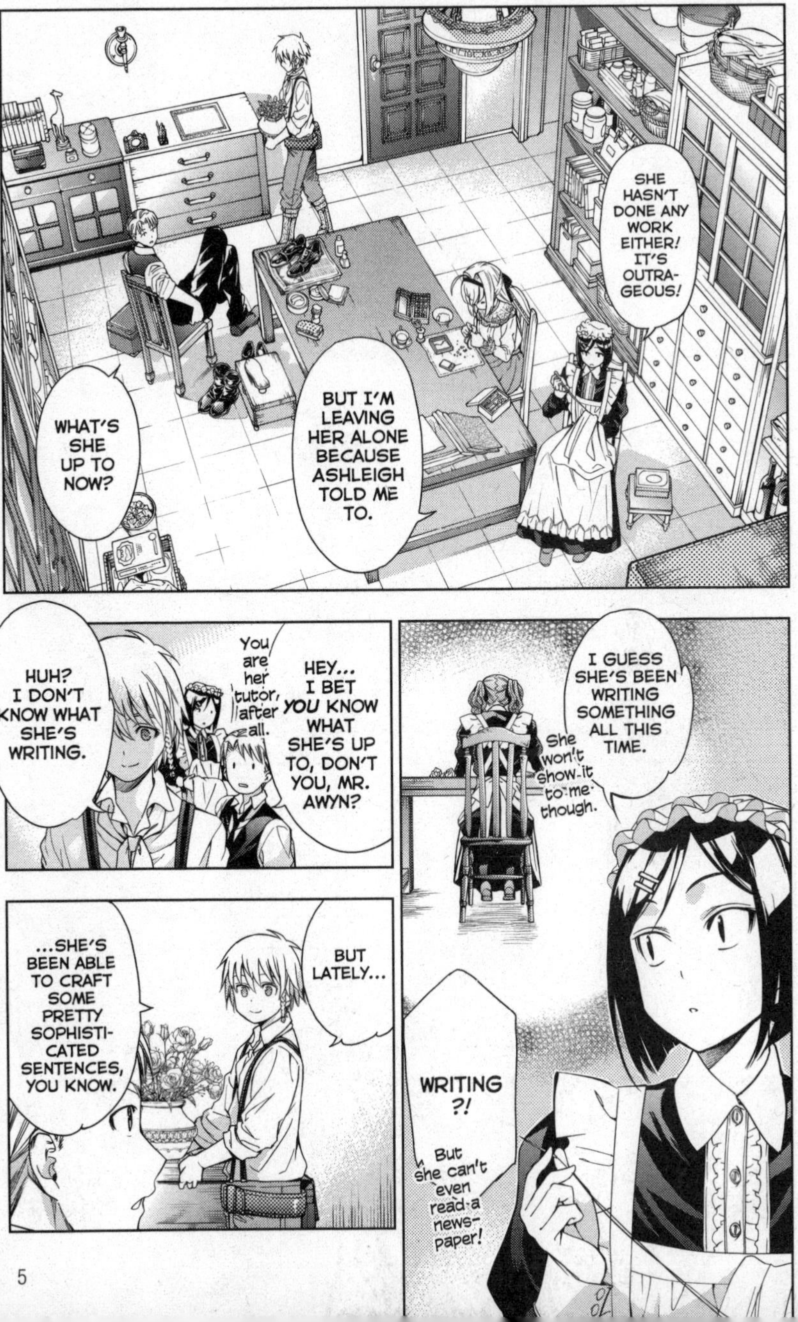
SHE HASN'T DONE ANY WORK EITHER! IT'S OUTRAGEOUS!
BUT I'M LEAVING HER ALONE BECAUSE ASHLEIGH TOLD ME TO.
WHAT'S SHE UP TO NOW?
I GUESS SHE'S BEEN WRITING SOMETHING ALL THIS TIME.
She won't show it to me though.
WRITING ?!
But she can't even read a news-paper!
HEY... I BET *YOU* KNOW WHAT SHE'S UP TO, DON'T YOU, MR. AWYN?
You are her tutor, after all.
HUH? I DON'T KNOW WHAT SHE'S WRITING.
BUT LATELY...
...SHE'S BEEN ABLE TO CRAFT SOME PRETTY SOPHISTI-CATED SENTENCES, YOU KNOW.

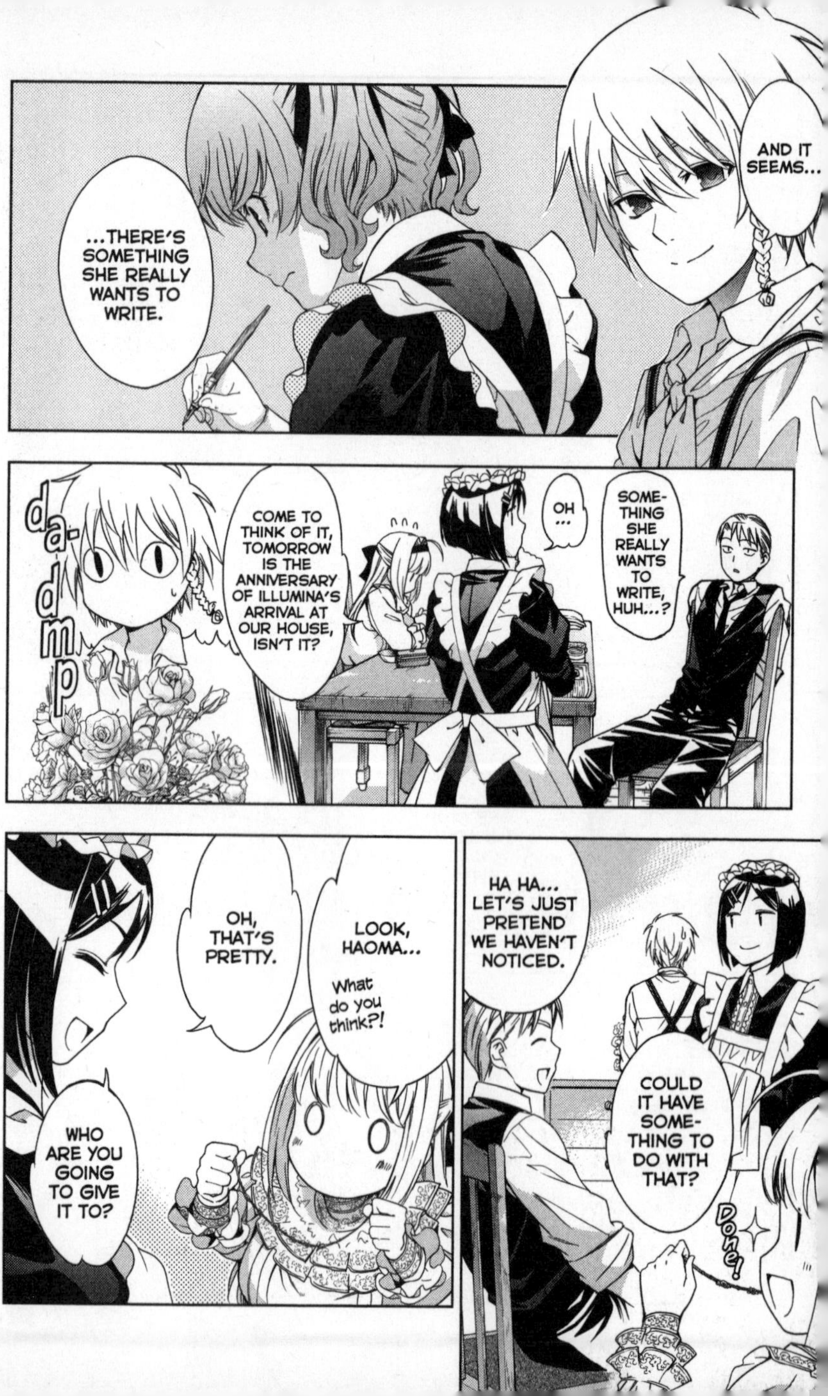
AND IT SEEMS...
...THERE'S SOMETHING SHE REALLY WANTS TO WRITE.
SOME-THING SHE REALLY WANTS TO WRITE, HUH...?
OH ...
COME TO THINK OF IT, TOMORROW IS THE ANNIVERSARY OF ILLUMINA'S ARRIVAL AT OUR HOUSE, ISN'T IT?
da-dump
HA HA... LET'S JUST PRETEND WE HAVEN'T NOTICED.
COULD IT HAVE SOME-THING TO DO WITH THAT?
Done!
LOOK, HAOMA...
What do you think?!
OH, THAT'S PRETTY.
WHO ARE YOU GOING TO GIVE IT TO?

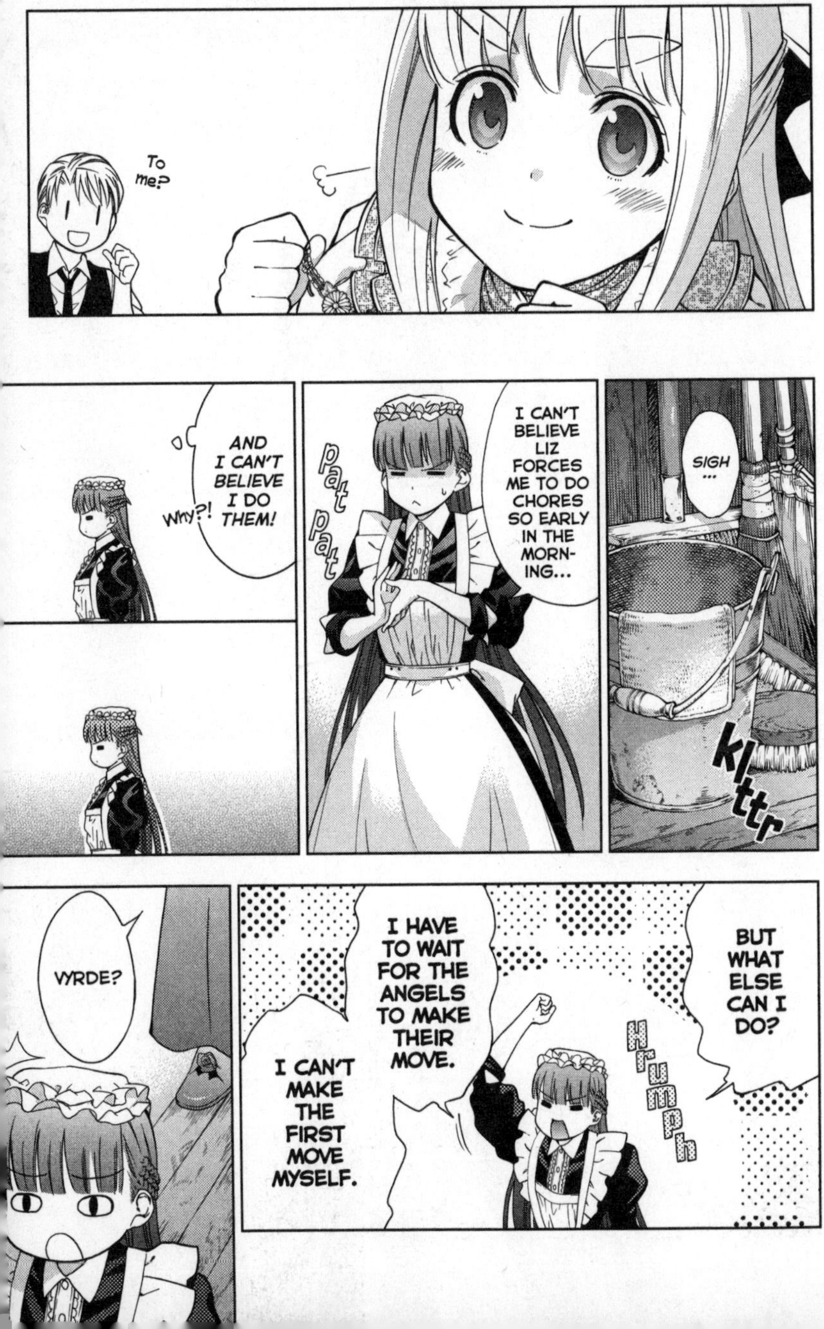
To me?
SIGH...
klttr
pat pat
I CAN'T BELIEVE LIZ FORCES ME TO DO CHORES SO EARLY IN THE MORNING...
AND I CAN'T BELIEVE I DO THEM!
Why?!
BUT WHAT ELSE CAN I DO?
Hrumph
I HAVE TO WAIT FOR THE ANGELS TO MAKE THEIR MOVE.
I CAN'T MAKE THE FIRST MOVE MYSELF.
VYRDE?

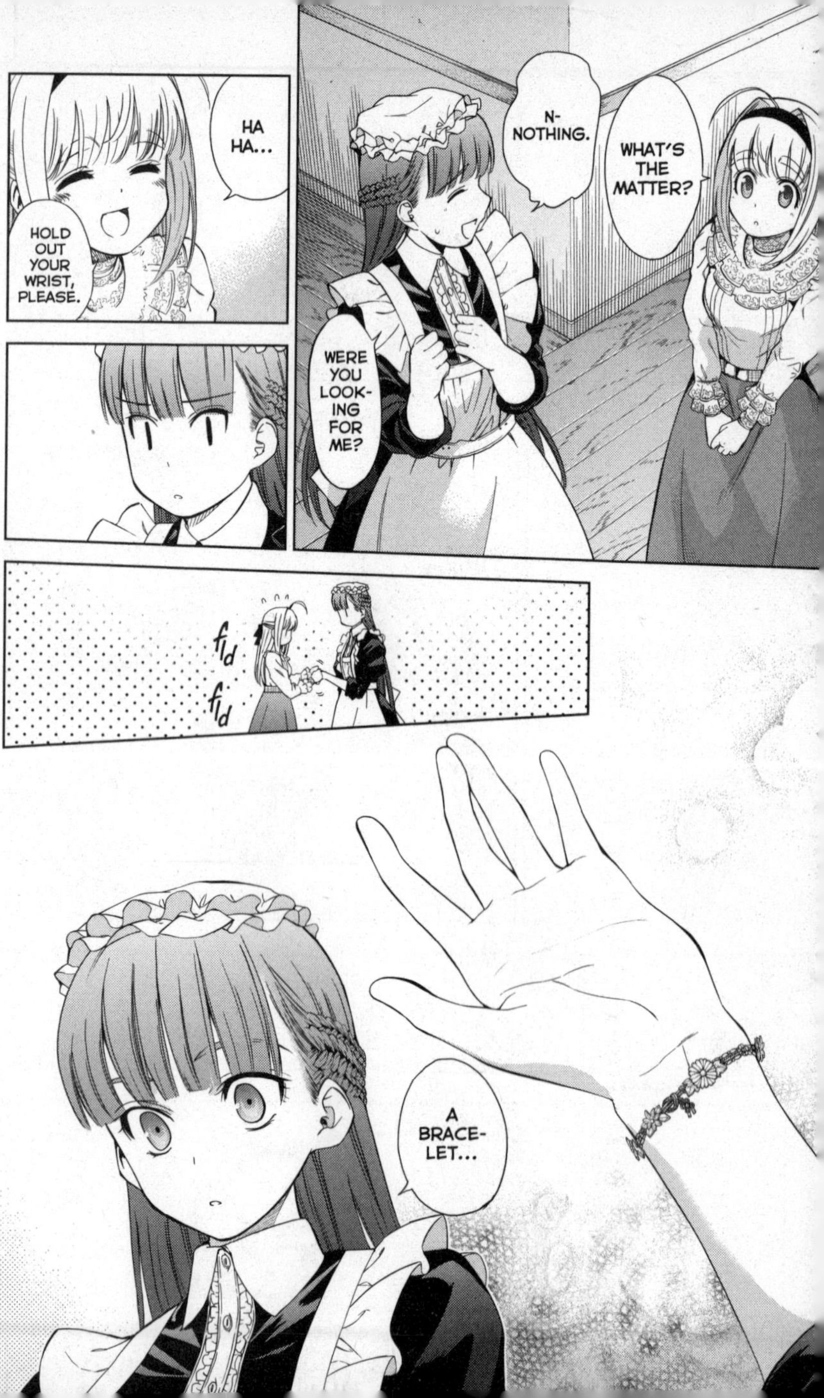
WHAT'S THE MATTER?
N-NOTHING.
WERE YOU LOOKING FOR ME?
HA HA...
HOLD OUT YOUR WRIST, PLEASE.
fid fid
A BRACE-LET...

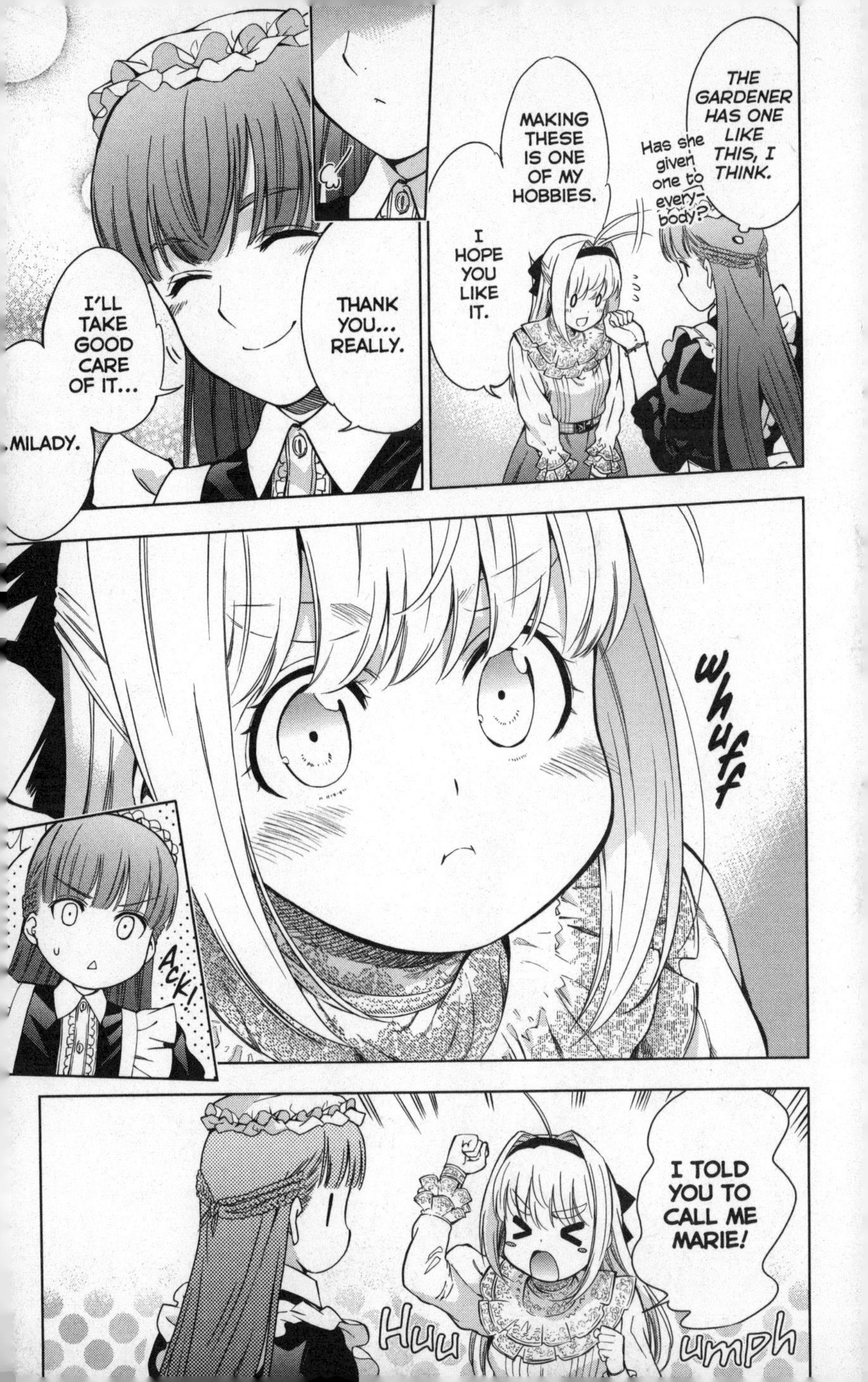

THE GARDENER HAS ONE LIKE THIS, I THINK.
Has she given one to every-body?
MAKING THESE IS ONE OF MY HOBBIES.
I HOPE YOU LIKE IT.
THANK YOU... REALLY.
I'LL TAKE GOOD CARE OF IT...
...MILADY.
whuff
ACK!
I TOLD YOU TO CALL ME MARIE!
Huuumph

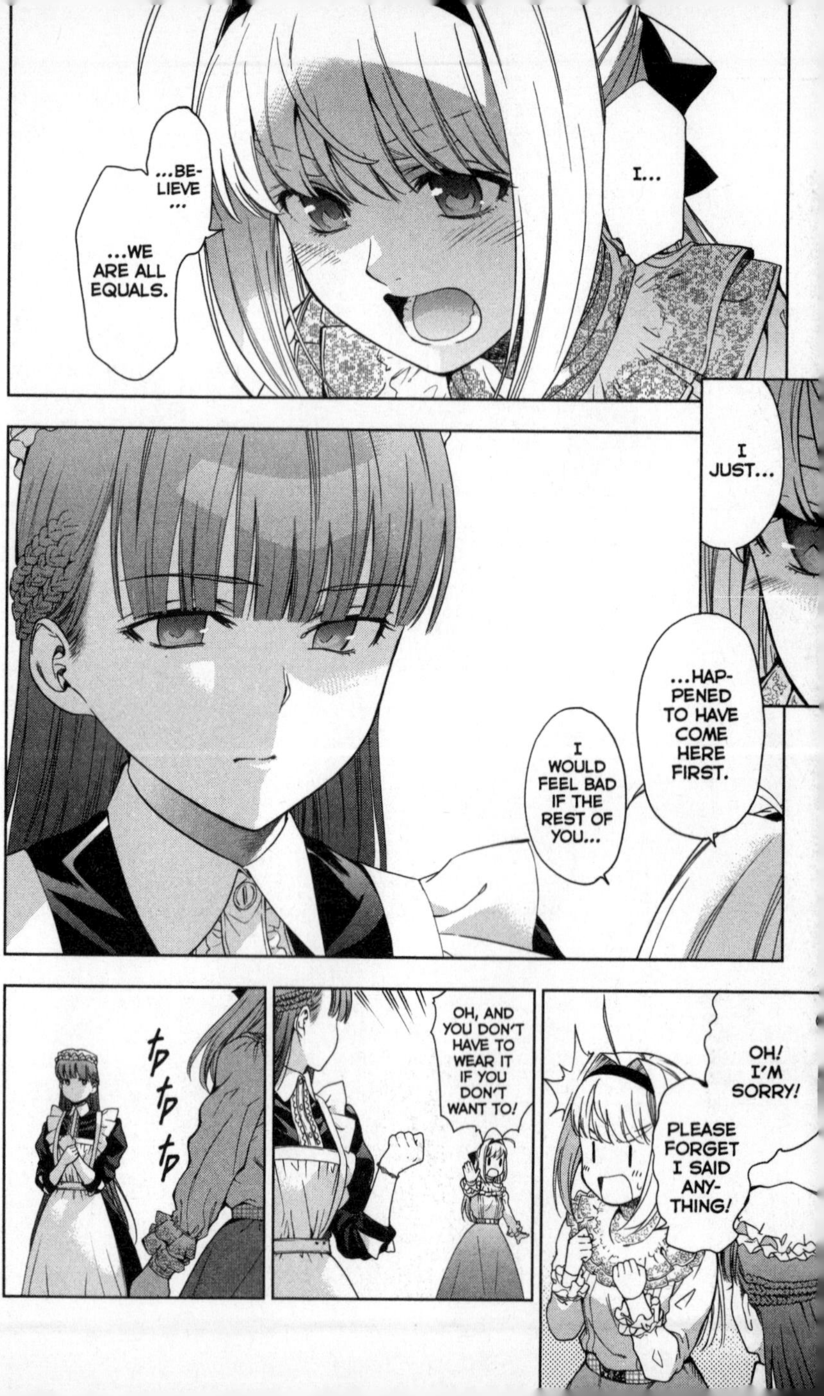
I...
...BE- LIEVE ...
...WE ARE ALL EQUALS.
I JUST...
...HAP- PENED TO HAVE COME HERE FIRST.
I WOULD FEEL BAD IF THE REST OF YOU...
OH! I'M SORRY!
PLEASE FORGET I SAID ANY- THING!
OH, AND YOU DON'T HAVE TO WEAR IT IF YOU DON'T WANT TO!

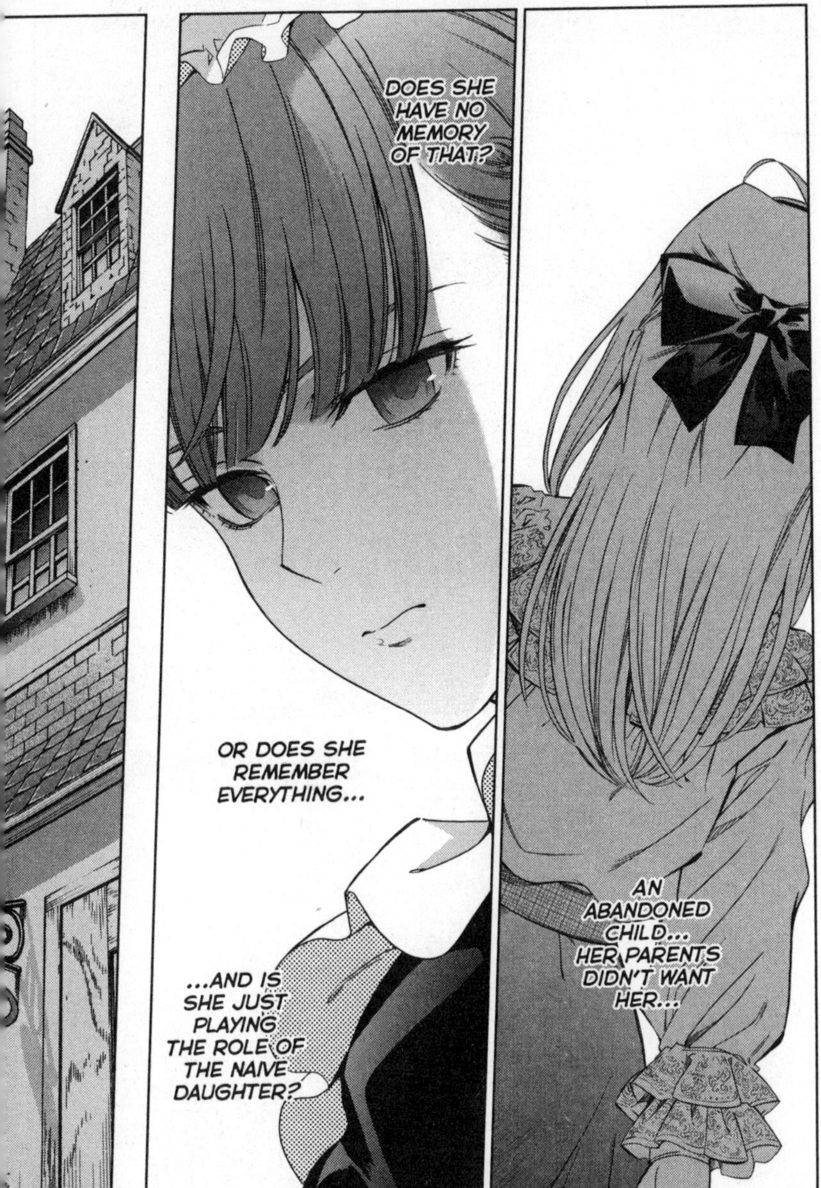
AN ABANDONED CHILD... HER PARENTS DIDN'T WANT HER...
DOES SHE HAVE NO MEMORY OF THAT?
OR DOES SHE REMEMBER EVERYTHING...
...AND IS SHE JUST PLAYING THE ROLE OF THE NAIVE DAUGHTER?

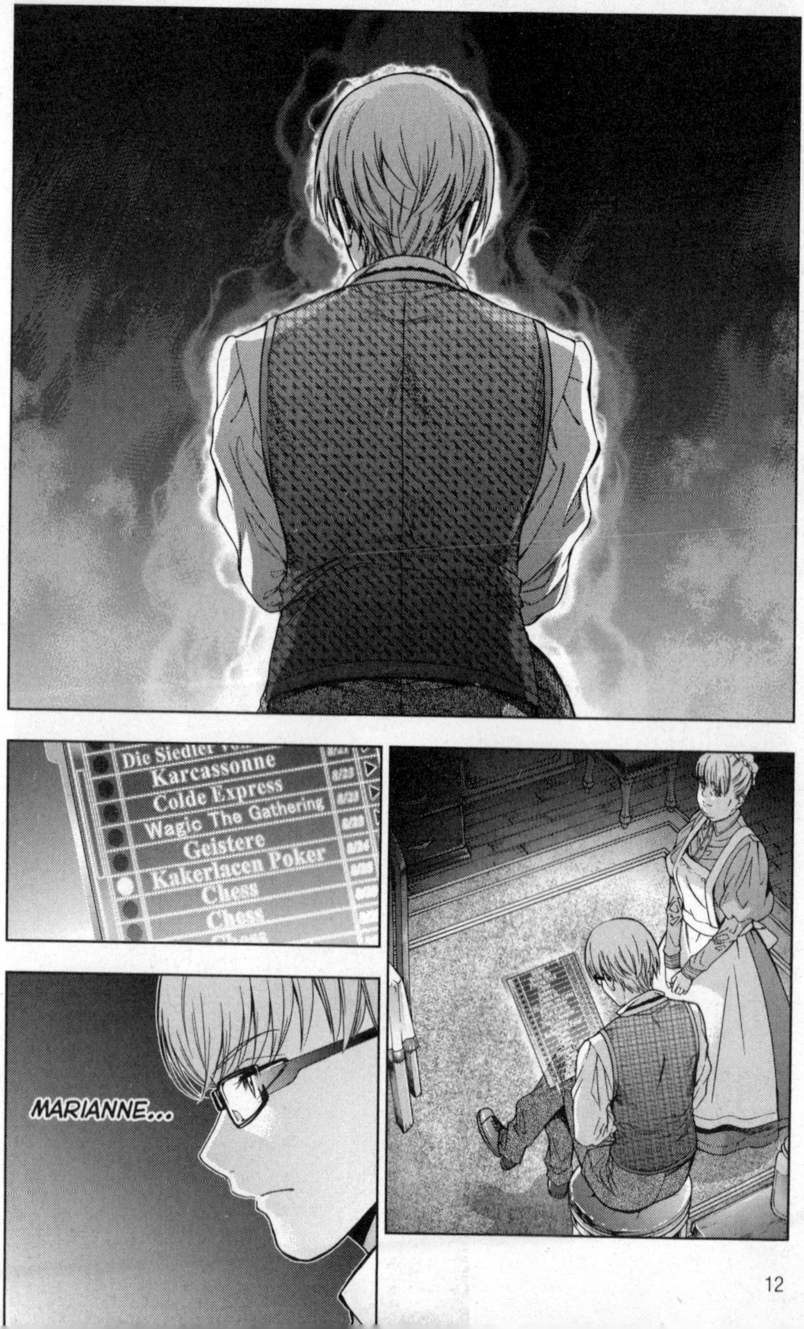

Die Siedler
Karcassonne
Colde Express
Wagic The Gathering
Geistere
Kakerlacen Poker
Chess
Chess
MARIANNE...

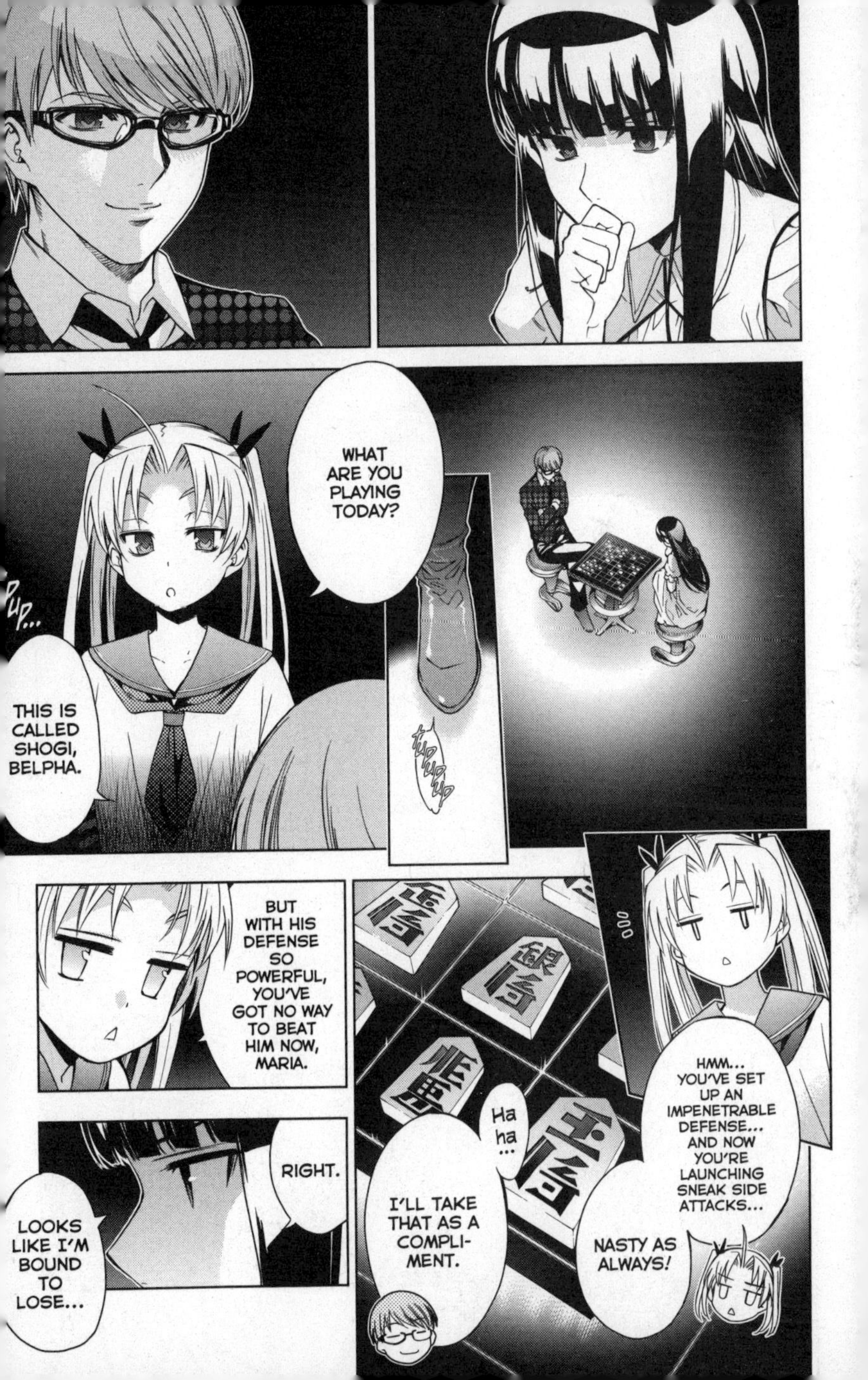
WHAT ARE YOU PLAYING TODAY?
PUP...
THIS IS CALLED SHOGI, BELPHA.
HMM... YOU'VE SET UP AN IMPENETRABLE DEFENSE... AND NOW YOU'RE LAUNCHING SNEAK SIDE ATTACKS...
NASTY AS ALWAYS!
Ha ha...
I'LL TAKE THAT AS A COMPLIMENT.
BUT WITH HIS DEFENSE SO POWERFUL, YOU'VE GOT NO WAY TO BEAT HIM NOW, MARIA.
RIGHT.
LOOKS LIKE I'M BOUND TO LOSE...

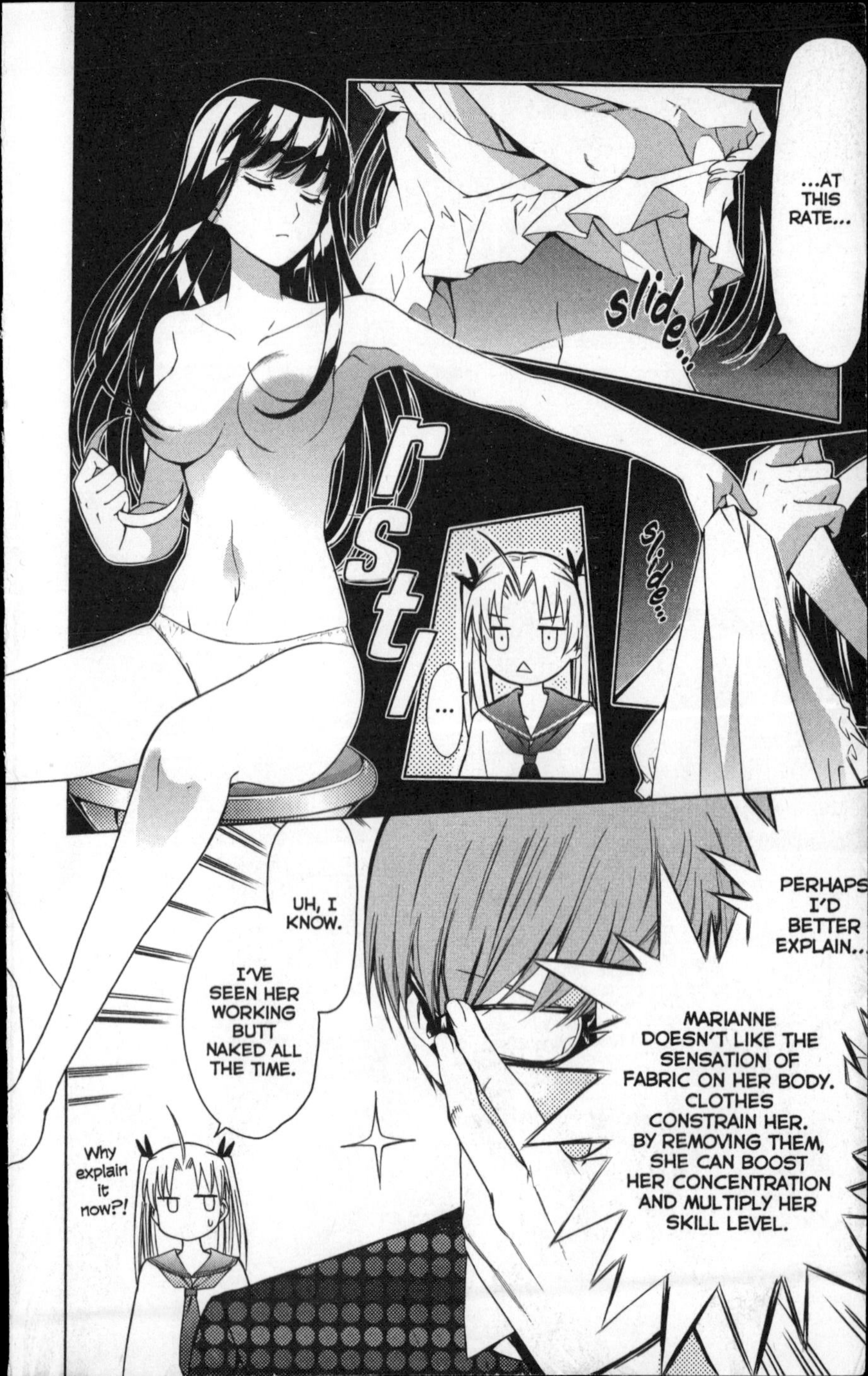
...AT THIS RATE...
slide...
slide...
...
rstl
PERHAPS I'D BETTER EXPLAIN...
MARIANNE DOESN'T LIKE THE SENSATION OF FABRIC ON HER BODY. CLOTHES CONSTRAIN HER. BY REMOVING THEM, SHE CAN BOOST HER CONCENTRATION AND MULTIPLY HER SKILL LEVEL.
UH, I KNOW.
I'VE SEEN HER WORKING BUTT NAKED ALL THE TIME.
Why explain it now?!

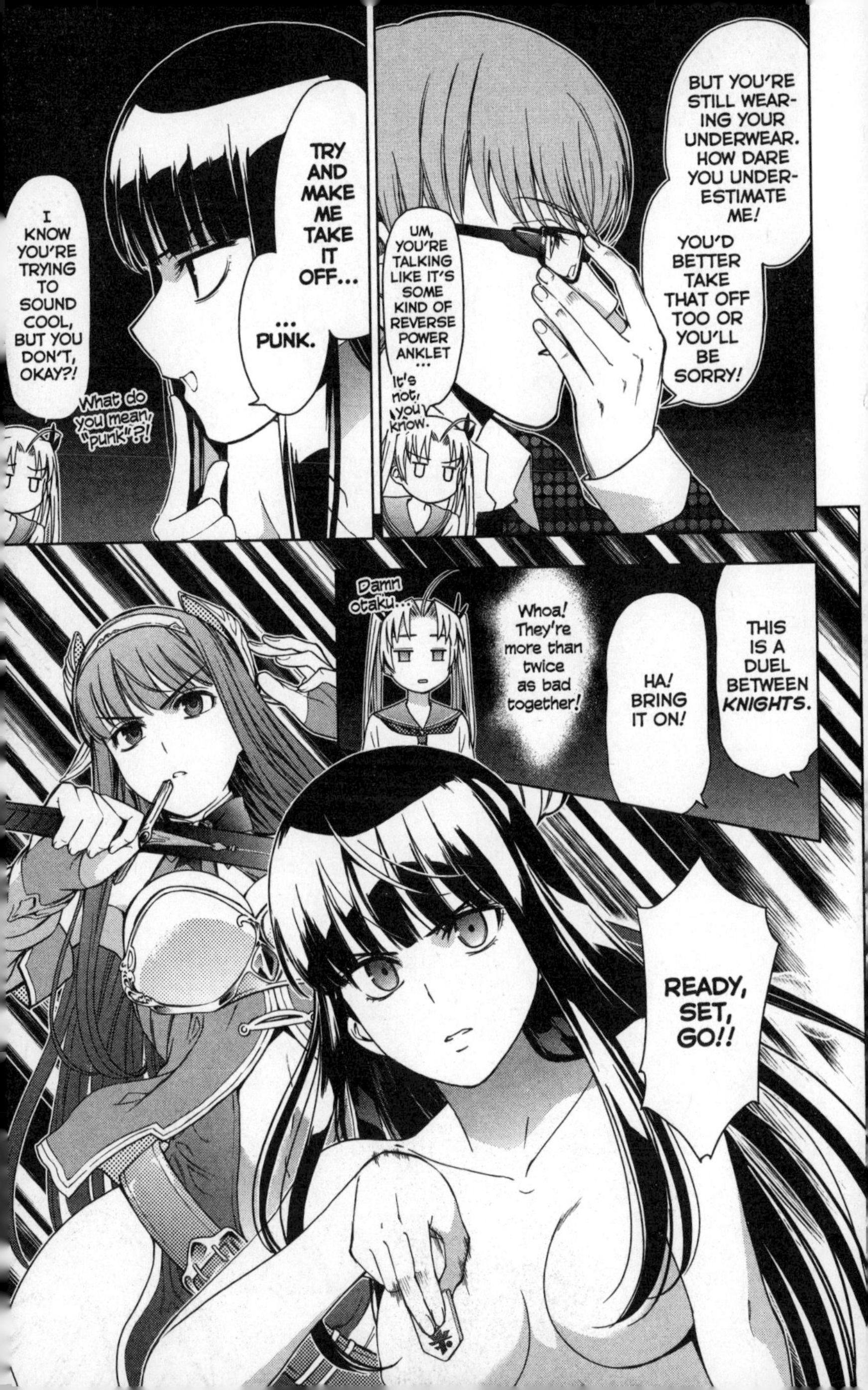
BUT YOU'RE STILL WEAR-ING YOUR UNDERWEAR. HOW DARE YOU UNDER-ESTIMATE ME!
YOU'D BETTER TAKE THAT OFF TOO OR YOU'LL BE SORRY!
UM, YOU'RE TALKING LIKE IT'S SOME KIND OF REVERSE POWER ANKLET...
It's not, you know.
TRY AND MAKE ME TAKE IT OFF...
... PUNK.
I KNOW YOU'RE TRYING TO SOUND COOL, BUT YOU DON'T, OKAY?!
What do you mean, "punk"?!
THIS IS A DUEL BETWEEN *KNIGHTS*.
HA! BRING IT ON!
Whoa! They're more than twice as bad together!
Damn otaku...
READY, SET, GO!!

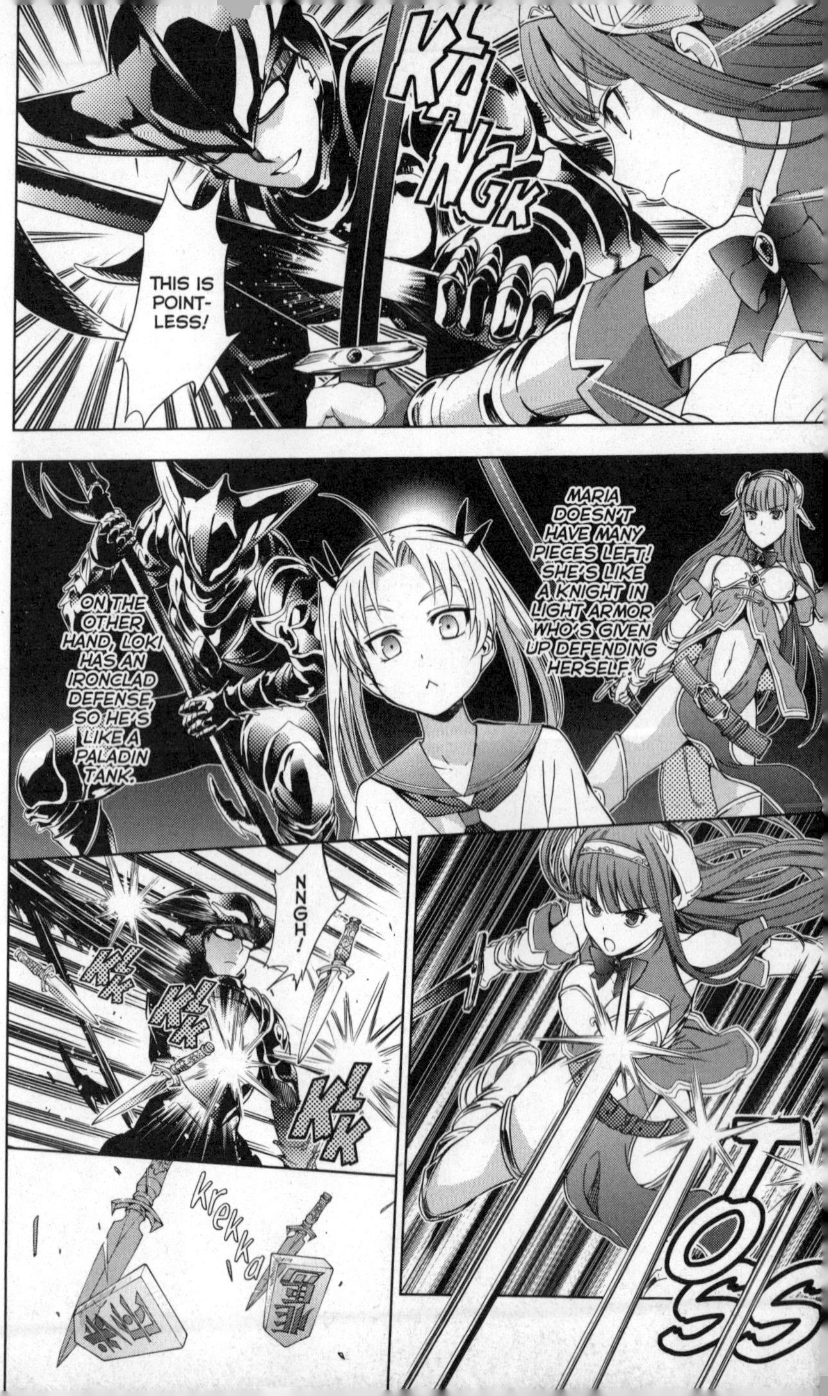
KANGK
THIS IS POINT-LESS!
MARIA DOESN'T HAVE MANY PIECES LEFT! SHE'S LIKE A KNIGHT IN LIGHT ARMOR WHO'S GIVEN UP DEFENDING HERSELF.
ON THE OTHER HAND, LOKI HAS AN IRONCLAD DEFENSE, SO HE'S LIKE A PALADIN TANK.
TOSS
NNGH!
krekka

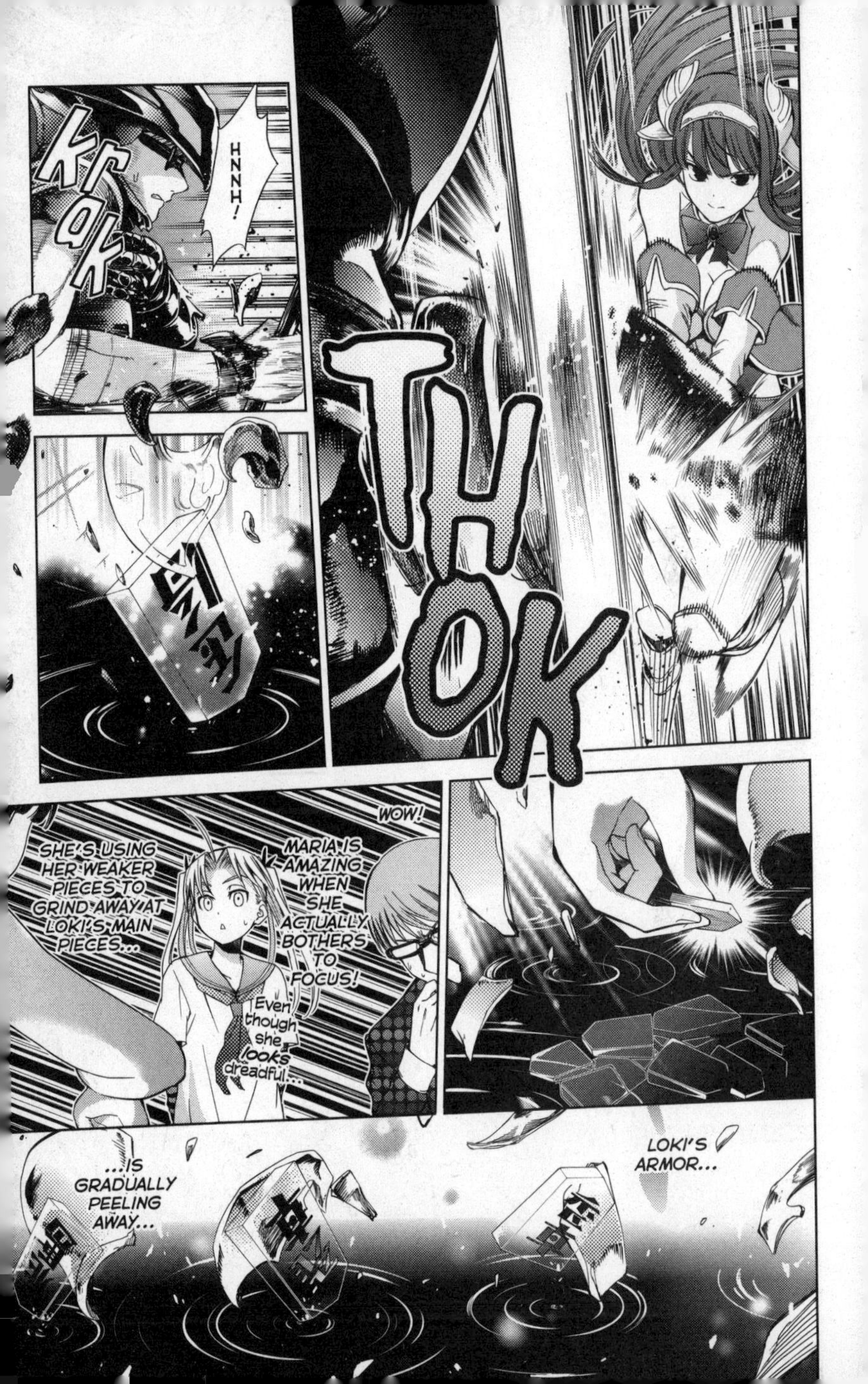
THOK
HNNH!
krrak
WOW!
MARIA IS AMAZING WHEN SHE ACTUALLY BOTHERS TO FOCUS!
SHE'S USING HER WEAKER PIECES TO GRIND AWAY AT LOKI'S MAIN PIECES...
Even though she looks dreadful...
LOKI'S ARMOR...
...IS GRADUALLY PEELING AWAY...

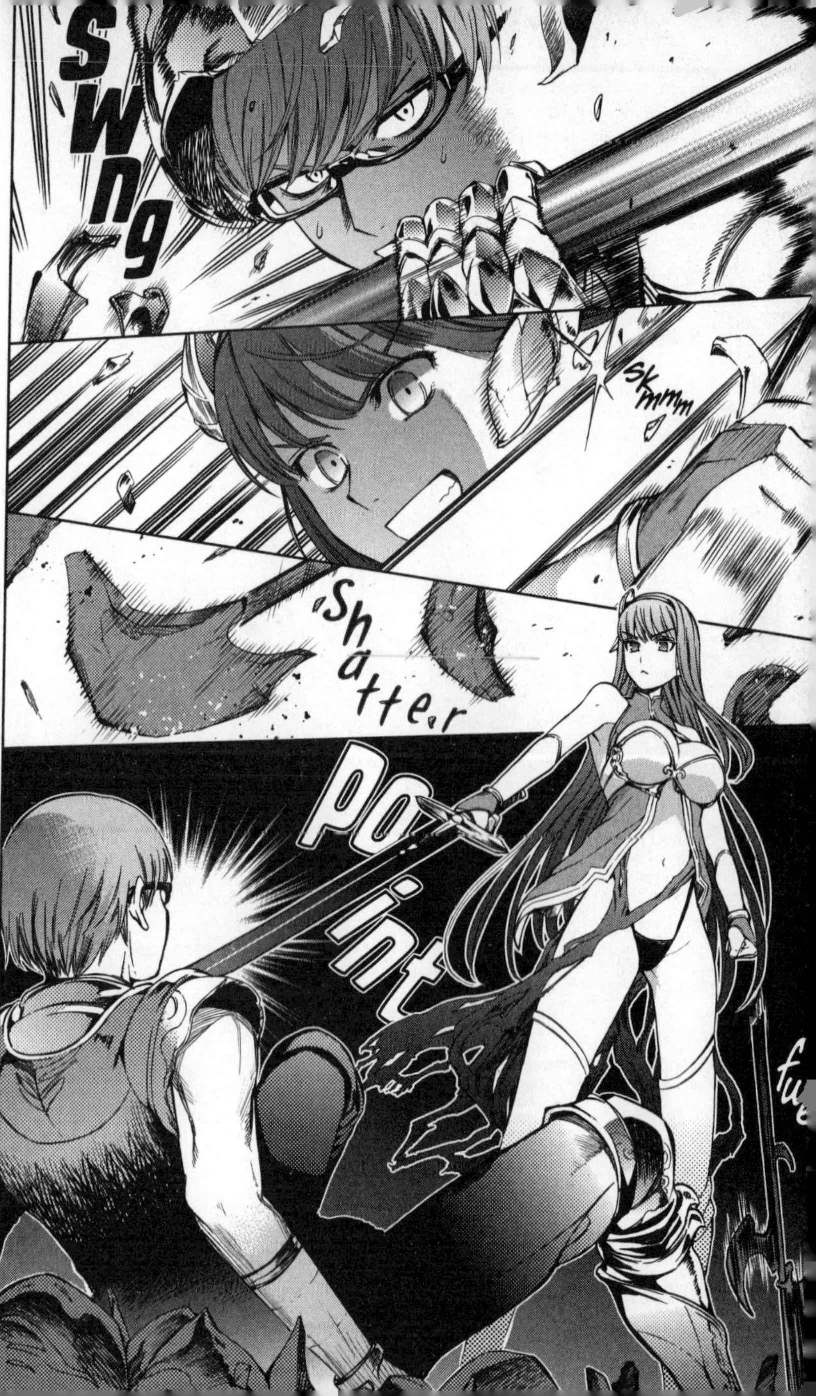
SWNG
SKMMM
Shatter
point

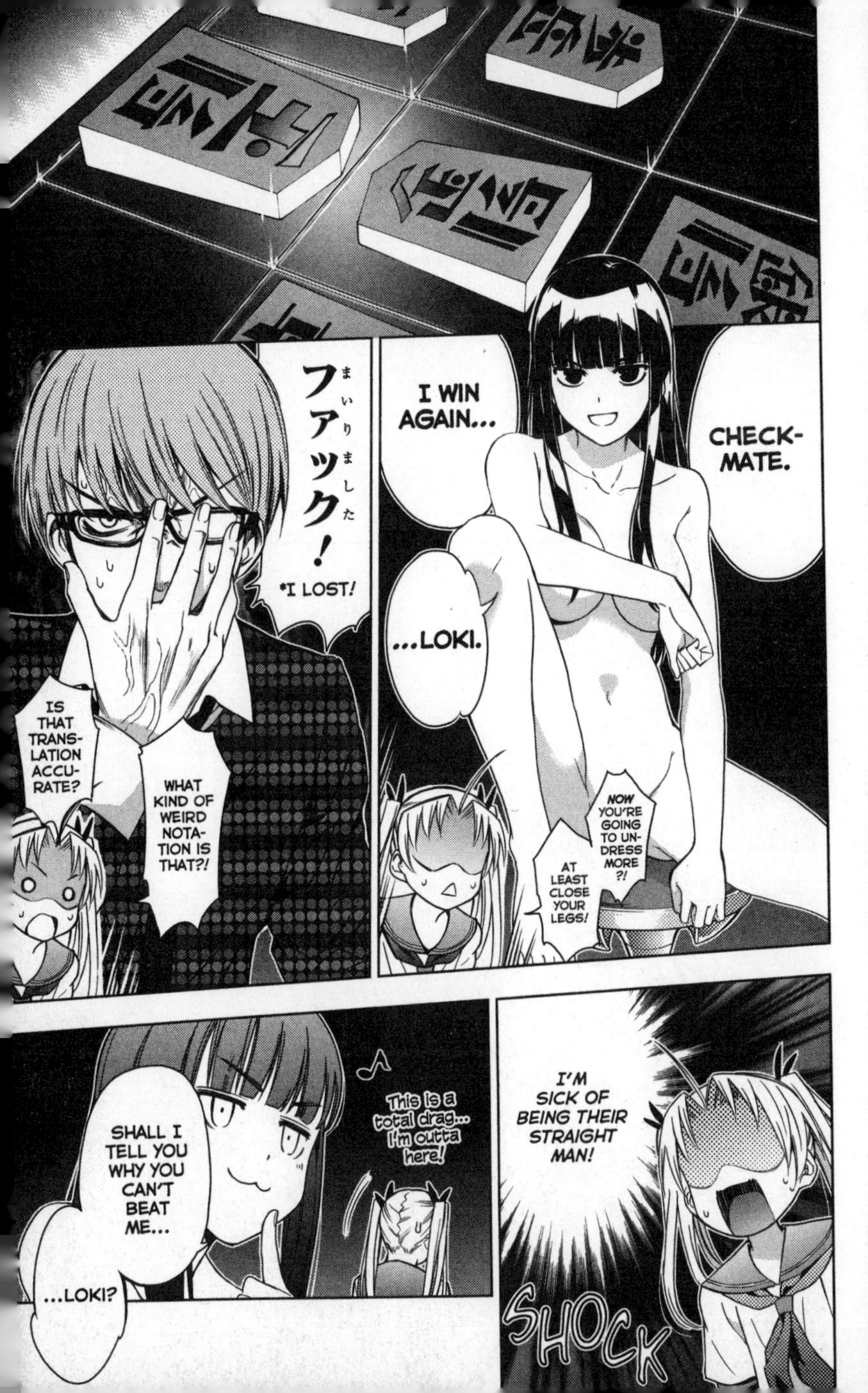
CHECK-MATE.
I WIN AGAIN...
...LOKI.
NOW YOU'RE GOING TO UNDRESS MORE?!
AT LEAST CLOSE YOUR LEGS!
ファック！(まいりました)
*I LOST!
WHAT KIND OF WEIRD NOTATION IS THAT?!
IS THAT TRANSLATION ACCURATE?
I'M SICK OF BEING THEIR STRAIGHT MAN!
SHOCK
This is a total drag... I'm outta here!
SHALL I TELL YOU WHY YOU CAN'T BEAT ME...
...LOKI?

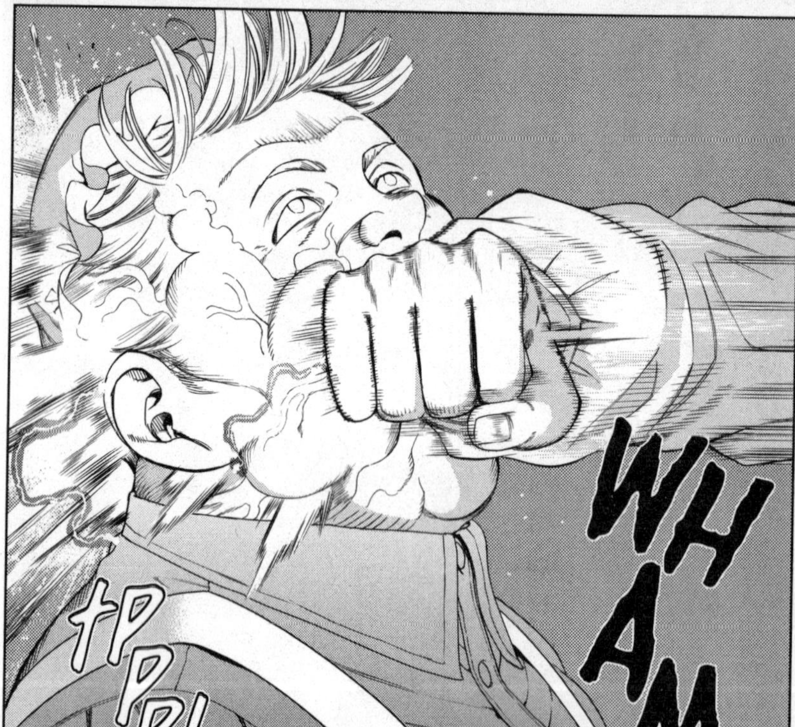
WHAM
tPPPI
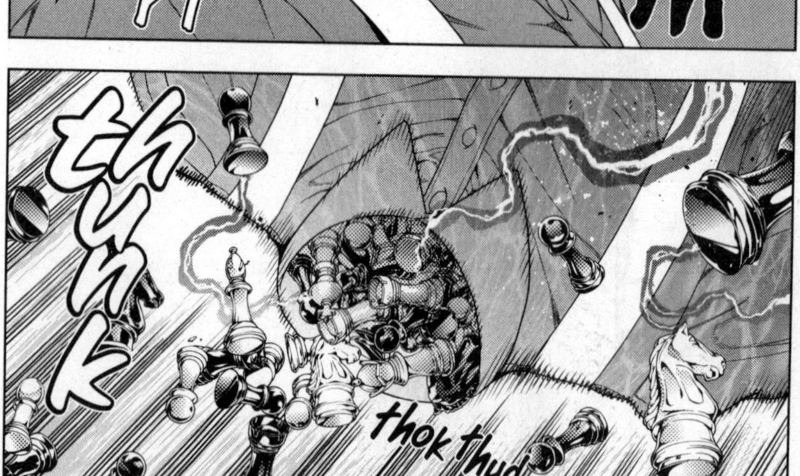
thunk
thok thud

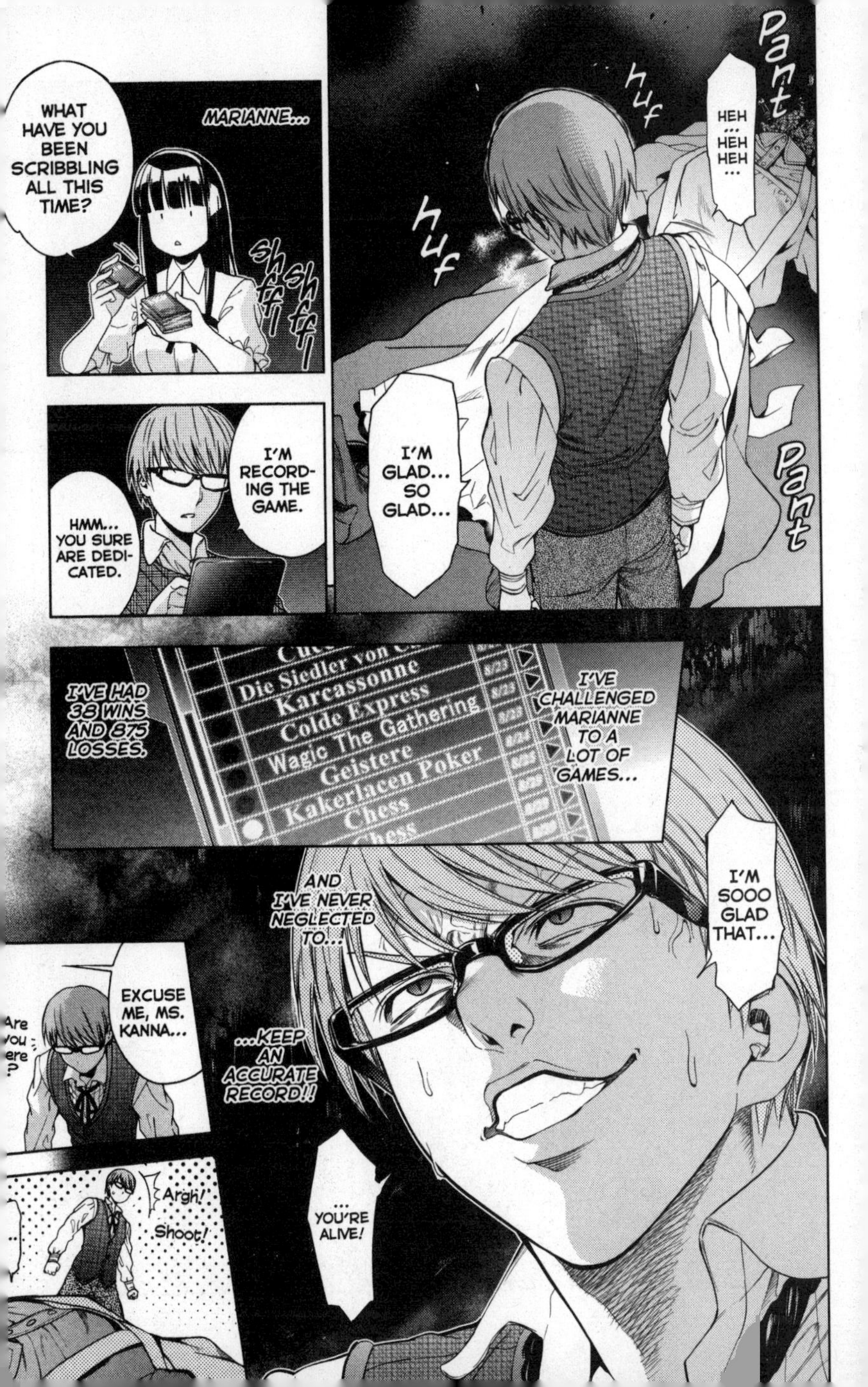
Pant
HEH... HEH HEH...
huf
huf
I'M GLAD... SO GLAD...
Pant
MARIANNE...
WHAT HAVE YOU BEEN SCRIBBLING ALL THIS TIME?
shffl shffl
I'M RECORDING THE GAME.
HMM... YOU SURE ARE DEDICATED.
I'VE CHALLENGED MARIANNE TO A LOT OF GAMES...
Karcassonne
Colde Express
Wagic The Gathering
Geistere
Kakerlacen Poker
Chess
I'VE HAD 38 WINS AND 875 LOSSES.
I'M SOOO GLAD THAT...
AND I'VE NEVER NEGLECTED TO..!
...KEEP AN ACCURATE RECORD!!
...YOU'RE ALIVE!
EXCUSE ME, MS. KANNA...
Argh!
Shoot!

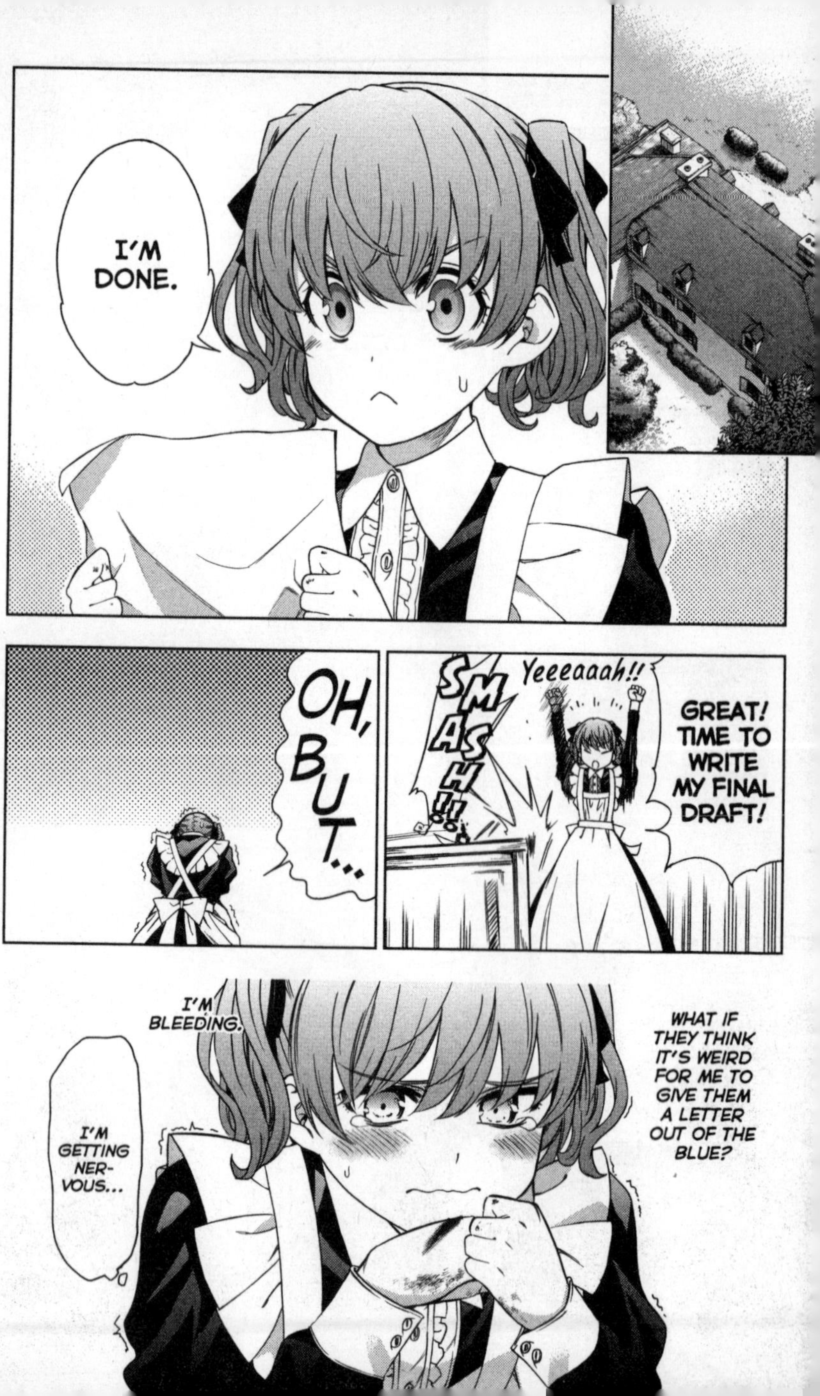

I'M DONE.
Yeeeaaah!!
GREAT! TIME TO WRITE MY FINAL DRAFT!
SMASH!!
OH, BUT...
WHAT IF THEY THINK IT'S WEIRD FOR ME TO GIVE THEM A LETTER OUT OF THE BLUE?
I'M BLEEDING.
I'M GETTING NER-VOUS...

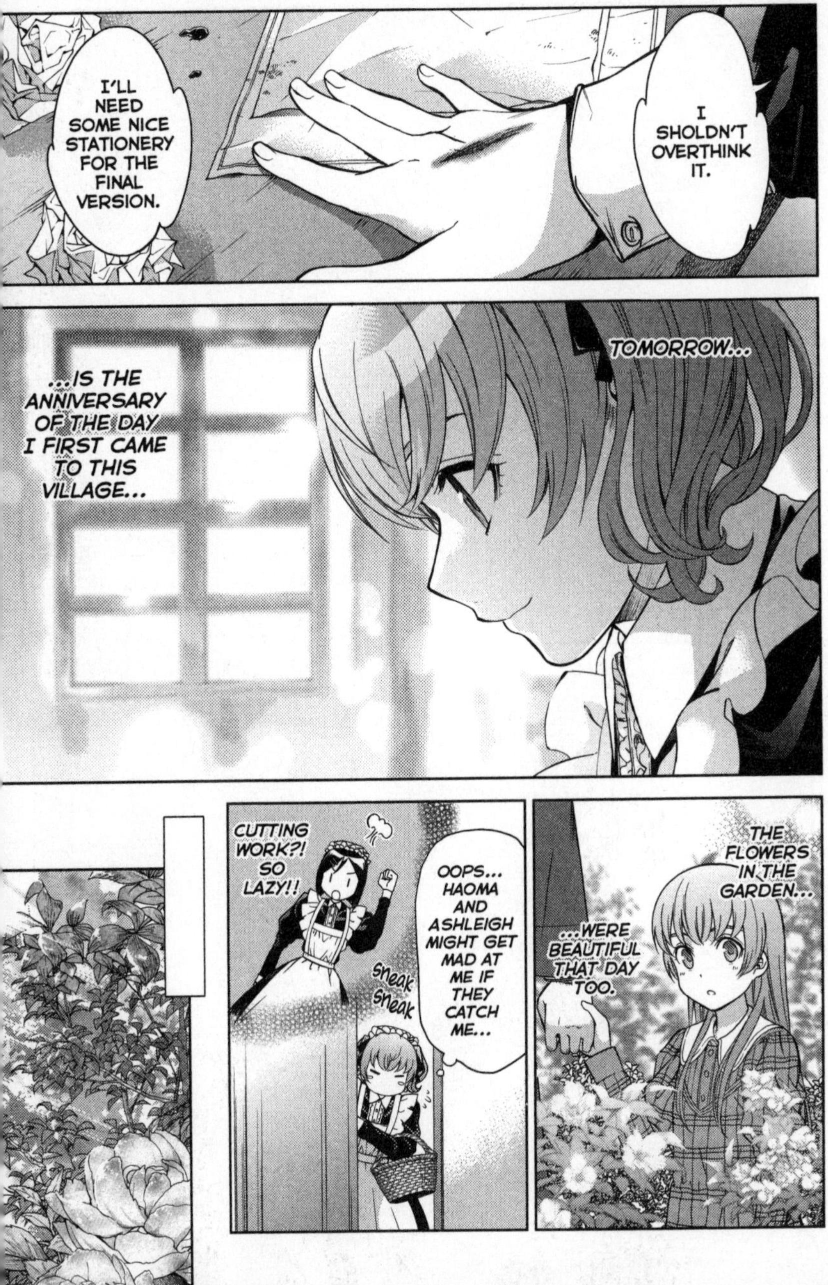
I SHOLDN'T OVERTHINK IT.
I'LL NEED SOME NICE STATIONERY FOR THE FINAL VERSION.
TOMORROW...
...IS THE ANNIVERSARY OF THE DAY I FIRST CAME TO THIS VILLAGE...
THE FLOWERS IN THE GARDEN...
...WERE BEAUTIFUL THAT DAY TOO.
OOPS... HAOMA AND ASHLEIGH MIGHT GET MAD AT ME IF THEY CATCH ME...
CUTTING WORK?! SO LAZY!!
sneak sneak

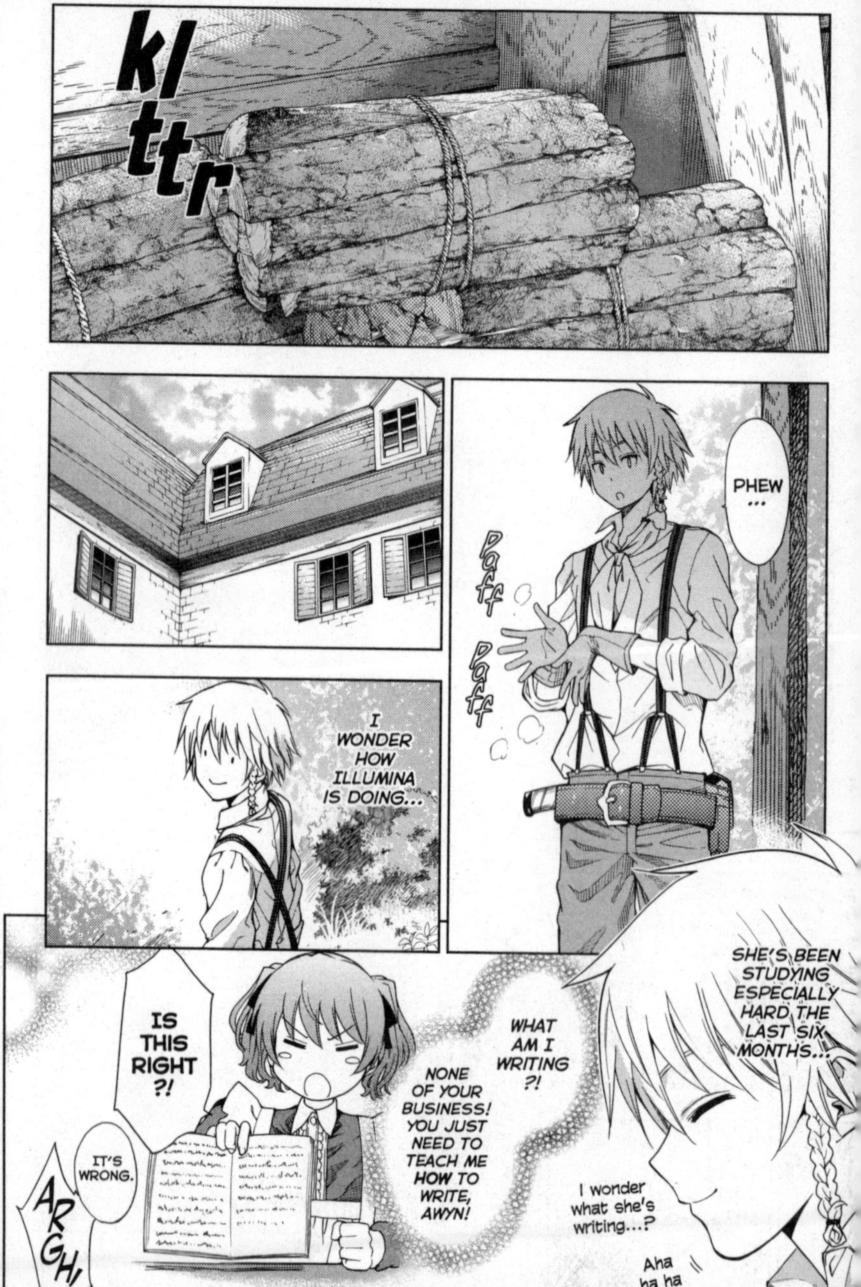
kl ttr
PHEW...
Paff Paff
I WONDER HOW ILLUMINA IS DOING...
SHE'S BEEN STUDYING ESPECIALLY HARD THE LAST SIX MONTHS...
I wonder what she's writing...?
Aha ha ha
WHAT AM I WRITING?!
NONE OF YOUR BUSINESS! YOU JUST NEED TO TEACH ME HOW TO WRITE, AWYN!
IS THIS RIGHT?!
IT'S WRONG.
ARGH!

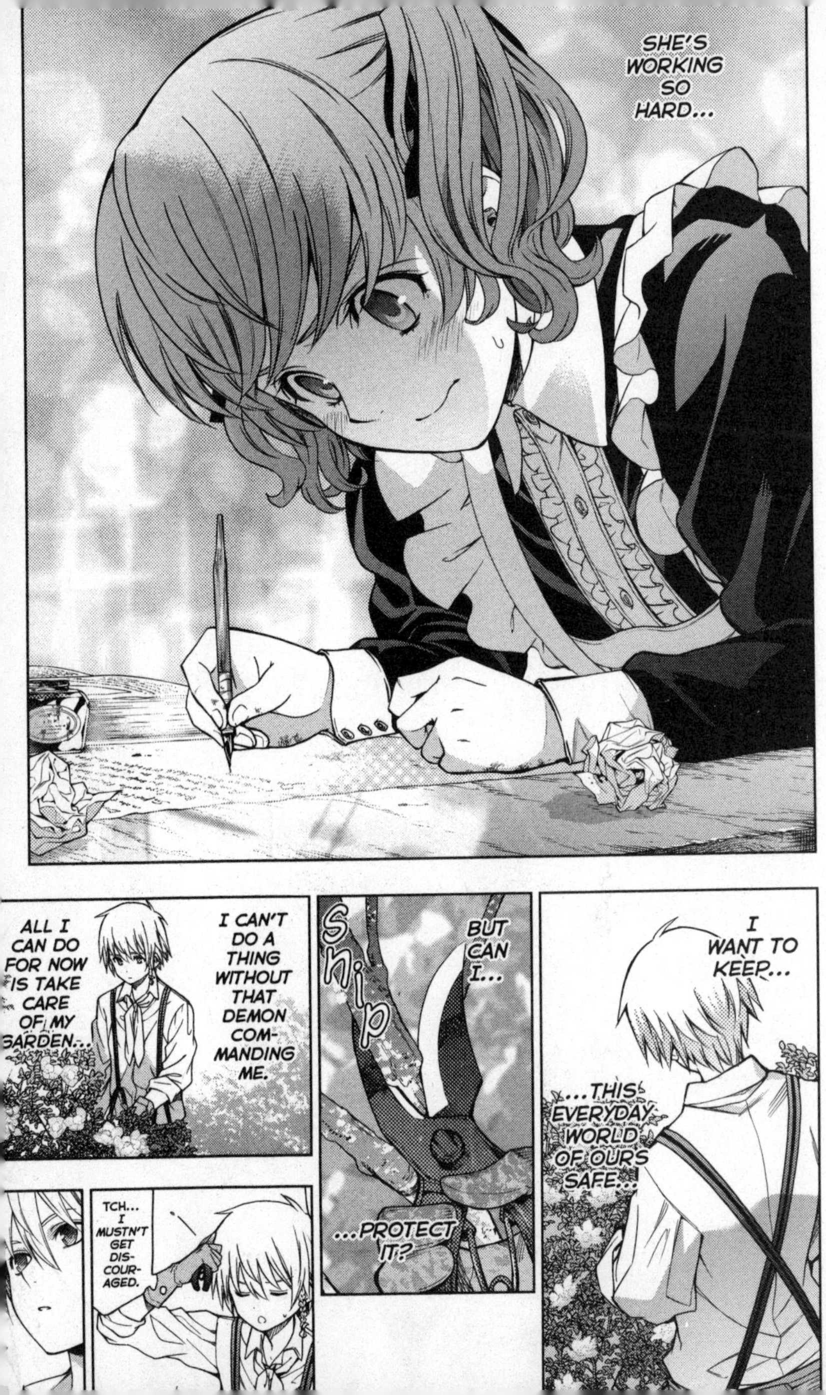
SHE'S WORKING SO HARD...
I WANT TO KEEP...
...THIS EVERYDAY WORLD OF OURS SAFE...
BUT CAN I...
Ship
...PROTECT IT?
I CAN'T DO A THING WITHOUT THAT DEMON COMMANDING ME.
ALL I CAN DO FOR NOW IS TAKE CARE OF MY GARDEN...
TCH... I MUSTN'T GET DISCOURAGED.

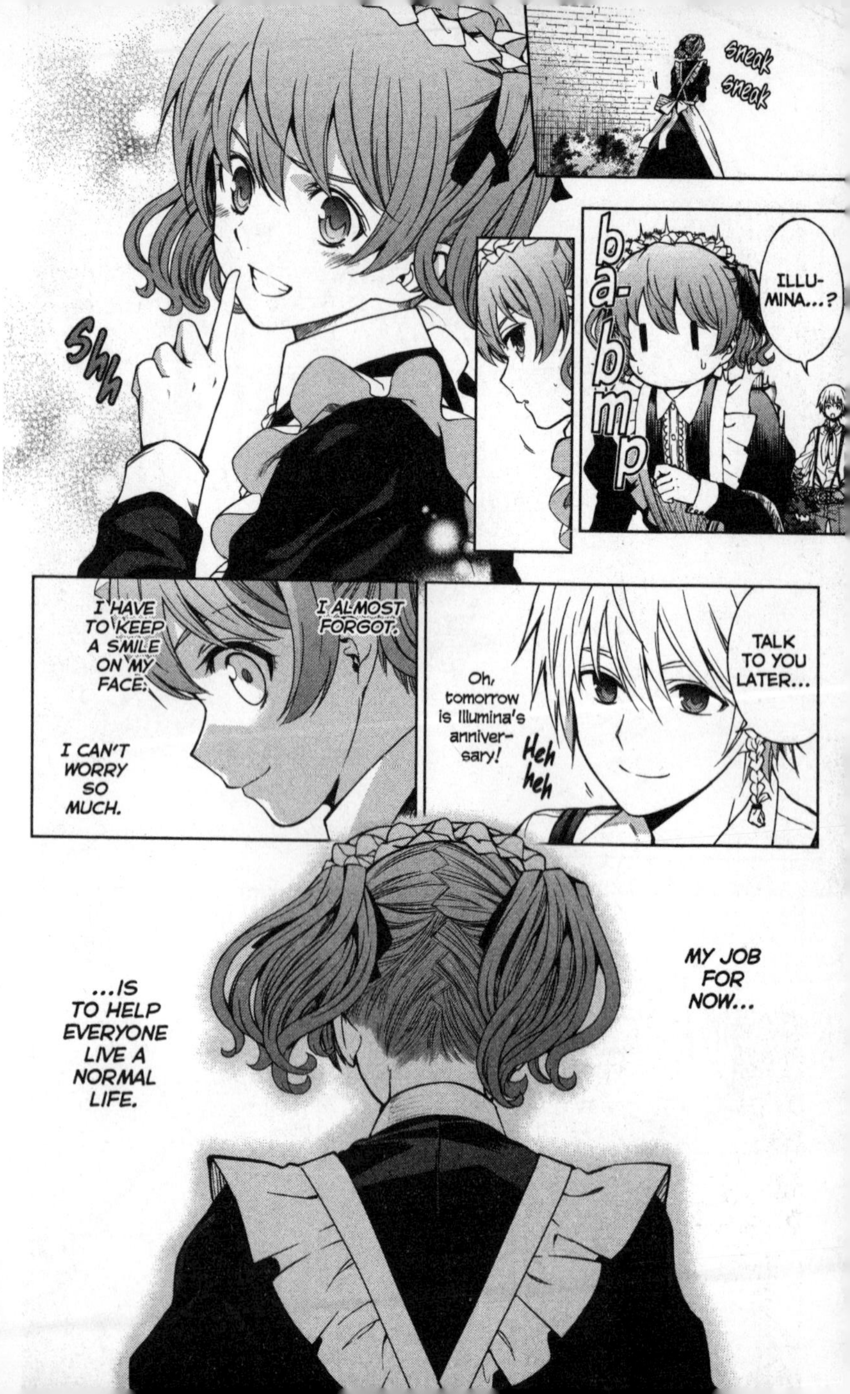
sneak sneak
ILLU-MINA...?
ba-bamp
Shh
TALK TO YOU LATER...
Oh, tomorrow is Illumina's anniver-sary!
Heh heh
I ALMOST FORGOT.
I HAVE TO KEEP A SMILE ON MY FACE.
I CAN'T WORRY SO MUCH.
MY JOB FOR NOW...
...IS TO HELP EVERYONE LIVE A NORMAL LIFE.

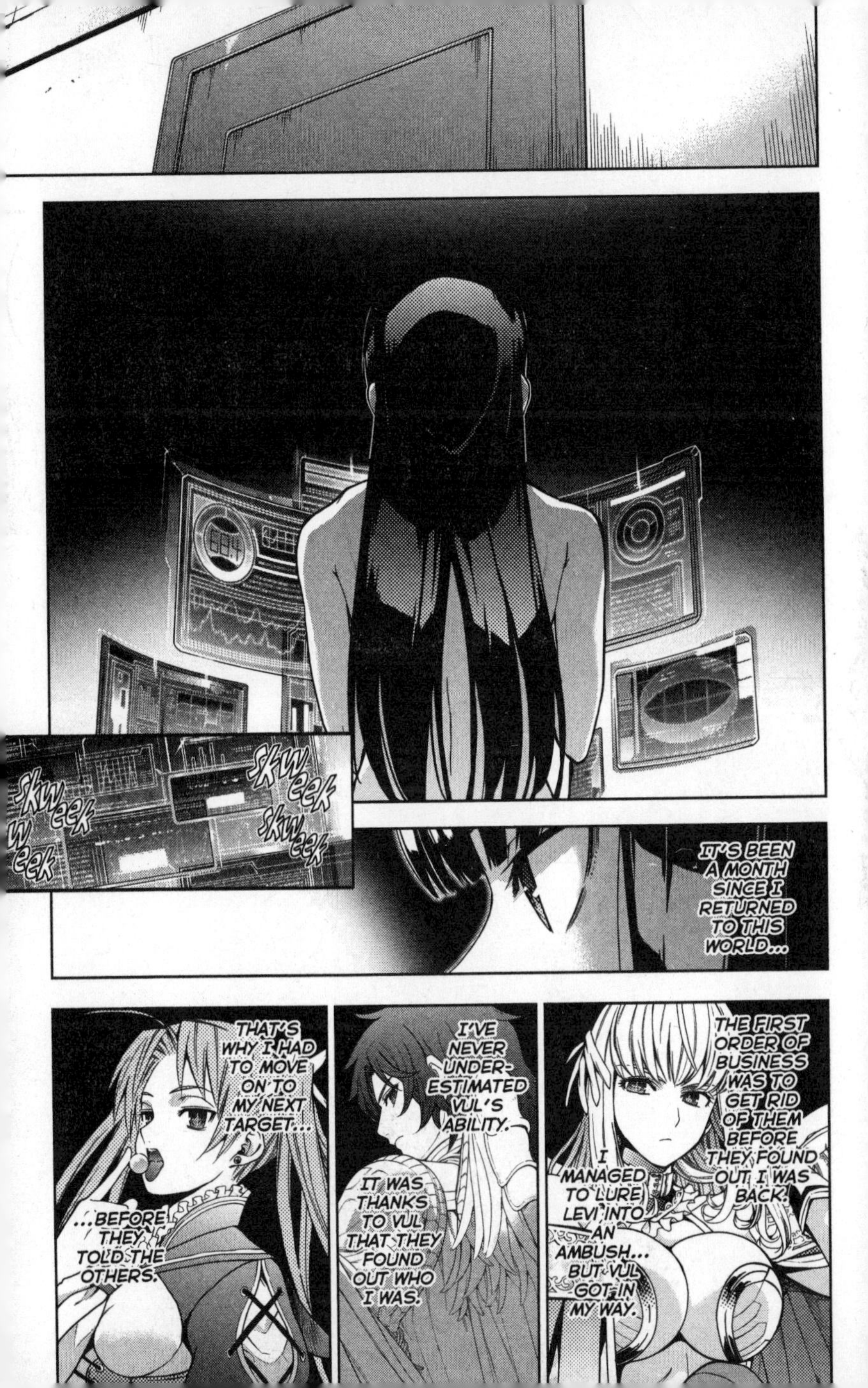
skweek
skweek
IT'S BEEN A MONTH SINCE I RETURNED TO THIS WORLD...
THE FIRST ORDER OF BUSINESS WAS TO GET RID OF THEM BEFORE THEY FOUND OUT I WAS BACK.
I MANAGED TO LURE LEVI INTO AN AMBUSH... BUT VUL GOT IN MY WAY.
I'VE NEVER UNDER-ESTIMATED VUL'S ABILITY.
IT WAS THANKS TO VUL THAT THEY FOUND OUT WHO I WAS.
THAT'S WHY I HAD TO MOVE ON TO MY NEXT TARGET...
...BEFORE THEY TOLD THE OTHERS.

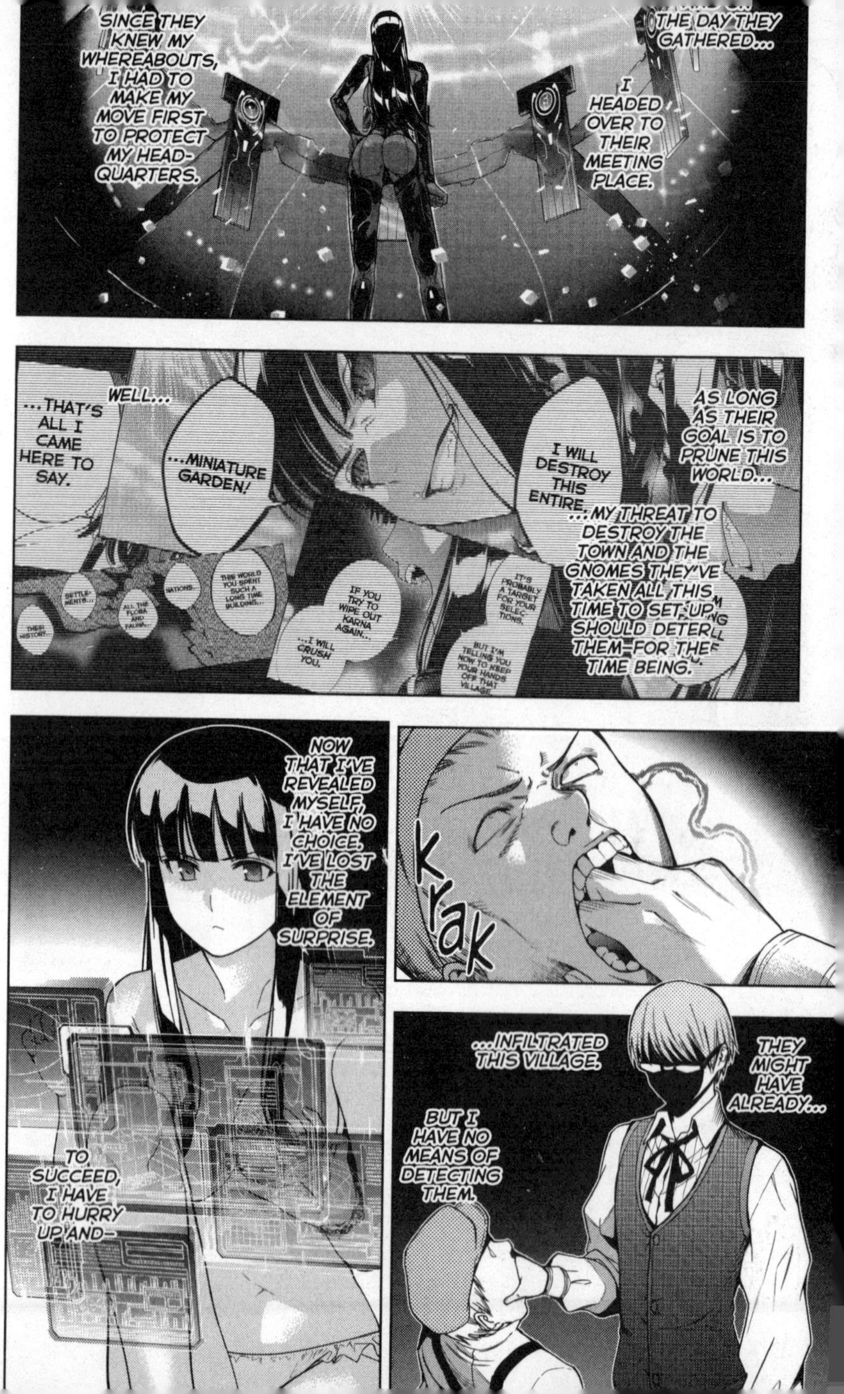
THE DAY THEY GATHERED...
I HEADED OVER TO THEIR MEETING PLACE.
SINCE THEY KNEW MY WHEREABOUTS, I HAD TO MAKE MY MOVE FIRST TO PROTECT MY HEAD-QUARTERS.
AS LONG AS THEIR GOAL IS TO PRUNE THIS WORLD...
...MY THREAT TO DESTROY THE TOWN AND THE GNOMES THEY'VE TAKEN ALL THIS TIME TO SET UP SHOULD DETER THEM FOR THE TIME BEING.
I WILL DESTROY THIS ENTIRE...
...MINIATURE GARDEN!
WELL...
...THAT'S ALL I CAME HERE TO SAY.
IT'S PROBABLY A TARGET FOR YOUR SELECTIONS.
BUT I'M TELLING YOU NOW TO KEEP YOUR HANDS OFF THAT VILLAGE.
IF YOU TRY TO WIPE OUT KARNA AGAIN...
...I WILL CRUSH YOU.
THE WORLD YOU SPENT SUCH A LONG TIME BUILDING...
NATIONS...
SETTLEMENTS...
ALL THE FLORA AND FAUNA...
THEIR HISTORY...
KRAK
THEY MIGHT HAVE ALREADY...
...INFILTRATED THIS VILLAGE.
BUT I HAVE NO MEANS OF DETECTING THEM.
NOW THAT I'VE REVEALED MYSELF, I HAVE NO CHOICE. I'VE LOST THE ELEMENT OF SURPRISE.
TO SUCCEED, I HAVE TO HURRY UP AND–

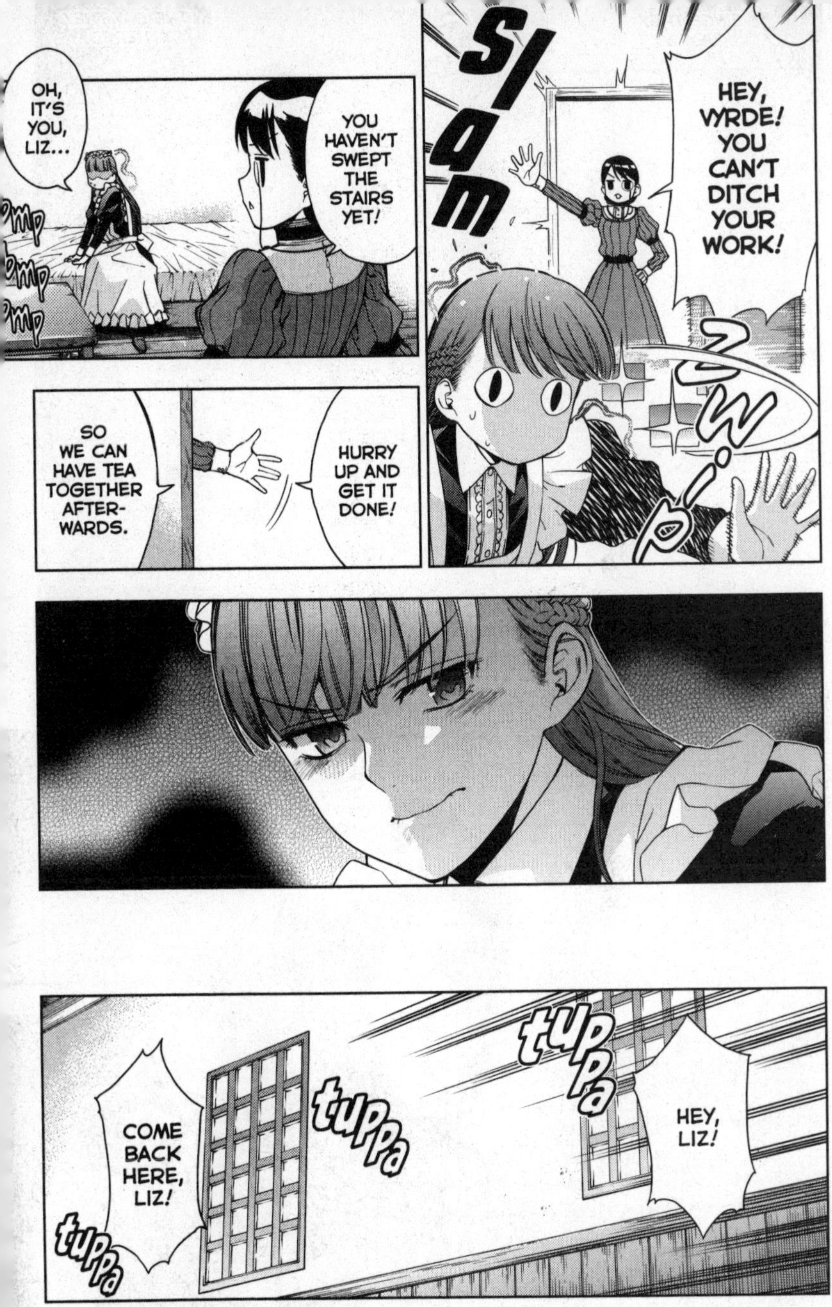
Slam
HEY, VYRDE! YOU CAN'T DITCH YOUR WORK!
zwip
YOU HAVEN'T SWEPT THE STAIRS YET!
OH, IT'S YOU, LIZ...
HURRY UP AND GET IT DONE!
SO WE CAN HAVE TEA TOGETHER AFTER-WARDS.
HEY, LIZ!
tuppa
tuppa
COME BACK HERE, LIZ!
tuppa

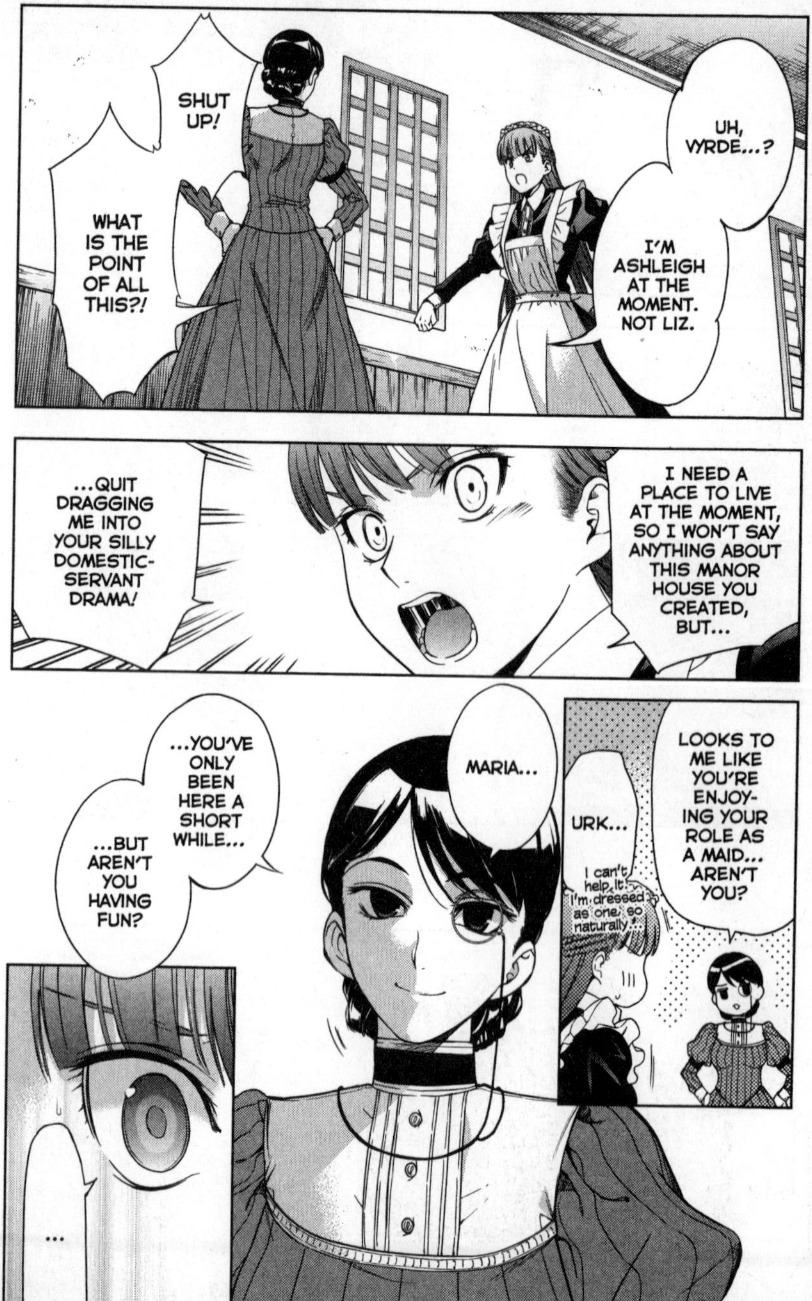
UH, VYRDE...?
I'M ASHLEIGH AT THE MOMENT. NOT LIZ.
SHUT UP!
WHAT IS THE POINT OF ALL THIS?!
I NEED A PLACE TO LIVE AT THE MOMENT, SO I WON'T SAY ANYTHING ABOUT THIS MANOR HOUSE YOU CREATED, BUT...
...QUIT DRAGGING ME INTO YOUR SILLY DOMESTIC-SERVANT DRAMA!
LOOKS TO ME LIKE YOU'RE ENJOYING YOUR ROLE AS A MAID... AREN'T YOU?
URK...
I can't help it. I'm dressed as one, so naturally...
MARIA...
...YOU'VE ONLY BEEN HERE A SHORT WHILE...
...BUT AREN'T YOU HAVING FUN?
...

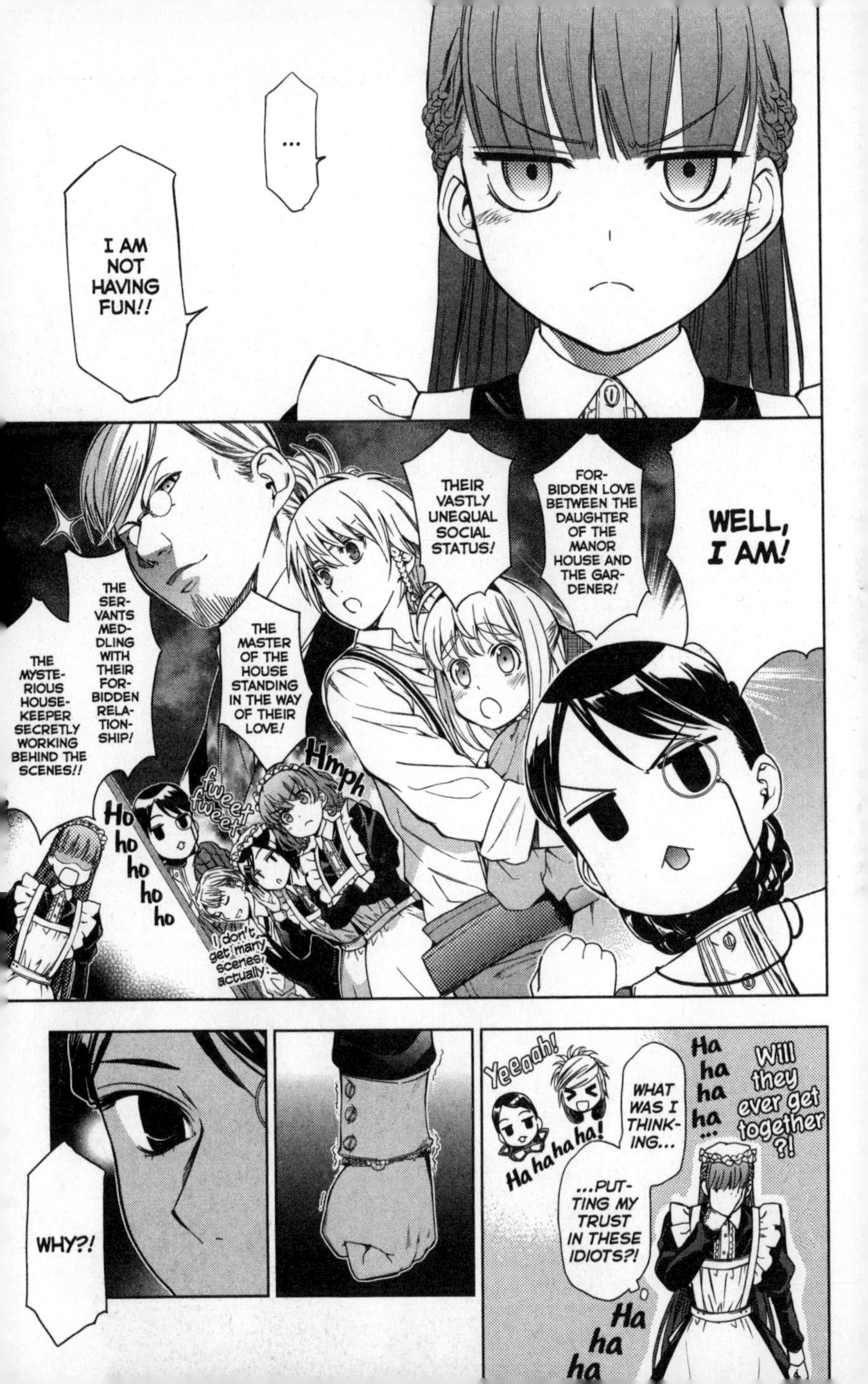
...
I AM NOT HAVING FUN!!
WELL, I AM!
FOR-BIDDEN LOVE BETWEEN THE DAUGHTER OF THE MANOR HOUSE AND THE GAR-DENER!
THEIR VASTLY UNEQUAL SOCIAL STATUS!
THE MASTER OF THE HOUSE STANDING IN THE WAY OF THEIR LOVE!
THE SER-VANTS MED-DLING WITH THEIR FOR-BIDDEN RELA-TION-SHIP!
THE MYSTE-RIOUS HOUSE-KEEPER SECRETLY WORKING BEHIND THE SCENES!!
Hmph
fweet fweet
Ho ho ho ho ho
I don't get many scenes actually!
Will they ever get together?!
Ha ha ha ha...
WHAT WAS I THINK-ING...
...PUT-TING MY TRUST IN THESE IDIOTS?!
Yeeaah!
Ha ha ha ha!
Ha ha ha
WHY?!

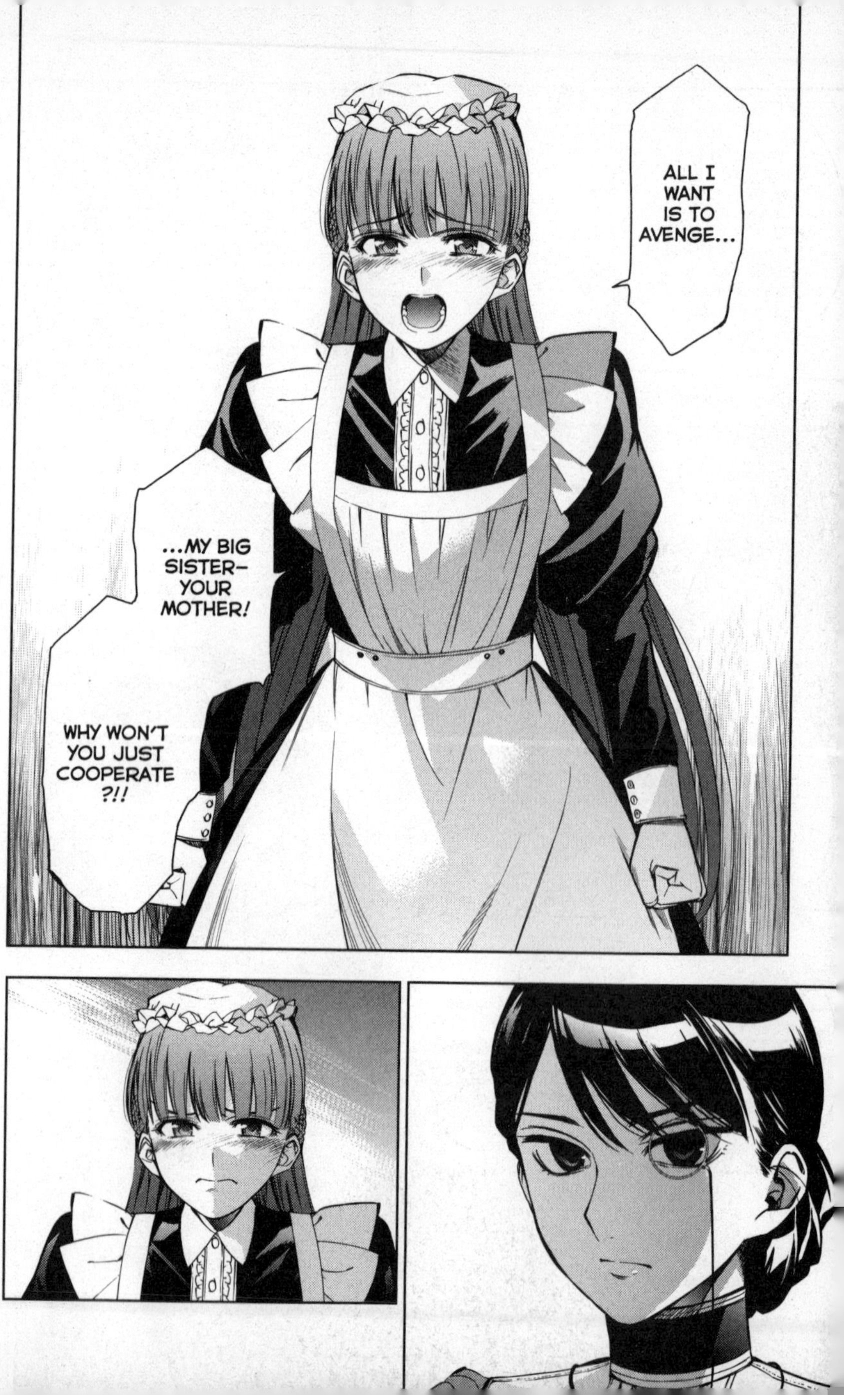
ALL I WANT IS TO AVENGE...
...MY BIG SISTER—YOUR MOTHER!
WHY WON'T YOU JUST COOPERATE ?!!

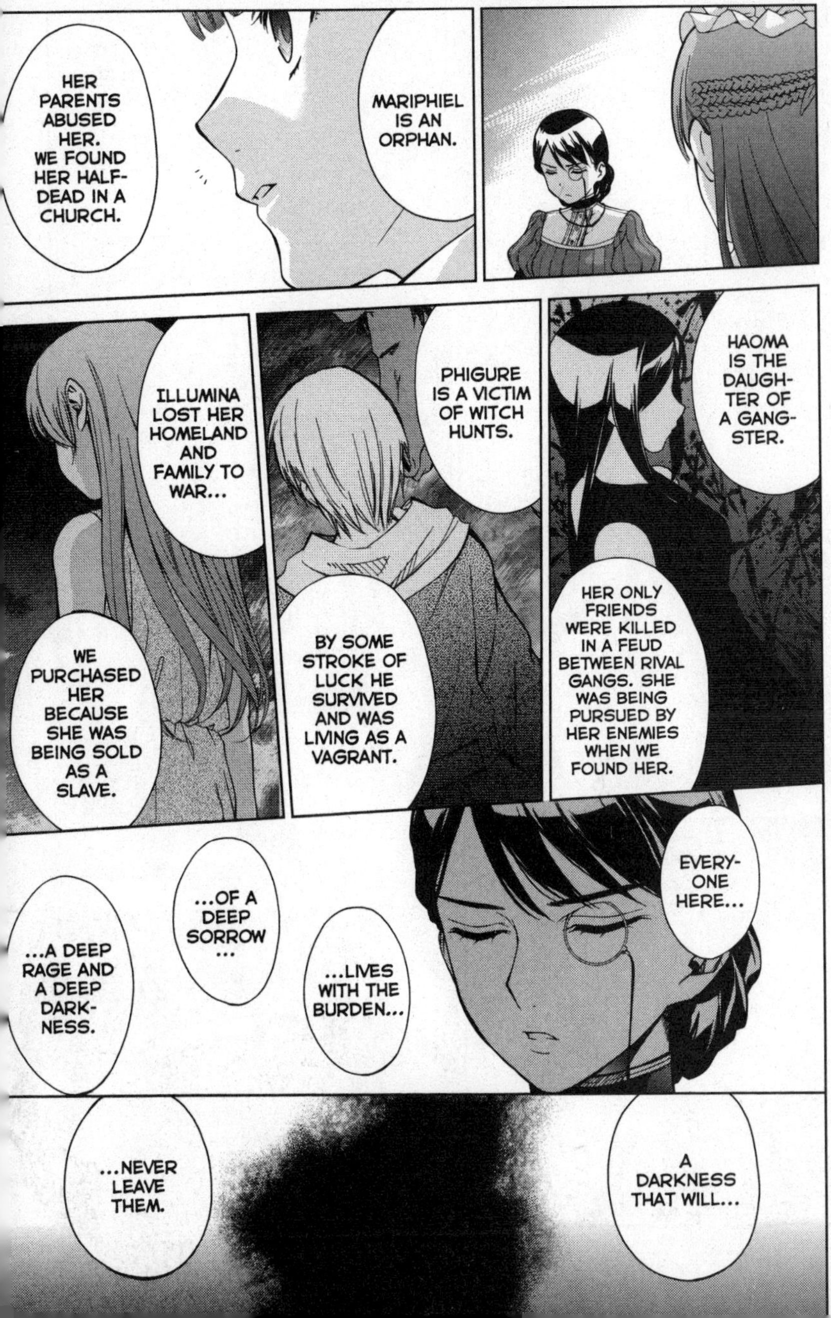
MARIPHIEL IS AN ORPHAN.
HER PARENTS ABUSED HER. WE FOUND HER HALF-DEAD IN A CHURCH.
HAOMA IS THE DAUGHTER OF A GANGSTER.
HER ONLY FRIENDS WERE KILLED IN A FEUD BETWEEN RIVAL GANGS. SHE WAS BEING PURSUED BY HER ENEMIES WHEN WE FOUND HER.
PHIGURE IS A VICTIM OF WITCH HUNTS.
BY SOME STROKE OF LUCK HE SURVIVED AND WAS LIVING AS A VAGRANT.
ILLUMINA LOST HER HOMELAND AND FAMILY TO WAR...
WE PURCHASED HER BECAUSE SHE WAS BEING SOLD AS A SLAVE.
EVERYONE HERE...
...LIVES WITH THE BURDEN...
...OF A DEEP SORROW...
...A DEEP RAGE AND A DEEP DARKNESS.
A DARKNESS THAT WILL...
...NEVER LEAVE THEM.

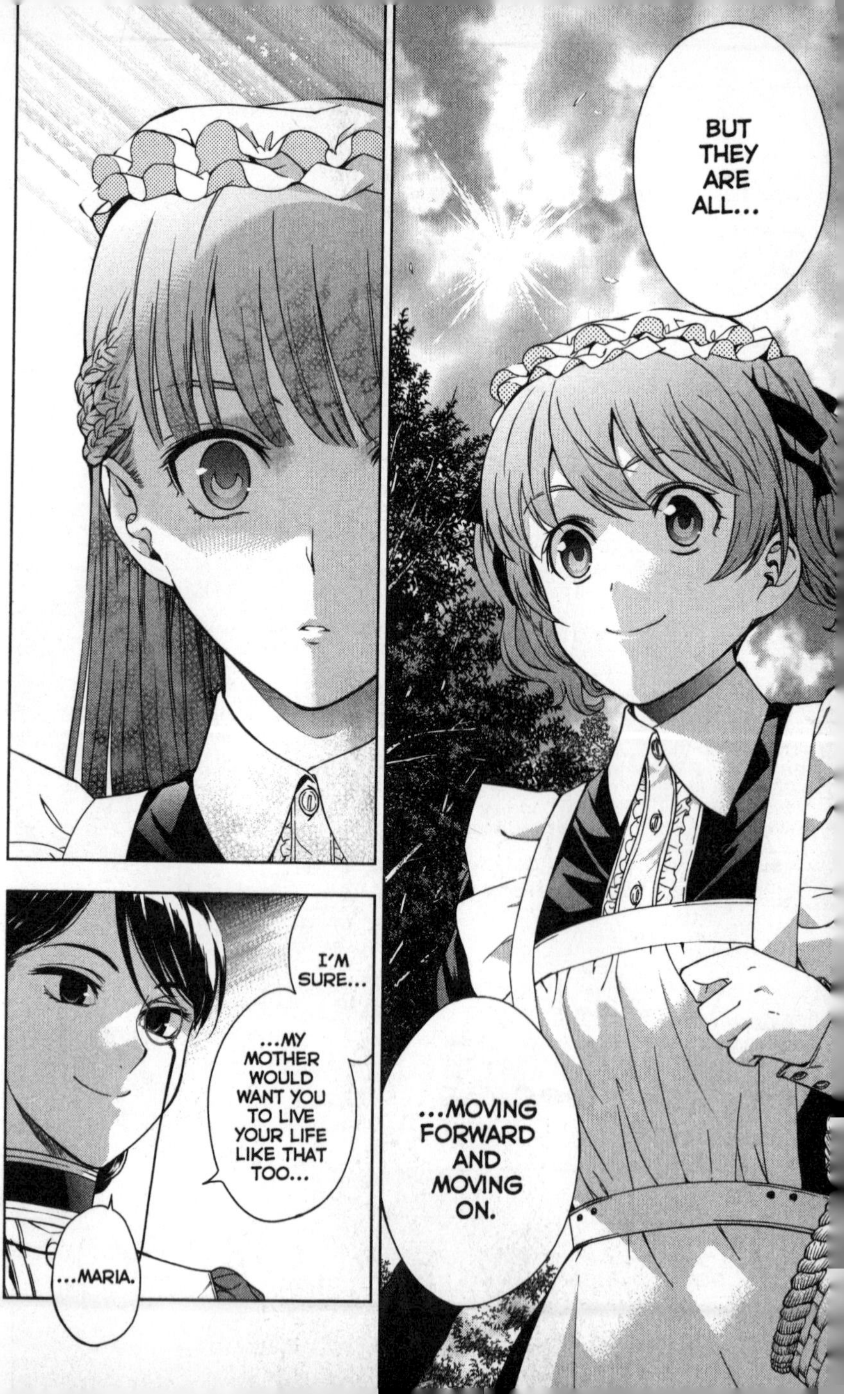
BUT THEY ARE ALL...
...MOVING FORWARD AND MOVING ON.
I'M SURE...
...MY MOTHER WOULD WANT YOU TO LIVE YOUR LIFE LIKE THAT TOO...
...MARIA.

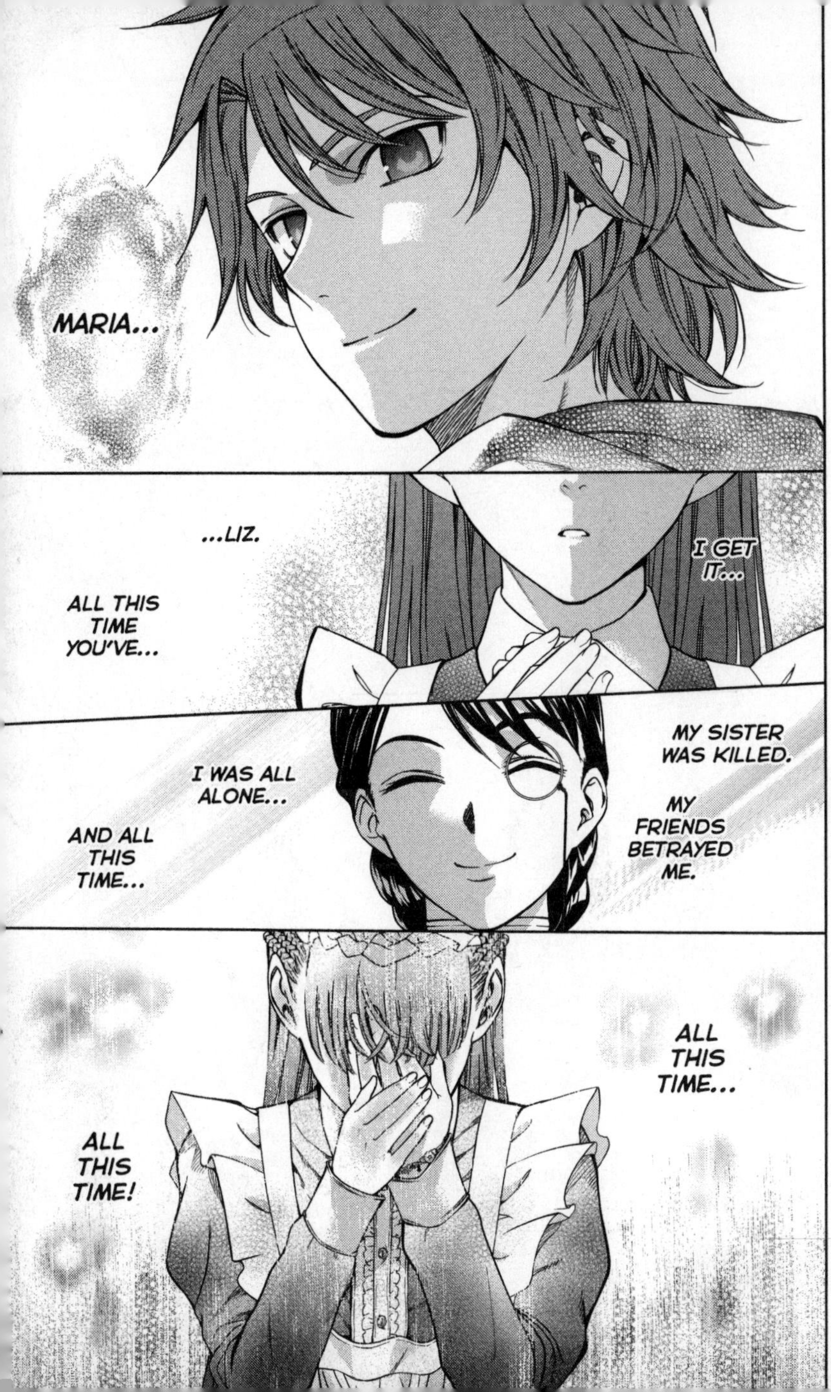
MARIA...
I GET IT...
...LIZ.
ALL THIS TIME YOU'VE...
MY SISTER WAS KILLED.
MY FRIENDS BETRAYED ME.
I WAS ALL ALONE...
AND ALL THIS TIME...
ALL THIS TIME...
ALL THIS TIME!

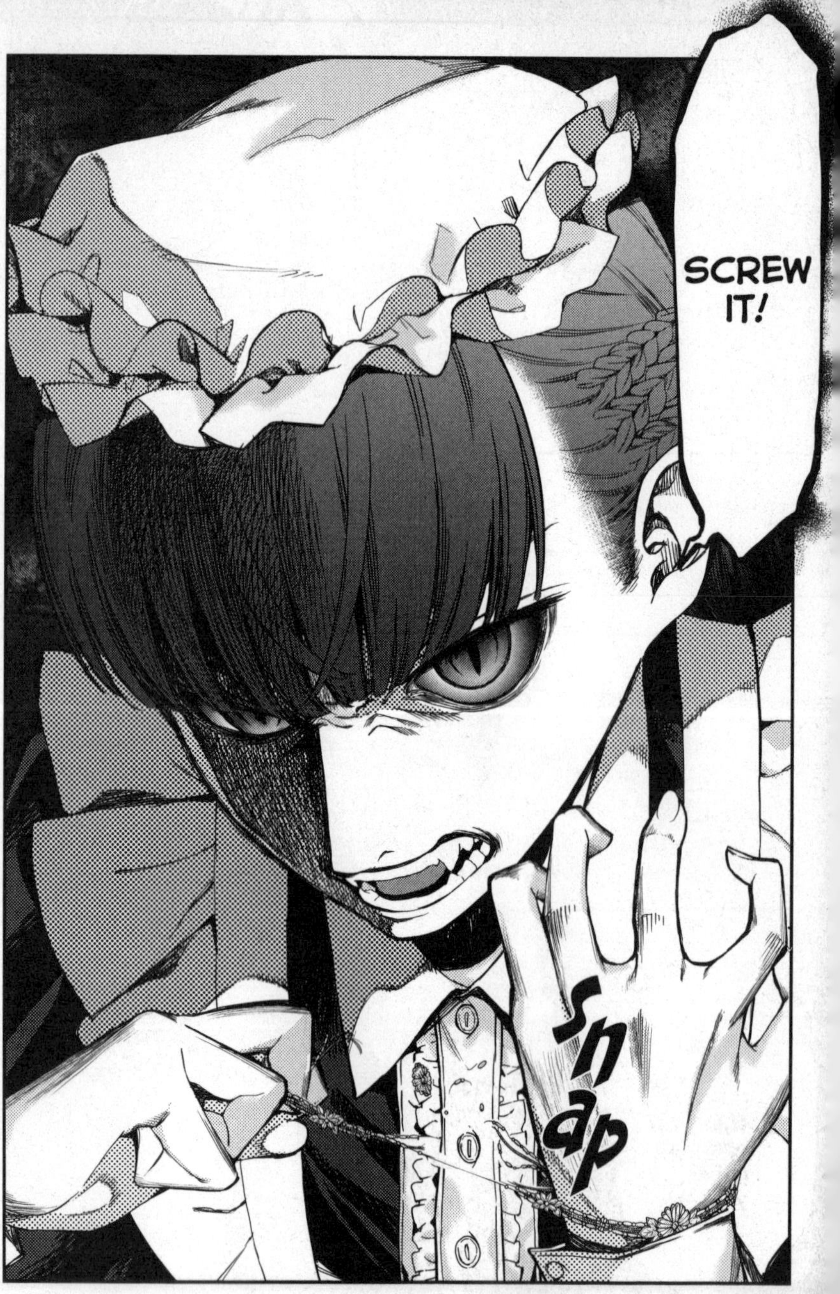
SCREW IT!
SNAP

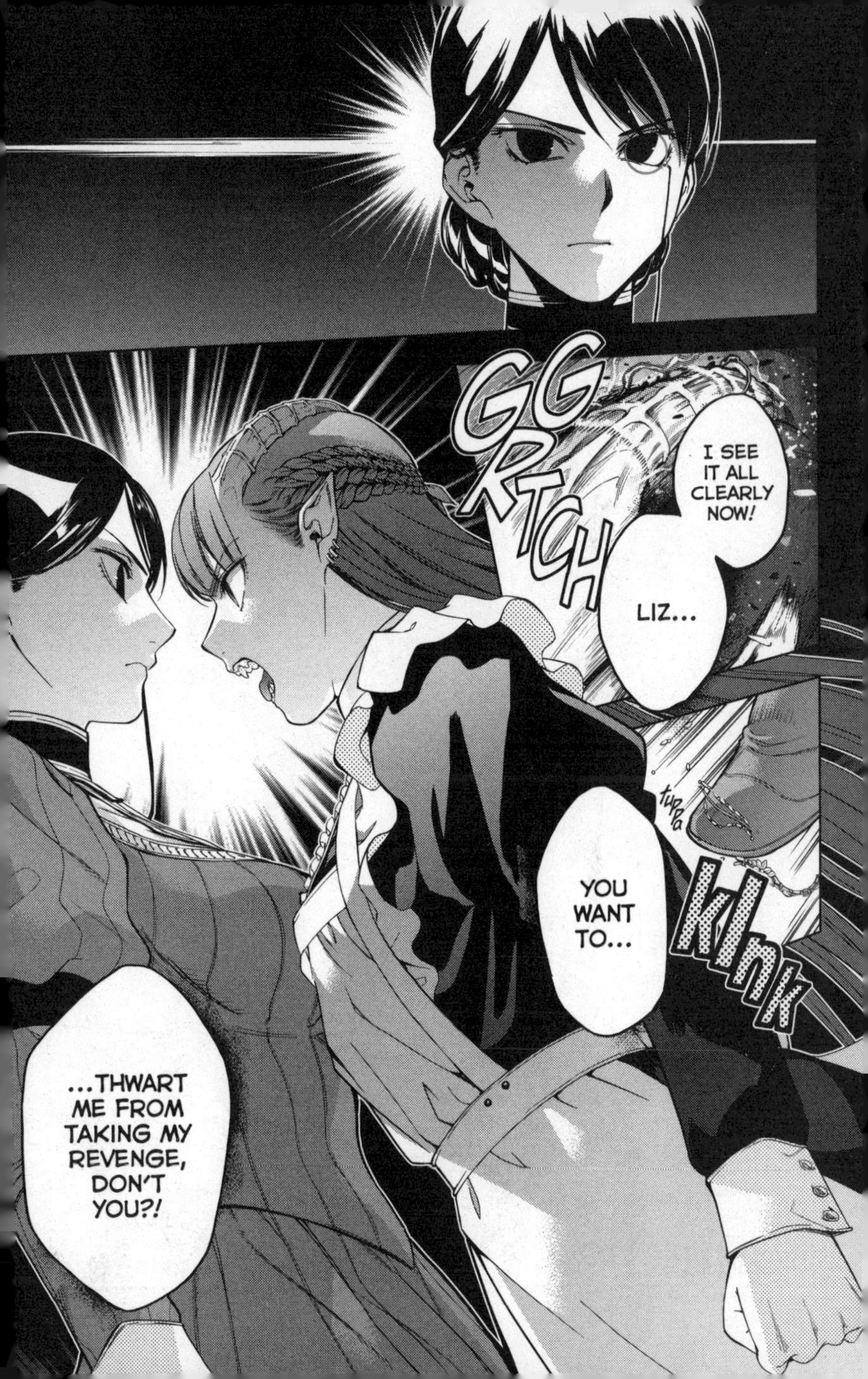
GGRTCH
I SEE IT ALL CLEARLY NOW!
LIZ...
tuppa
klink
YOU WANT TO...
...THWART ME FROM TAKING MY REVENGE, DON'T YOU?!

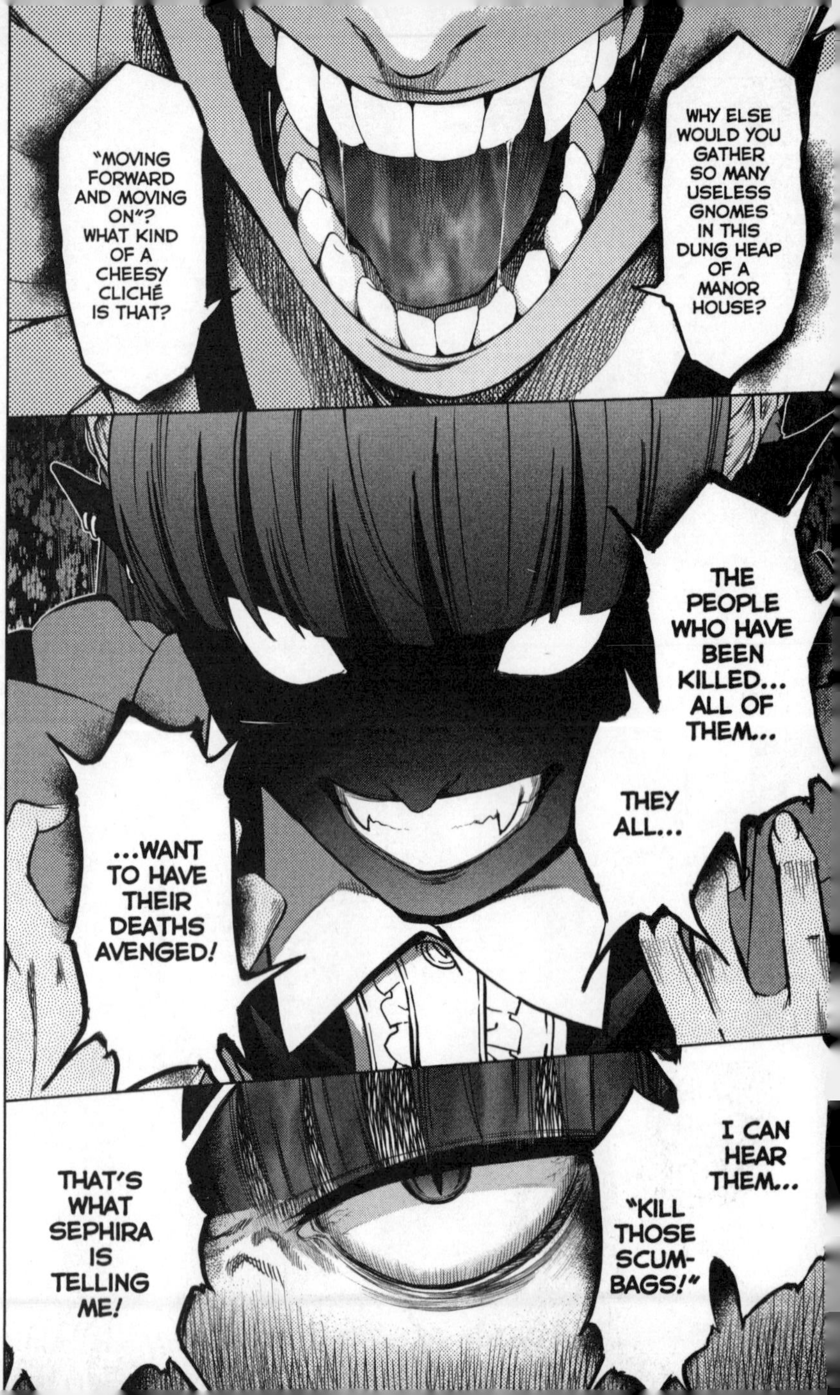
WHY ELSE WOULD YOU GATHER SO MANY USELESS GNOMES IN THIS DUNG HEAP OF A MANOR HOUSE?
"MOVING FORWARD AND MOVING ON"? WHAT KIND OF A CHEESY CLICHÉ IS THAT?
THE PEOPLE WHO HAVE BEEN KILLED... ALL OF THEM...
THEY ALL...
...WANT TO HAVE THEIR DEATHS AVENGED!
I CAN HEAR THEM...
"KILL THOSE SCUM-BAGS!"
THAT'S WHAT SEPHIRA IS TELLING ME!

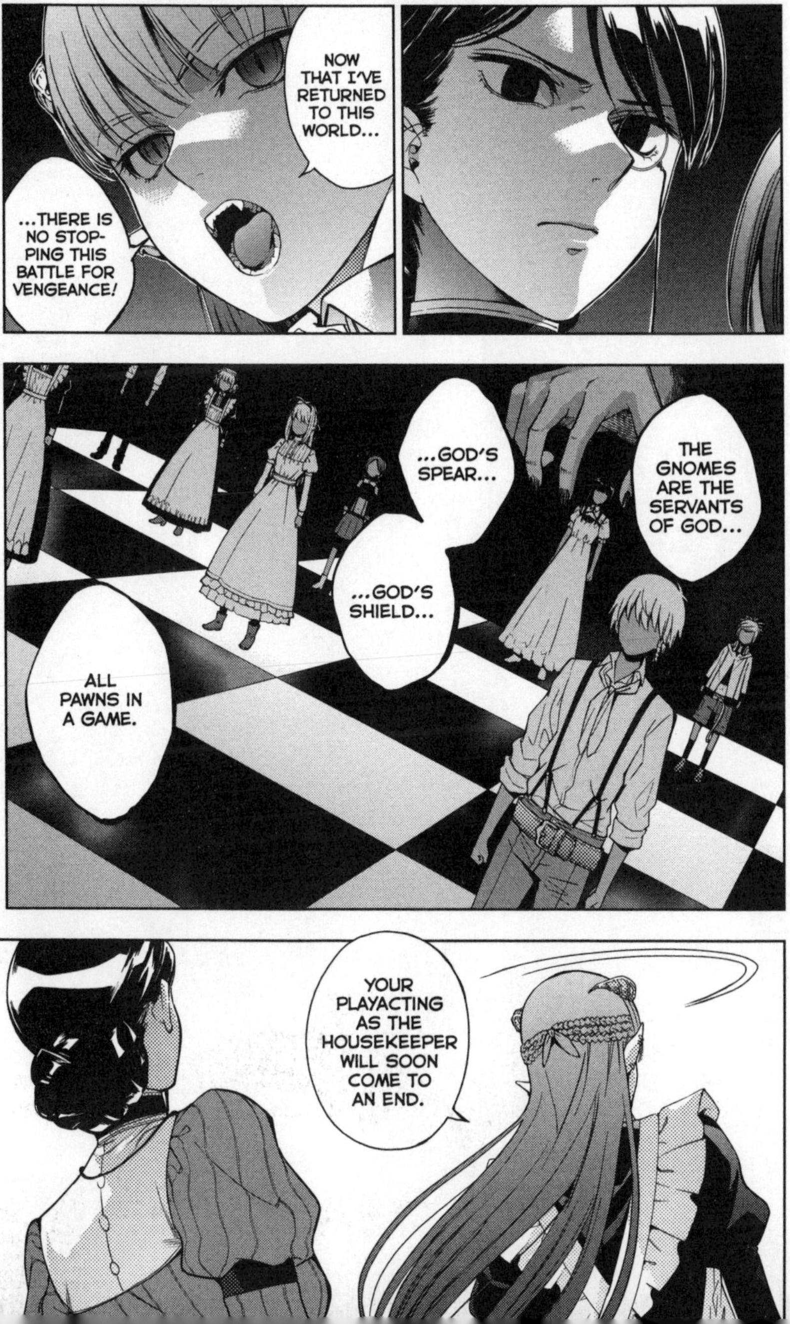
NOW THAT I'VE RETURNED TO THIS WORLD...
...THERE IS NO STOP-PING THIS BATTLE FOR VENGEANCE!
THE GNOMES ARE THE SERVANTS OF GOD...
...GOD'S SPEAR...
...GOD'S SHIELD...
ALL PAWNS IN A GAME.
YOUR PLAYACTING AS THE HOUSEKEEPER WILL SOON COME TO AN END.

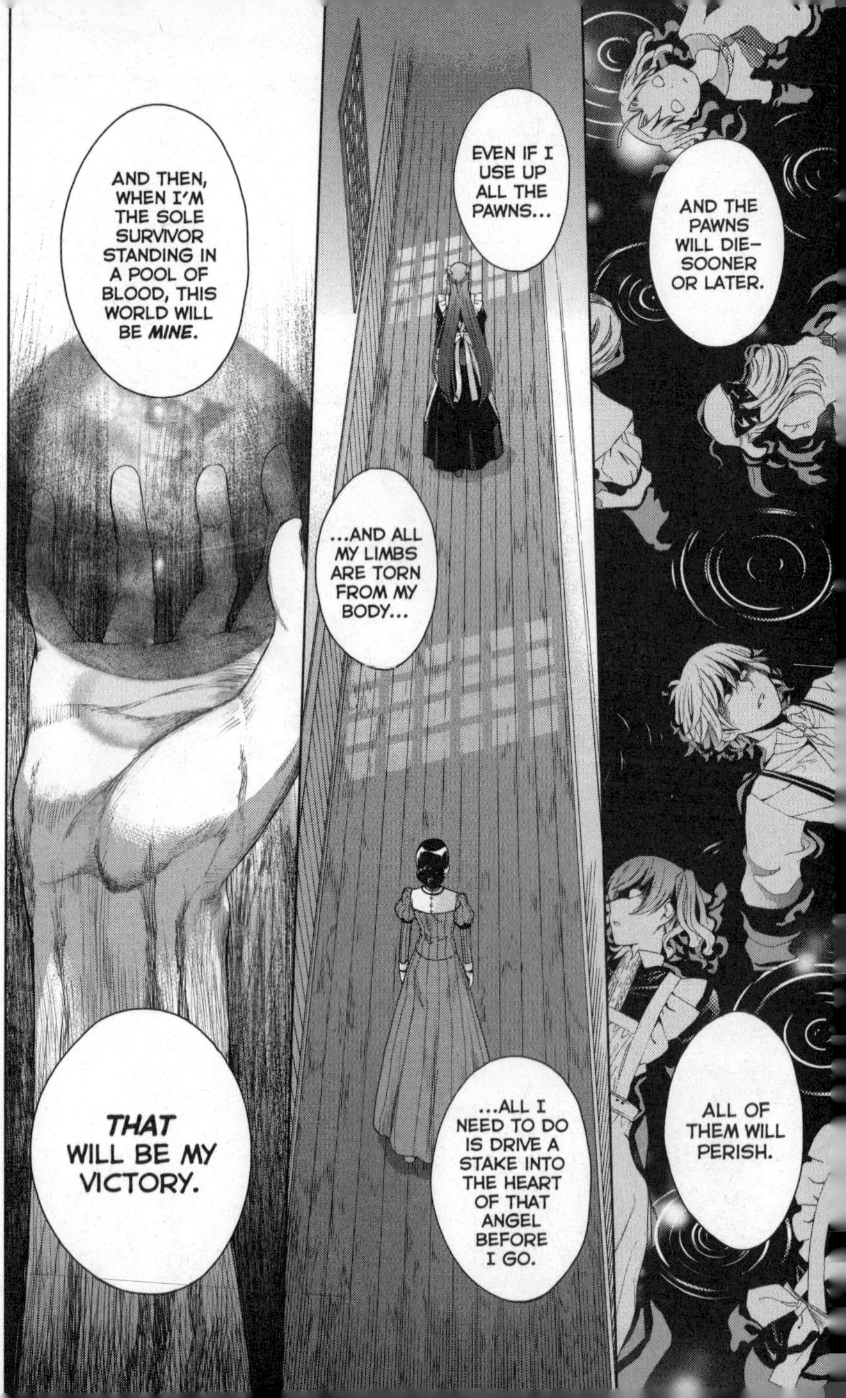
AND THE PAWNS WILL DIE—SOONER OR LATER.
ALL OF THEM WILL PERISH.
EVEN IF I USE UP ALL THE PAWNS...
...AND ALL MY LIMBS ARE TORN FROM MY BODY...
...ALL I NEED TO DO IS DRIVE A STAKE INTO THE HEART OF THAT ANGEL BEFORE I GO.
AND THEN, WHEN I'M THE SOLE SURVIVOR STANDING IN A POOL OF BLOOD, THIS WORLD WILL BE *MINE*.
THAT WILL BE MY VICTORY.

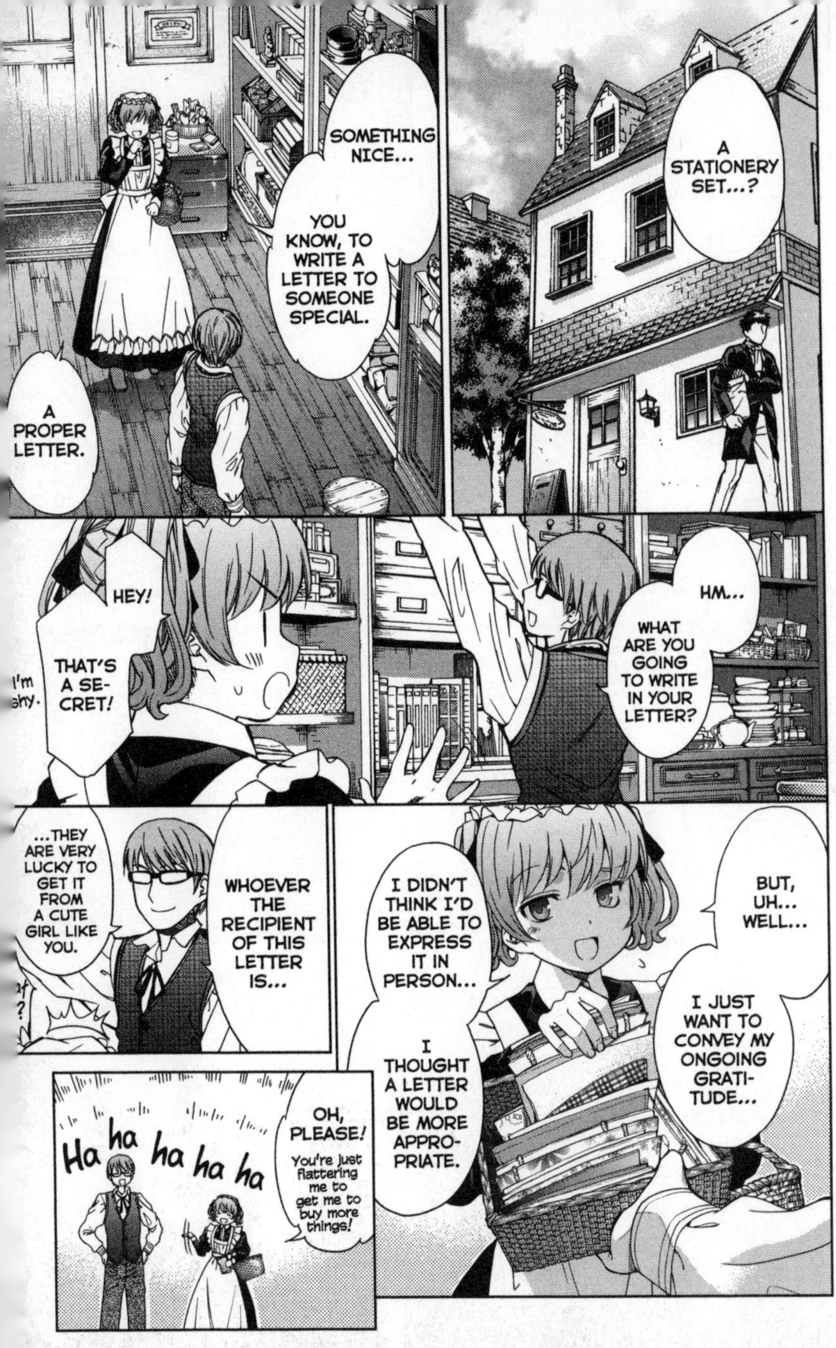
A STATIONERY SET...?
SOMETHING NICE...
YOU KNOW, TO WRITE A LETTER TO SOMEONE SPECIAL.
A PROPER LETTER.
HM...
WHAT ARE YOU GOING TO WRITE IN YOUR LETTER?
HEY!
THAT'S A SE-CRET!
I'm shy.
BUT, UH... WELL...
I JUST WANT TO CONVEY MY ONGOING GRATI-TUDE...
I DIDN'T THINK I'D BE ABLE TO EXPRESS IT IN PERSON...
I THOUGHT A LETTER WOULD BE MORE APPRO-PRIATE.
WHOEVER THE RECIPIENT OF THIS LETTER IS...
...THEY ARE VERY LUCKY TO GET IT FROM A CUTE GIRL LIKE YOU.
OH, PLEASE!
You're just flattering me to get me to buy more things!
Ha ha ha ha ha

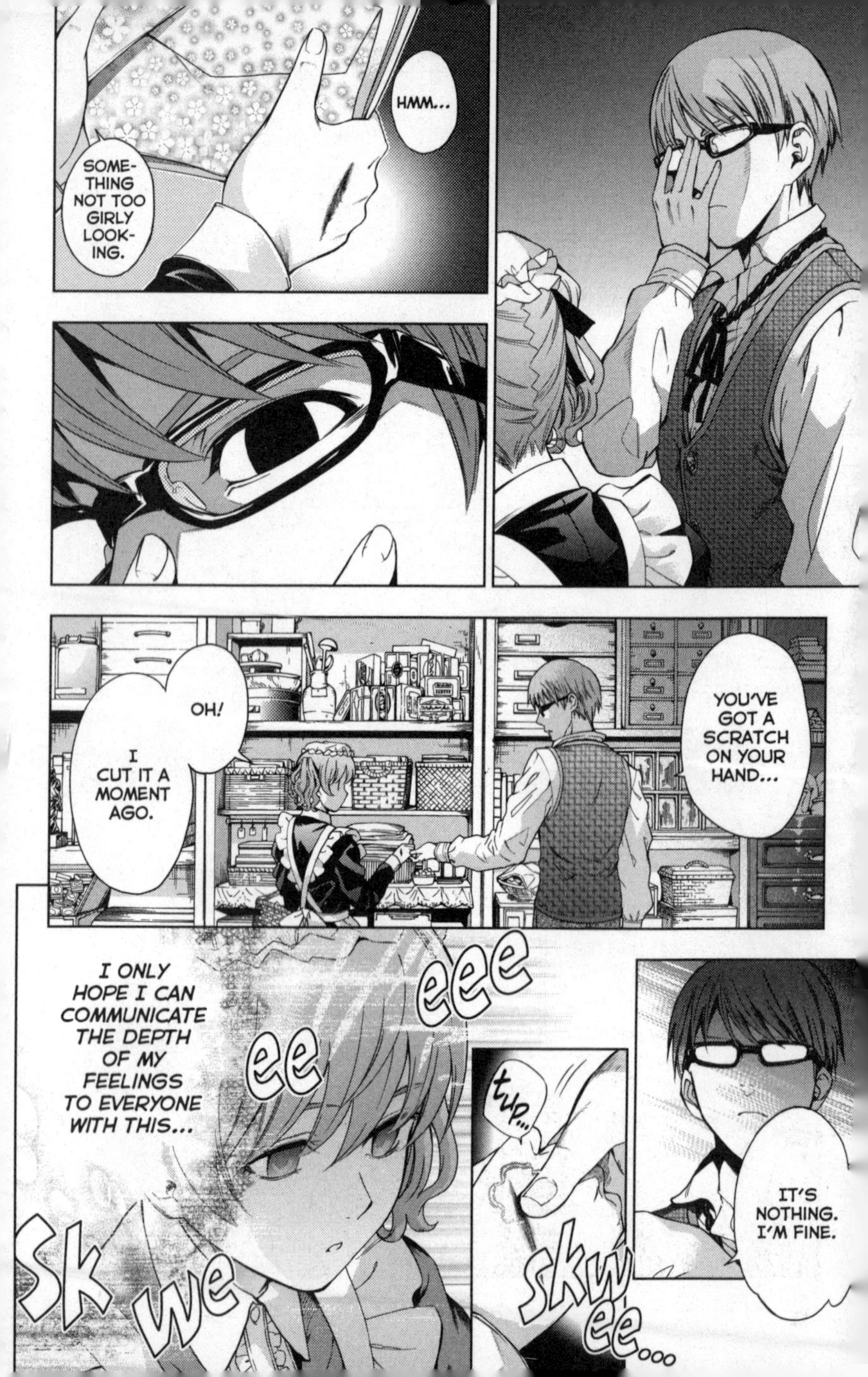
HMM...
SOME-THING NOT TOO GIRLY LOOK-ING.
YOU'VE GOT A SCRATCH ON YOUR HAND...
OH!
I CUT IT A MOMENT AGO.
IT'S NOTHING. I'M FINE.
tup...
skwee...
eee
ee
I ONLY HOPE I CAN COMMUNICATE THE DEPTH OF MY FEELINGS TO EVERYONE WITH THIS...
Skwe

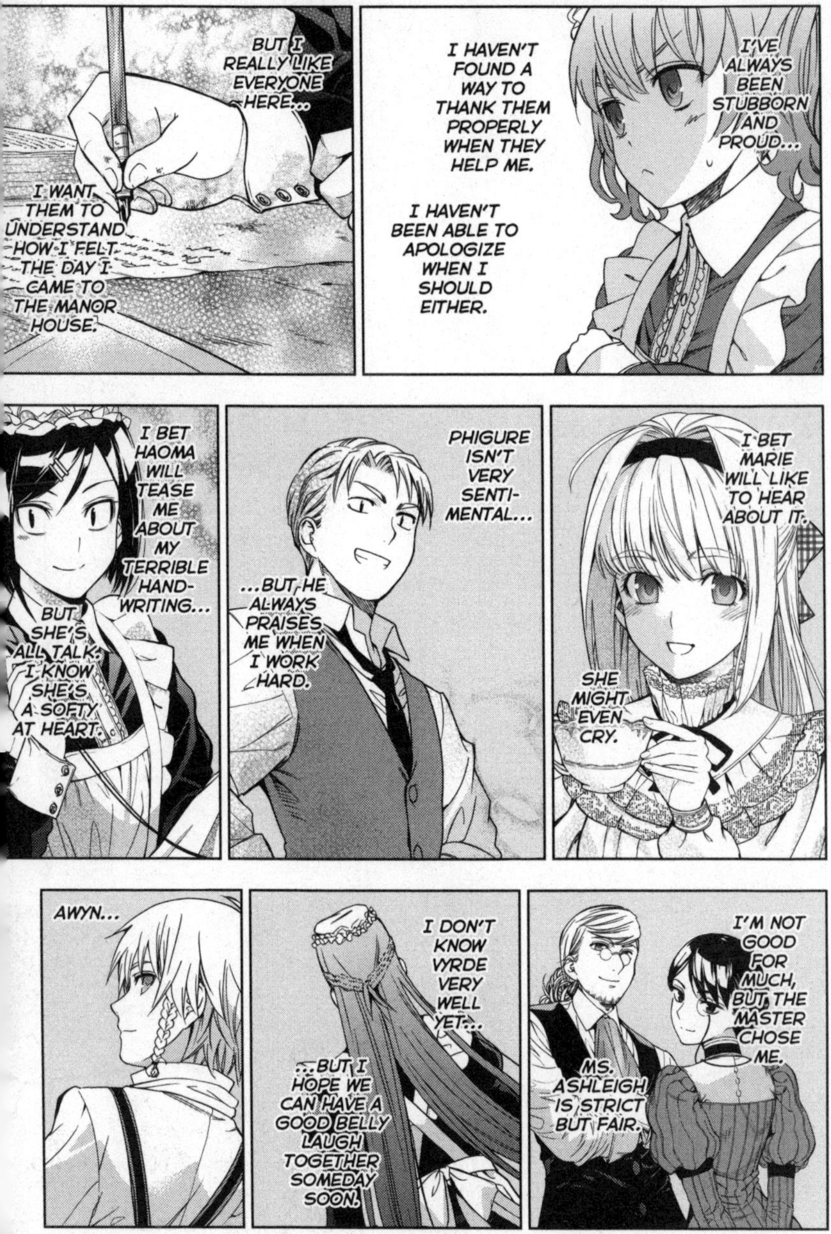
I'VE ALWAYS BEEN STUBBORN AND PROUD...
I HAVEN'T FOUND A WAY TO THANK THEM PROPERLY WHEN THEY HELP ME.
I HAVEN'T BEEN ABLE TO APOLOGIZE WHEN I SHOULD EITHER.
BUT I REALLY LIKE EVERYONE HERE...
I WANT THEM TO UNDERSTAND HOW I FELT THE DAY I CAME TO THE MANOR HOUSE.
I BET MARIE WILL LIKE TO HEAR ABOUT IT.
SHE MIGHT EVEN CRY.
PHIGURE ISN'T VERY SENTI-MENTAL...
...BUT HE ALWAYS PRAISES ME WHEN I WORK HARD.
I BET HAOMA WILL TEASE ME ABOUT MY TERRIBLE HAND-WRITING...
BUT SHE'S ALL TALK. I KNOW SHE'S A SOFTY AT HEART.
I'M NOT GOOD FOR MUCH, BUT THE MASTER CHOSE ME.
MS. ASHLEIGH IS STRICT BUT FAIR.
I DON'T KNOW VYRDE VERY WELL YET...
...BUT I HOPE WE CAN HAVE A GOOD BELLY LAUGH TOGETHER SOMEDAY SOON.
AWYN...

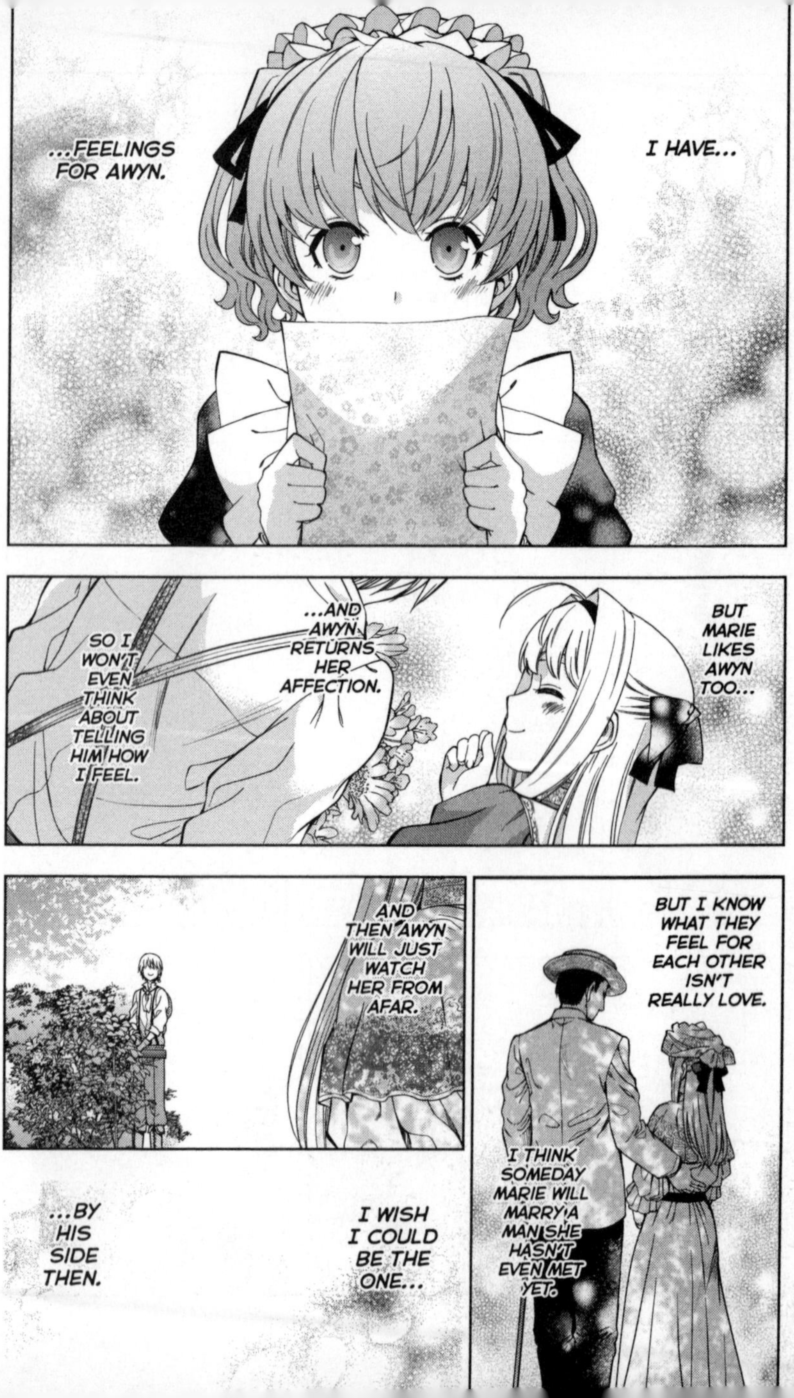
I HAVE...
...FEELINGS FOR AWYN.
BUT MARIE LIKES AWYN TOO...
...AND AWYN RETURNS HER AFFECTION.
SO I WON'T EVEN THINK ABOUT TELLING HIM HOW I FEEL.
BUT I KNOW WHAT THEY FEEL FOR EACH OTHER ISN'T REALLY LOVE.
I THINK SOMEDAY MARIE WILL MARRY A MAN SHE HASN'T EVEN MET YET.
AND THEN AWYN WILL JUST WATCH HER FROM AFAR.
I WISH I COULD BE THE ONE...
...BY HIS SIDE THEN.

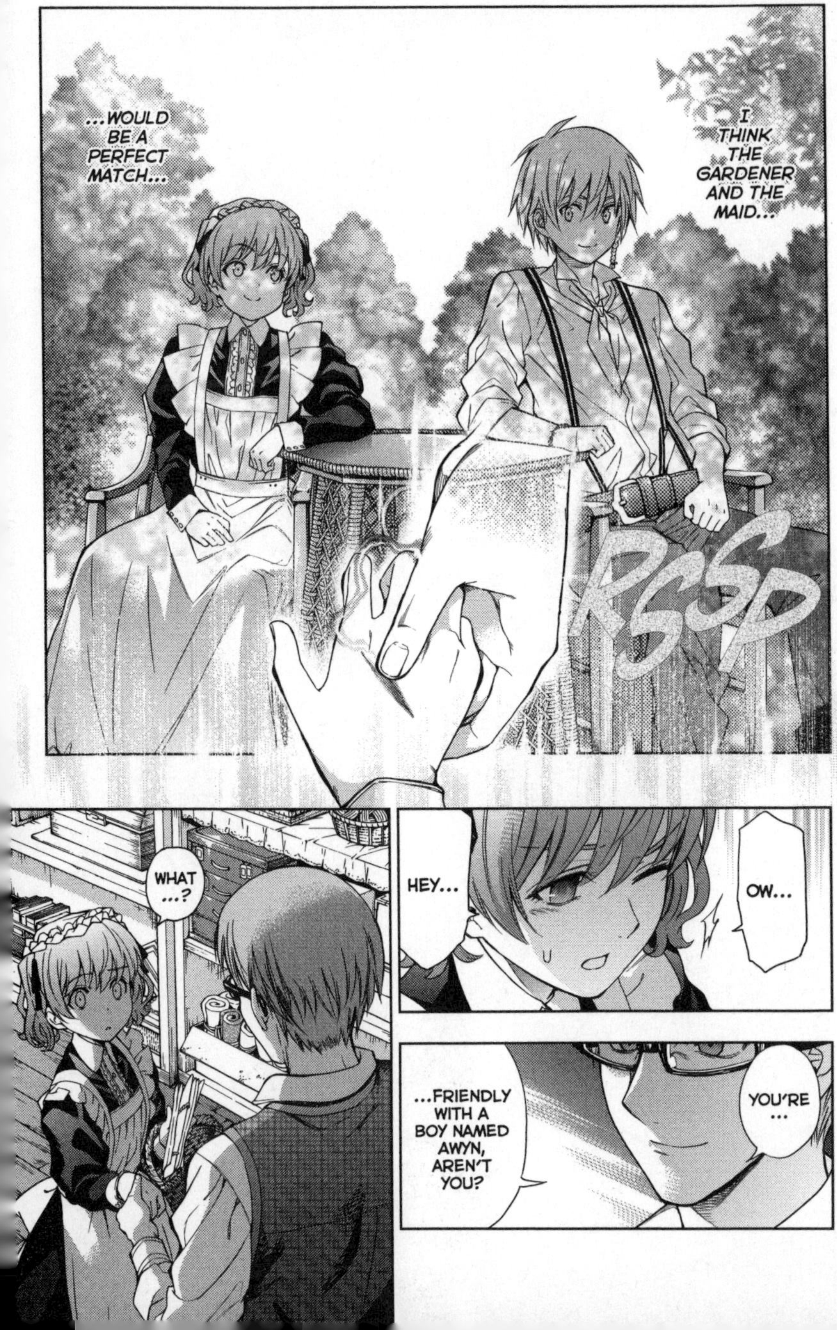
I THINK THE GARDENER AND THE MAID...
...WOULD BE A PERFECT MATCH...
RSSP
OW...
HEY...
YOU'RE ...
...FRIENDLY WITH A BOY NAMED AWYN, AREN'T YOU?
WHAT ...?

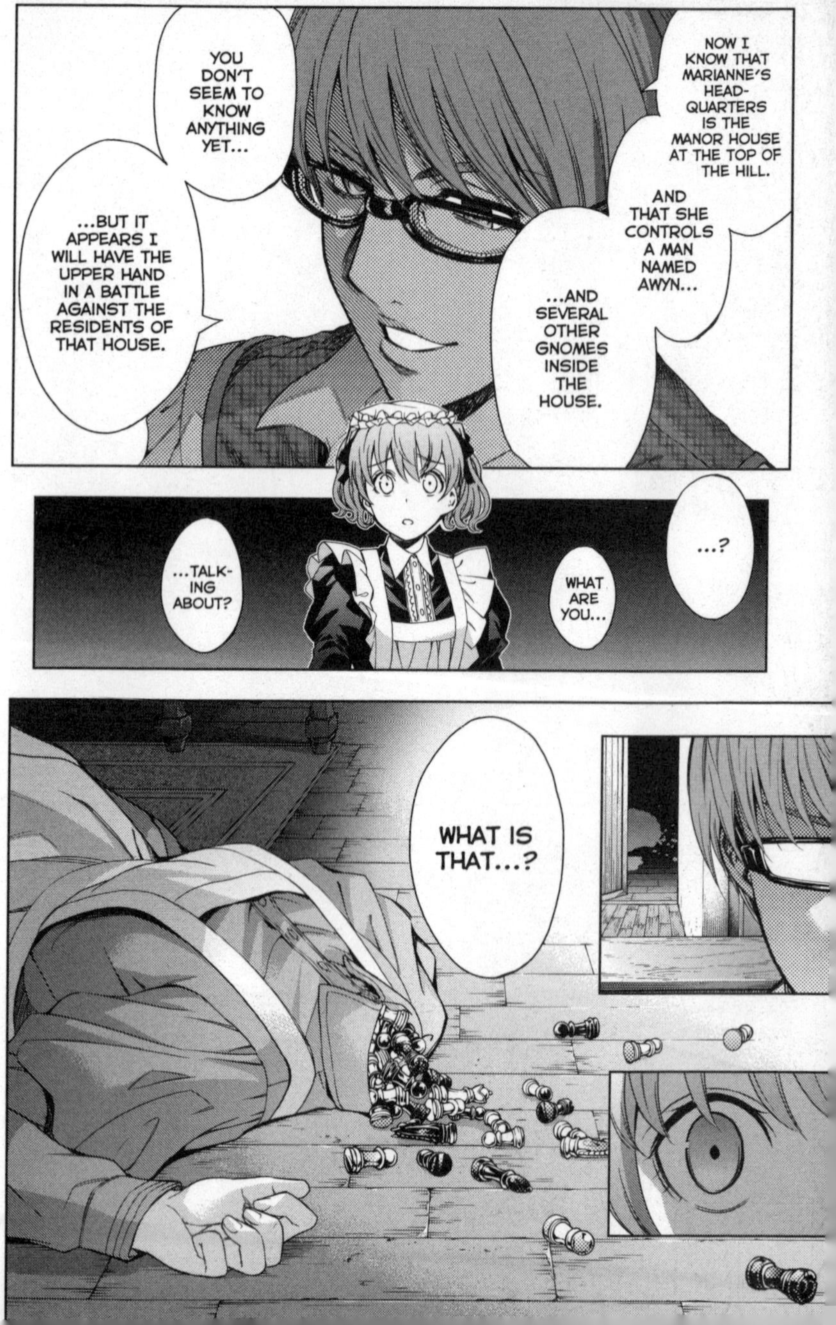
NOW I KNOW THAT MARIANNE'S HEAD-QUARTERS IS THE MANOR HOUSE AT THE TOP OF THE HILL.
AND THAT SHE CONTROLS A MAN NAMED AWYN...
...AND SEVERAL OTHER GNOMES INSIDE THE HOUSE.
YOU DON'T SEEM TO KNOW ANYTHING YET...
...BUT IT APPEARS I WILL HAVE THE UPPER HAND IN A BATTLE AGAINST THE RESIDENTS OF THAT HOUSE.
...?
WHAT ARE YOU...
...TALK-ING ABOUT?
WHAT IS THAT...?

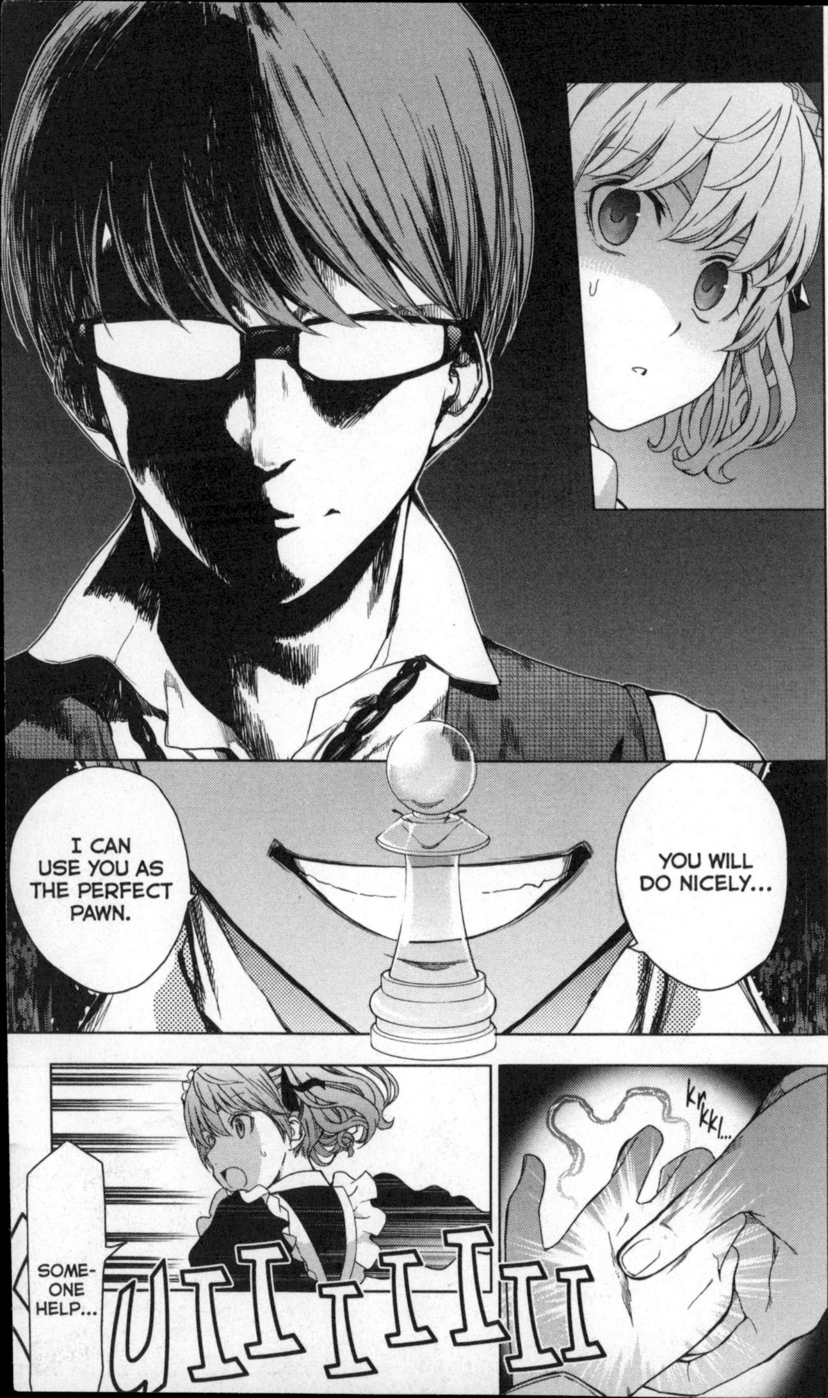
YOU WILL DO NICELY...
I CAN USE YOU AS THE PERFECT PAWN.
KRKKI...
SOME-ONE HELP...
UIIIIIIII

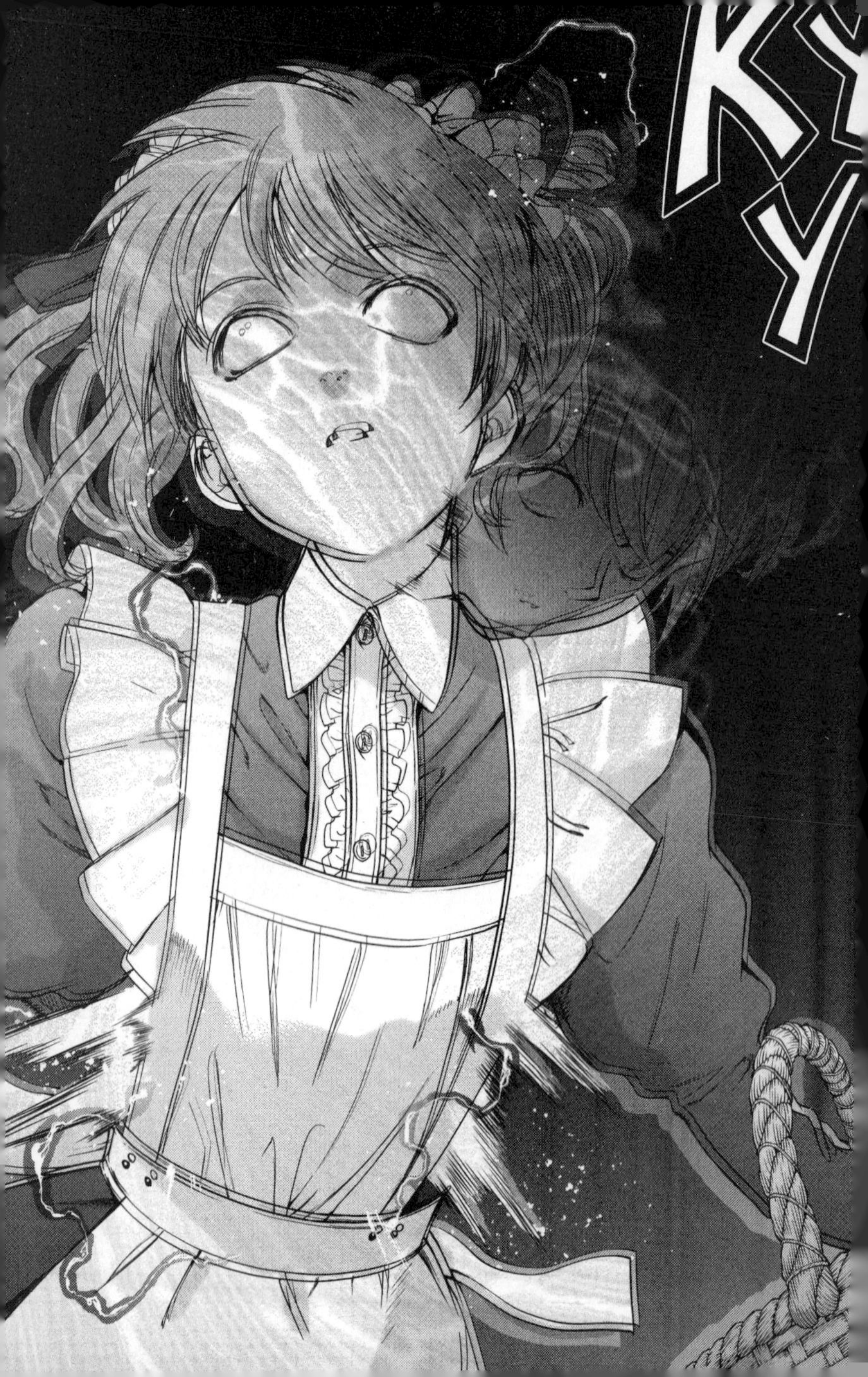

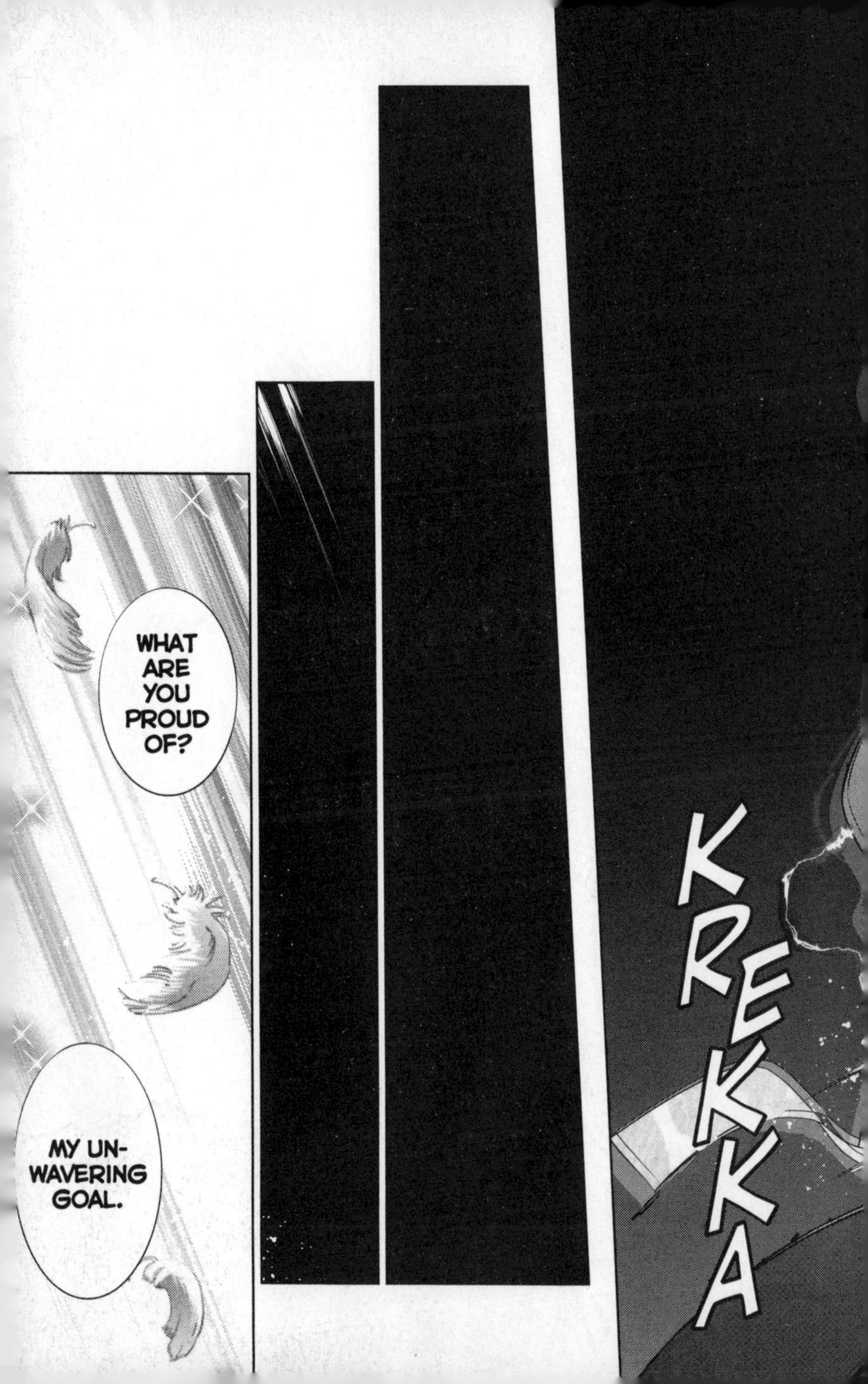
KREKKA
WHAT ARE YOU PROUD OF?
MY UN-WAVERING GOAL.

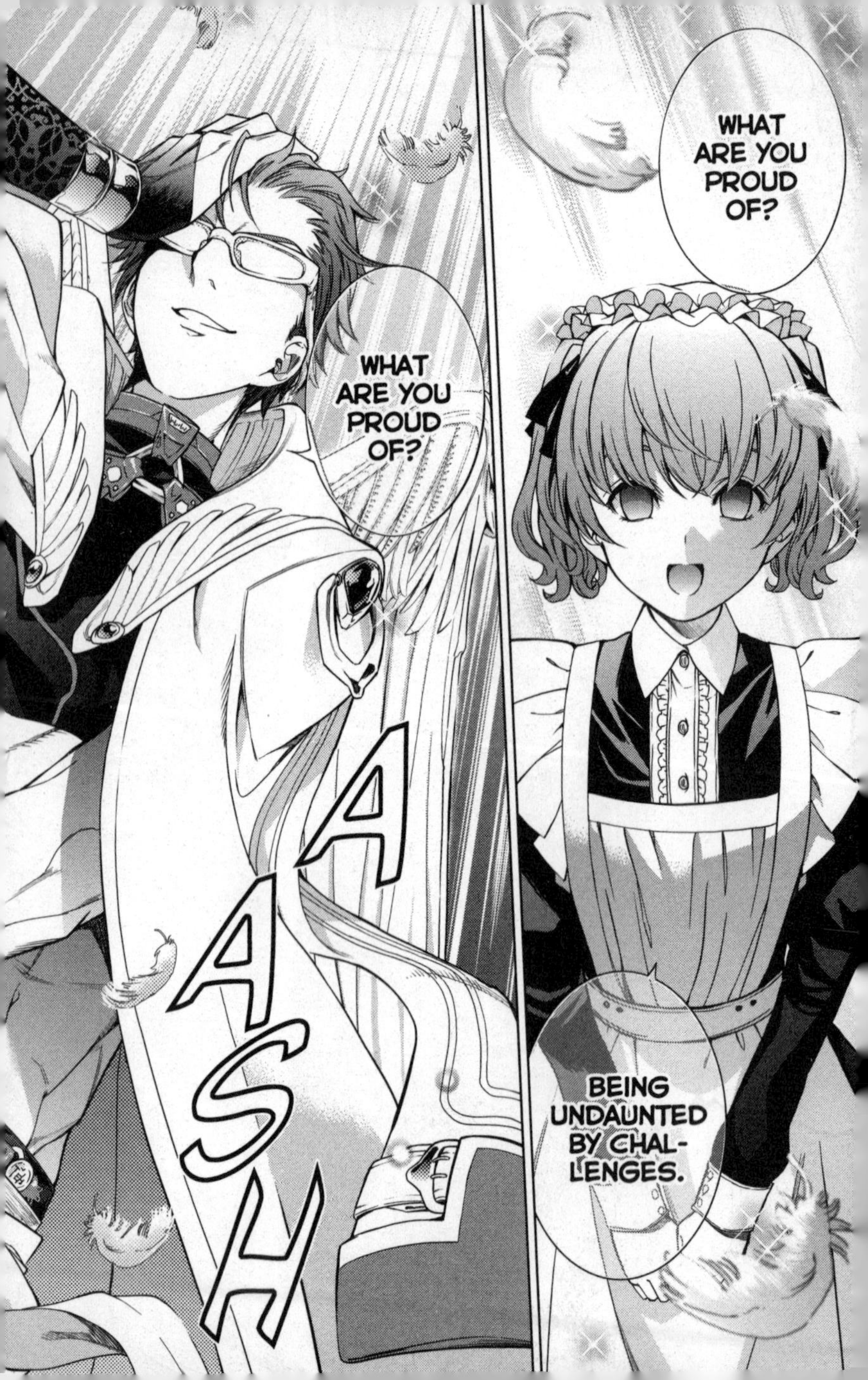
WHAT ARE YOU PROUD OF?
BEING UNDAUNTED BY CHAL-LENGES.
WHAT ARE YOU PROUD OF?
AASH

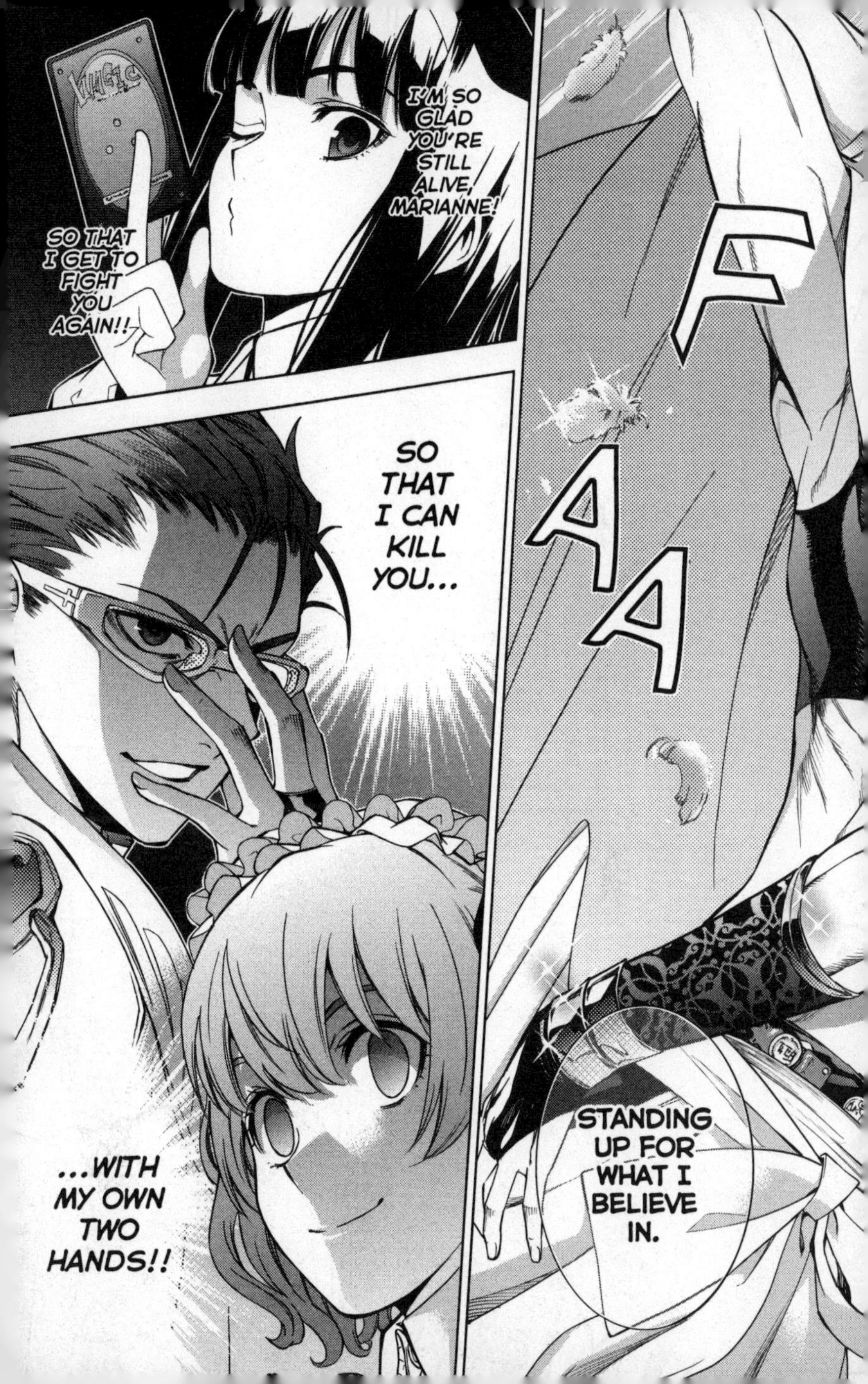
FAAA
STANDING UP FOR WHAT I BELIEVE IN.
I'M SO GLAD YOU'RE STILL ALIVE, MARIANNE!
SO THAT I GET TO FIGHT YOU AGAIN!!
SO THAT I CAN KILL YOU...
...WITH MY OWN TWO HANDS!!

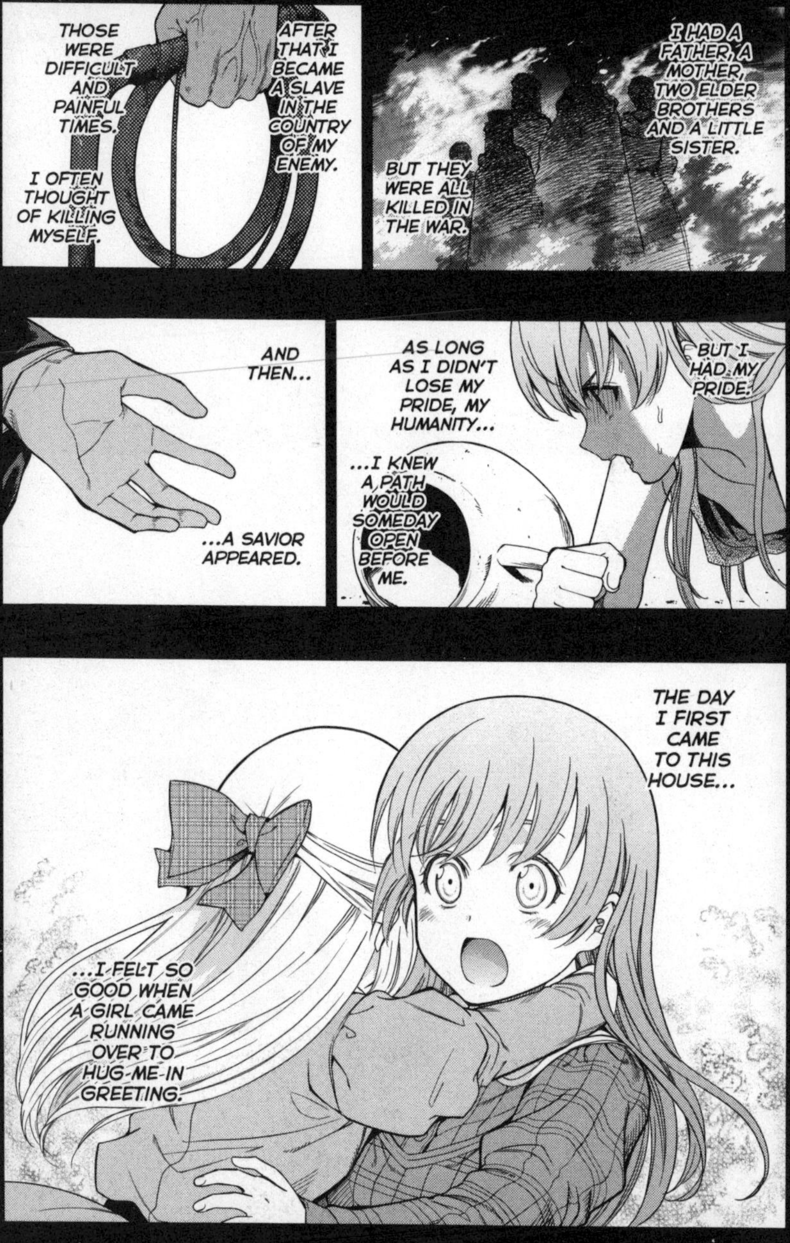
I HAD A FATHER, A MOTHER, TWO ELDER BROTHERS AND A LITTLE SISTER.
BUT THEY WERE ALL KILLED IN THE WAR.
AFTER THAT I BECAME A SLAVE IN THE COUNTRY OF MY ENEMY.
THOSE WERE DIFFICULT AND PAINFUL TIMES.
I OFTEN THOUGHT OF KILLING MYSELF.
BUT I HAD MY PRIDE.
AS LONG AS I DIDN'T LOSE MY PRIDE, MY HUMANITY...
...I KNEW A PATH WOULD SOMEDAY OPEN BEFORE ME.
AND THEN...
...A SAVIOR APPEARED.
THE DAY I FIRST CAME TO THIS HOUSE...
...I FELT SO GOOD WHEN A GIRL CAME RUNNING OVER TO HUG ME IN GREETING.

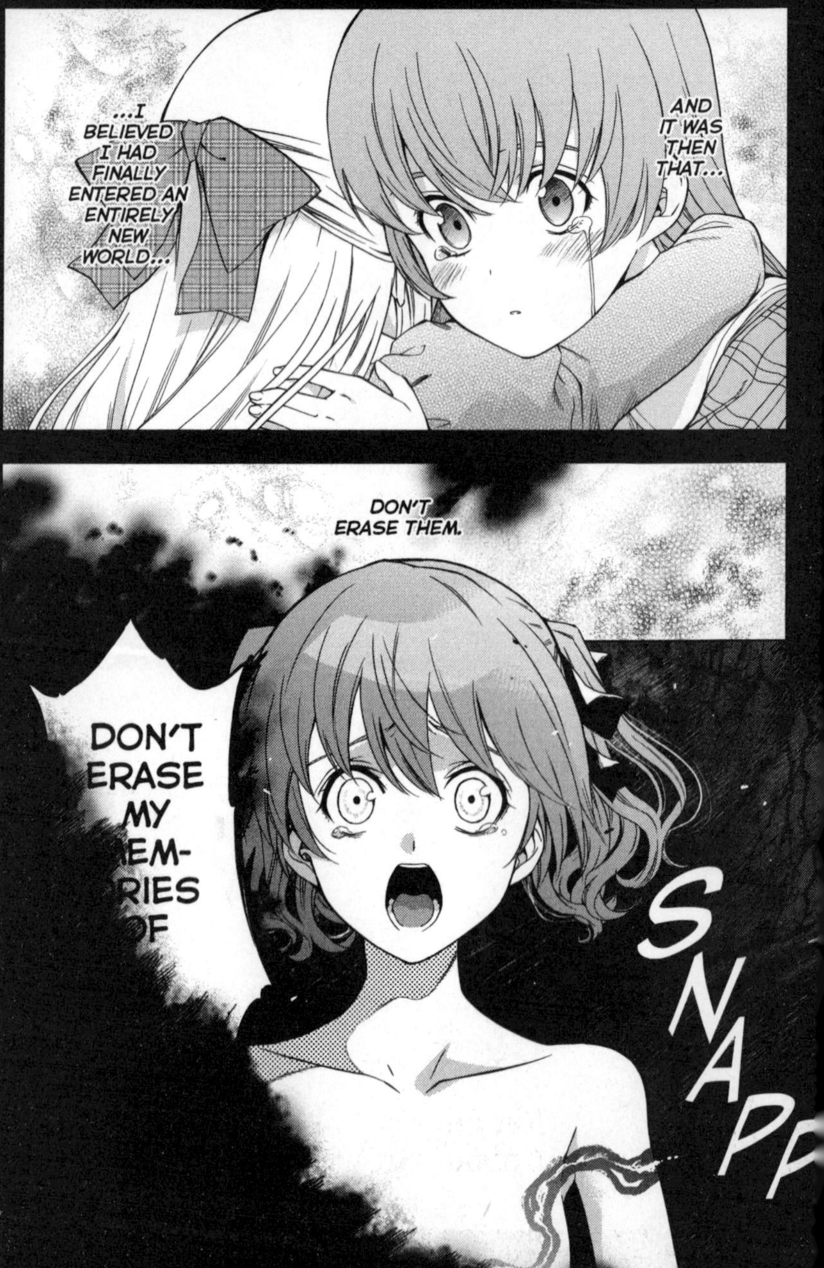
AND IT WAS THEN THAT...
...I BELIEVED I HAD FINALLY ENTERED AN ENTIRELY NEW WORLD...
DON'T ERASE THEM.
SNAPP
DON'T ERASE MY MEM- ORIES OF

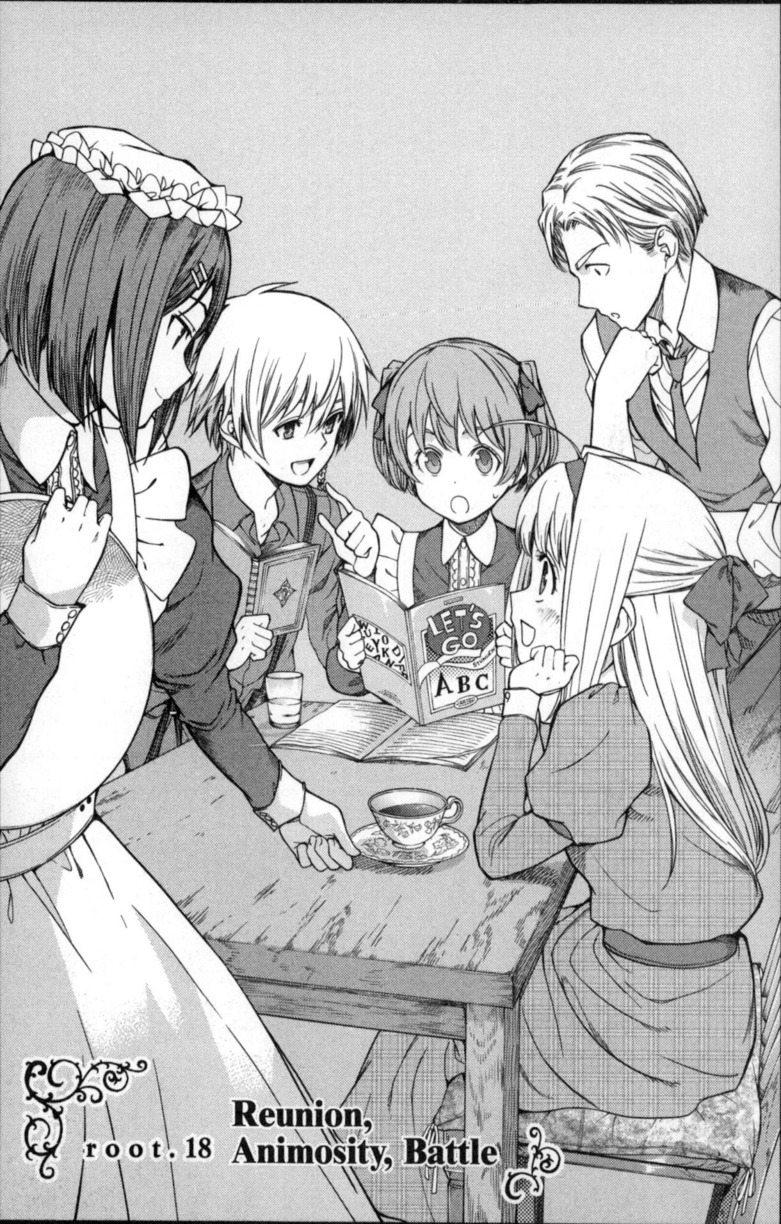
LET'S GO
ABC

root. 18 Reunion, Animosity, Battle

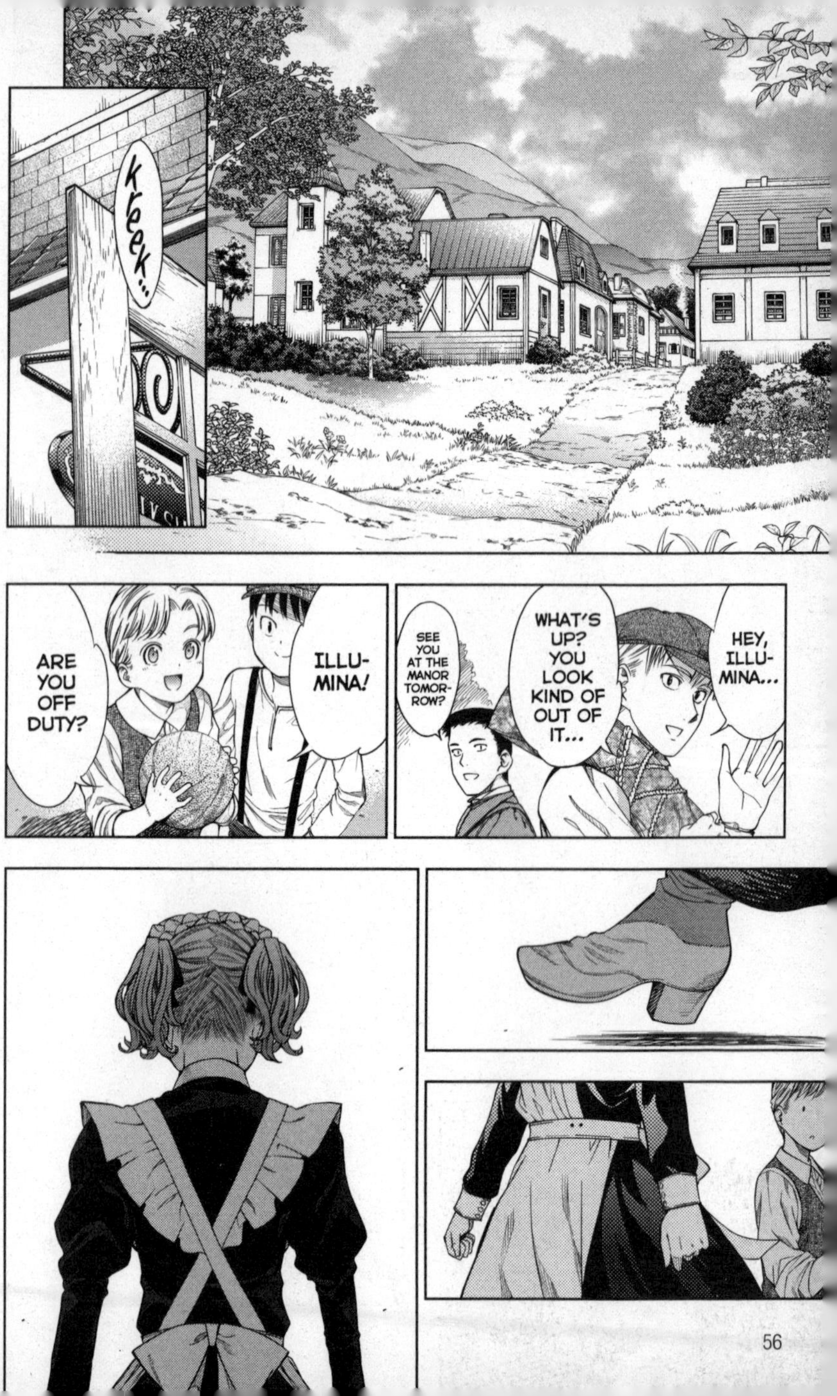
kreek...
HEY, ILLUMINA...
WHAT'S UP? YOU LOOK KIND OF OUT OF IT...
SEE YOU AT THE MANOR TOMORROW?
ILLUMINA!
ARE YOU OFF DUTY?

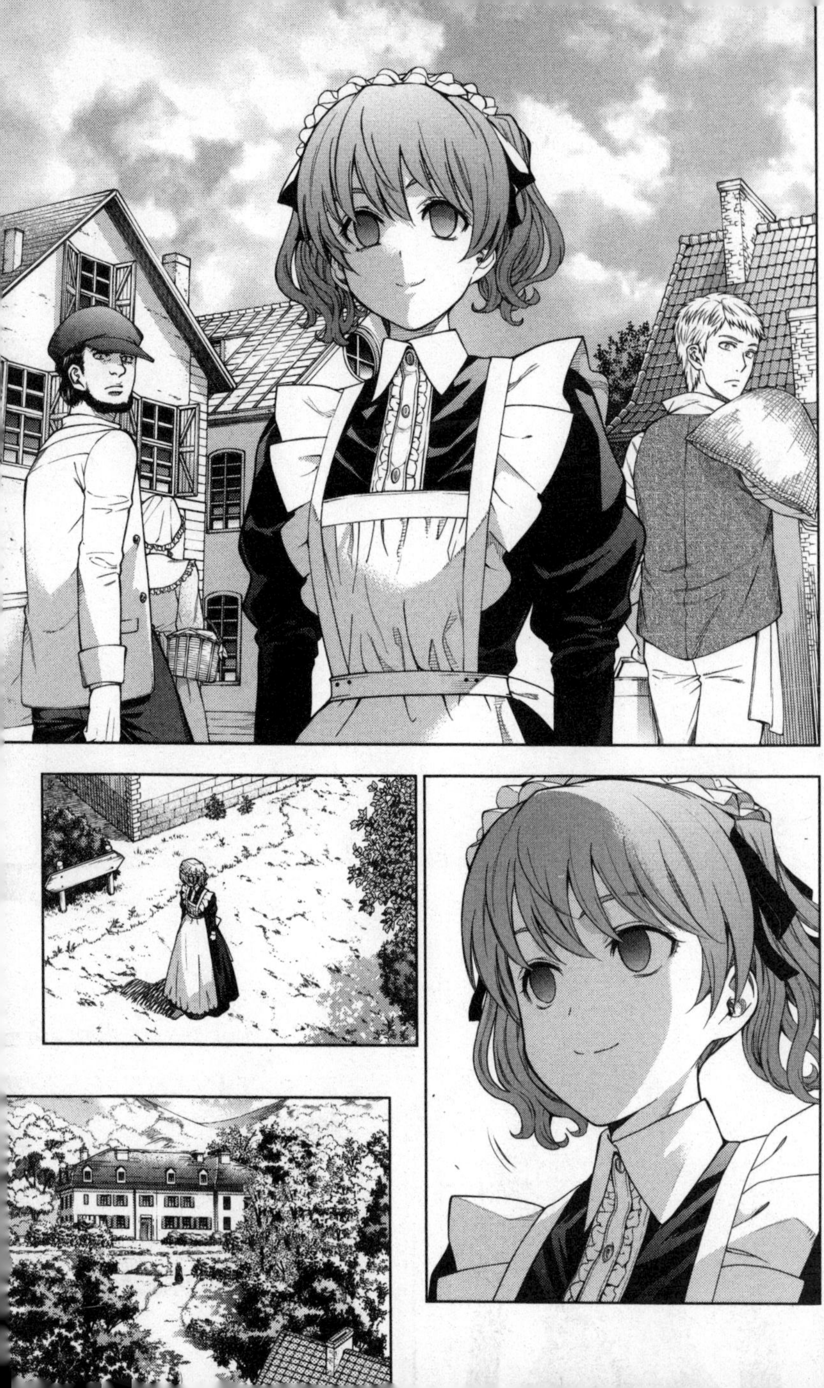

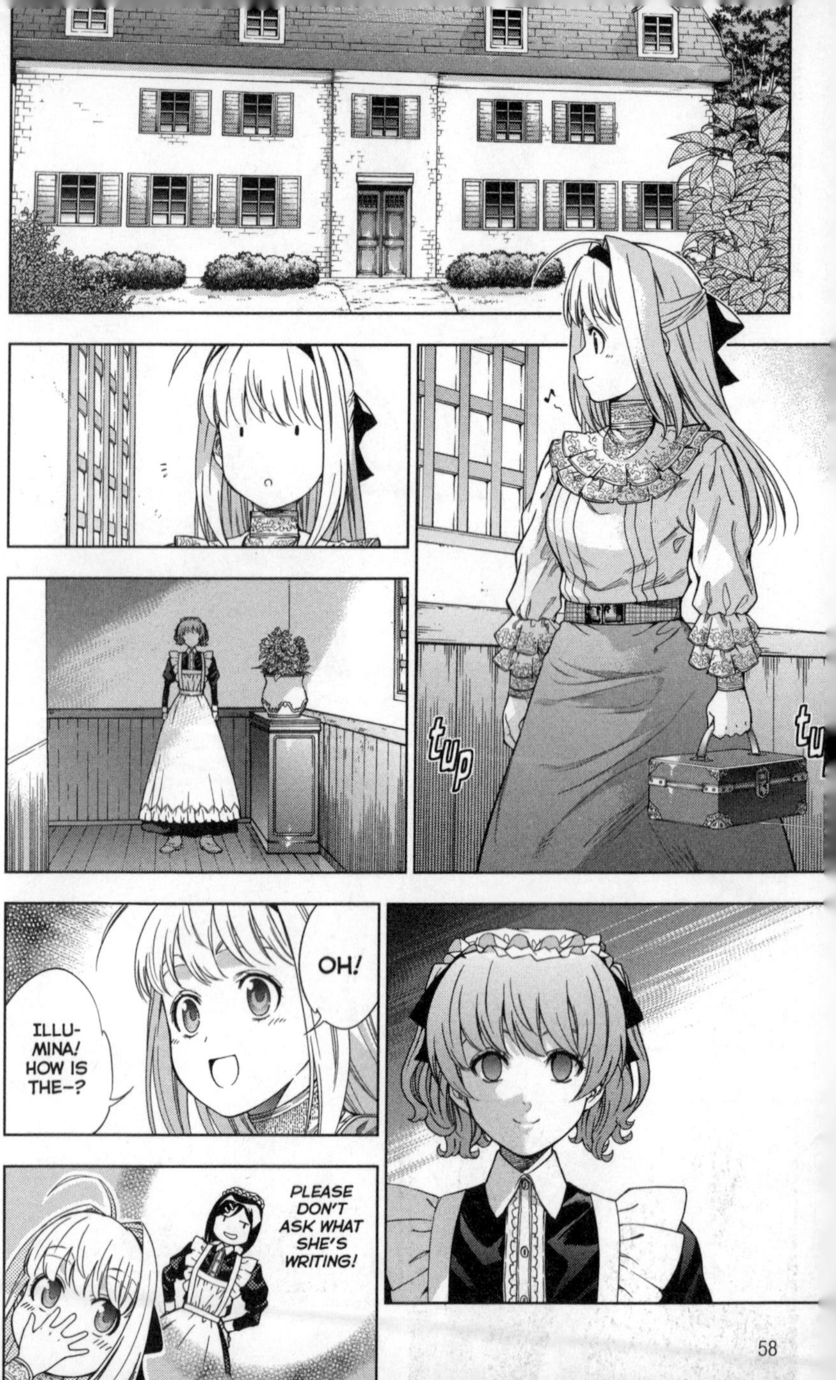
tup
tu
OH!
ILLU-MINA! HOW IS THE–?
PLEASE DON'T ASK WHAT SHE'S WRITING!

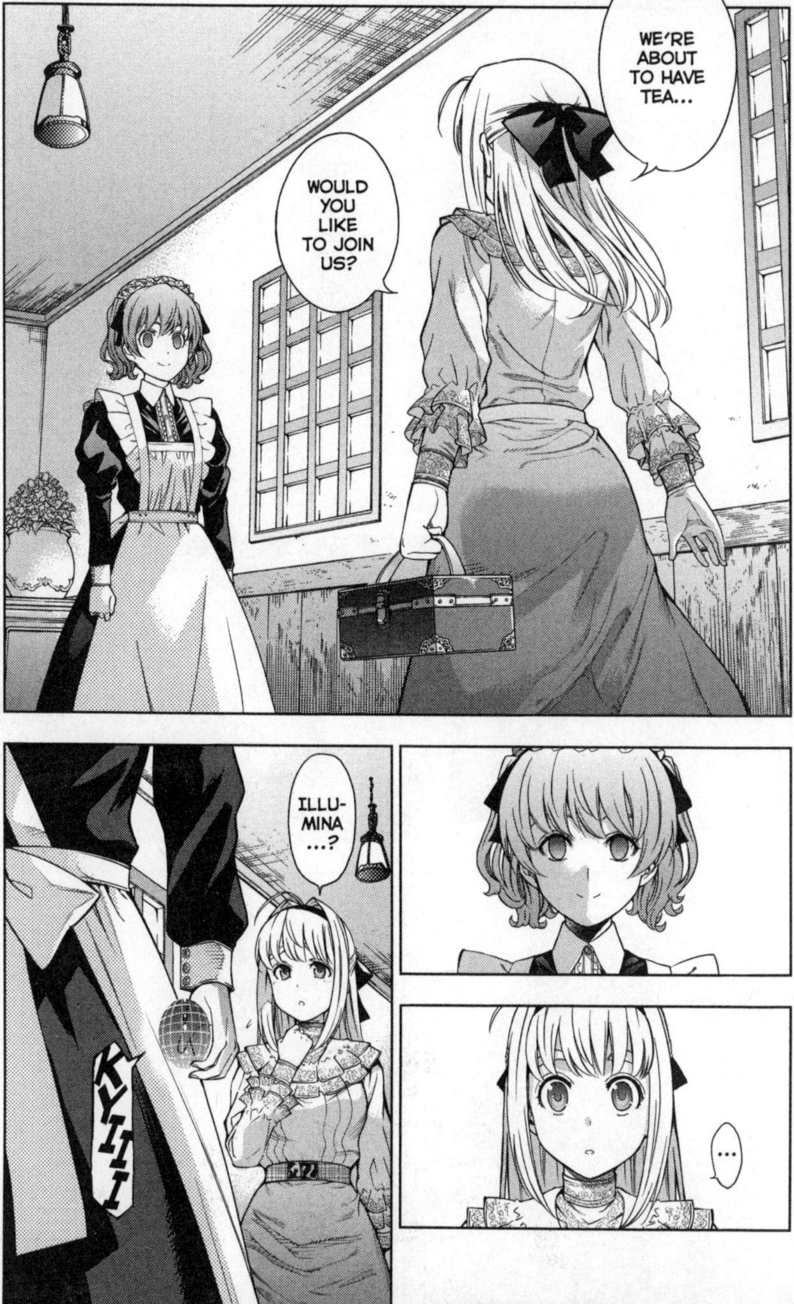
WE'RE ABOUT TO HAVE TEA...
WOULD YOU LIKE TO JOIN US?
...
ILLUMINA...?
KYIII

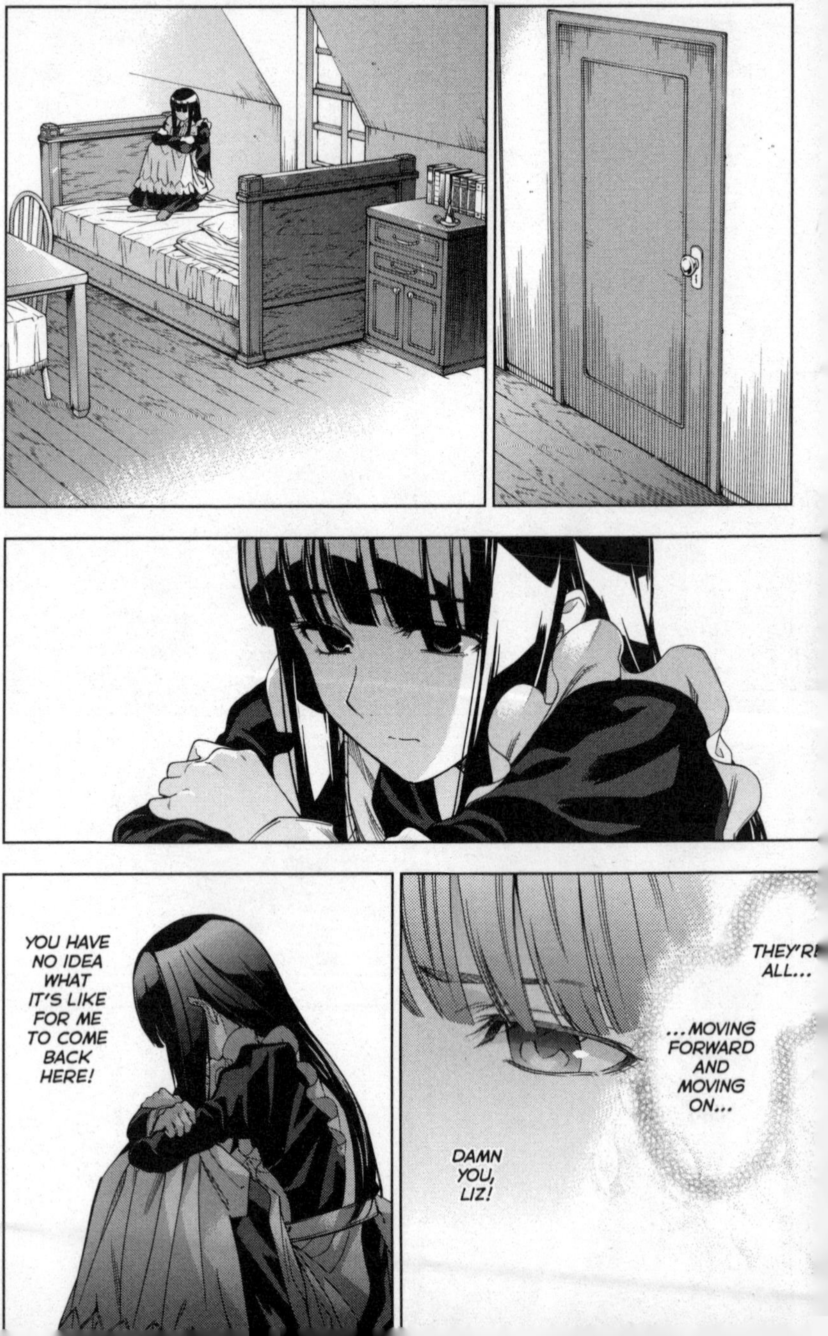
THEY'RE ALL...
...MOVING FORWARD AND MOVING ON...
DAMN YOU, LIZ!
YOU HAVE NO IDEA WHAT IT'S LIKE FOR ME TO COME BACK HERE!

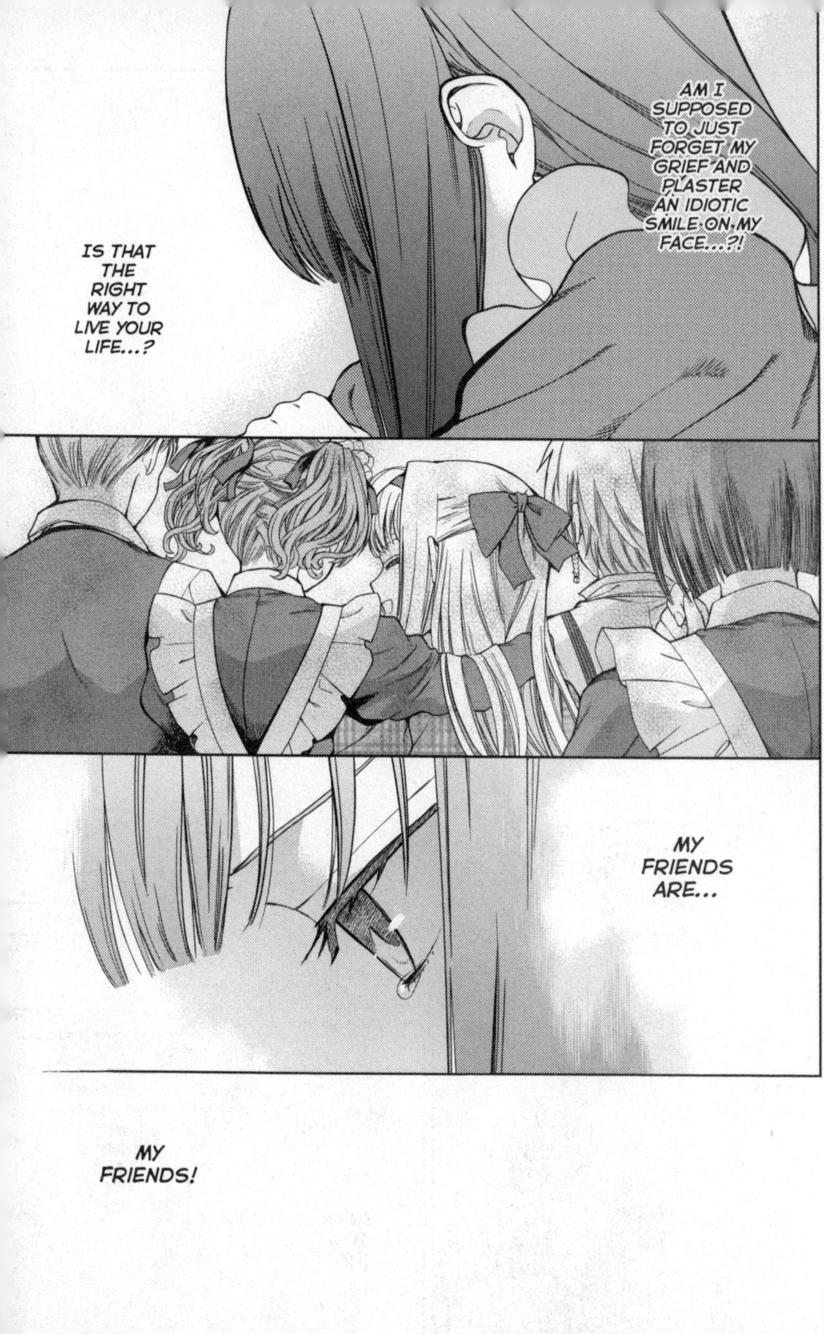
AM I SUPPOSED TO JUST FORGET MY GRIEF AND PLASTER AN IDIOTIC SMILE ON MY FACE...?!
IS THAT THE RIGHT WAY TO LIVE YOUR LIFE...?
MY FRIENDS ARE...
MY FRIENDS!

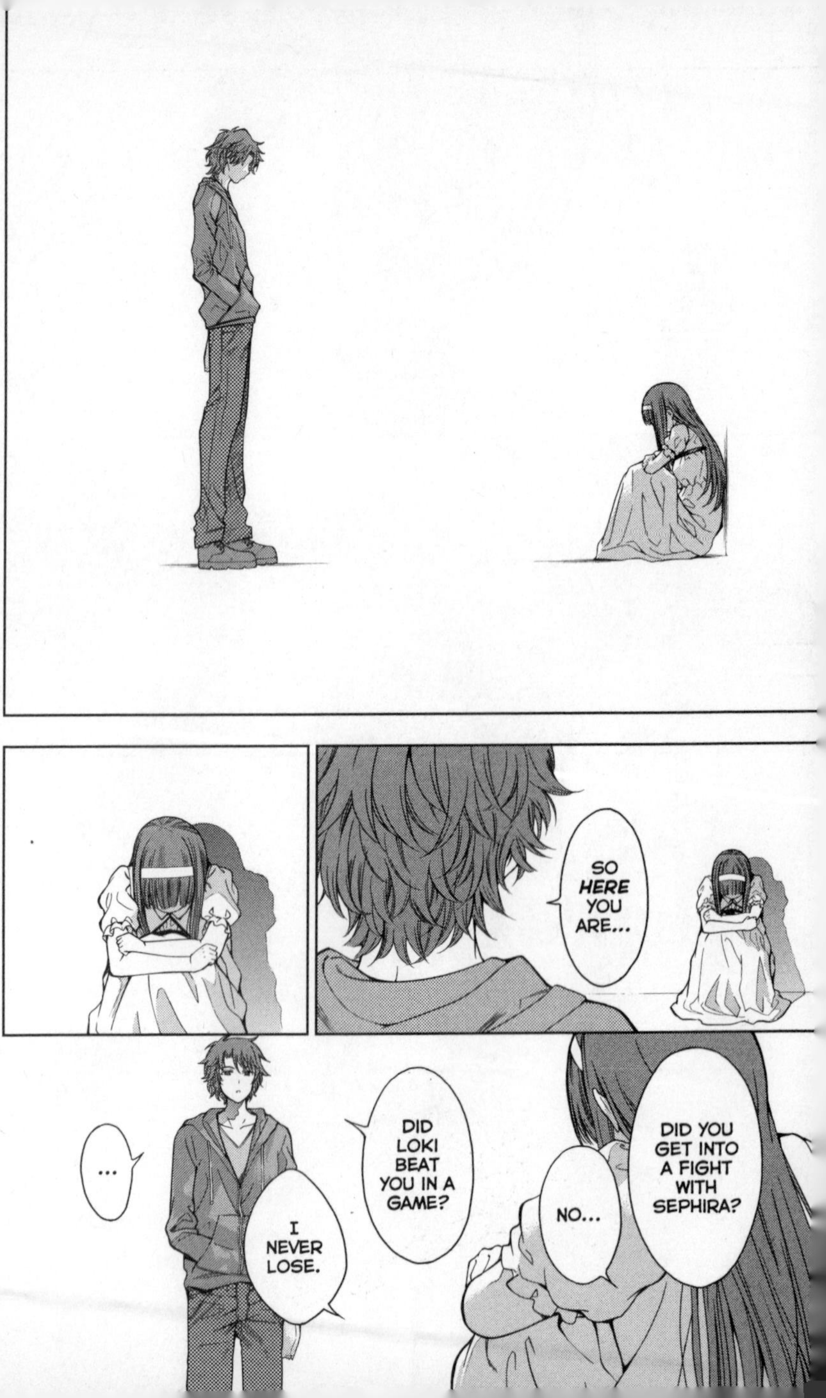
SO *HERE* YOU ARE...
DID YOU GET INTO A FIGHT WITH SEPHIRA?
NO...
DID LOKI BEAT YOU IN A GAME?
I NEVER LOSE.
...

WANT A SNACK?

Comes with a collectible card.

VUL...

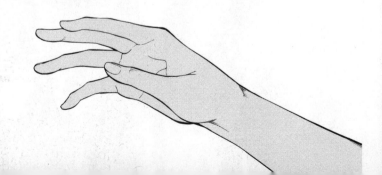

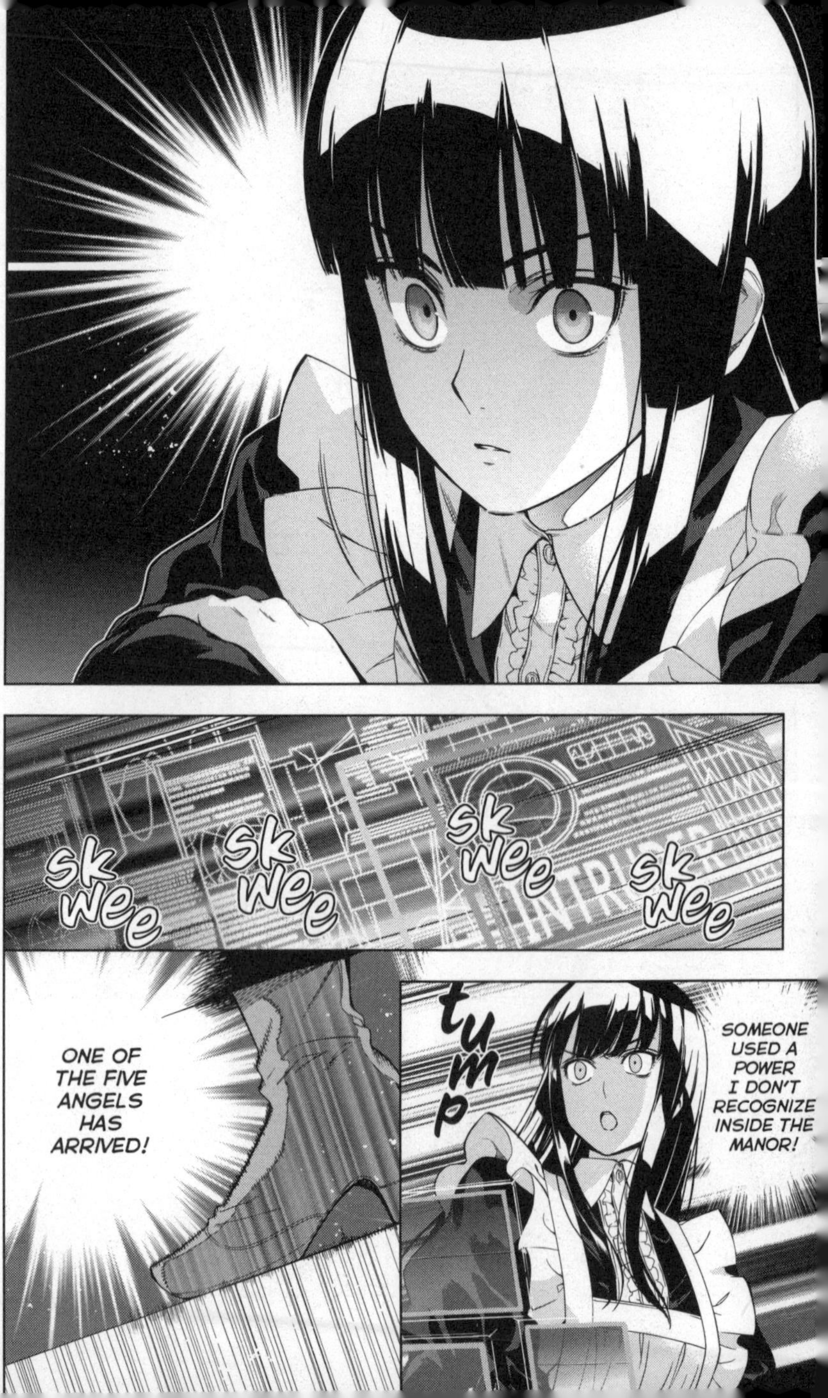
sk wee
sk wee
sk wee
sk wee
SOMEONE USED A POWER I DON'T RECOGNIZE INSIDE THE MANOR!
tump
ONE OF THE FIVE ANGELS HAS ARRIVED!

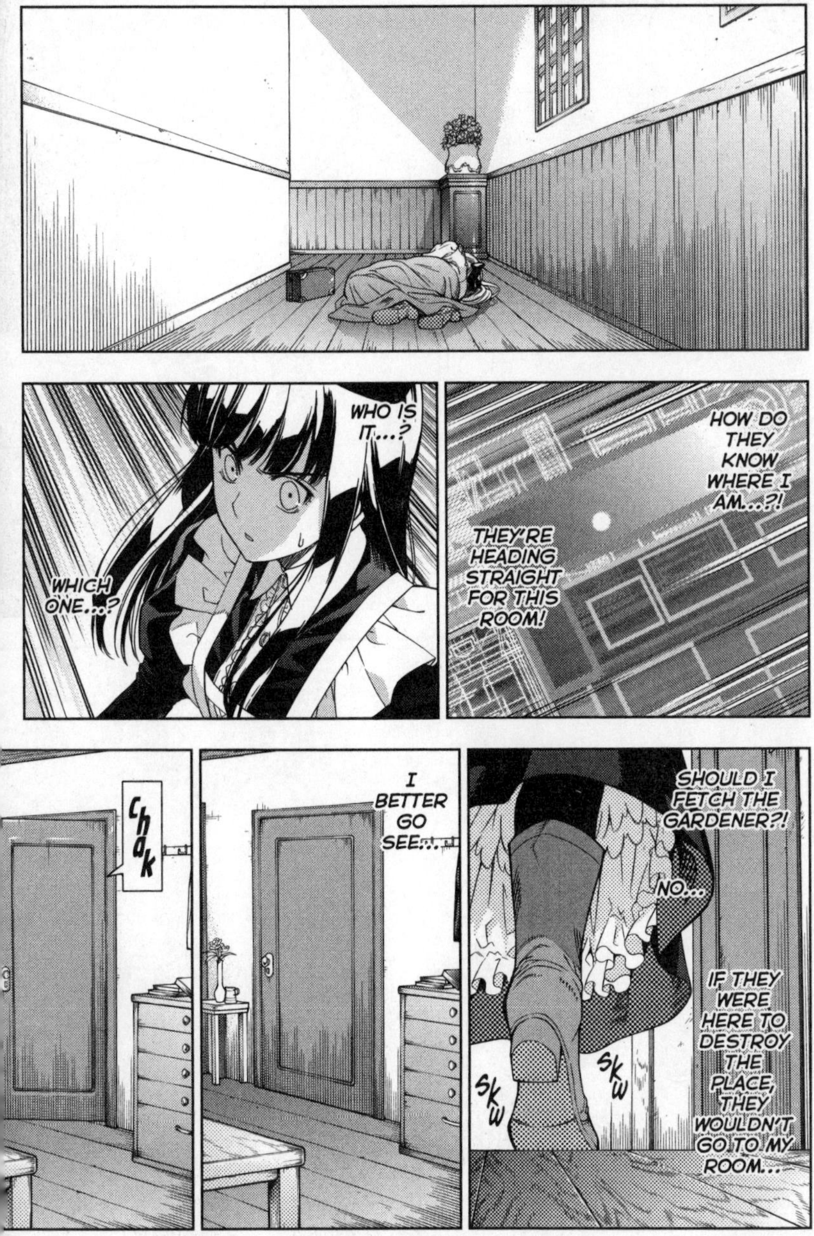
HOW DO THEY KNOW WHERE I AM...?!
THEY'RE HEADING STRAIGHT FOR THIS ROOM!
WHO IS IT...?
WHICH ONE...?
SHOULD I FETCH THE GARDENER?!
NO...
IF THEY WERE HERE TO DESTROY THE PLACE, THEY WOULDN'T GO TO MY ROOM...
SKW
SKW
I BETTER GO SEE...
CHAK

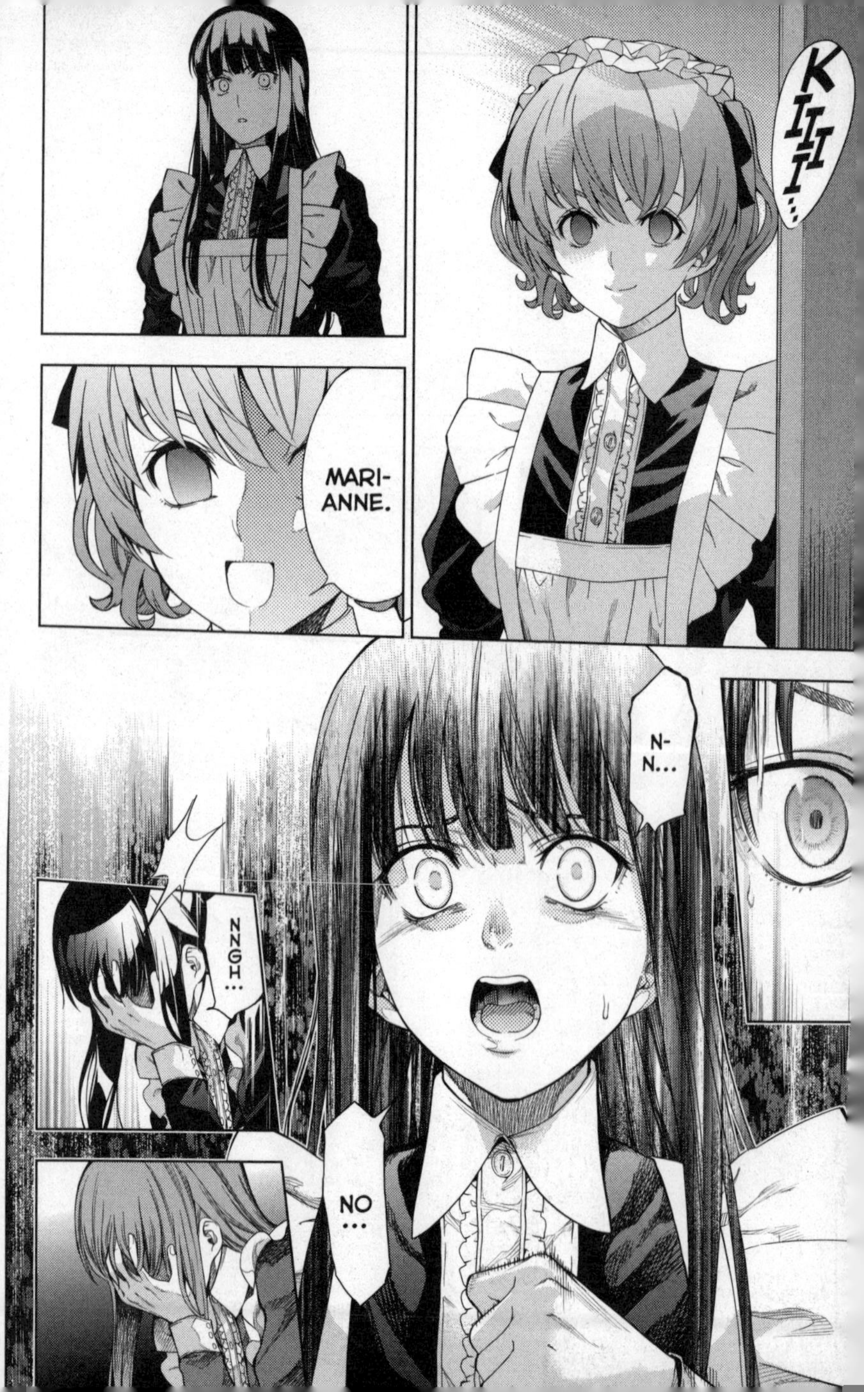
KIIII...
MARI-
ANNE.
N-
N...
NNGH
...
NO
...

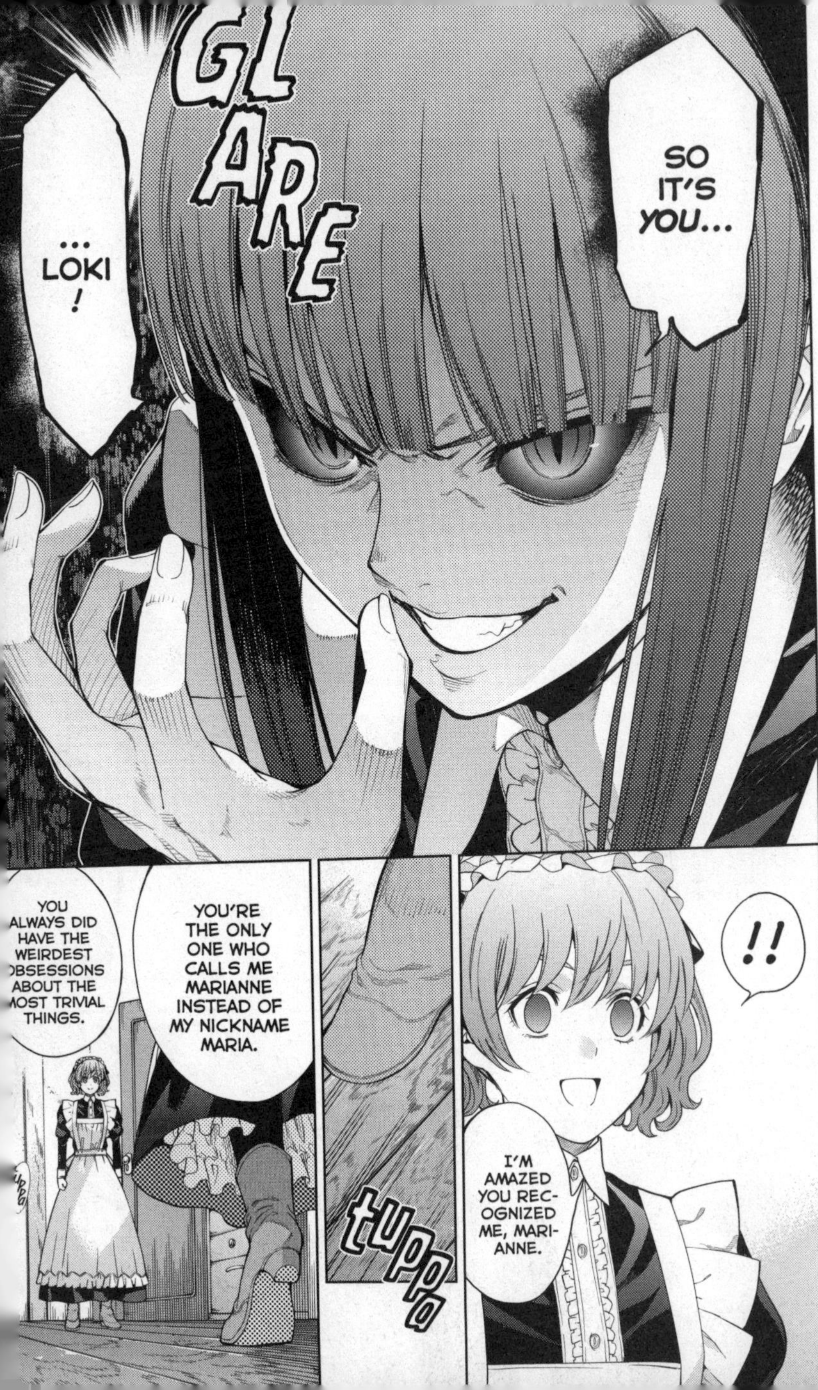
SO IT'S YOU...
... LOKI!
GLARE
!!
I'M AMAZED YOU RECOGNIZED ME, MARIANNE.
tuppa
YOU'RE THE ONLY ONE WHO CALLS ME MARIANNE INSTEAD OF MY NICKNAME MARIA.
YOU ALWAYS DID HAVE THE WEIRDEST OBSESSIONS ABOUT THE MOST TRIVIAL THINGS.

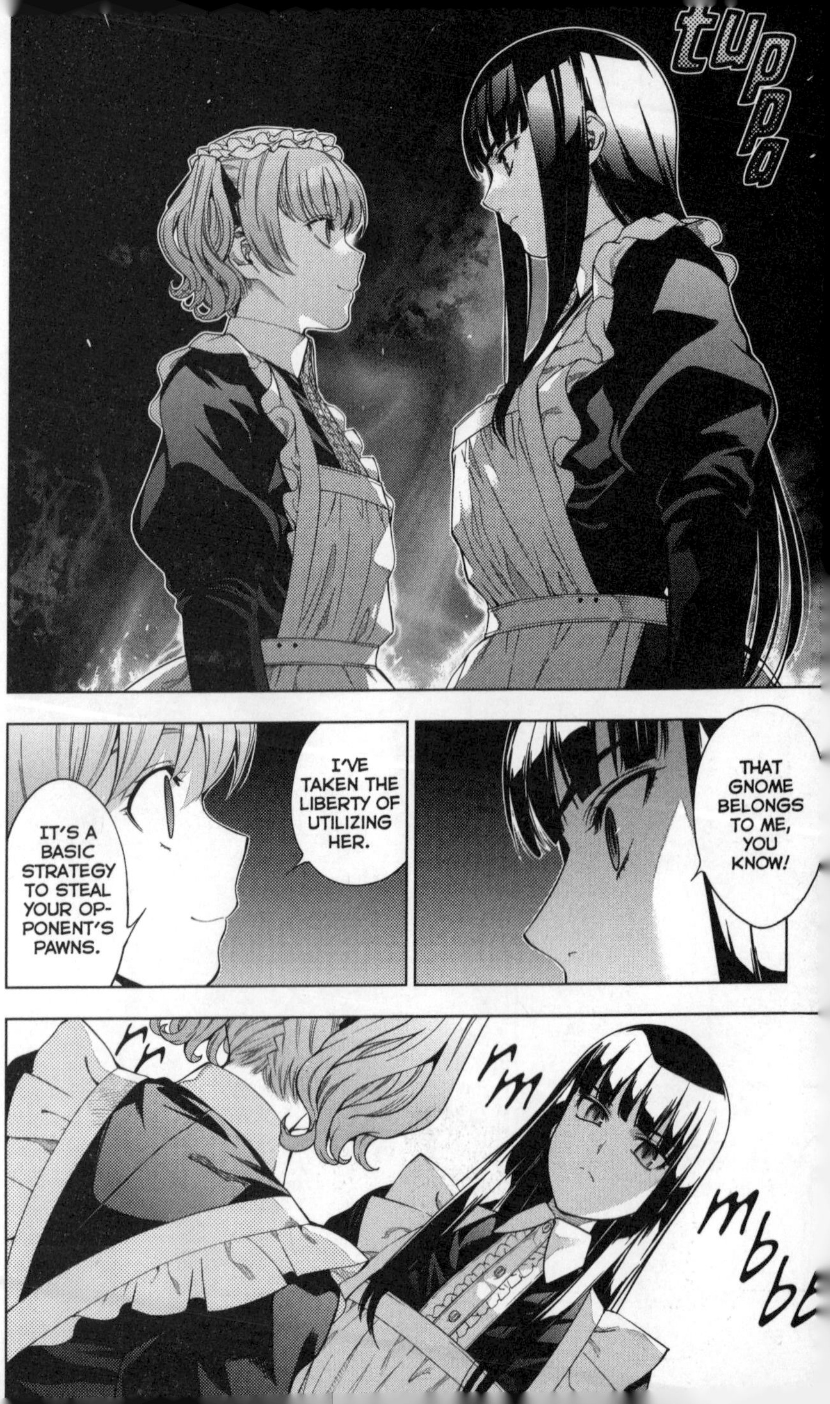
tuppa
THAT GNOME BELONGS TO ME, YOU KNOW!
I'VE TAKEN THE LIBERTY OF UTILIZING HER.
IT'S A BASIC STRATEGY TO STEAL YOUR OPPONENT'S PAWNS.
rm
rr
mbb

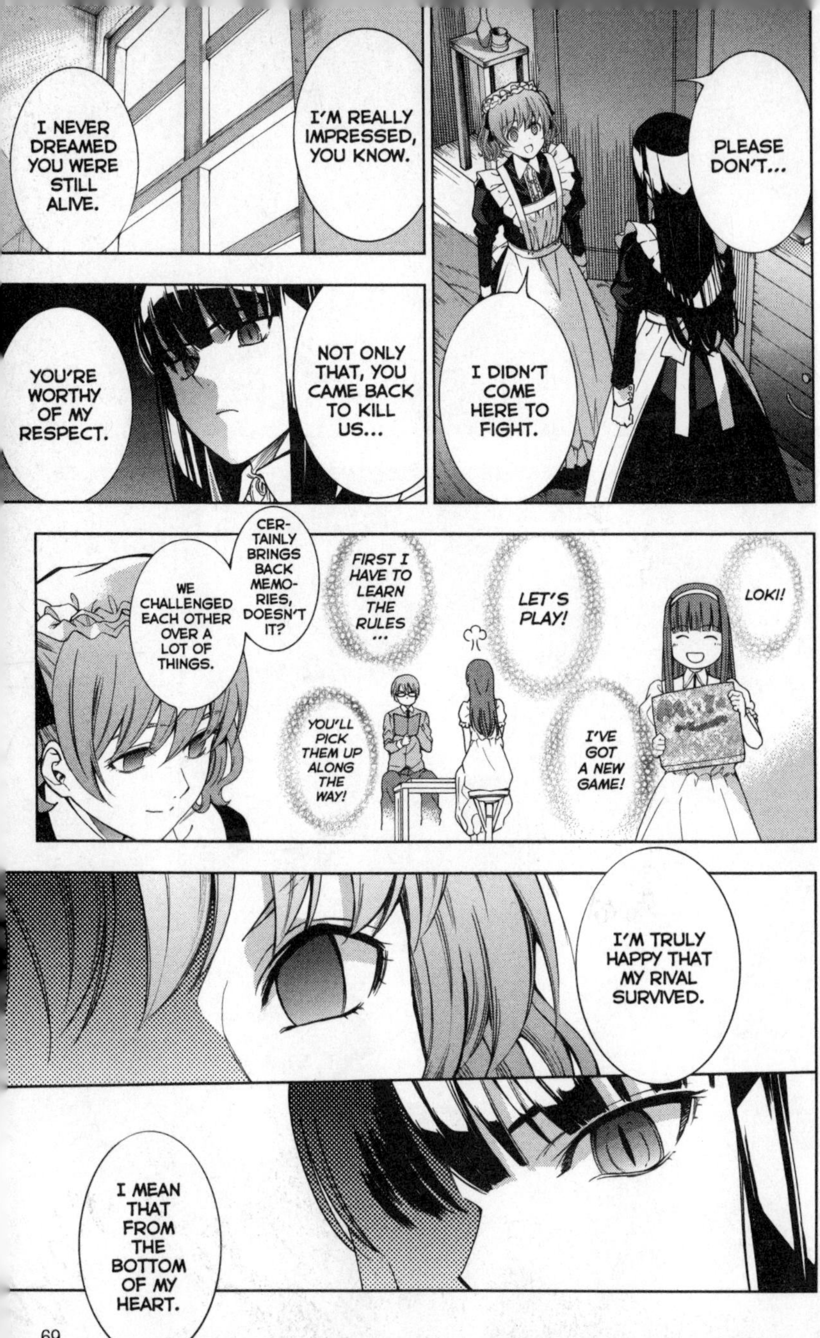
PLEASE DON'T...
I DIDN'T COME HERE TO FIGHT.
I'M REALLY IMPRESSED, YOU KNOW.
I NEVER DREAMED YOU WERE STILL ALIVE.
NOT ONLY THAT, YOU CAME BACK TO KILL US...
YOU'RE WORTHY OF MY RESPECT.
LOKI!
I'VE GOT A NEW GAME!
LET'S PLAY!
FIRST I HAVE TO LEARN THE RULES...
YOU'LL PICK THEM UP ALONG THE WAY!
CER-TAINLY BRINGS BACK MEMO-RIES, DOESN'T IT?
WE CHALLENGED EACH OTHER OVER A LOT OF THINGS.
I'M TRULY HAPPY THAT MY RIVAL SURVIVED.
I MEAN THAT FROM THE BOTTOM OF MY HEART.

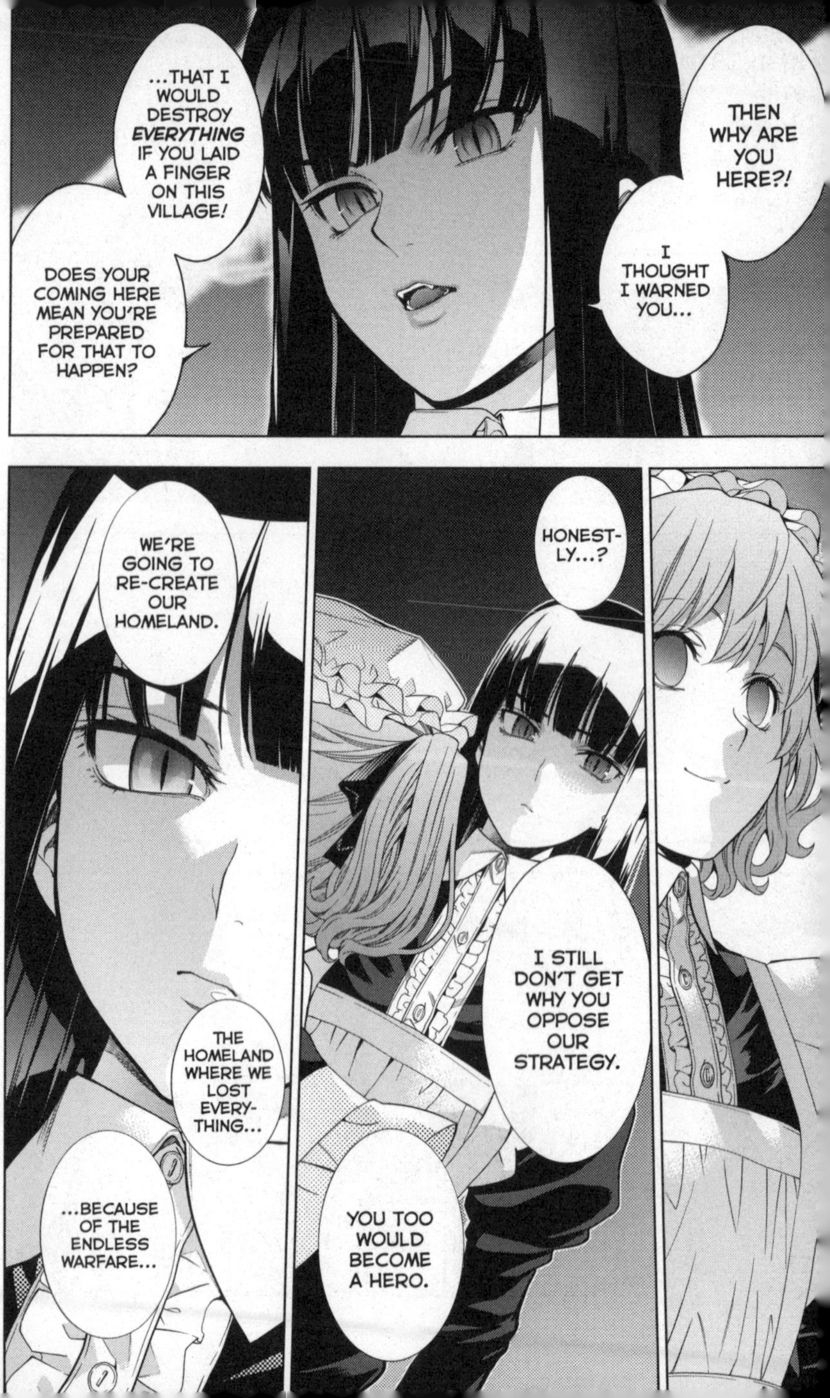
THEN WHY ARE YOU HERE?!
I THOUGHT I WARNED YOU...
...THAT I WOULD DESTROY *EVERYTHING* IF YOU LAID A FINGER ON THIS VILLAGE!
DOES YOUR COMING HERE MEAN YOU'RE PREPARED FOR THAT TO HAPPEN?
HONEST-LY...?
I STILL DON'T GET WHY YOU OPPOSE OUR STRATEGY.
YOU TOO WOULD BECOME A HERO.
WE'RE GOING TO RE-CREATE OUR HOMELAND.
THE HOMELAND WHERE WE LOST EVERY-THING...
...BECAUSE OF THE ENDLESS WARFARE...

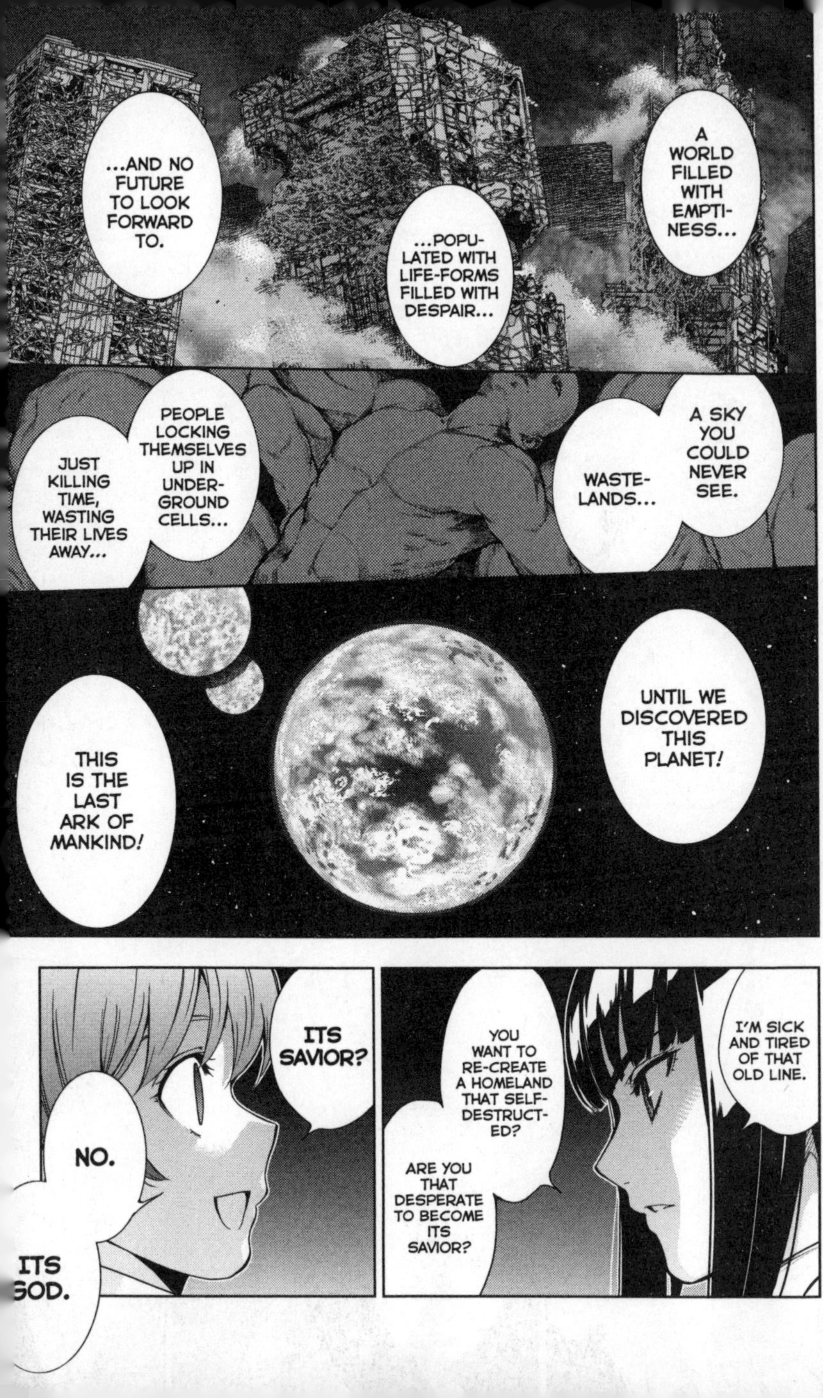
A WORLD FILLED WITH EMPTINESS...
...POPULATED WITH LIFE-FORMS FILLED WITH DESPAIR...
...AND NO FUTURE TO LOOK FORWARD TO.
A SKY YOU COULD NEVER SEE.
WASTELANDS...
PEOPLE LOCKING THEMSELVES UP IN UNDERGROUND CELLS...
JUST KILLING TIME, WASTING THEIR LIVES AWAY...
UNTIL WE DISCOVERED THIS PLANET!
THIS IS THE LAST ARK OF MANKIND!
I'M SICK AND TIRED OF THAT OLD LINE.
YOU WANT TO RE-CREATE A HOMELAND THAT SELF-DESTRUCTED?
ARE YOU THAT DESPERATE TO BECOME ITS SAVIOR?
ITS SAVIOR?
NO.
ITS GOD.

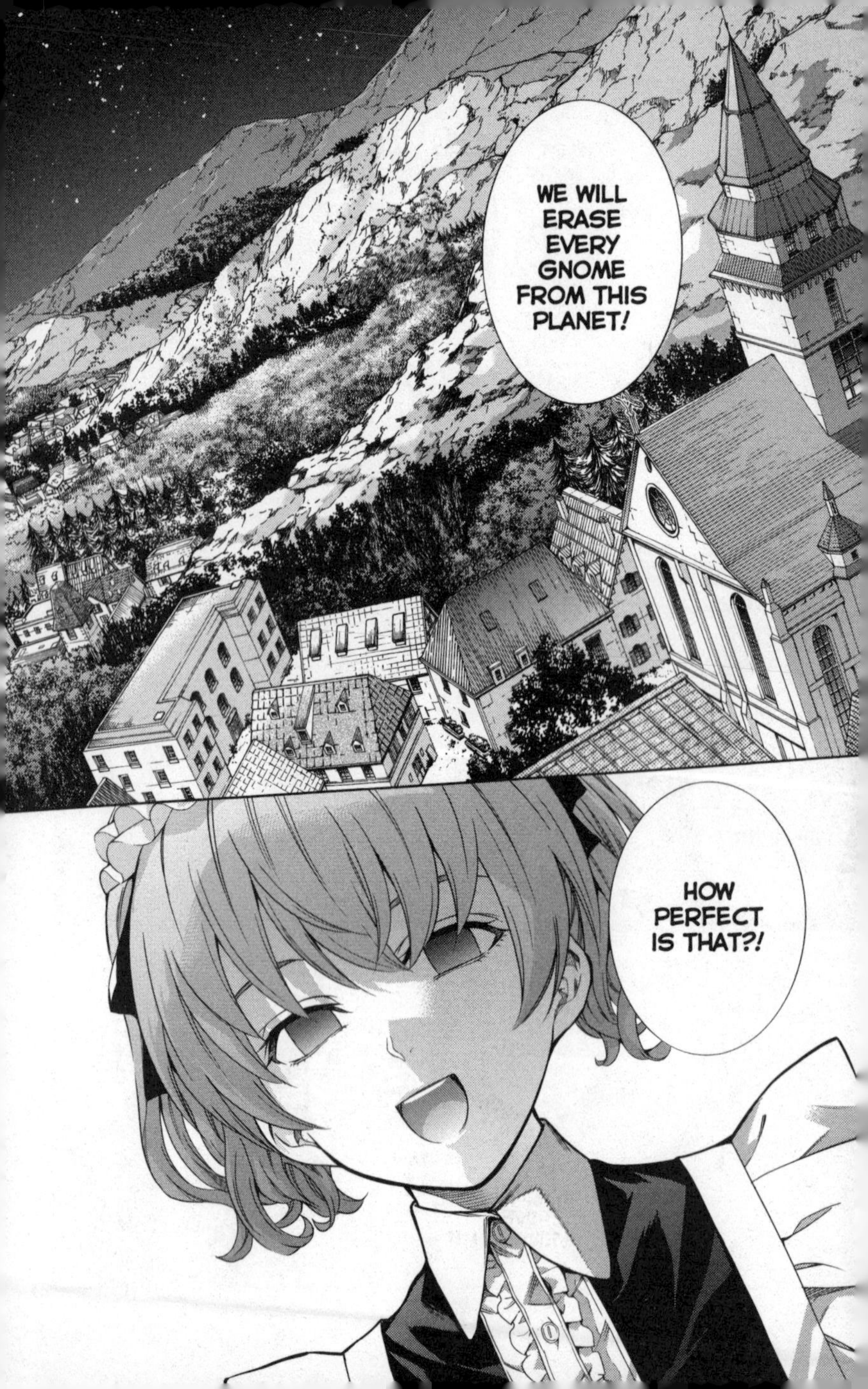
WE WILL ERASE EVERY GNOME FROM THIS PLANET!
HOW PERFECT IS THAT?!

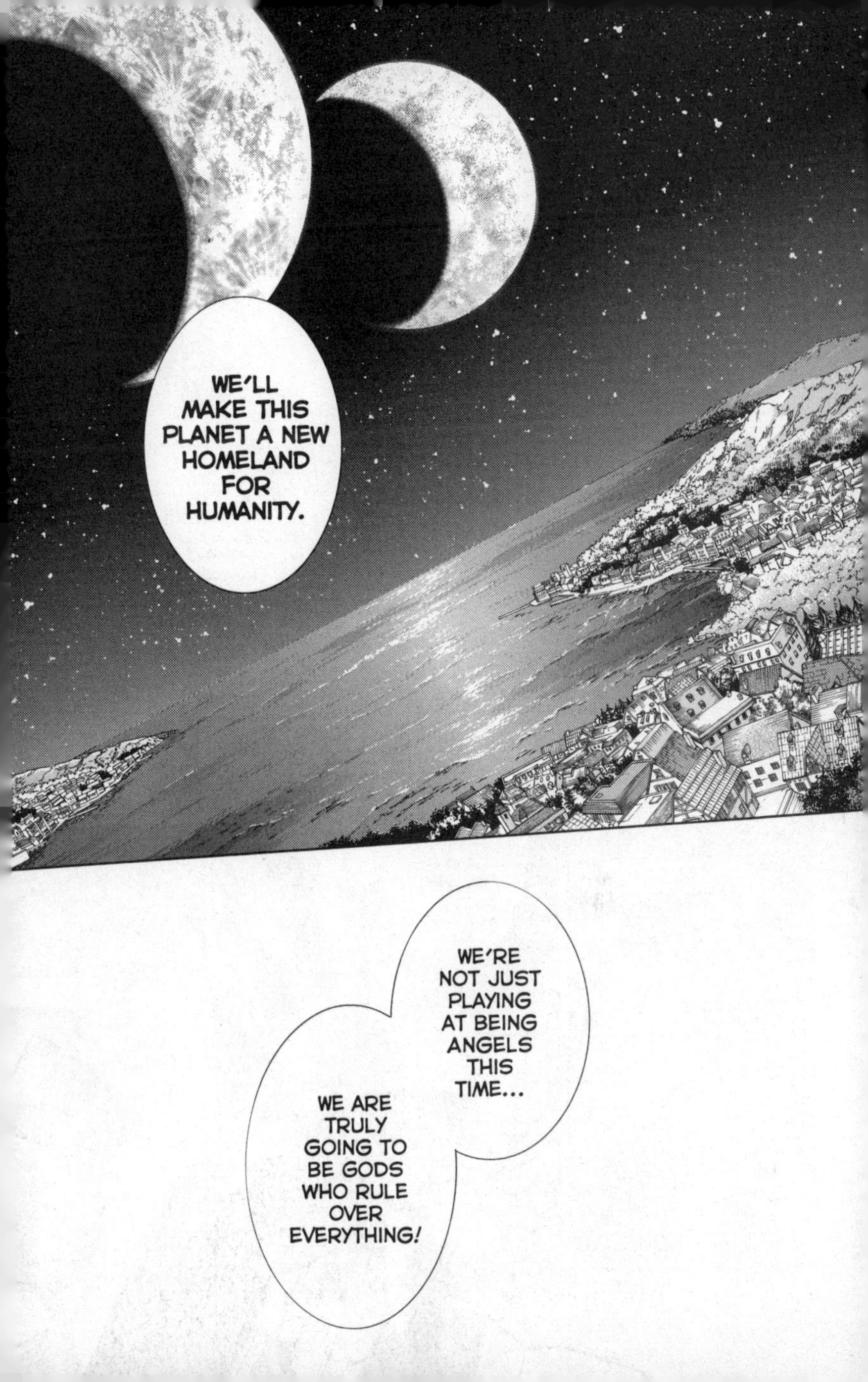
WE'LL MAKE THIS PLANET A NEW HOMELAND FOR HUMANITY.
WE'RE NOT JUST PLAYING AT BEING ANGELS THIS TIME...
WE ARE TRULY GOING TO BE GODS WHO RULE OVER EVERYTHING!

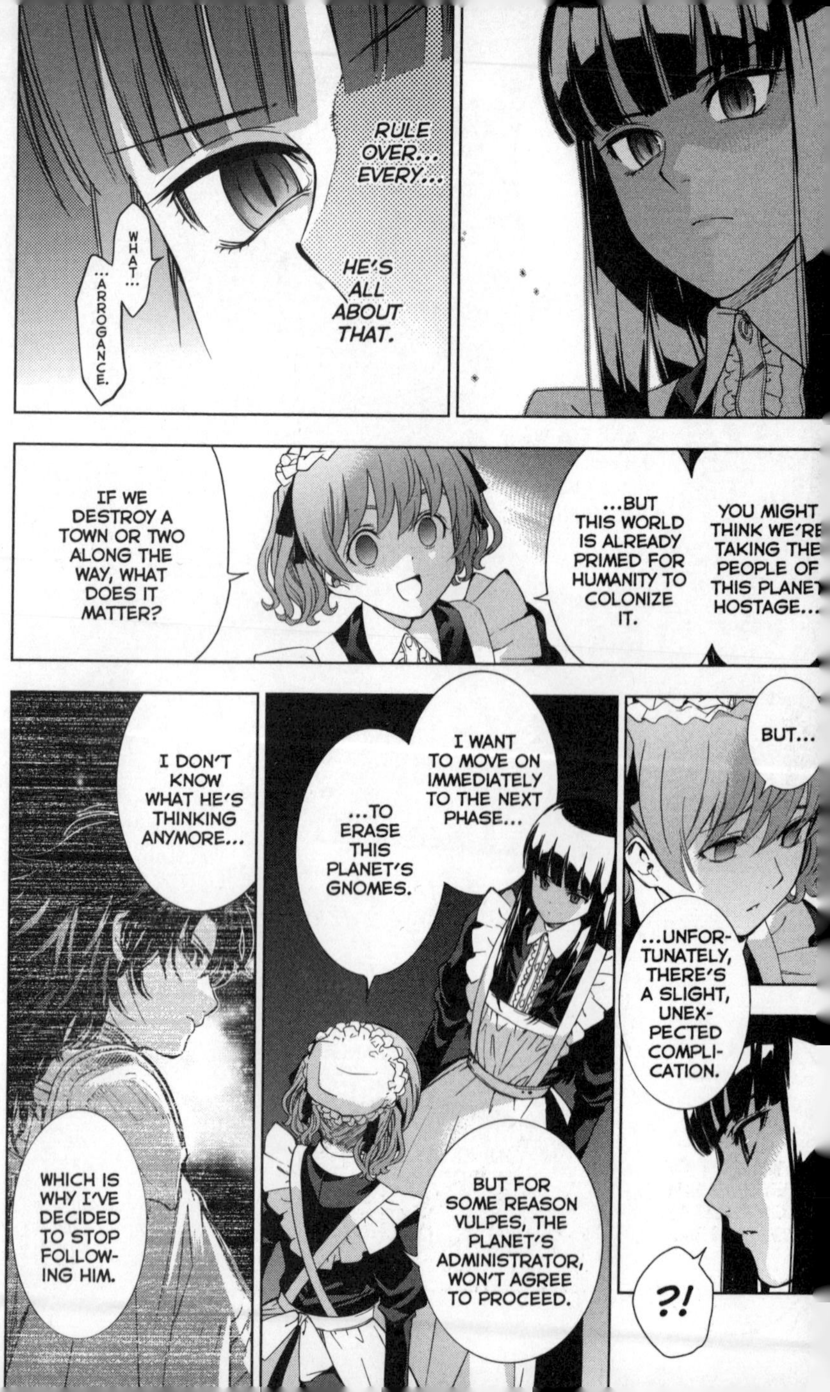
RULE OVER... EVERY...
HE'S ALL ABOUT THAT.
WHAT... ...ARROGANCE.
YOU MIGHT THINK WE'RE TAKING THE PEOPLE OF THIS PLANET HOSTAGE...
...BUT THIS WORLD IS ALREADY PRIMED FOR HUMANITY TO COLONIZE IT.
IF WE DESTROY A TOWN OR TWO ALONG THE WAY, WHAT DOES IT MATTER?
BUT...
...UNFORTUNATELY, THERE'S A SLIGHT, UNEXPECTED COMPLICATION.
?!
I WANT TO MOVE ON IMMEDIATELY TO THE NEXT PHASE...
...TO ERASE THIS PLANET'S GNOMES.
BUT FOR SOME REASON VULPES, THE PLANET'S ADMINISTRATOR, WON'T AGREE TO PROCEED.
I DON'T KNOW WHAT HE'S THINKING ANYMORE...
WHICH IS WHY I'VE DECIDED TO STOP FOLLOWING HIM.

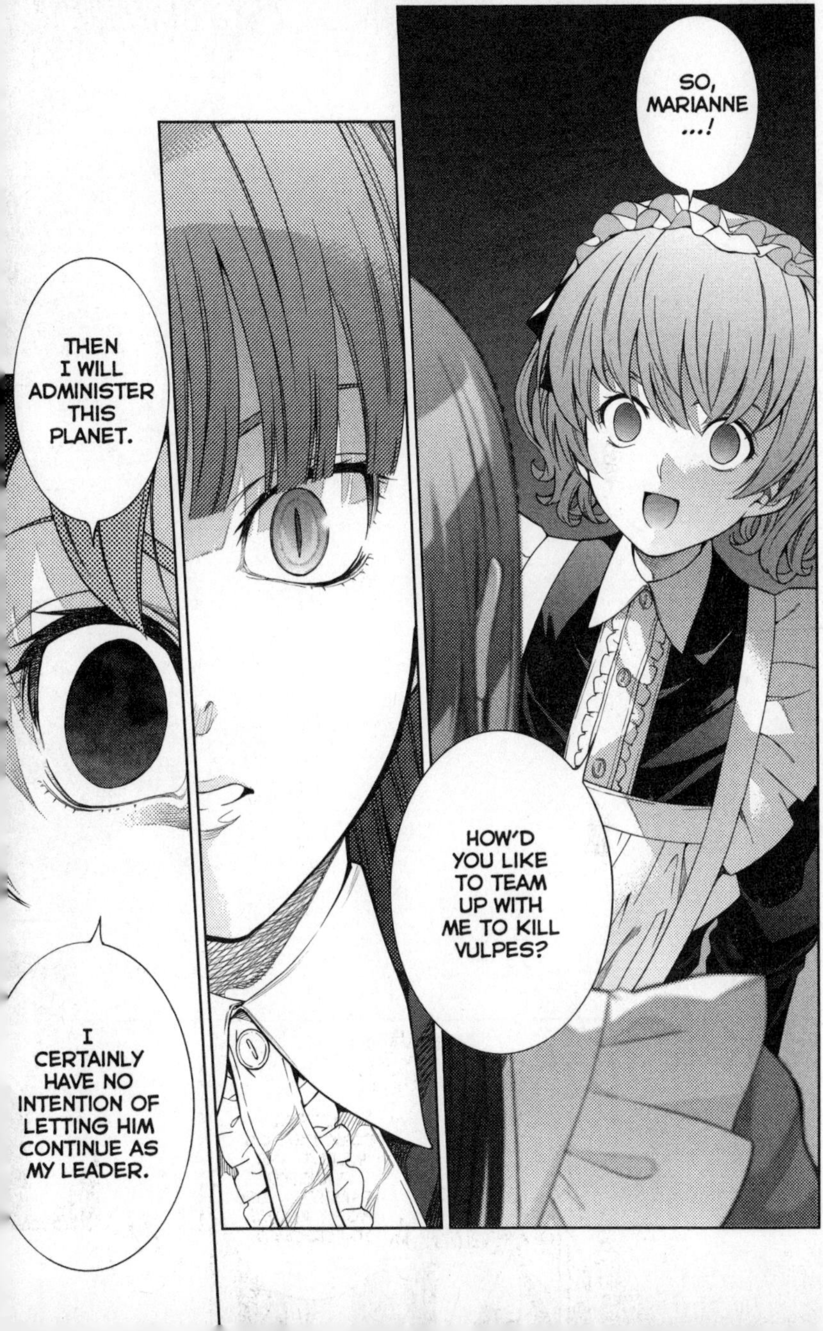
SO, MARIANNE ...!
HOW'D YOU LIKE TO TEAM UP WITH ME TO KILL VULPES?
THEN I WILL ADMINISTER THIS PLANET.
I CERTAINLY HAVE NO INTENTION OF LETTING HIM CONTINUE AS MY LEADER.

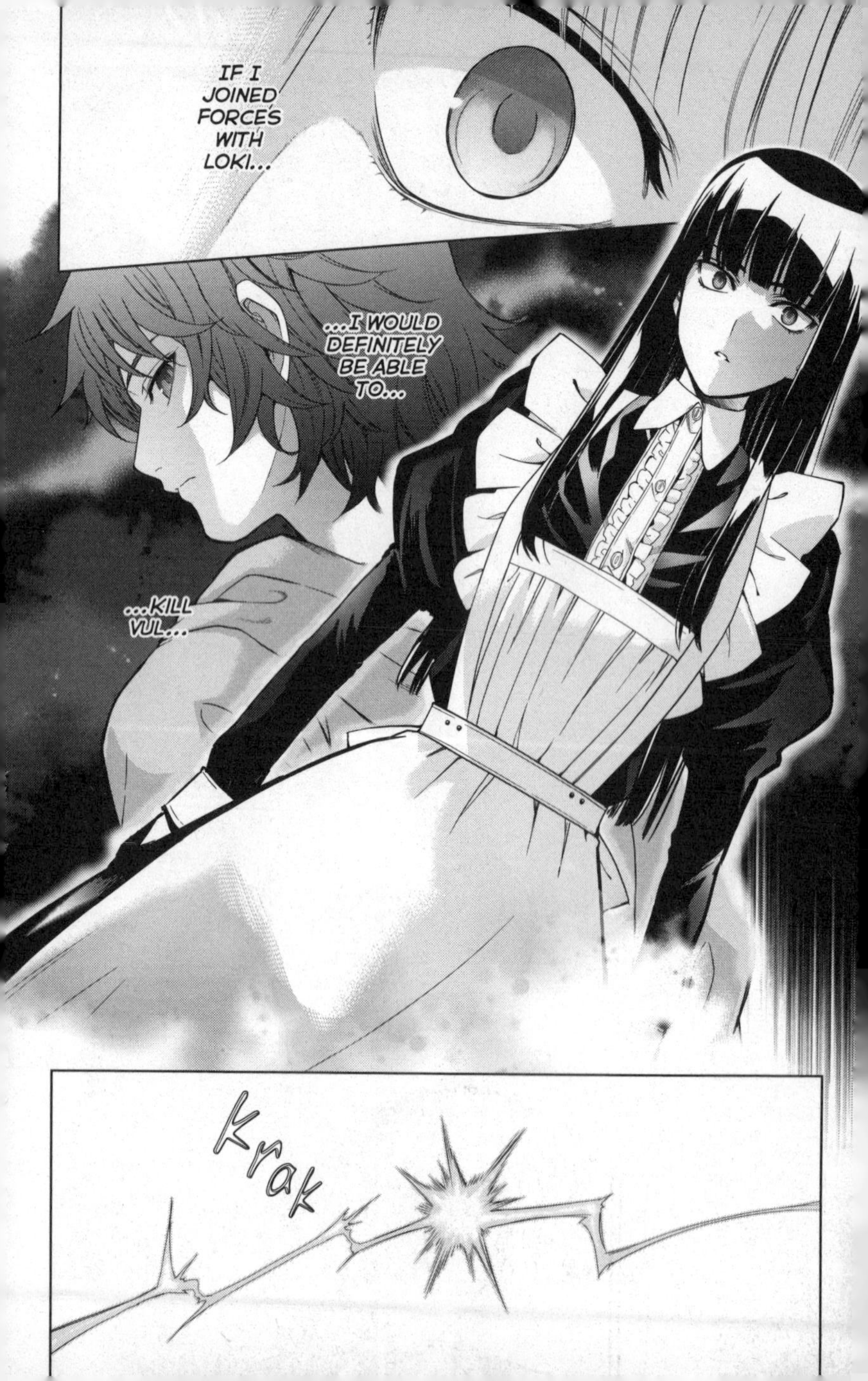
IF I JOINED FORCES WITH LOKI...
...I WOULD DEFINITELY BE ABLE TO...
...KILL VUL...
Krak

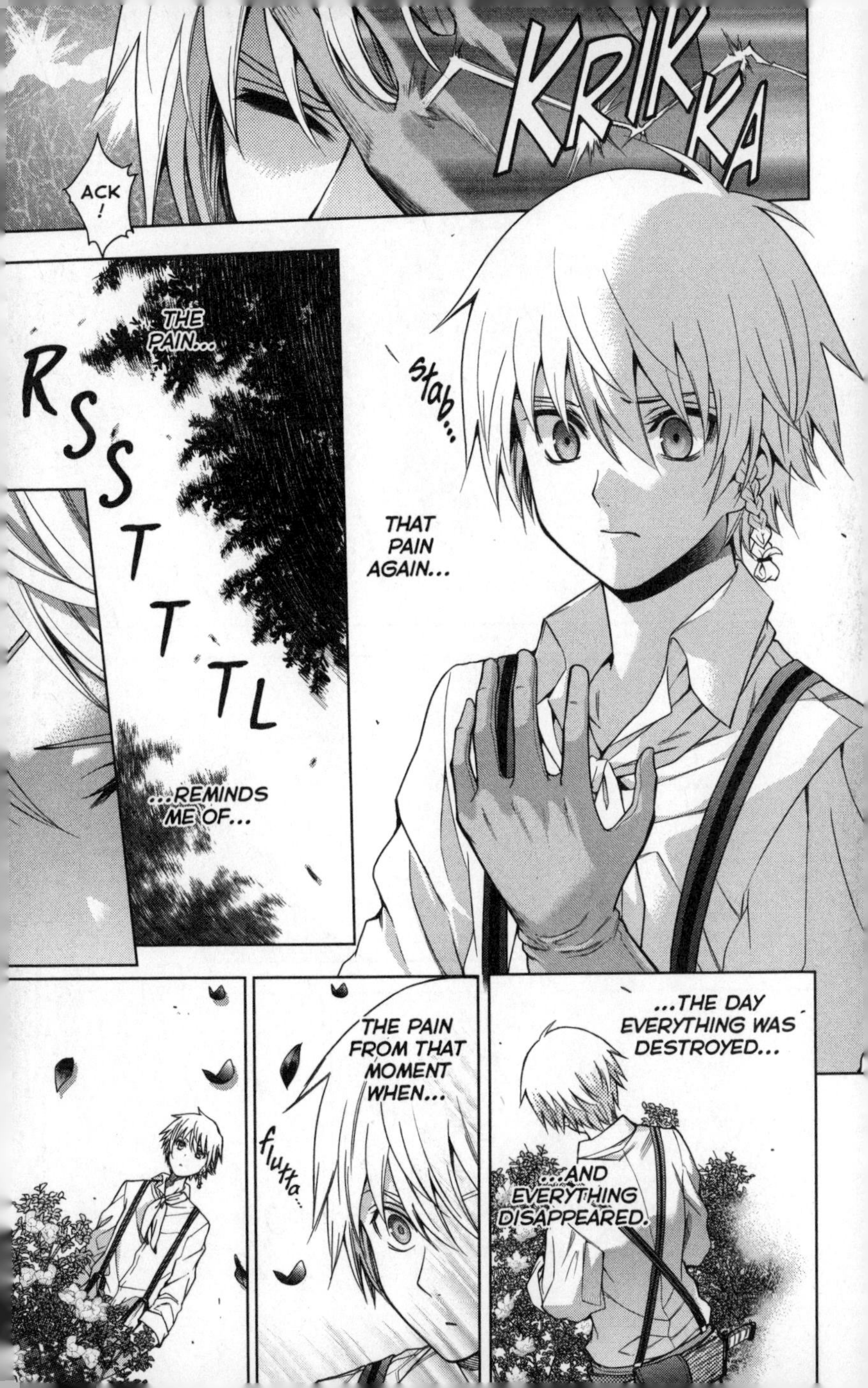
KRIKKA
ACK!
stab...
THAT PAIN AGAIN...
THE PAIN...
RSSTTTL
...REMINDS ME OF...
...THE DAY EVERYTHING WAS DESTROYED...
...AND EVERYTHING DISAPPEARED.
THE PAIN FROM THAT MOMENT WHEN...
fluxxa...

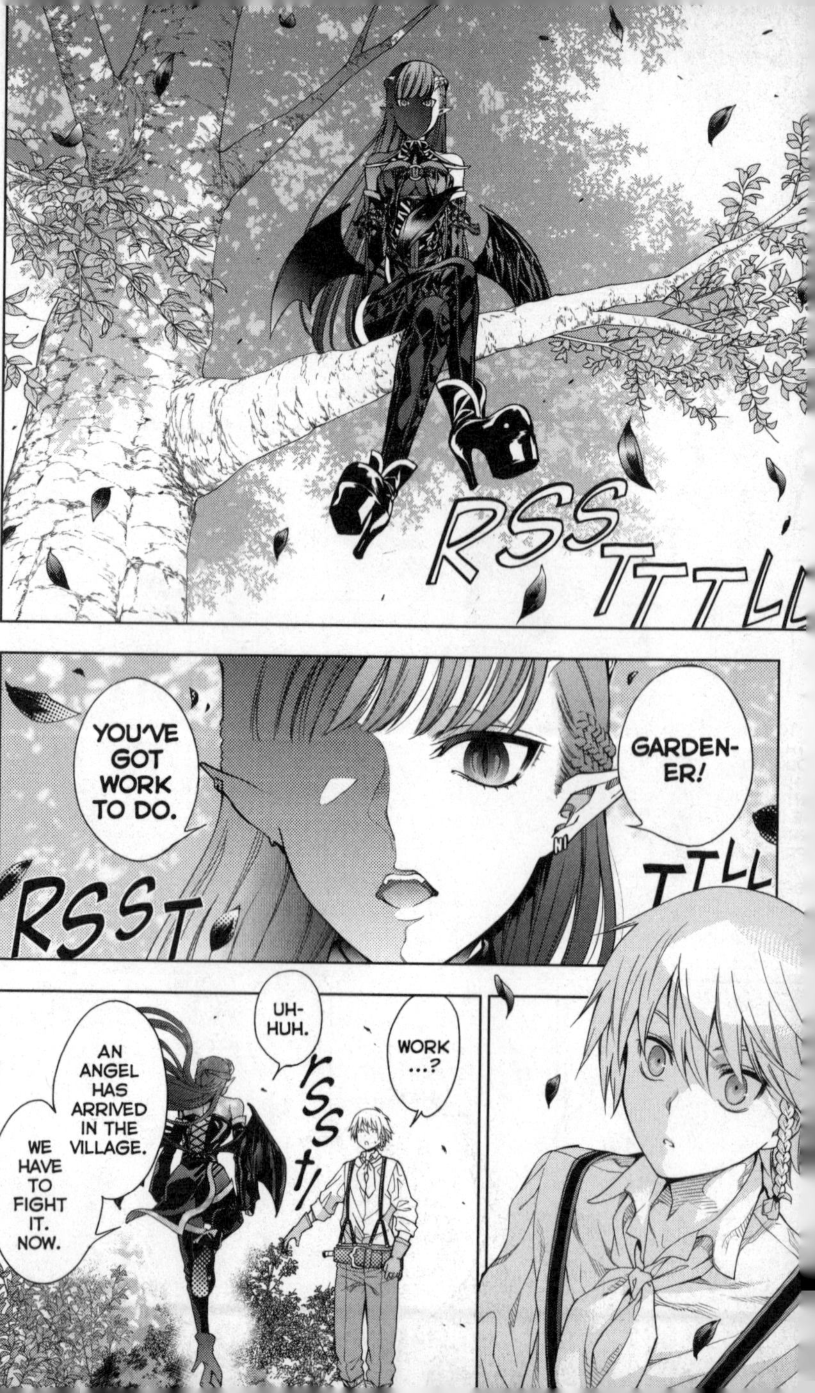
RSSTTTLL
GARDEN-
ER!
YOU'VE GOT WORK TO DO.
TTLL
RSST
WORK ...?
UH-HUH.
AN ANGEL HAS ARRIVED IN THE VILLAGE.
WE HAVE TO FIGHT IT. NOW.
RSSTL

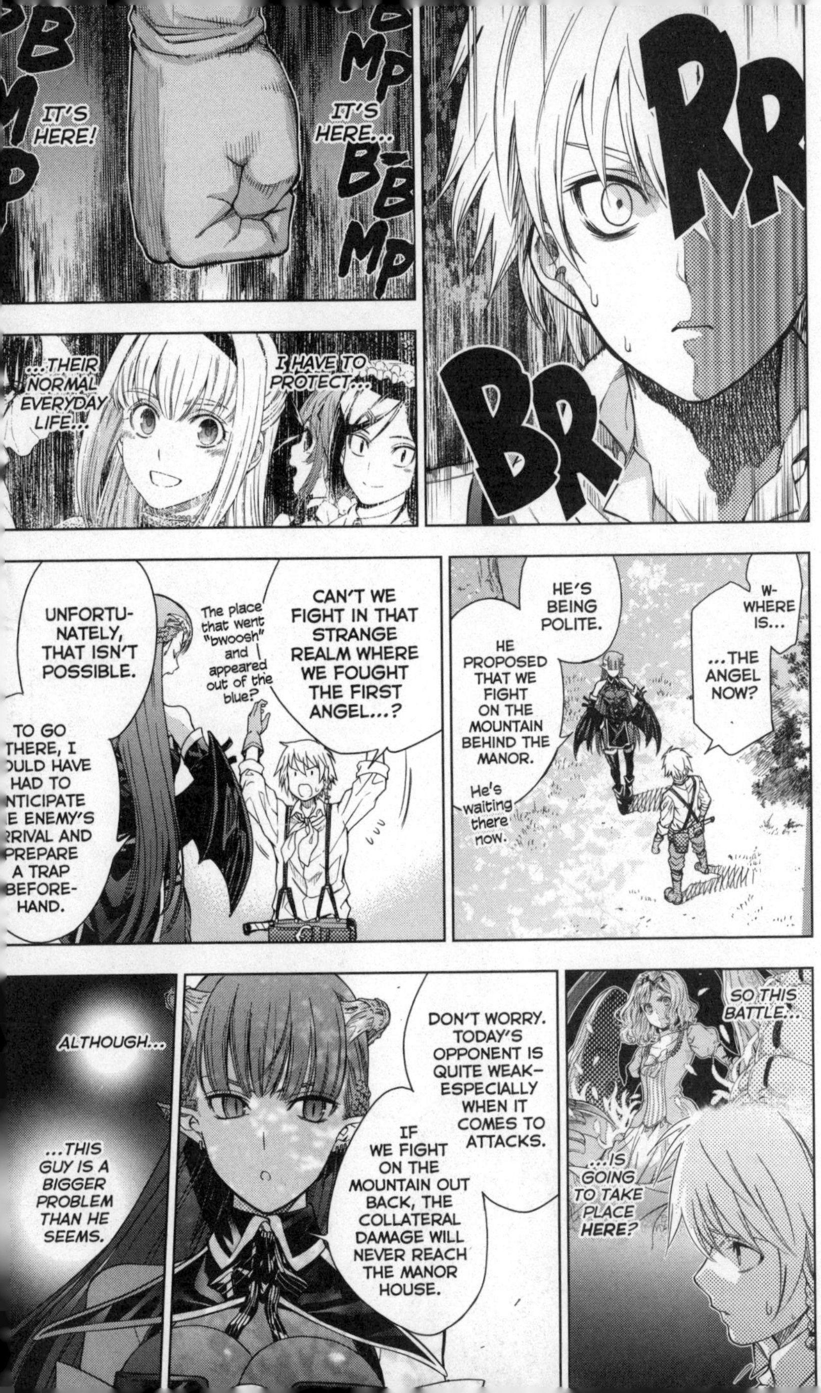
RR
BR
IT'S HERE...
B-BMP
IT'S HERE!
I HAVE TO PROTECT...
...THEIR NORMAL EVERYDAY LIFE...
W-WHERE IS...
...THE ANGEL NOW?
HE'S BEING POLITE.
HE PROPOSED THAT WE FIGHT ON THE MOUNTAIN BEHIND THE MANOR.
He's waiting there now.
CAN'T WE FIGHT IN THAT STRANGE REALM WHERE WE FOUGHT THE FIRST ANGEL...?
The place that went "bwoosh" and appeared out of the blue?
UNFORTU-NATELY, THAT ISN'T POSSIBLE.
TO GO THERE, I OULD HAVE HAD TO NTICIPATE E ENEMY'S RRIVAL AND PREPARE A TRAP BEFORE-HAND.
SO THIS BATTLE...
...IS GOING TO TAKE PLACE HERE?
DON'T WORRY. TODAY'S OPPONENT IS QUITE WEAK—ESPECIALLY WHEN IT COMES TO ATTACKS.
IF WE FIGHT ON THE MOUNTAIN OUT BACK, THE COLLATERAL DAMAGE WILL NEVER REACH THE MANOR HOUSE.
ALTHOUGH...
...THIS GUY IS A BIGGER PROBLEM THAN HE SEEMS.

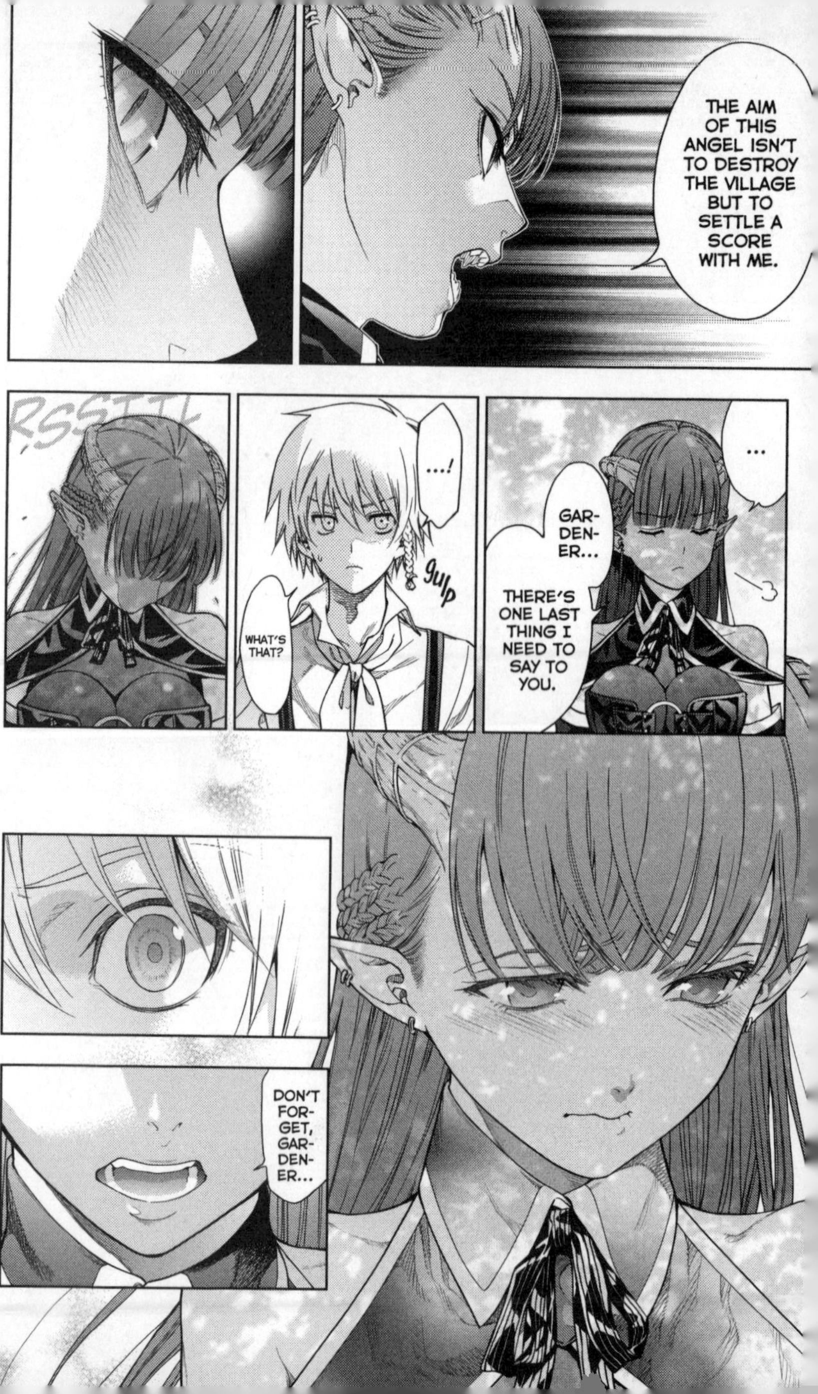
THE AIM OF THIS ANGEL ISN'T TO DESTROY THE VILLAGE BUT TO SETTLE A SCORE WITH ME.
...
GAR-DEN-ER...
THERE'S ONE LAST THING I NEED TO SAY TO YOU.
...!
gulp
WHAT'S THAT?
RSSTL
DON'T FOR-GET, GAR-DEN-ER...

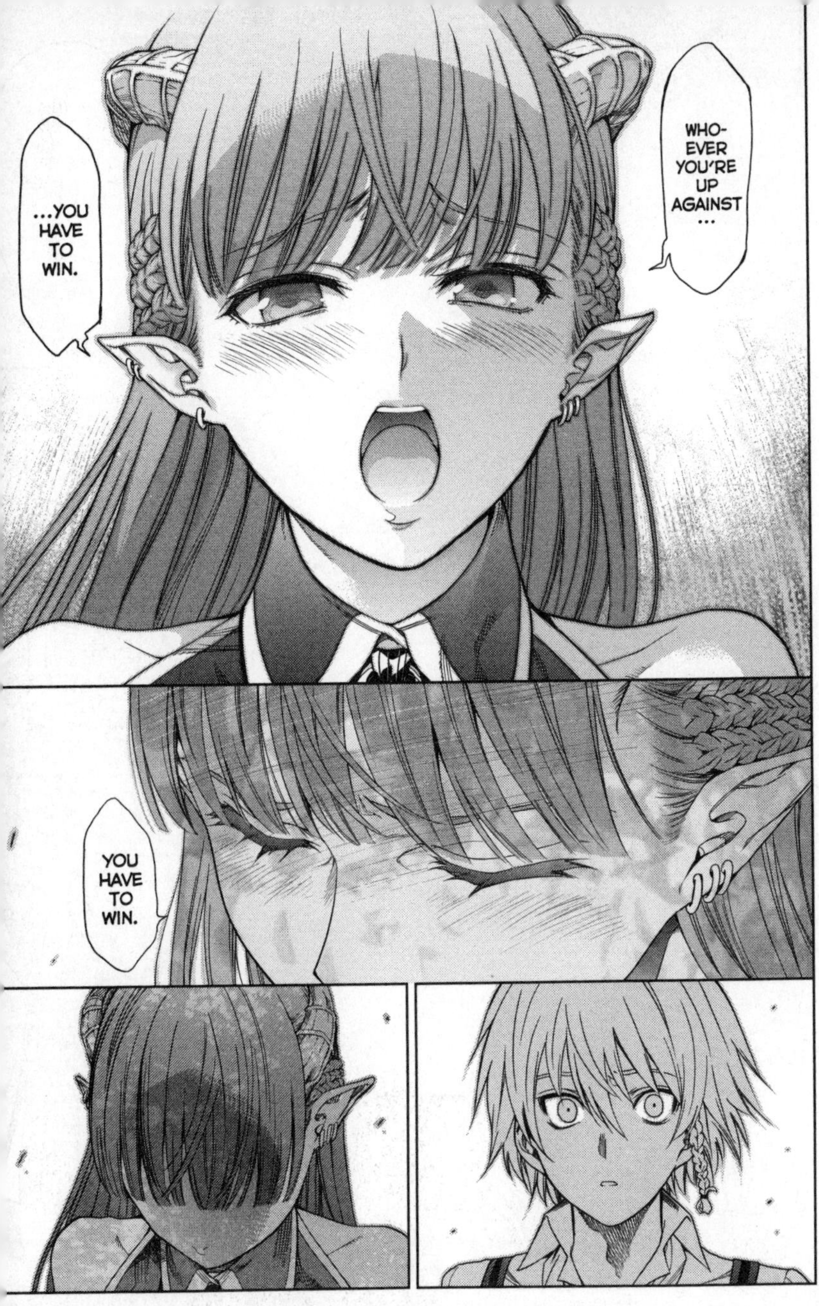
WHO-EVER YOU'RE UP AGAINST...
...YOU HAVE TO WIN.
YOU HAVE TO WIN.

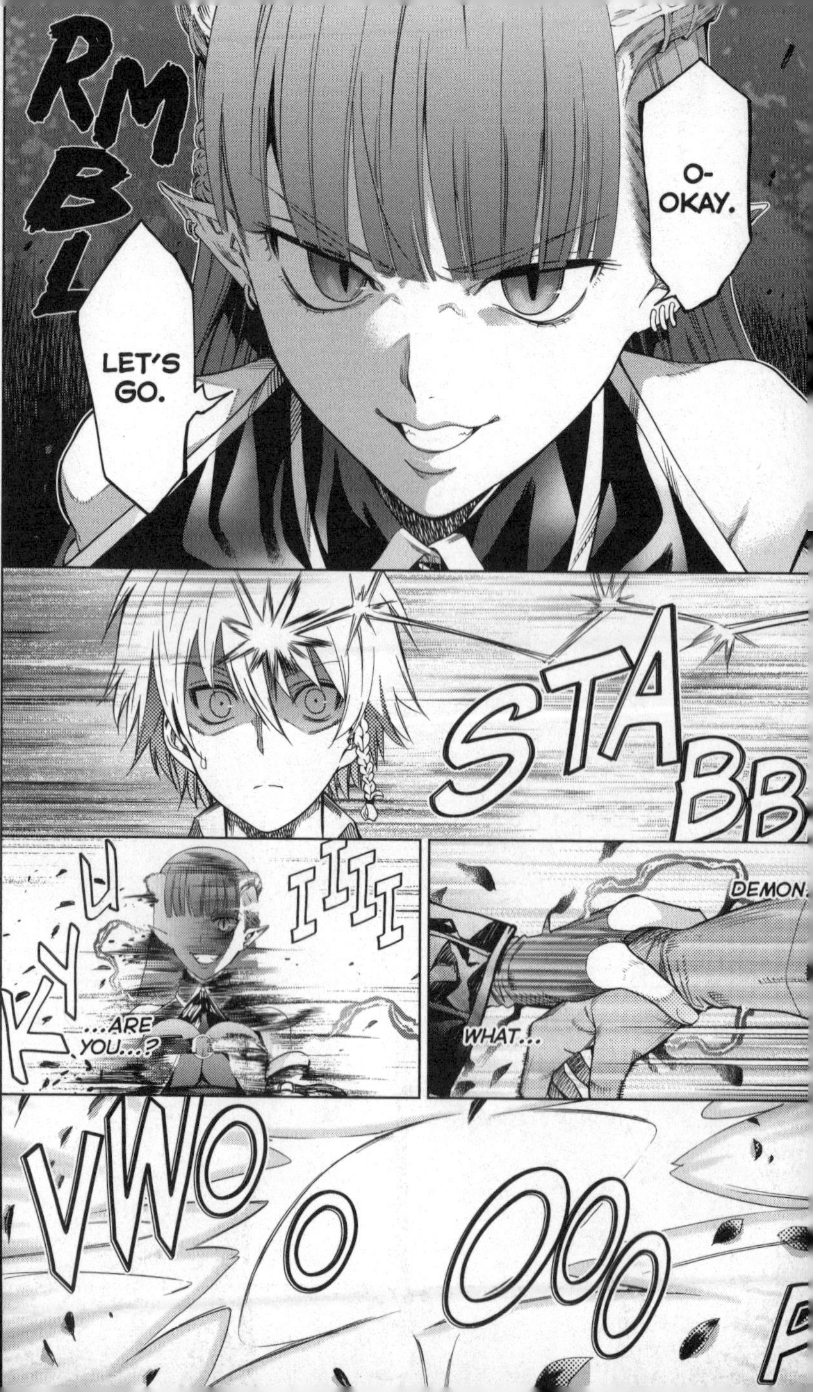
O-
OKAY.
RMBL
LET'S GO.
STABB
DEMON.
WHAT...
KYUIIII
...ARE YOU...?
VWOOOOO

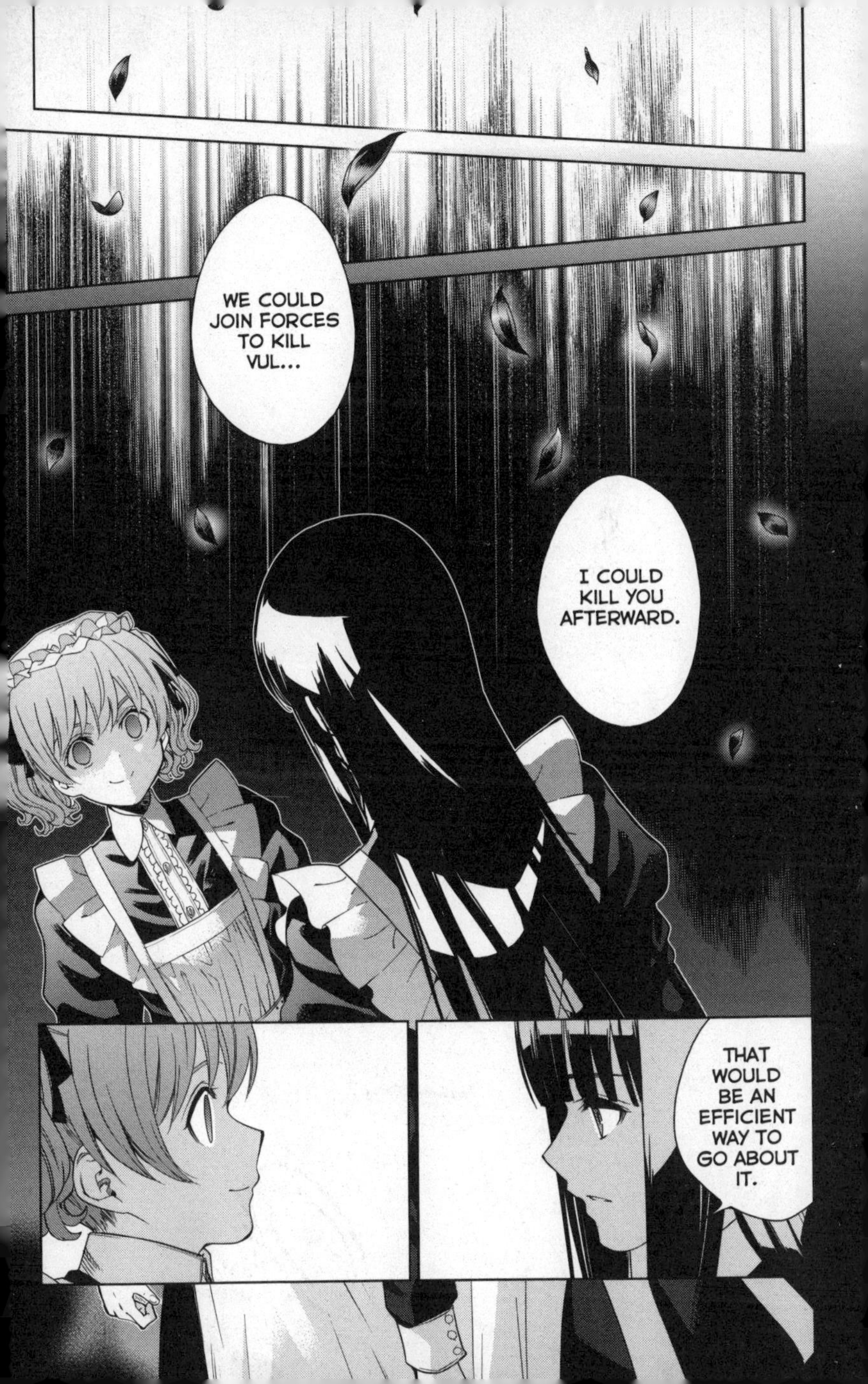
WE COULD JOIN FORCES TO KILL VUL...
I COULD KILL YOU AFTERWARD.
THAT WOULD BE AN EFFICIENT WAY TO GO ABOUT IT.

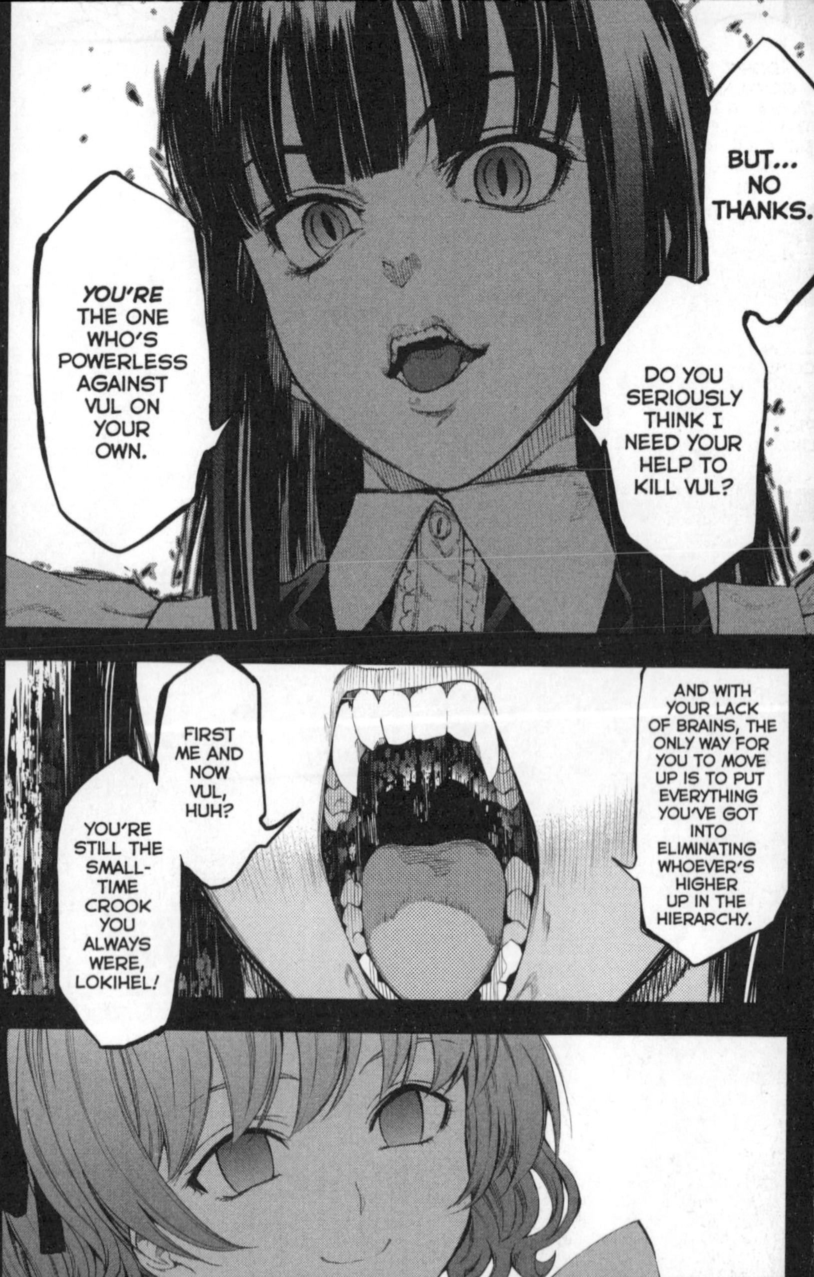
BUT... NO THANKS.
DO YOU SERIOUSLY THINK I NEED YOUR HELP TO KILL VUL?
YOU'RE THE ONE WHO'S POWERLESS AGAINST VUL ON YOUR OWN.
AND WITH YOUR LACK OF BRAINS, THE ONLY WAY FOR YOU TO MOVE UP IS TO PUT EVERYTHING YOU'VE GOT INTO ELIMINATING WHOEVER'S HIGHER UP IN THE HIERARCHY.
FIRST ME AND NOW VUL, HUH?
YOU'RE STILL THE SMALL-TIME CROOK YOU ALWAYS WERE, LOKIHEL!

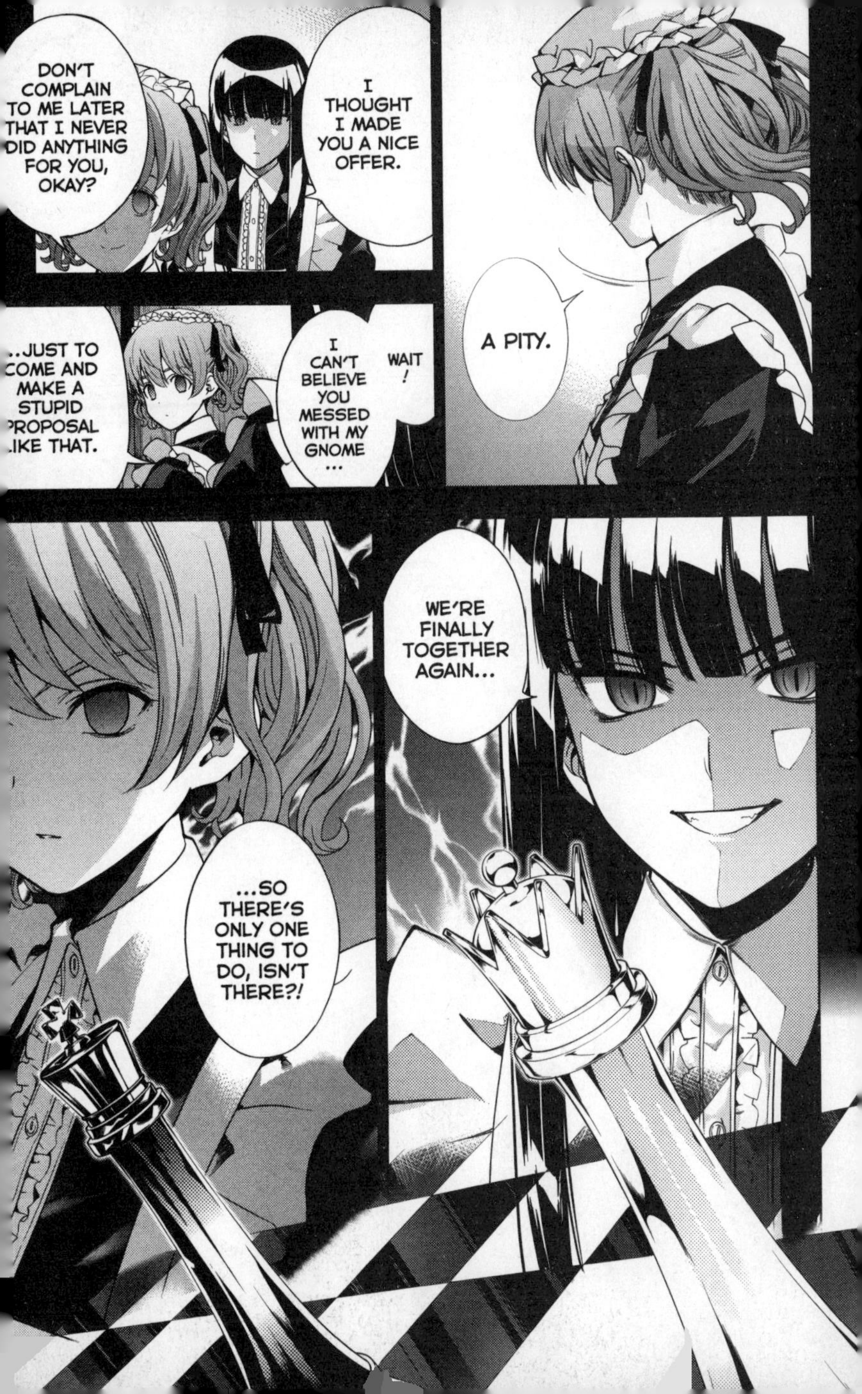
A PITY.
I THOUGHT I MADE YOU A NICE OFFER.
DON'T COMPLAIN TO ME LATER THAT I NEVER DID ANYTHING FOR YOU, OKAY?
WAIT!
I CAN'T BELIEVE YOU MESSED WITH MY GNOME...
...JUST TO COME AND MAKE A STUPID PROPOSAL LIKE THAT.
WE'RE FINALLY TOGETHER AGAIN...
...SO THERE'S ONLY ONE THING TO DO, ISN'T THERE?!

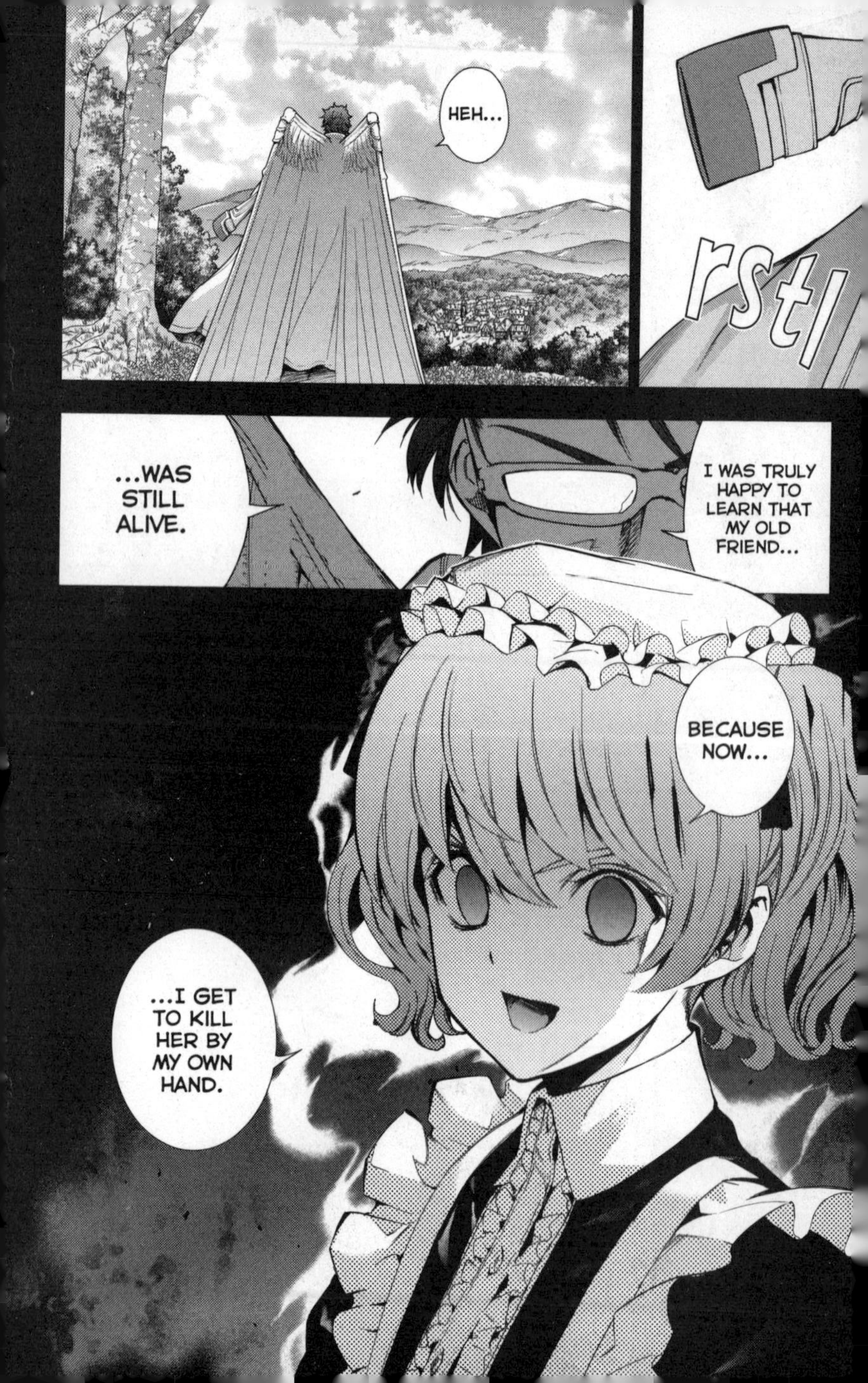
rstl
HEH...
I WAS TRULY HAPPY TO LEARN THAT MY OLD FRIEND...
...WAS STILL ALIVE.
BECAUSE NOW...
...I GET TO KILL HER BY MY OWN HAND.

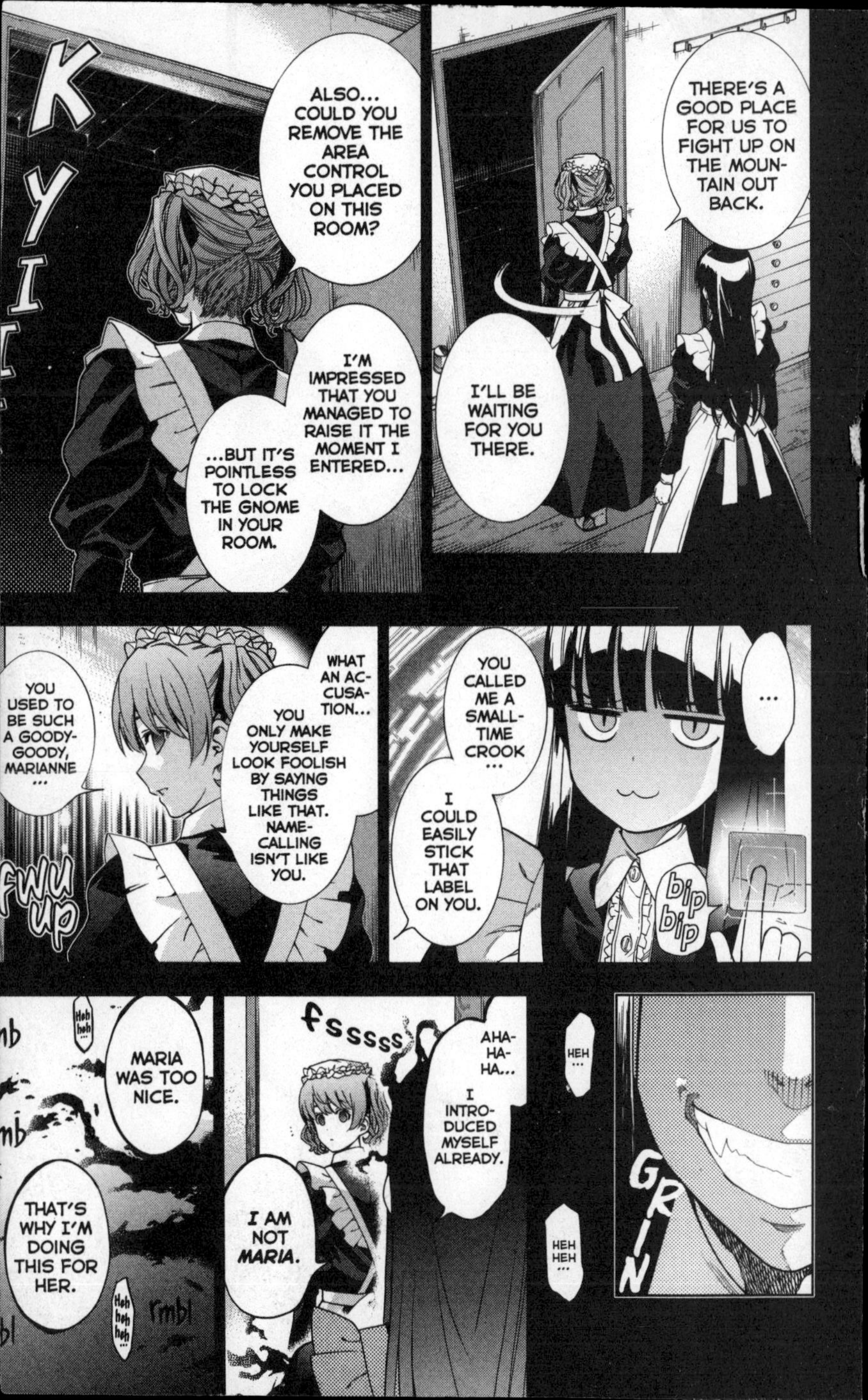
THERE'S A GOOD PLACE FOR US TO FIGHT UP ON THE MOUNTAIN OUT BACK.
I'LL BE WAITING FOR YOU THERE.
ALSO... COULD YOU REMOVE THE AREA CONTROL YOU PLACED ON THIS ROOM?
KYII
I'M IMPRESSED THAT YOU MANAGED TO RAISE IT THE MOMENT I ENTERED...
...BUT IT'S POINTLESS TO LOCK THE GNOME IN YOUR ROOM.
...
YOU CALLED ME A SMALL-TIME CROOK...
I COULD EASILY STICK THAT LABEL ON YOU.
bip bip
WHAT AN ACCUSATION... YOU ONLY MAKE YOURSELF LOOK FOOLISH BY SAYING THINGS LIKE THAT. NAME-CALLING ISN'T LIKE YOU.
YOU USED TO BE SUCH A GOODY-GOODY, MARIANNE...
fwuup
HEH...
GRIN
HEH HEH...
fsssss
AHAHAHA... I INTRODUCED MYSELF ALREADY.
I AM NOT *MARIA*.
Heh heh...
MARIA WAS TOO NICE.
THAT'S WHY I'M DOING THIS FOR HER.
Heh heh heh...
rmbl

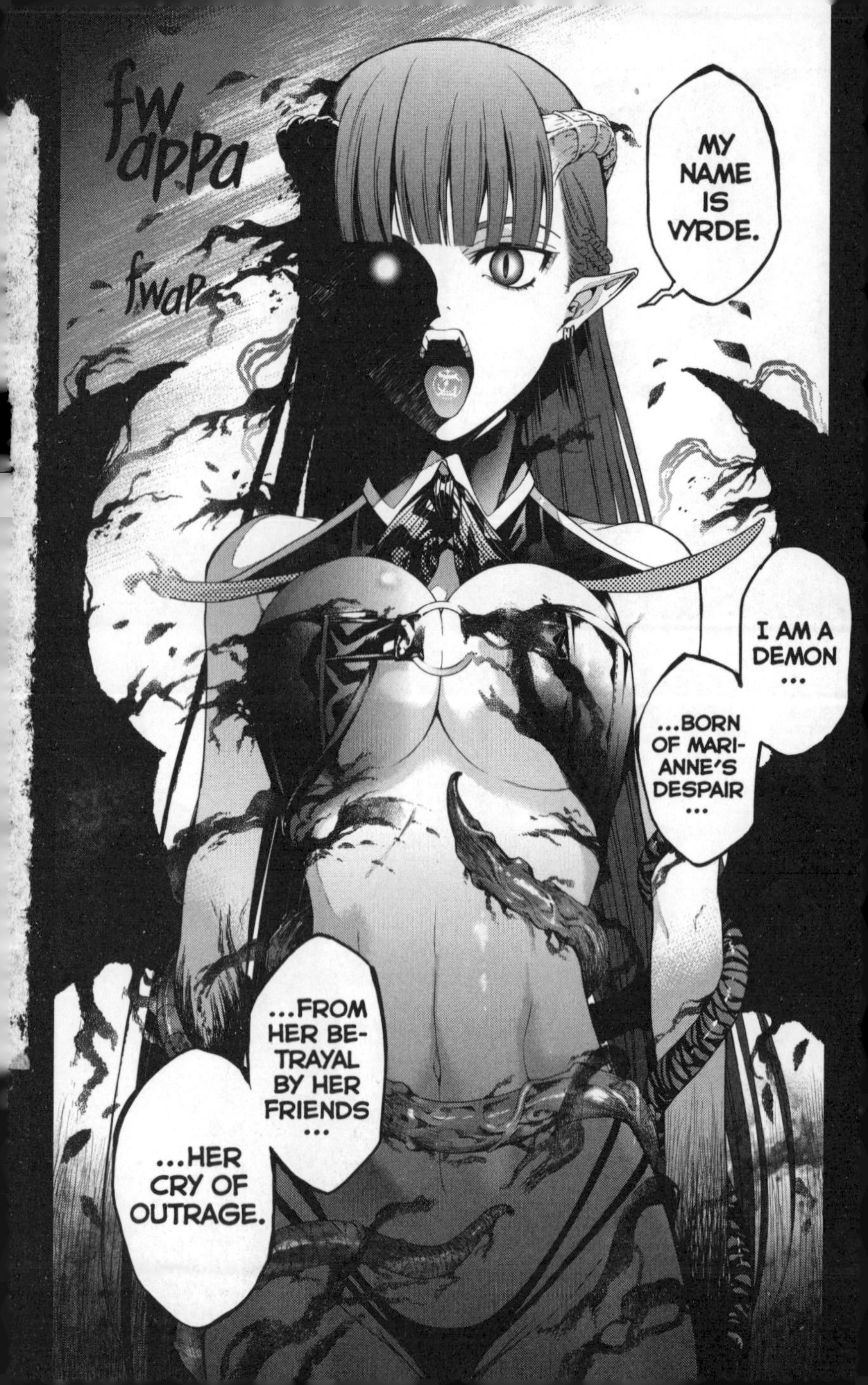
MY NAME IS VYRDE.
fw appa
fwap
I AM A DEMON ...
...BORN OF MARI-ANNE'S DESPAIR ...
...FROM HER BE-TRAYAL BY HER FRIENDS ...
...HER CRY OF OUTRAGE.

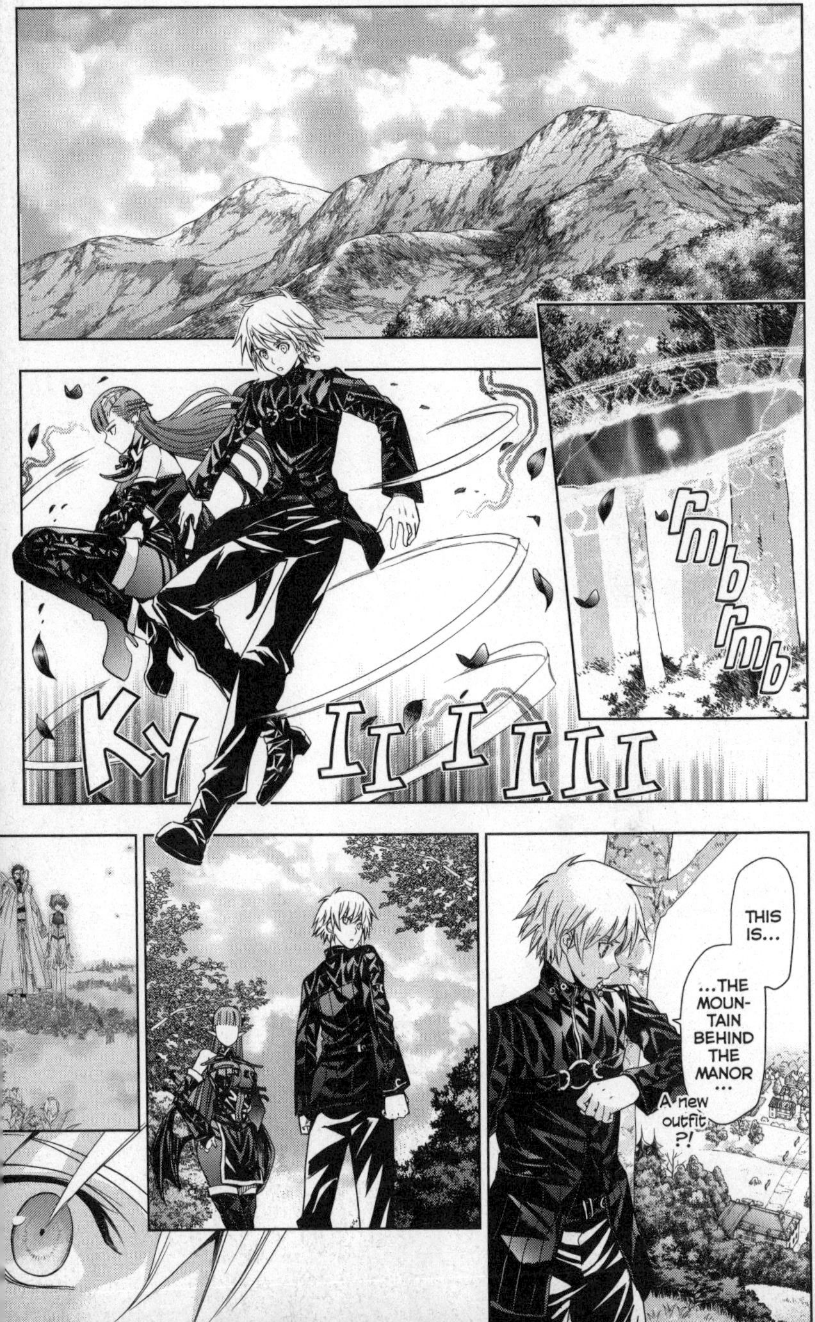
rmbrmb
KYIIIIII
THIS IS...
...THE MOUNTAIN BEHIND THE MANOR...
A new outfit?!

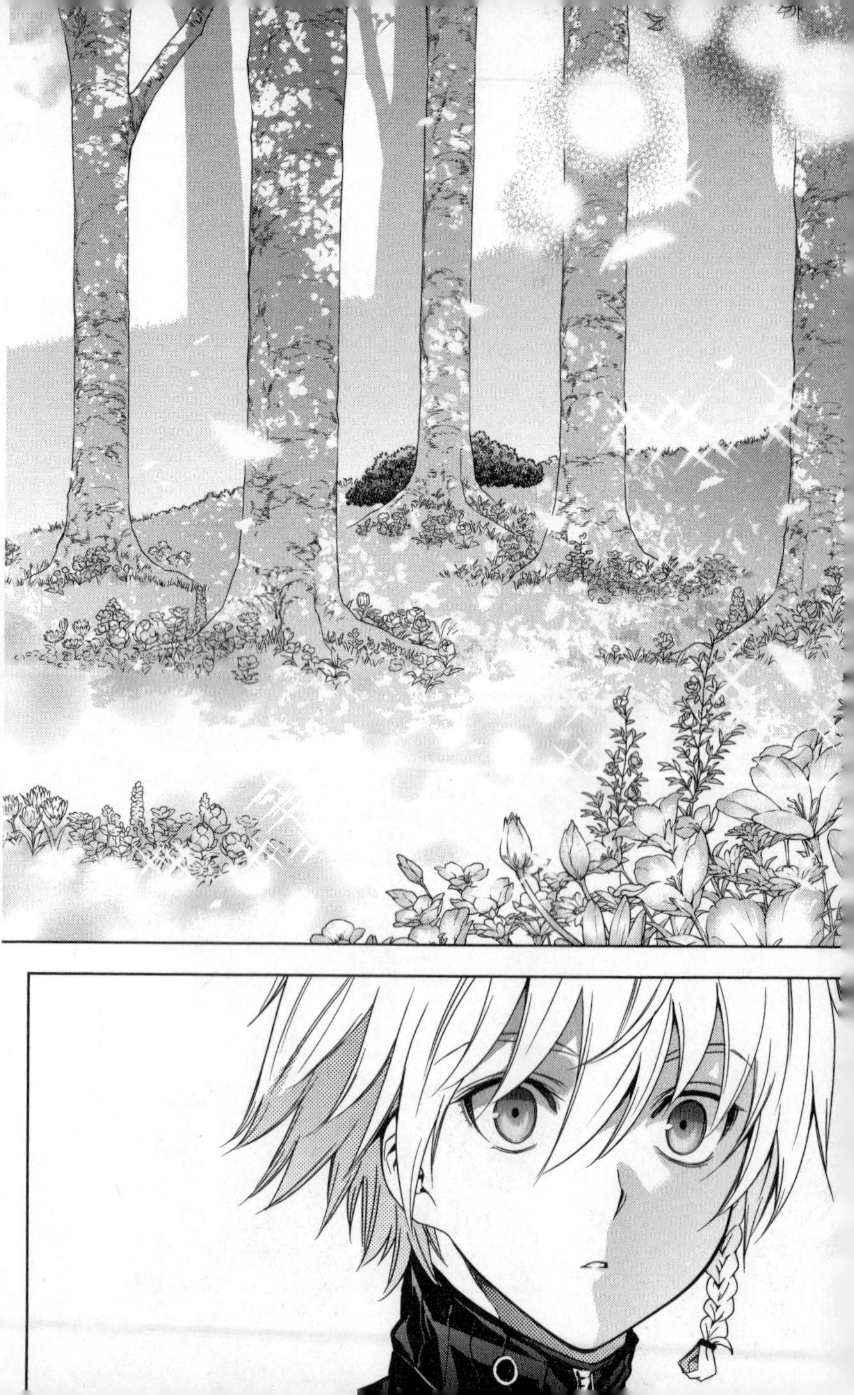

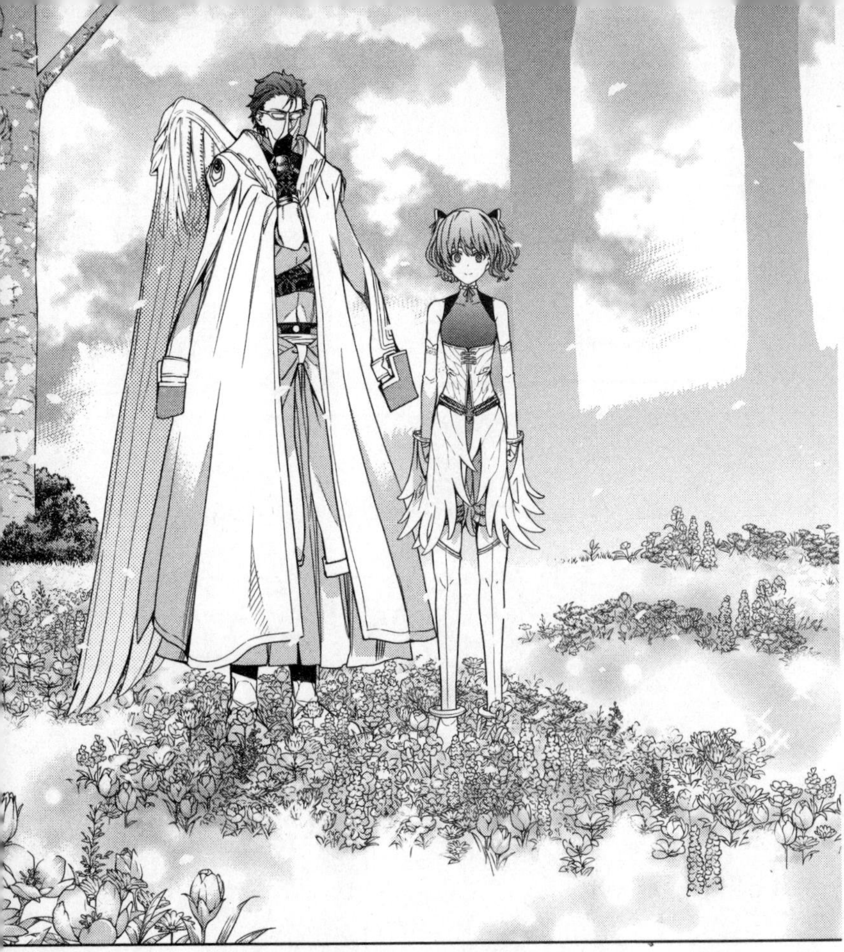

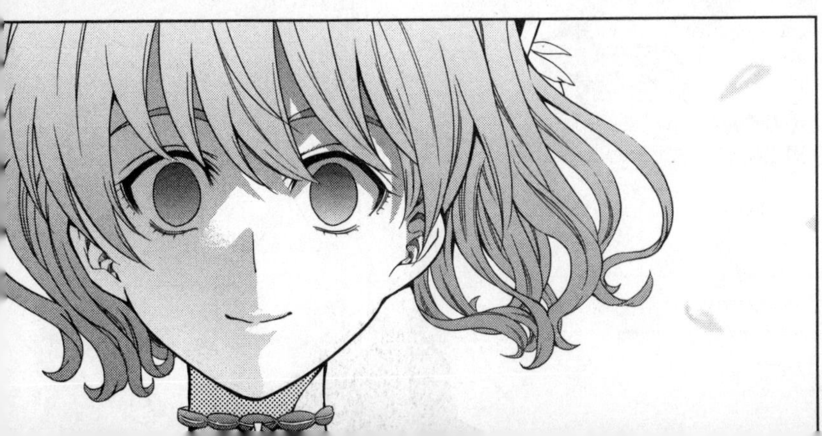

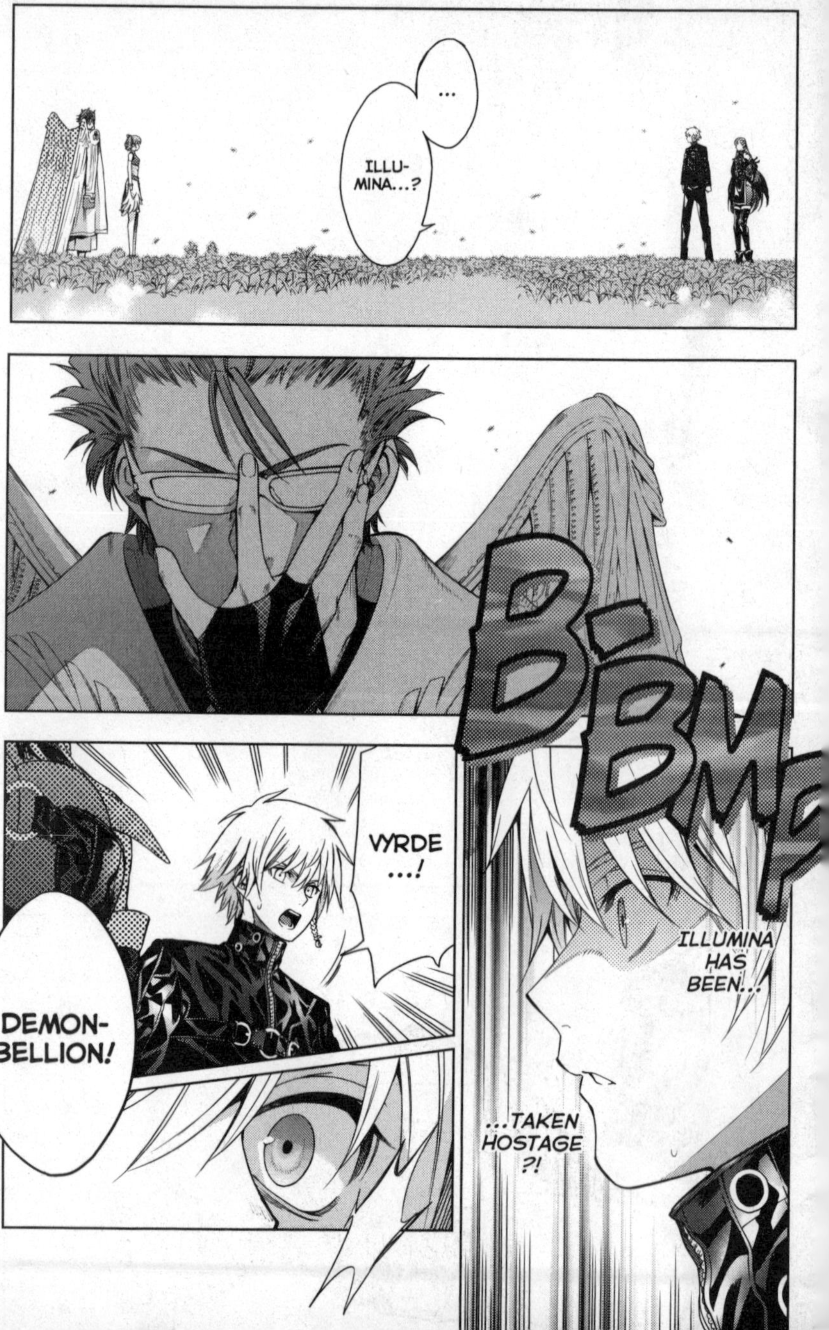
...
ILLUMINA...?
B-BM
ILLUMINA HAS BEEN...
...TAKEN HOSTAGE?!
VYRDE...!
DEMONBELLION!

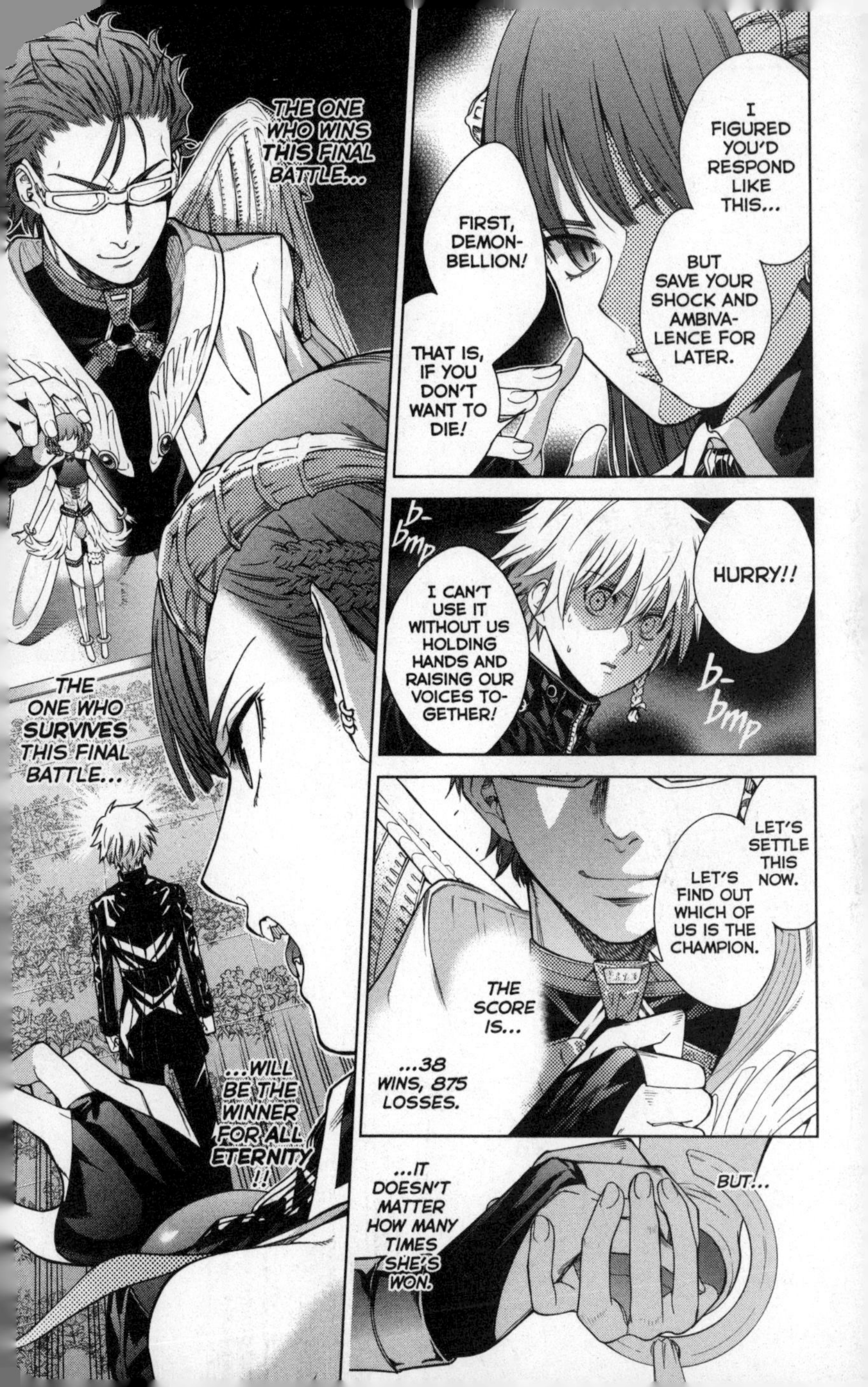

I FIGURED YOU'D RESPOND LIKE THIS...
BUT SAVE YOUR SHOCK AND AMBIVALENCE FOR LATER.
FIRST, DEMONBELLION!
THAT IS, IF YOU DON'T WANT TO DIE!
HURRY!!
b-bmp
I CAN'T USE IT WITHOUT US HOLDING HANDS AND RAISING OUR VOICES TOGETHER!
b-bmp
LET'S SETTLE THIS NOW.
LET'S FIND OUT WHICH OF US IS THE CHAMPION.
THE SCORE IS...
...38 WINS, 875 LOSSES.
BUT...
...IT DOESN'T MATTER HOW MANY TIMES SHE'S WON.
THE ONE WHO WINS THIS FINAL BATTLE...
THE ONE WHO SURVIVES THIS FINAL BATTLE...
...WILL BE THE WINNER FOR ALL ETERNITY!!

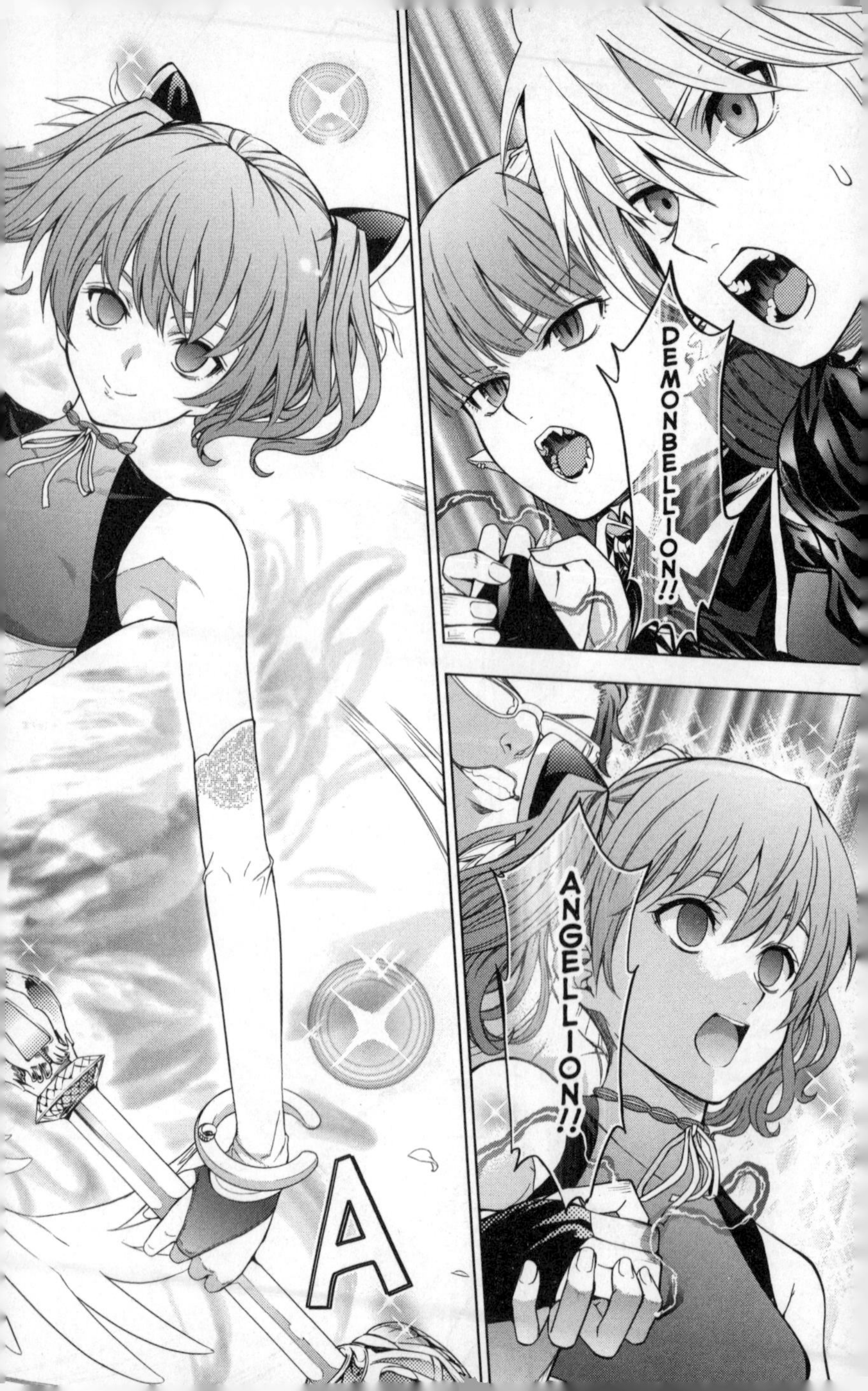
DEMONBELLION!!
ANGELLION!!
A

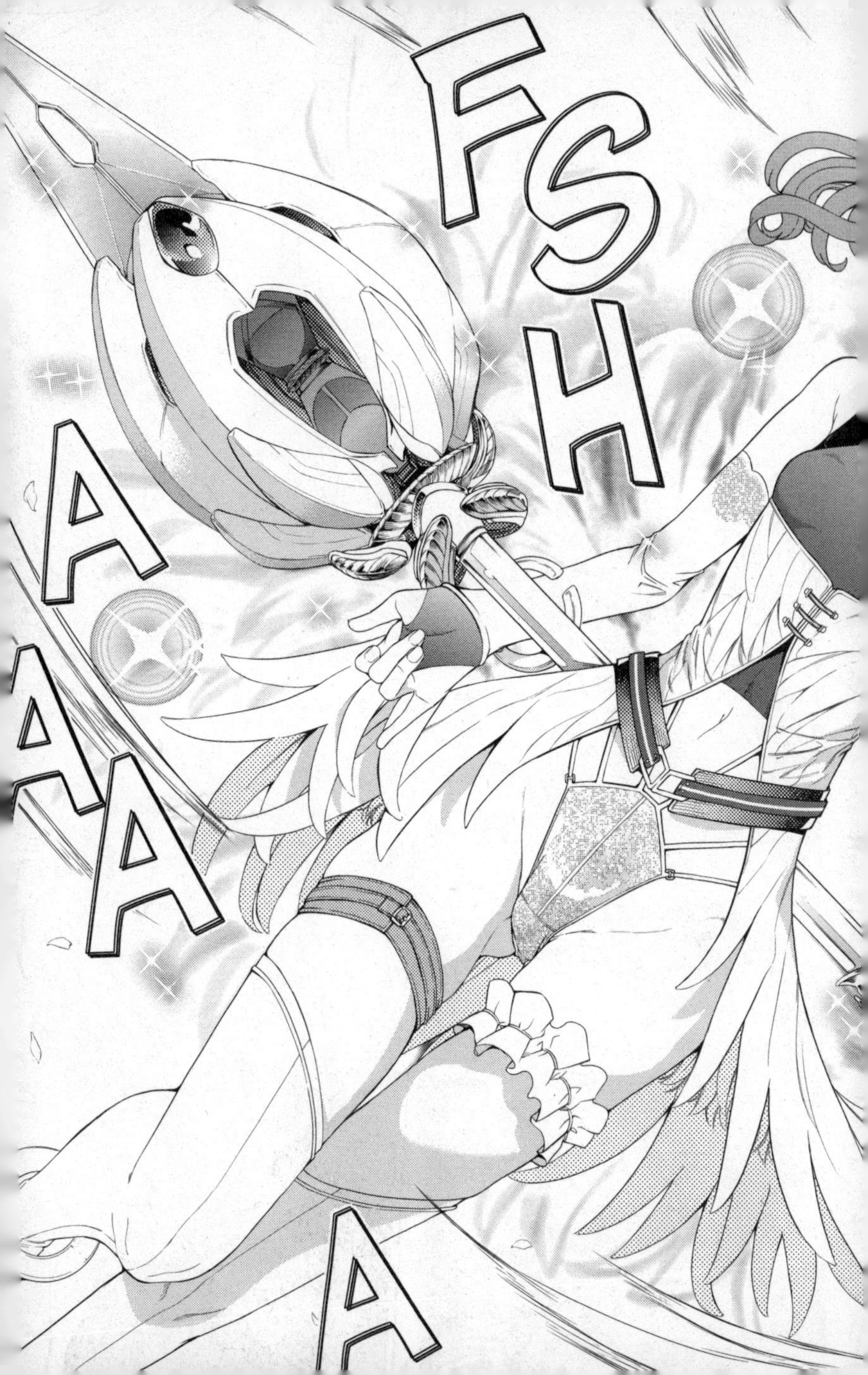
FSH
AAAAA

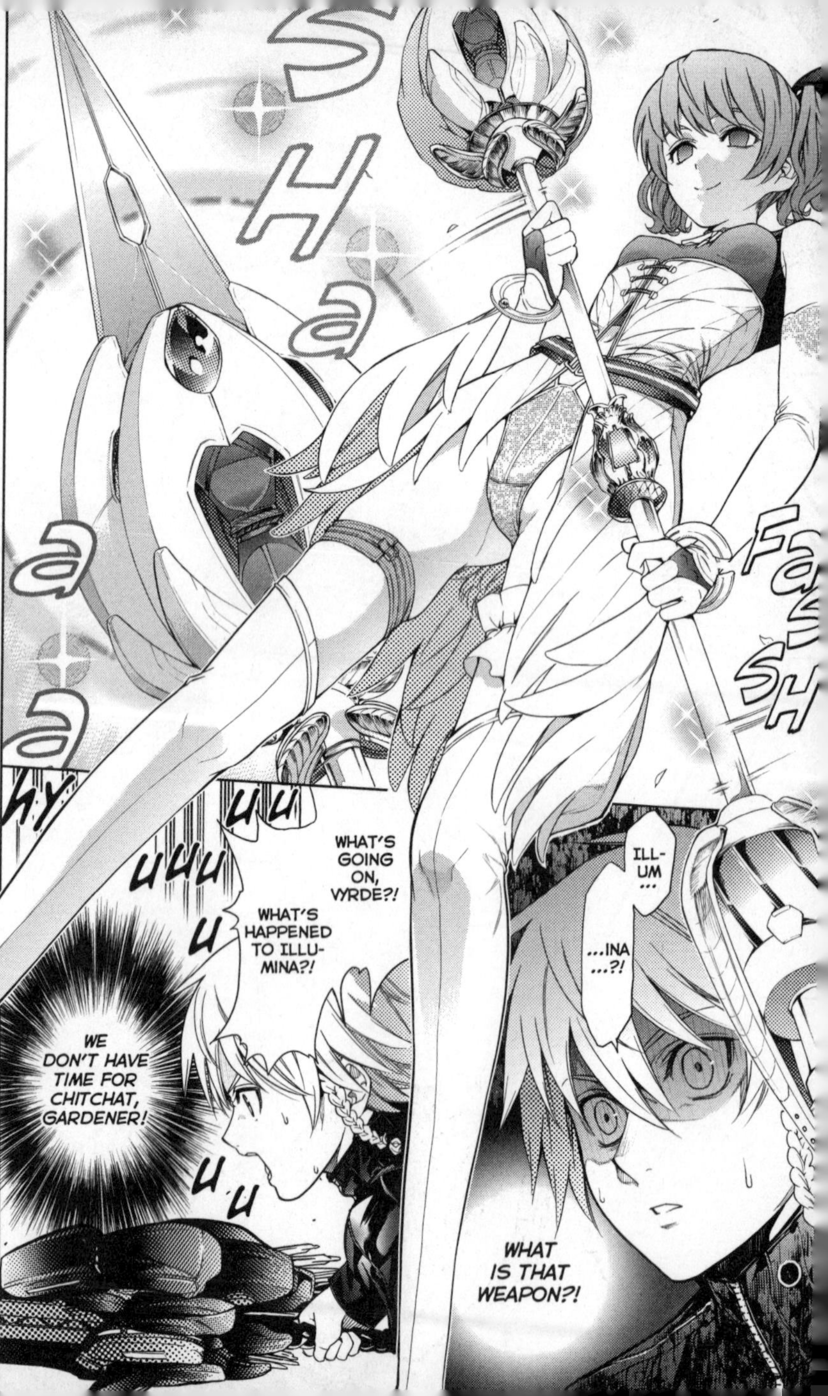
FaSH
SHaaaa
ILLUM...
...INA...?!
WHAT IS THAT WEAPON?!
hyuuuuuu
WHAT'S GOING ON, VYRDE?!
WHAT'S HAPPENED TO ILLUMINA?!
WE DON'T HAVE TIME FOR CHITCHAT, GARDENER!

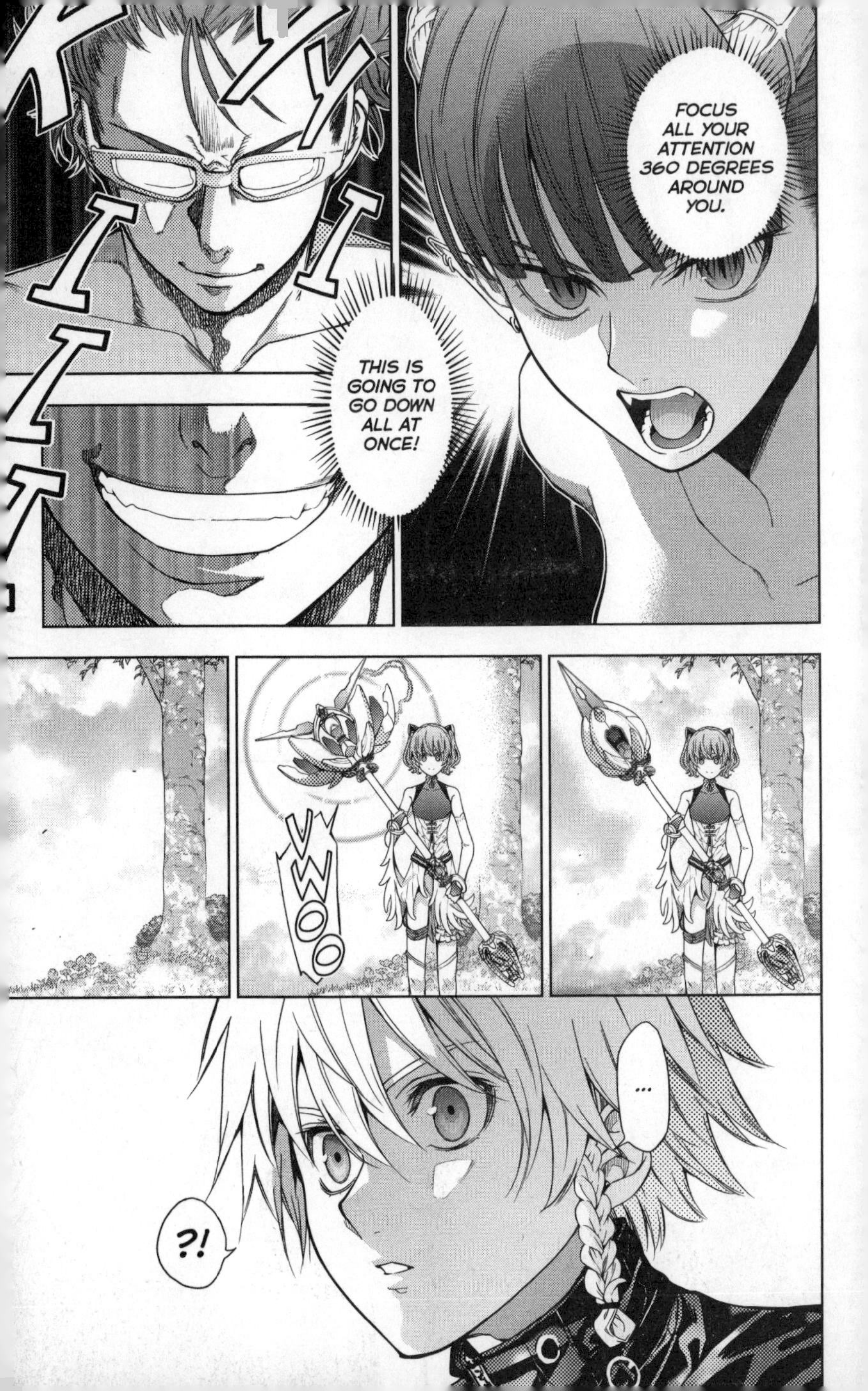
FOCUS ALL YOUR ATTENTION 360 DEGREES AROUND YOU.
THIS IS GOING TO GO DOWN ALL AT ONCE!
VWOO
...
?!

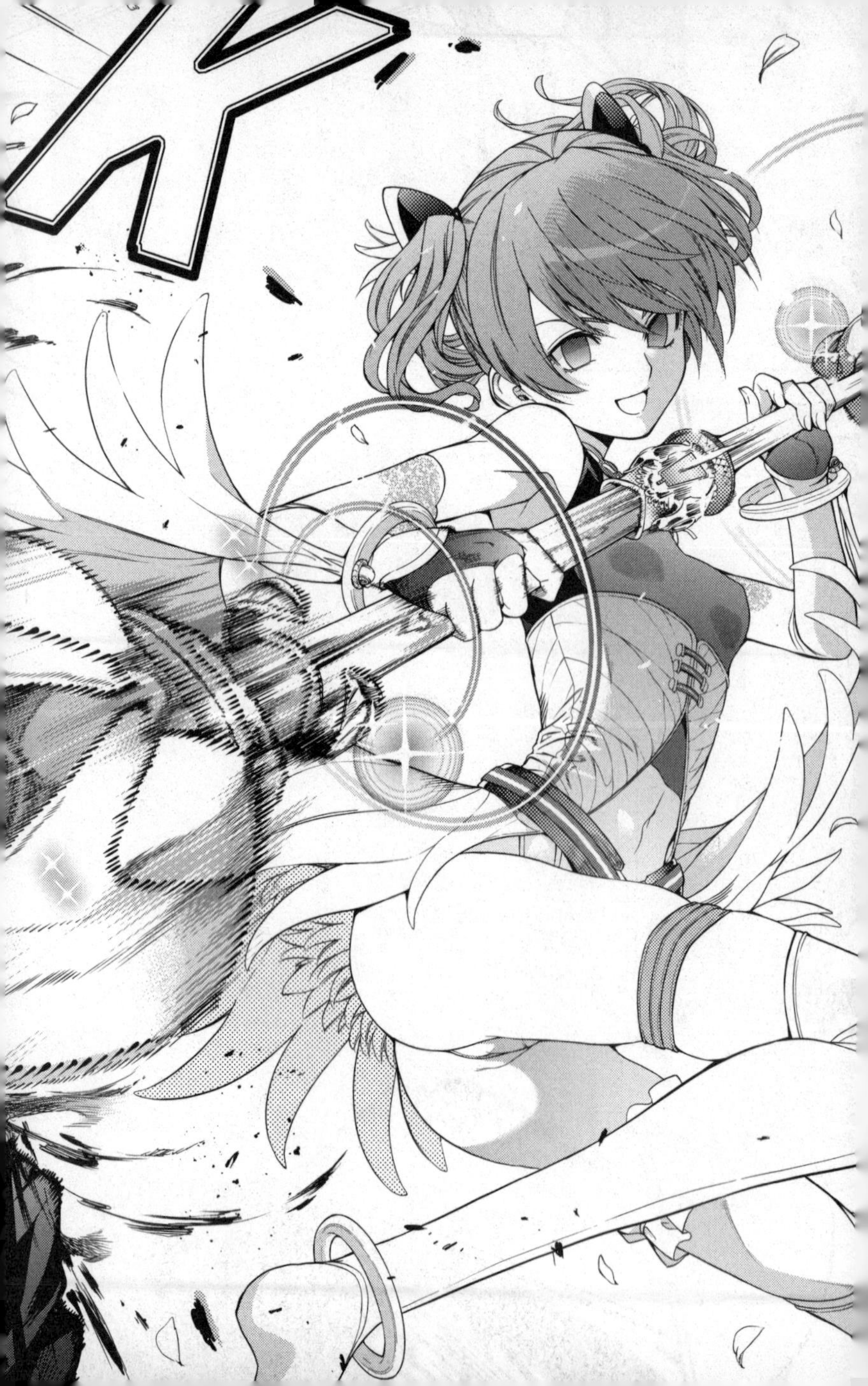

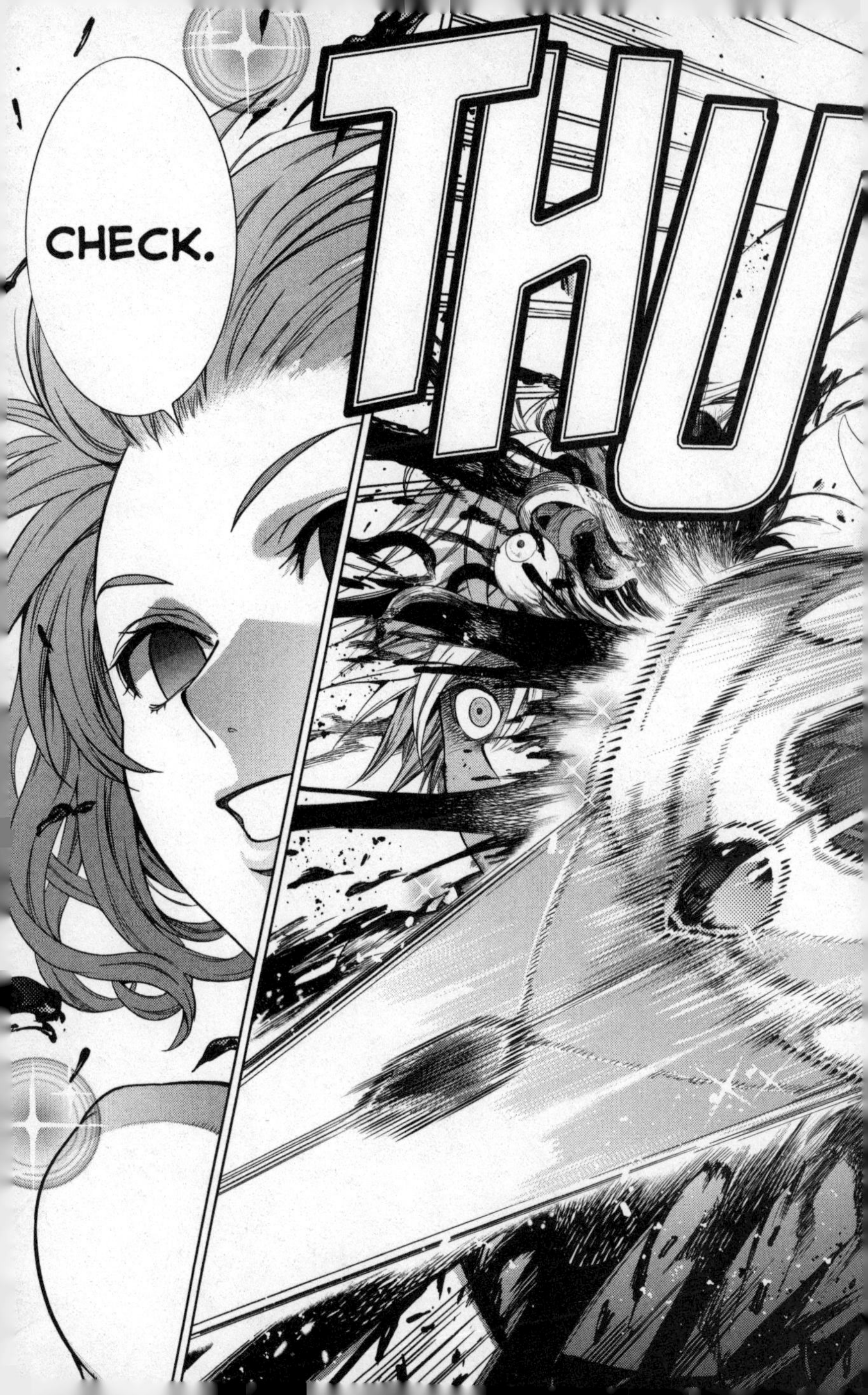
THU
CHECK.

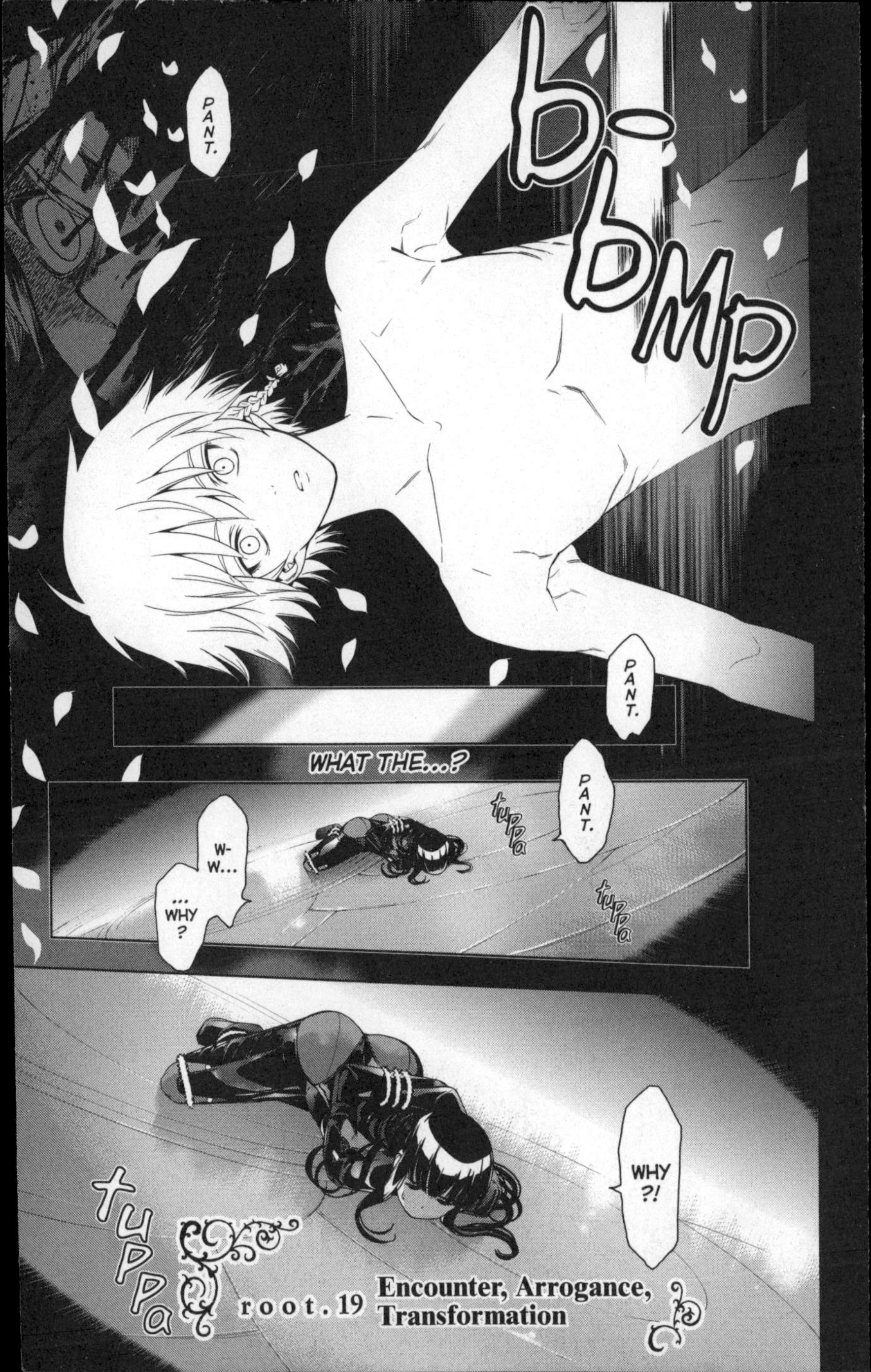
b-bmp
PANT.
PANT.
WHAT THE...?
PANT.
tuppa
tuppa
W-W...
...WHY?
WHY?!
tuppa
root. 19 Encounter, Arrogance, Transformation

WHOSE MEMORY IS THIS—?

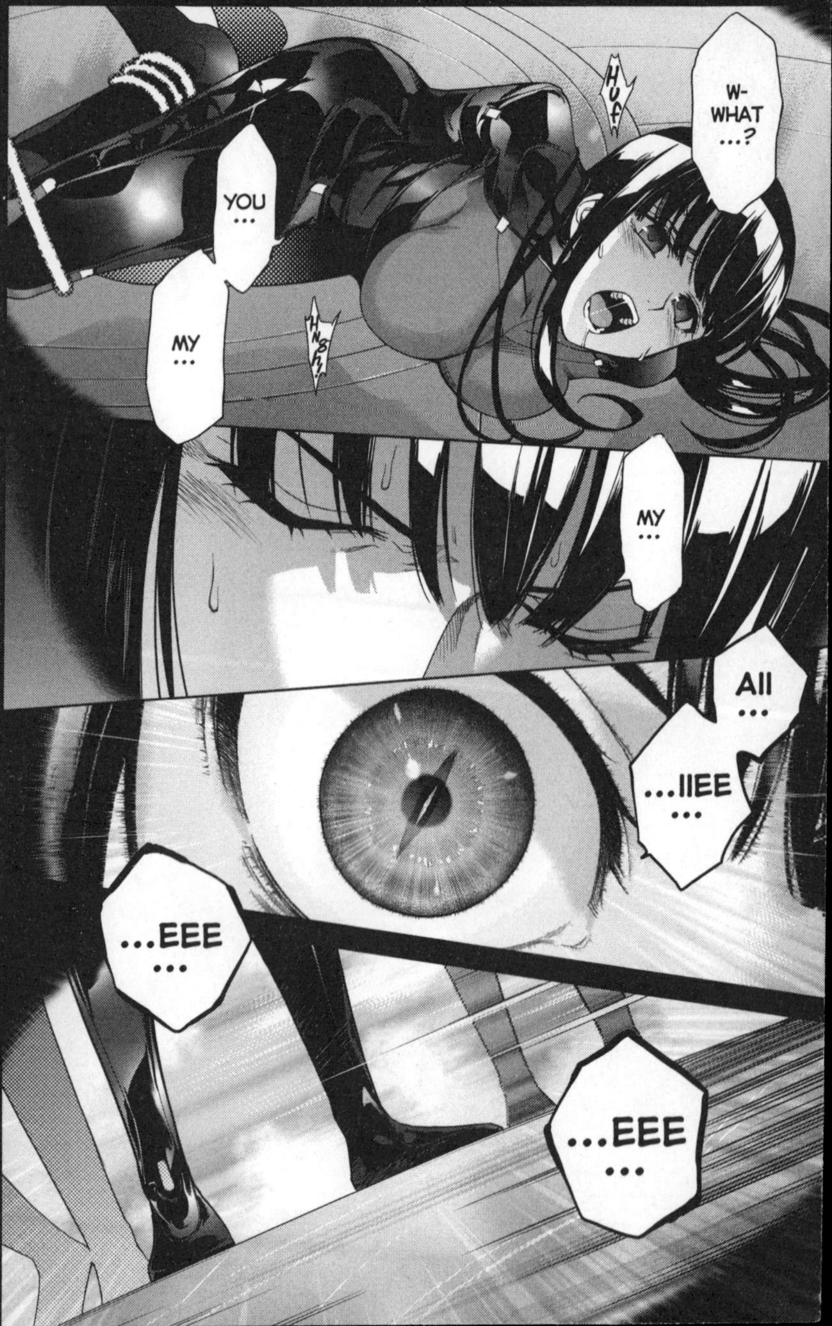
W-WHAT...?
Huf
YOU...
MY...
MY...
All...
...IIEE...
...EEE...
...EEE...

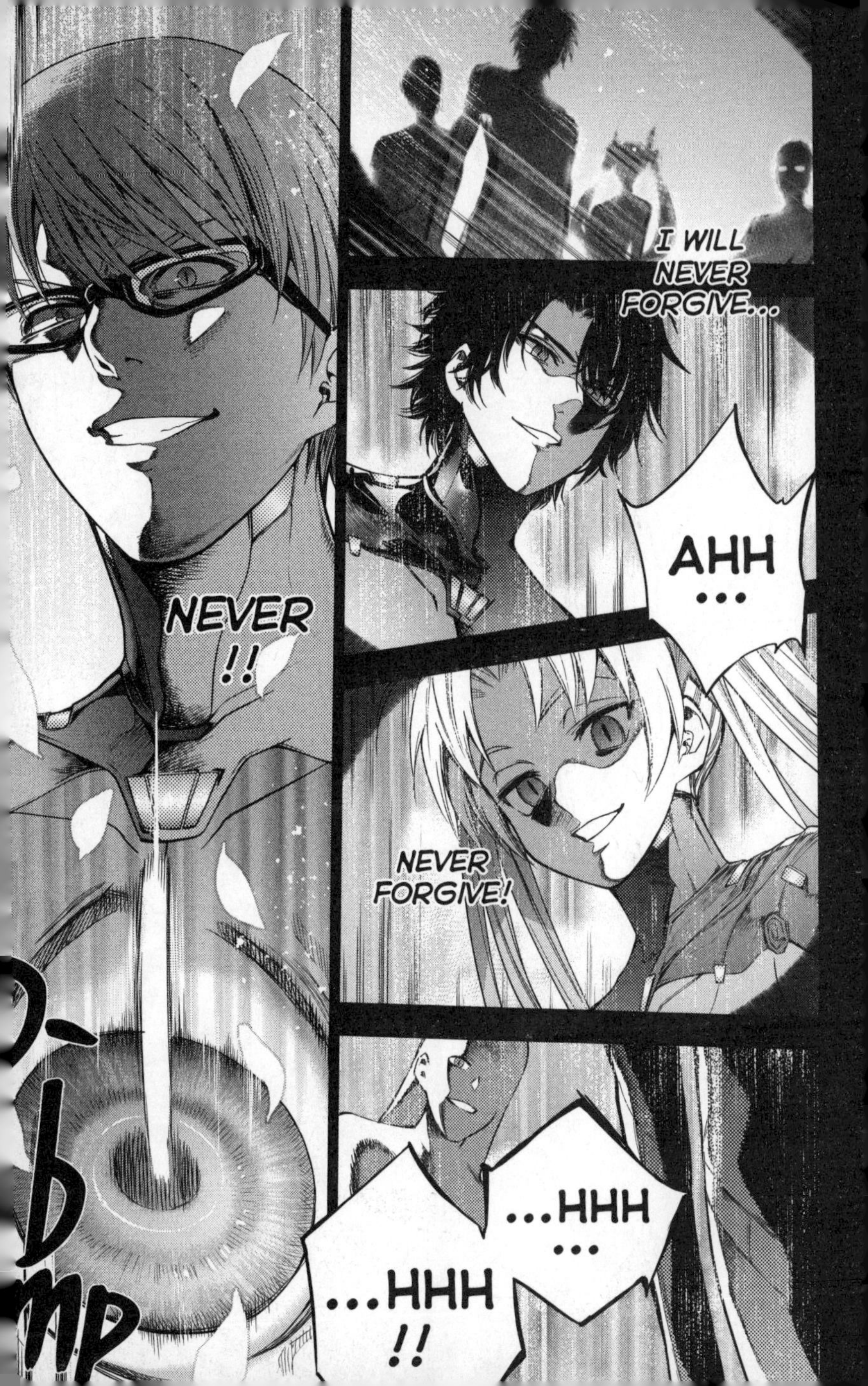
I WILL NEVER FORGIVE...
AHH...
NEVER FORGIVE!
...HHH...
...HHH!!
NEVER!!

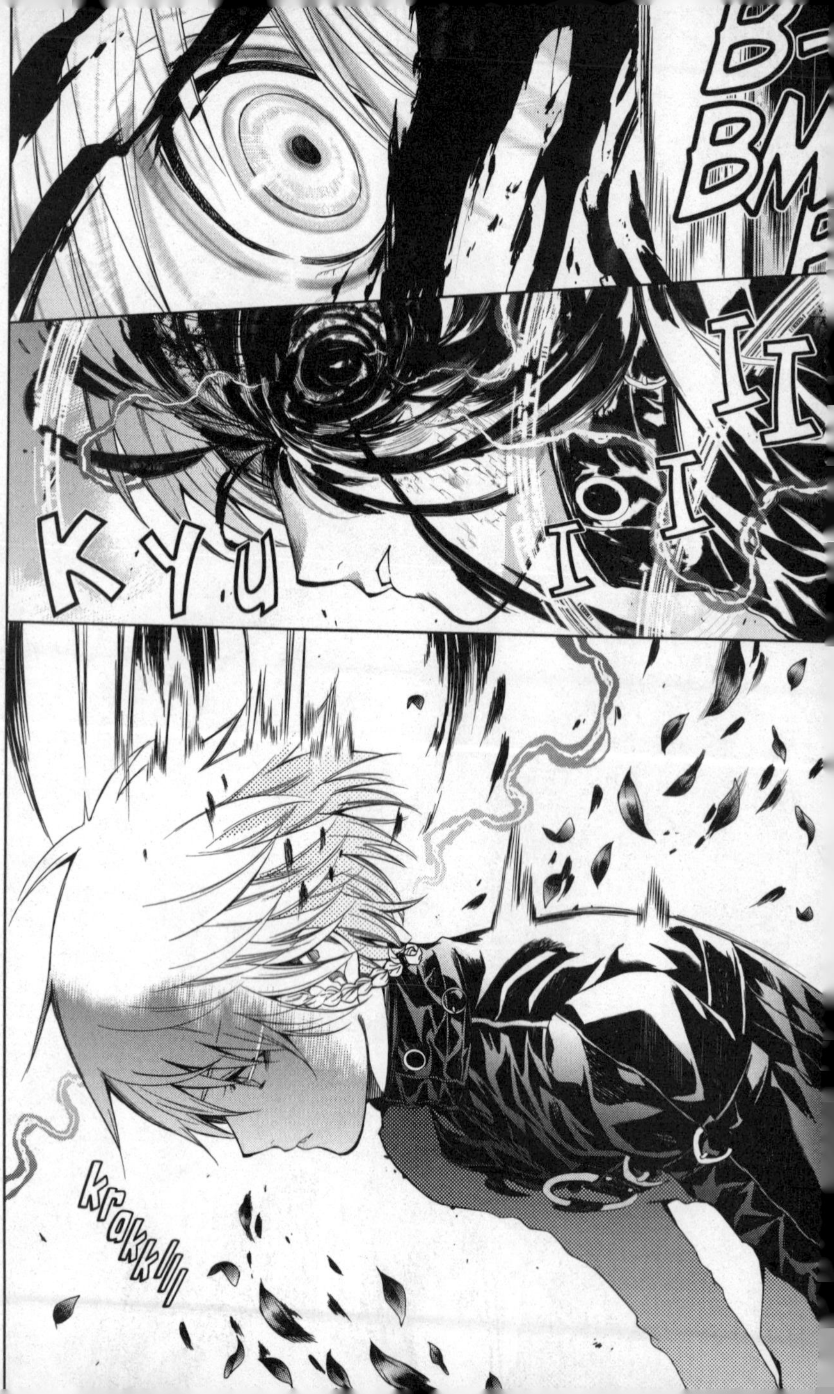
KYUIIII
krakklll

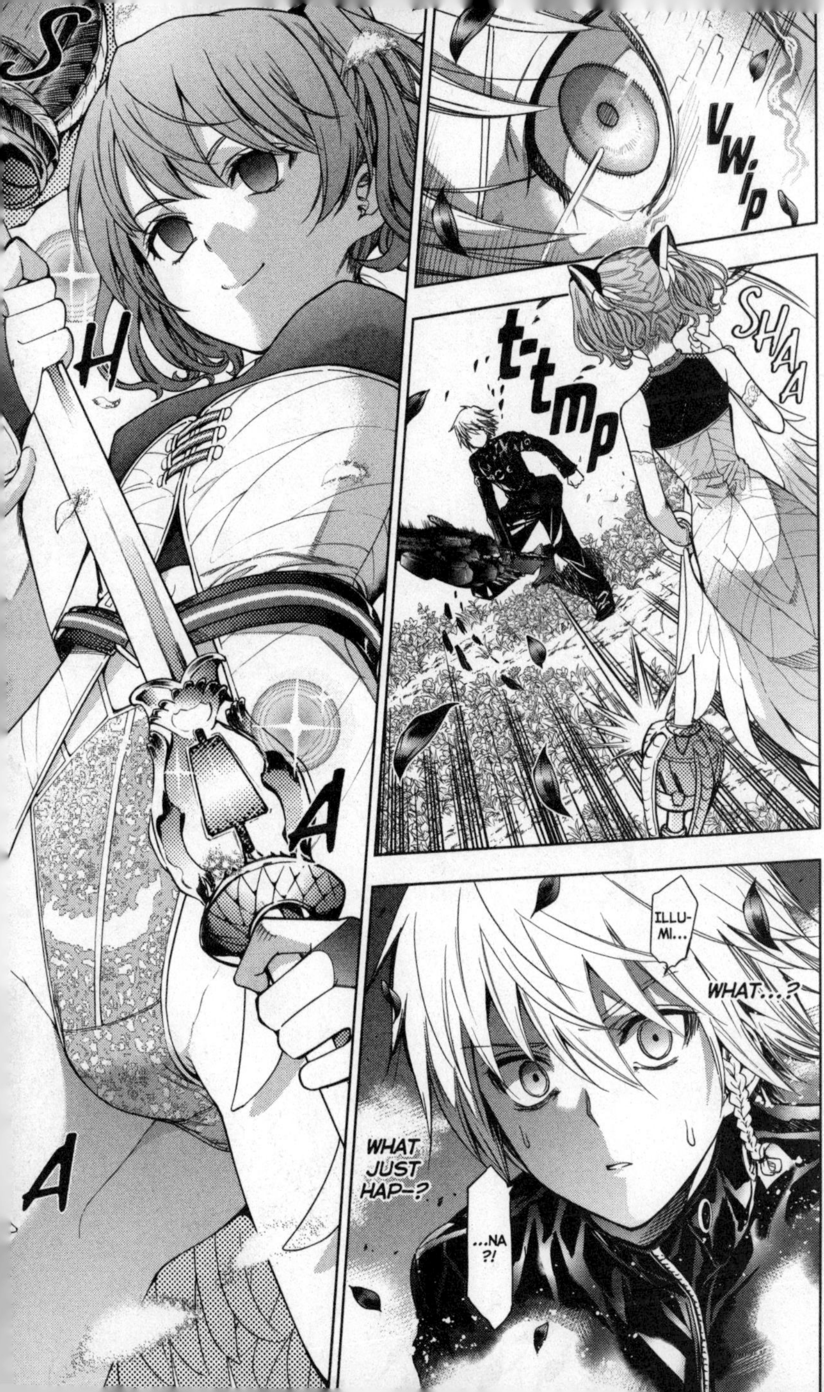
VWIP
SHAA
t-ttmp
ILLUMI...
WHAT...?
WHAT JUST HAP–?
...NA ?!
SHAA

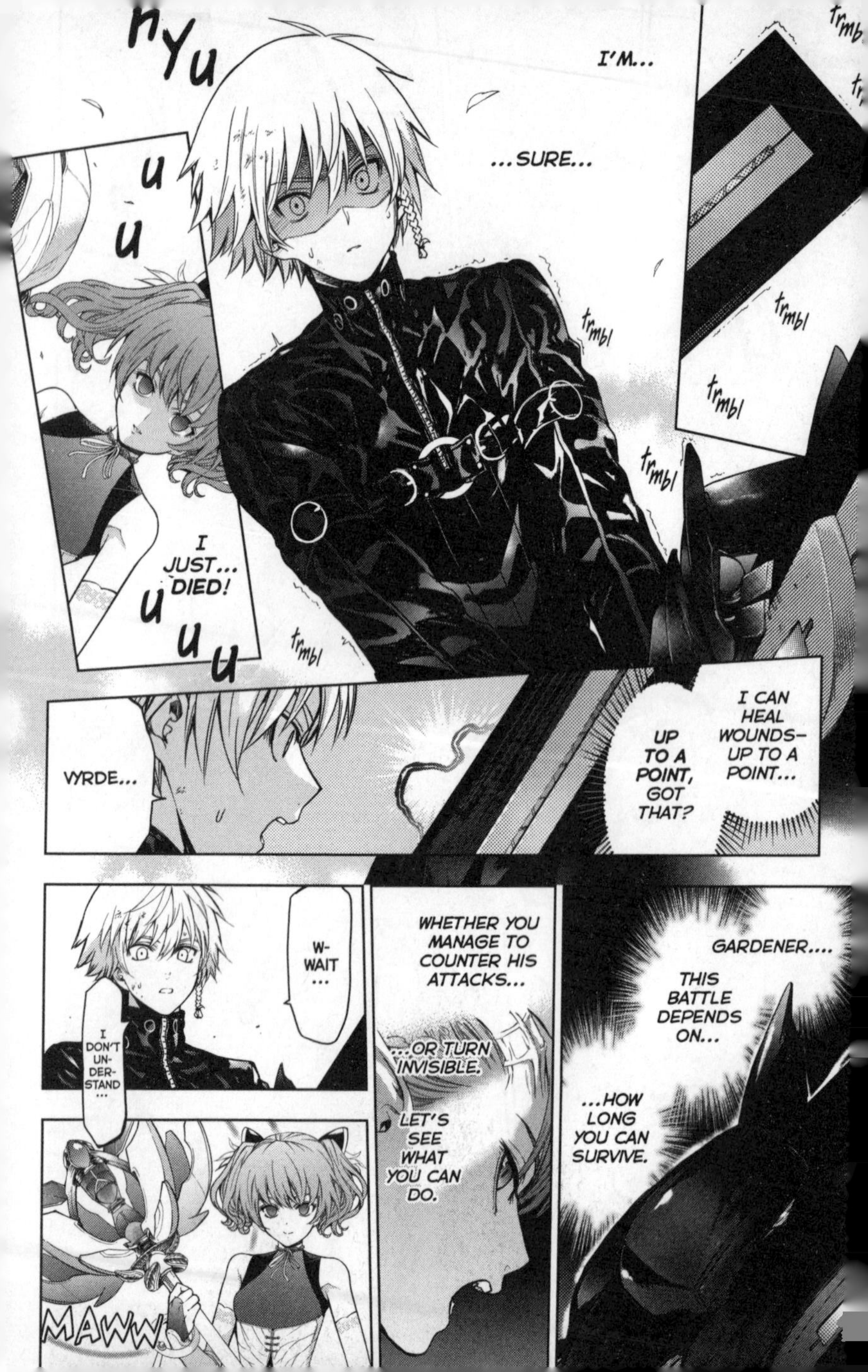
I'M...
...SURE...
trmbl
trmbl
trmbl
trmbl
nYu u u
I JUST... DIED!
u u u
trmbl
I CAN HEAL WOUNDS— UP TO A POINT...
UP TO A POINT, GOT THAT?
VYRDE...
GARDENER....
THIS BATTLE DEPENDS ON...
...HOW LONG YOU CAN SURVIVE.
WHETHER YOU MANAGE TO COUNTER HIS ATTACKS...
...OR TURN INVISIBLE.
LET'S SEE WHAT YOU CAN DO.
W-WAIT...
I DON'T UNDERSTAND...
MAWW

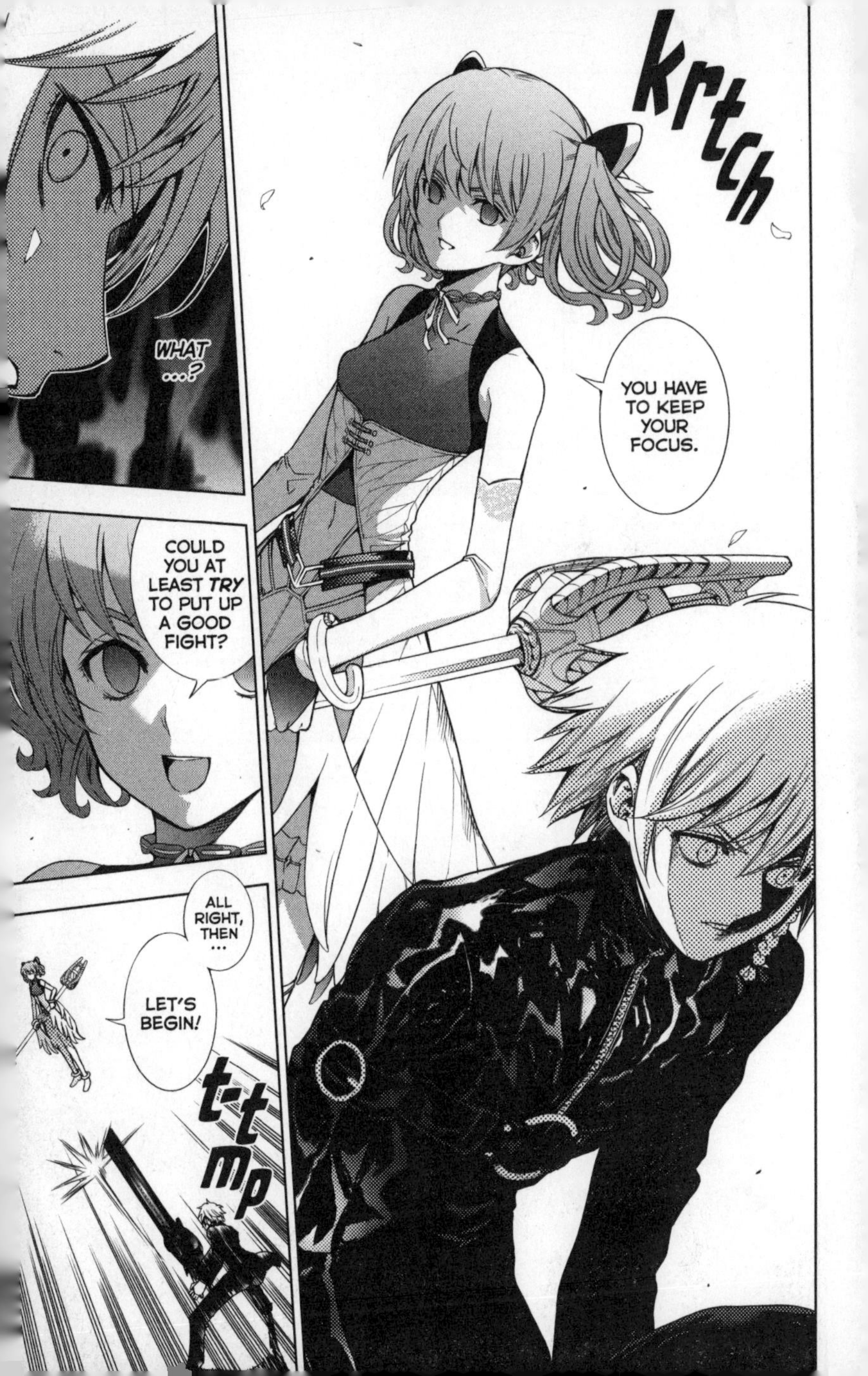
krtch
YOU HAVE TO KEEP YOUR FOCUS.
WHAT ...?
COULD YOU AT LEAST *TRY* TO PUT UP A GOOD FIGHT?
ALL RIGHT, THEN ...
LET'S BEGIN!
t-tmp

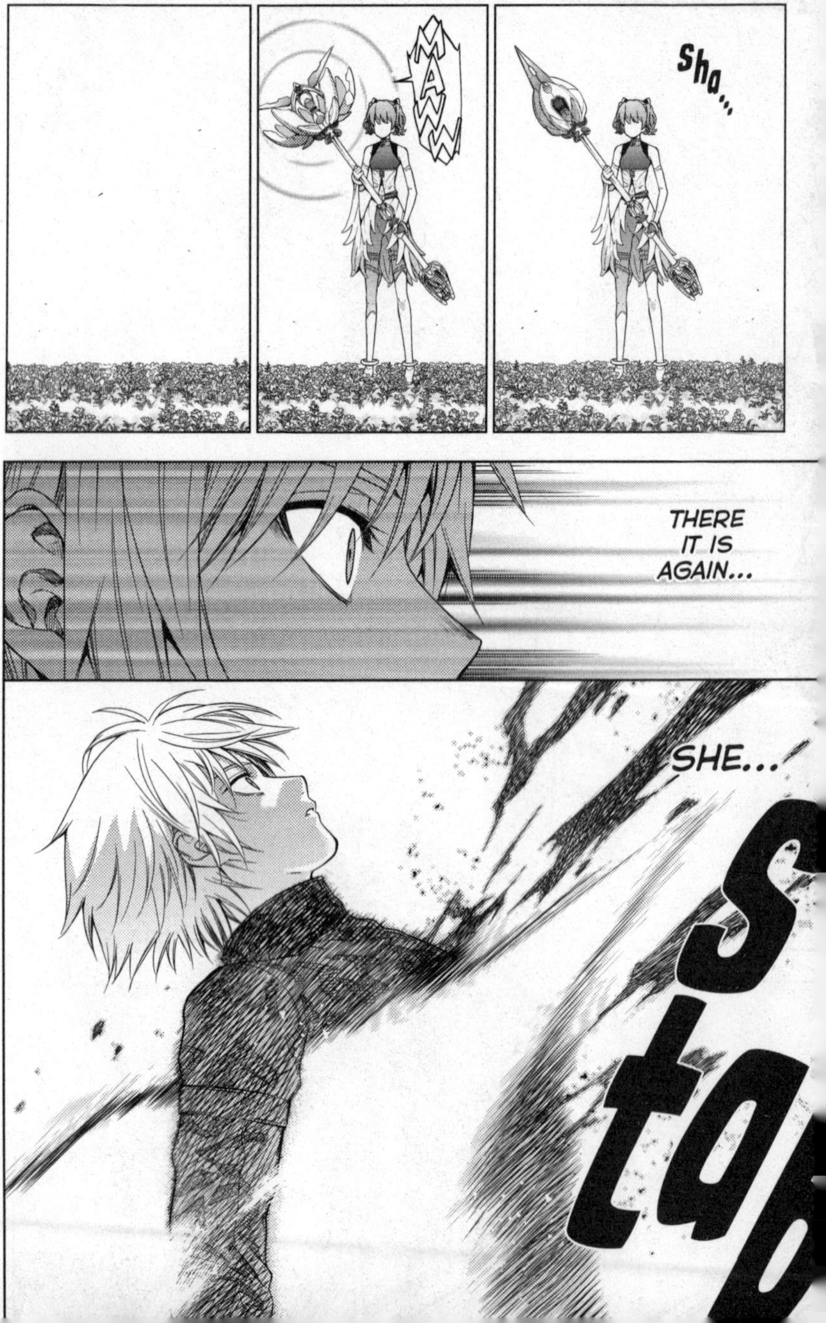
Sha...
THERE IT IS AGAIN...
SHE...

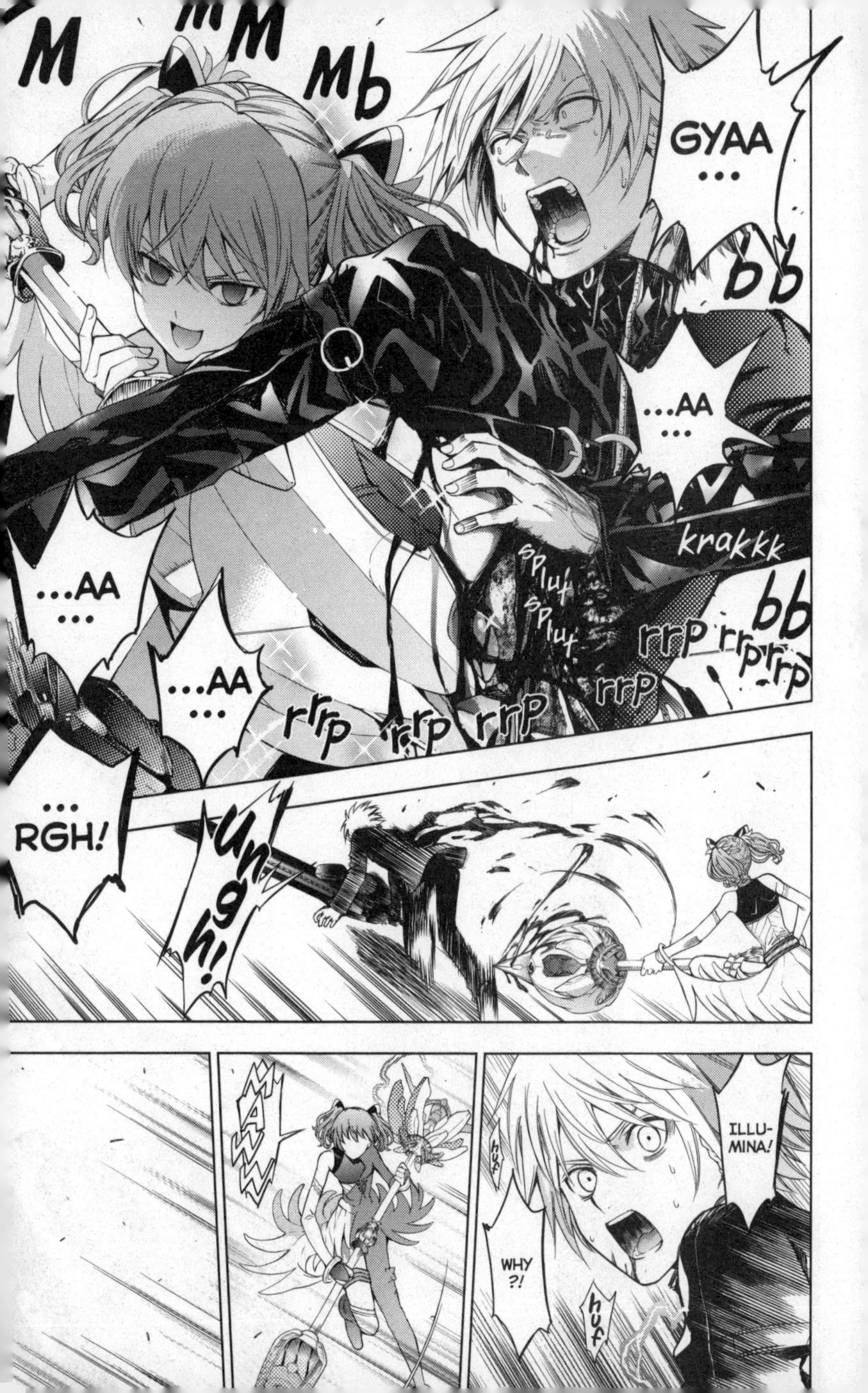
GYAA...
bb
Mb
mM
M
...AA...
krakkk
bb
splut
splut
rrp rrp rrp
rrp
rrp rrp rrp rrp
...AA...
...AA...
Ungh!
...RGH!
ILLU-MINA!
huf
WHY?!
huf

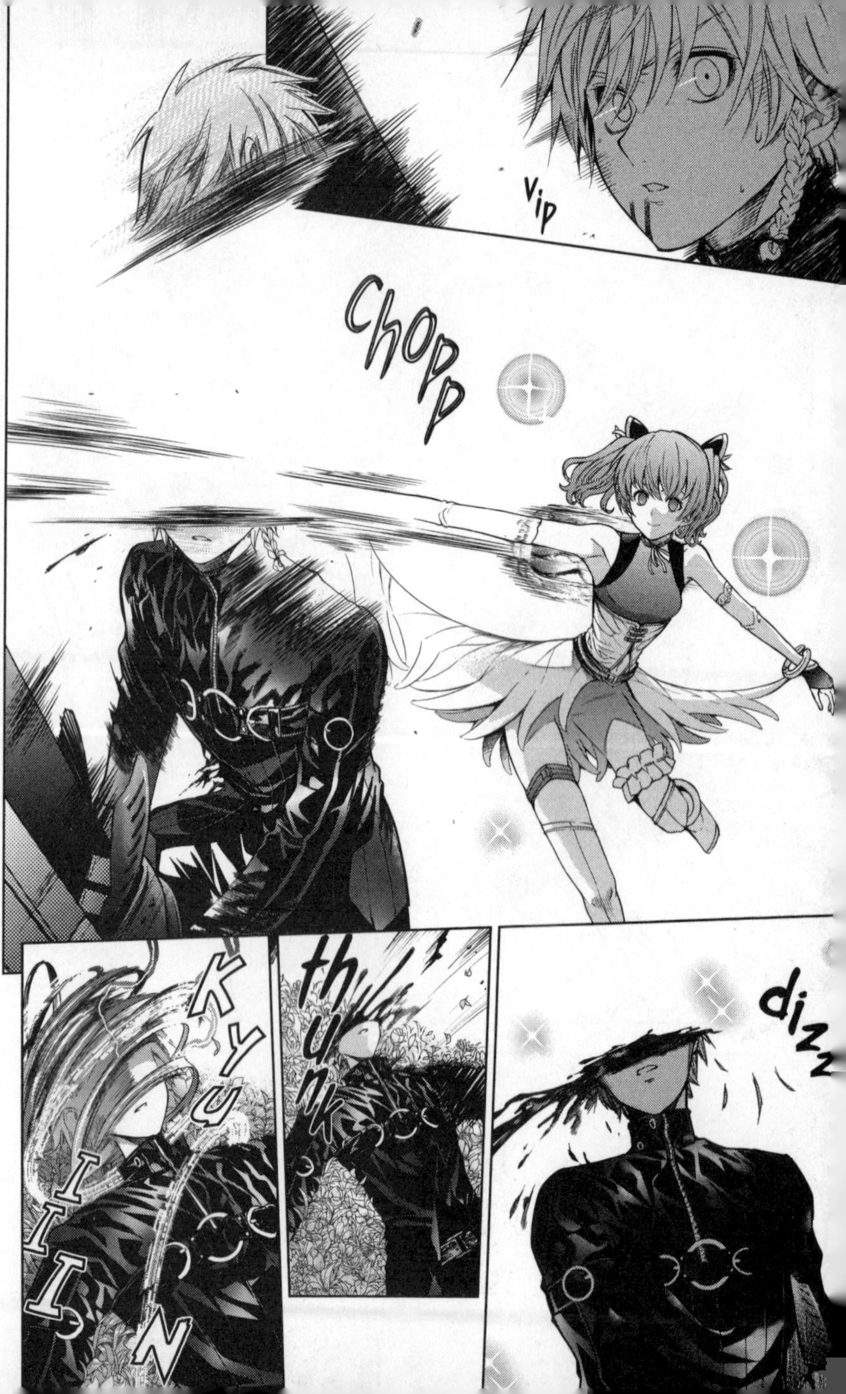
vip
Chopp
dizz
thunk
kyuIIIN

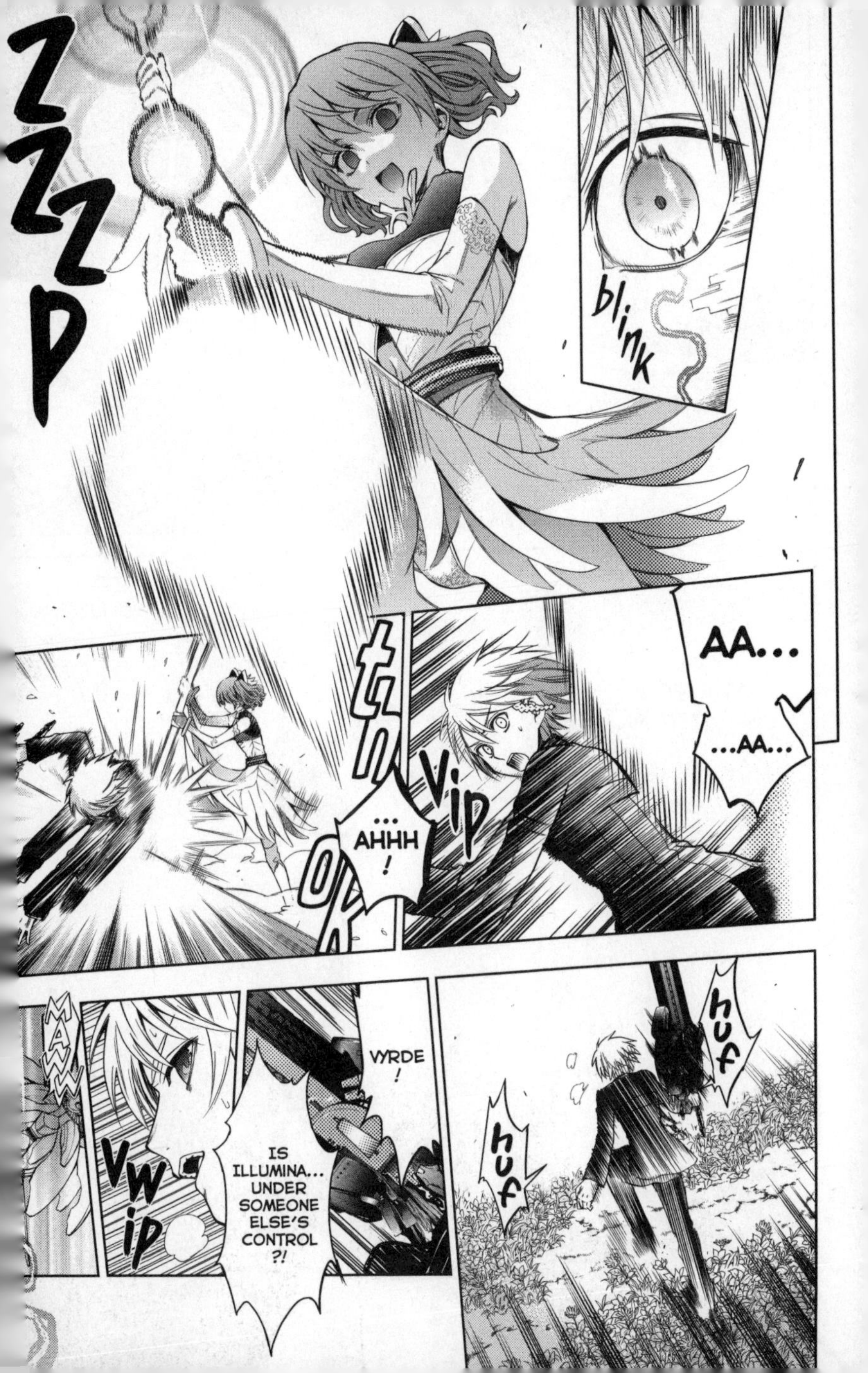
blink
ZZZP
AA...
...AA...
Vip
...AHHH!
huf
huf
VYRDE!
IS ILLUMINA... UNDER SOMEONE ELSE'S CONTROL?!
Vwip

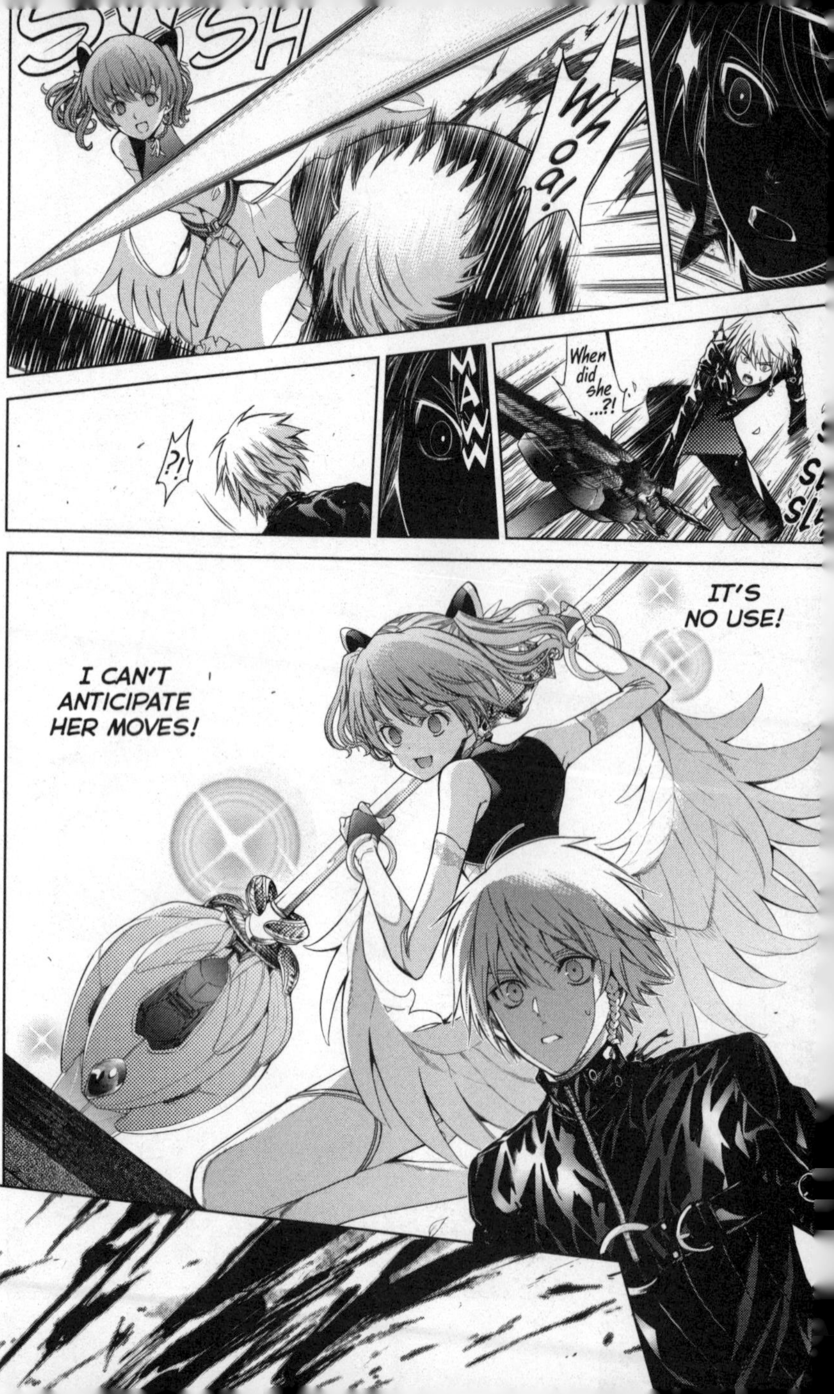
SWISH
Whoa!
When did she ...?!
MAWW
?!
IT'S NO USE!
I CAN'T ANTICIPATE HER MOVES!

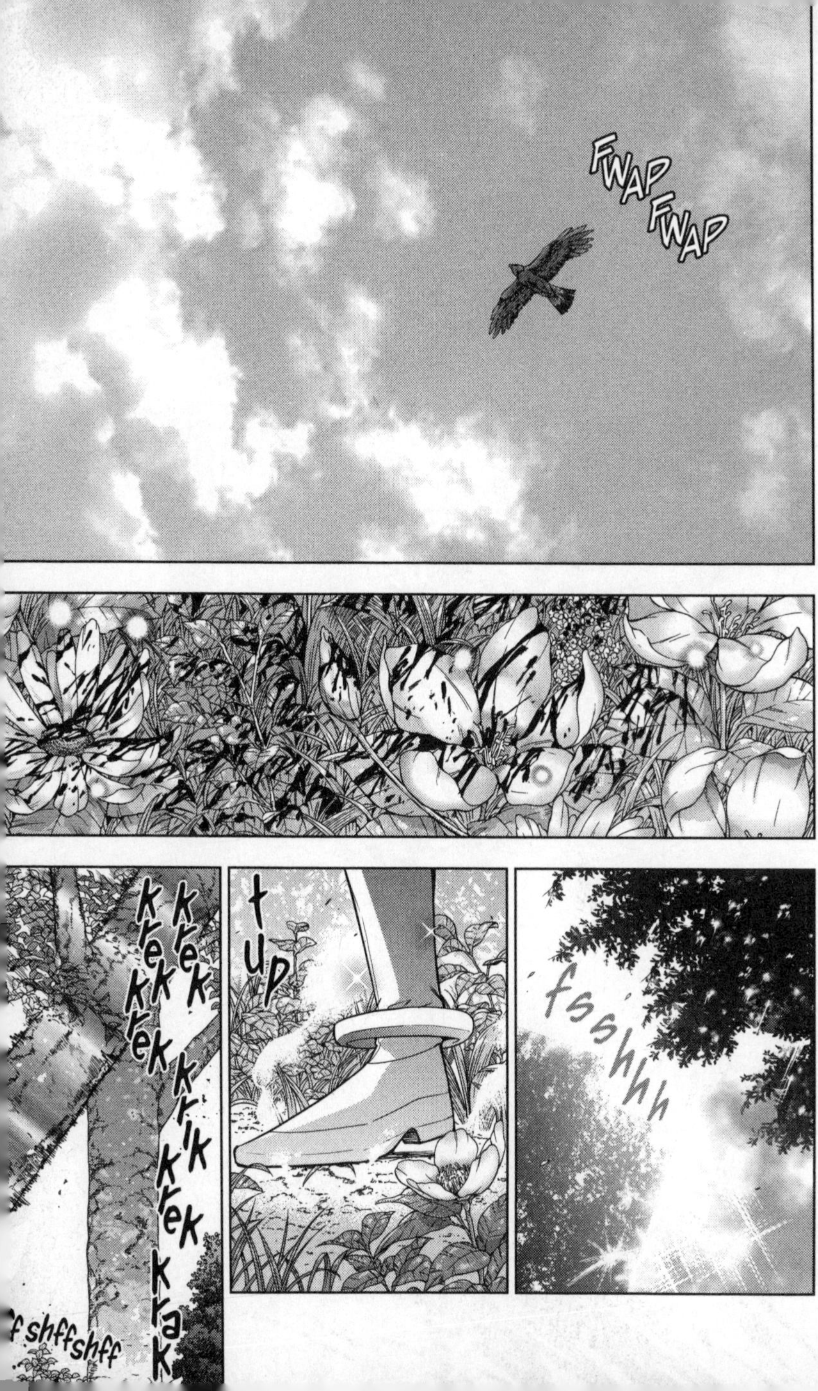
FWAP FWAP
fsshhh
tup
krek krek
krek krek
krrik
krek krek
krak
shffshff

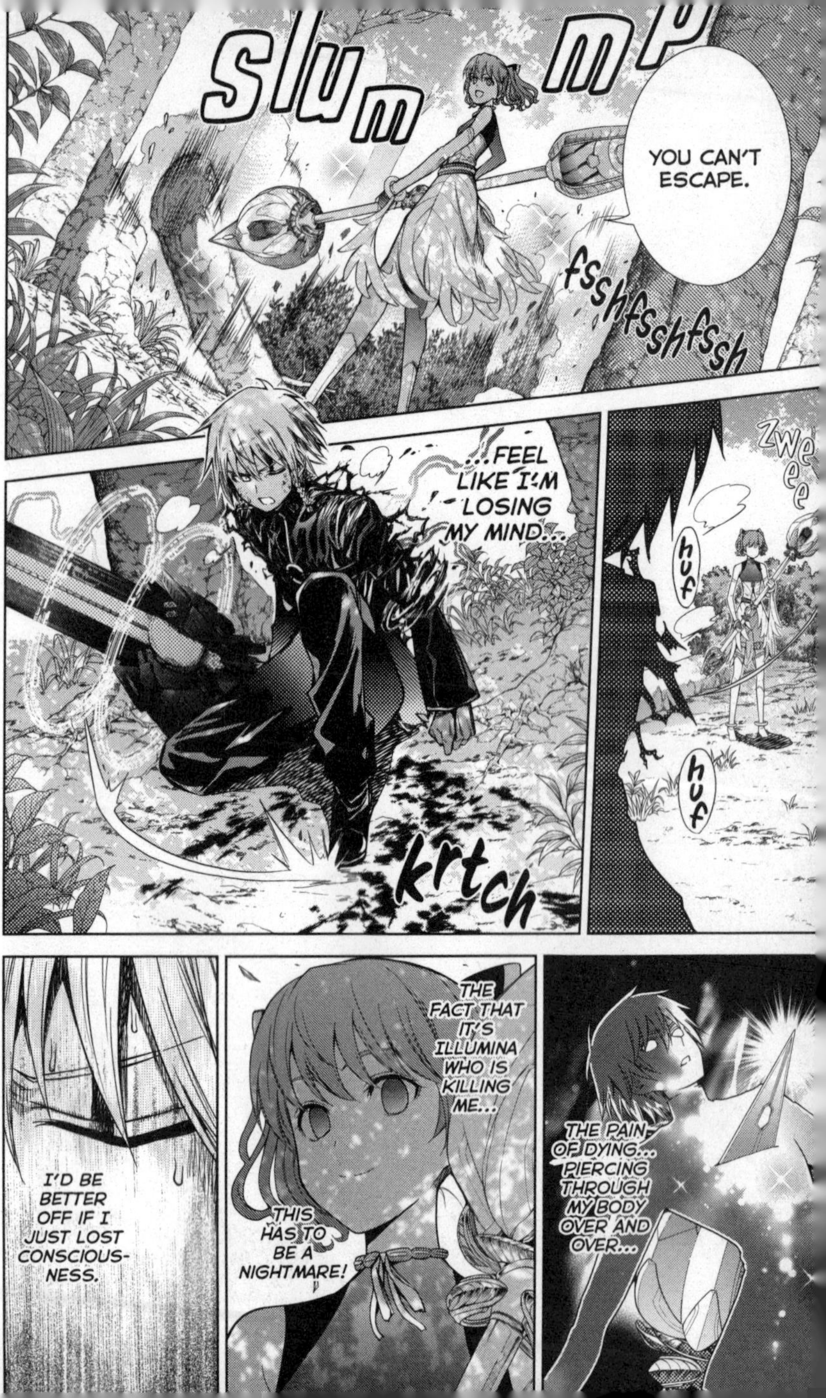
SLUMMP
YOU CAN'T ESCAPE.
FSSHFSSHFSSH
ZWEEE
HUF
HUF
...FEEL LIKE I'M LOSING MY MIND...
KRTCH
THE PAIN OF DYING... PIERCING THROUGH MY BODY OVER AND OVER...
THE FACT THAT IT'S ILLUMINA WHO IS KILLING ME...
THIS HAS TO BE A NIGHTMARE!
I'D BE BETTER OFF IF I JUST LOST CONSCIOUS-NESS.

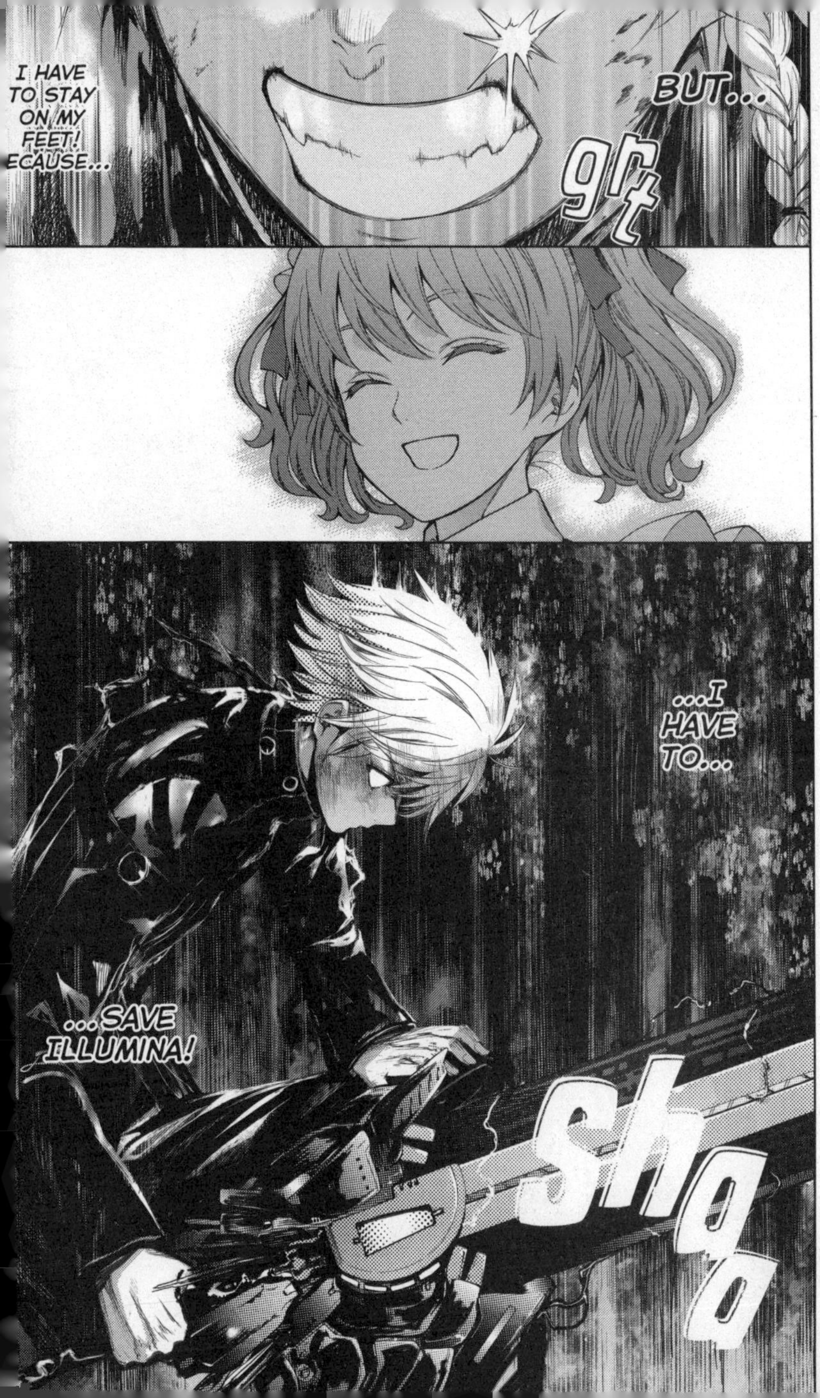
BUT...
grt
I HAVE TO STAY ON MY FEET! ECAUSE...
...I HAVE TO...
...SAVE ILLUMINA!
sha

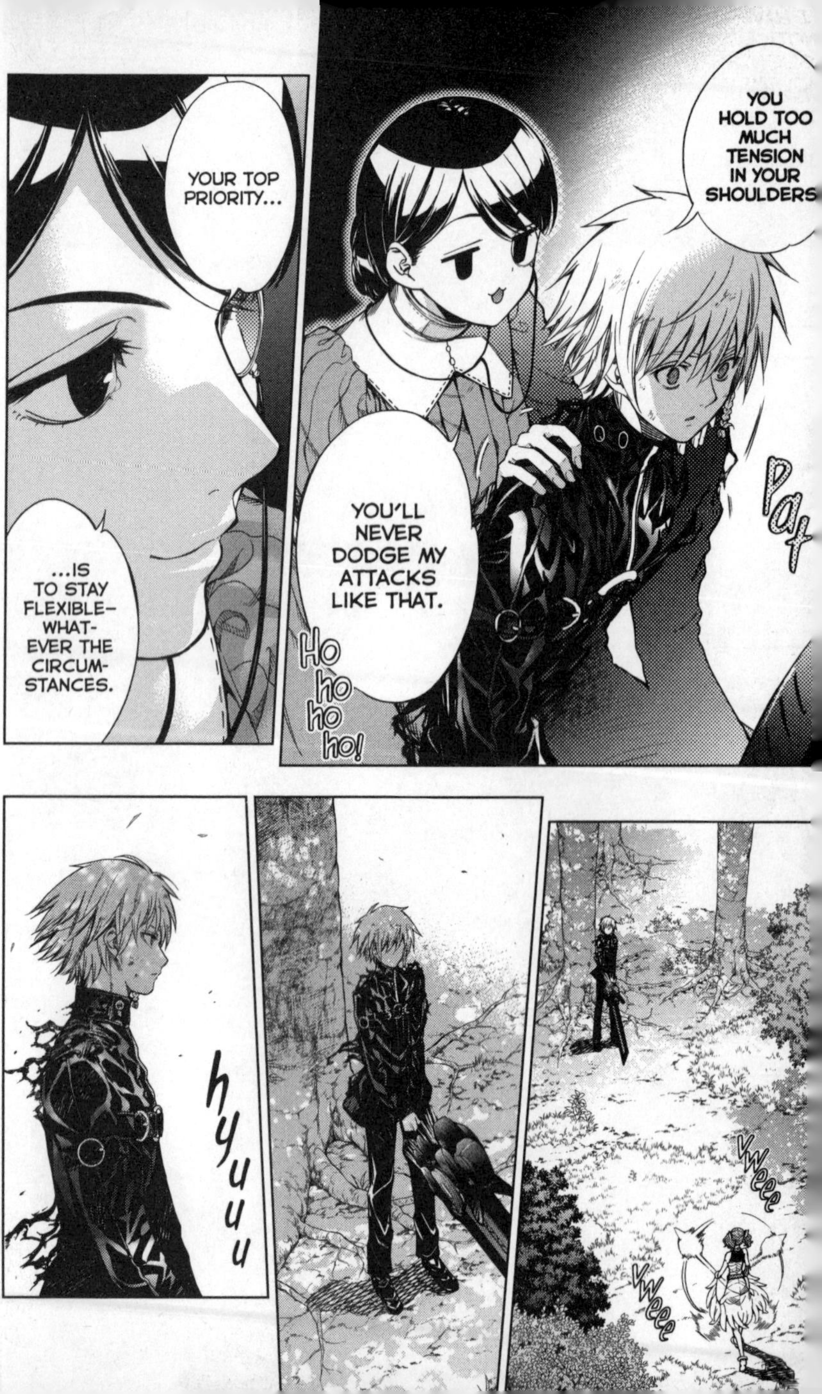
YOU HOLD TOO MUCH TENSION IN YOUR SHOULDERS
Pat
YOU'LL NEVER DODGE MY ATTACKS LIKE THAT.
Ho ho ho ho!
YOUR TOP PRIORITY...
...IS TO STAY FLEXIBLE— WHAT-EVER THE CIRCUM-STANCES.
Vweee
Vweee
hyuuuu

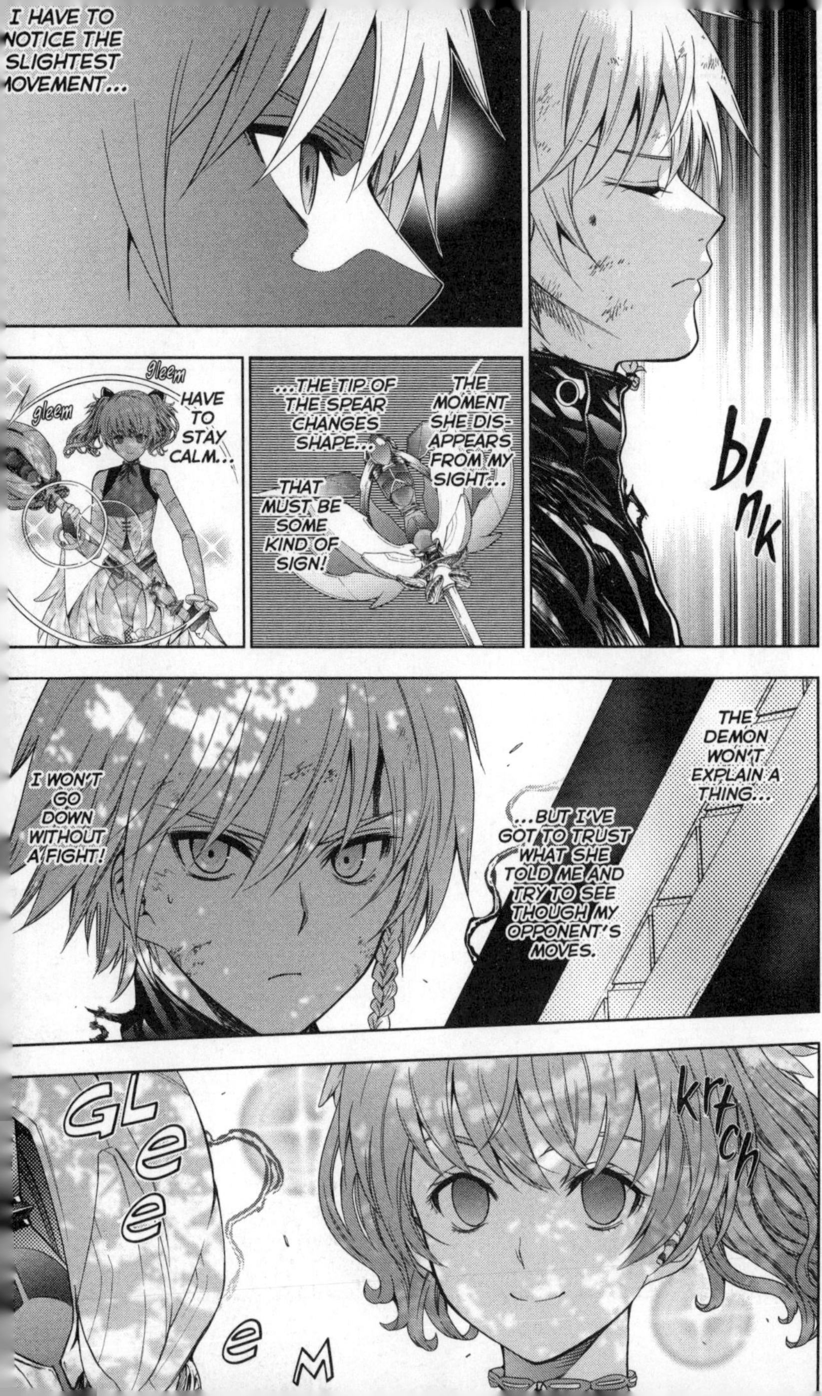
blink
I HAVE TO NOTICE THE SLIGHTEST MOVEMENT...
THE MOMENT SHE DIS-APPEARS FROM MY SIGHT...
...THE TIP OF THE SPEAR CHANGES SHAPE...
THAT MUST BE SOME KIND OF SIGN!
gleem
gleem
HAVE TO STAY CALM...
THE DEMON WON'T EXPLAIN A THING...
...BUT I'VE GOT TO TRUST WHAT SHE TOLD ME AND TRY TO SEE THOUGH MY OPPONENT'S MOVES.
I WON'T GO DOWN WITHOUT A FIGHT!
krtch
GLeeeeM

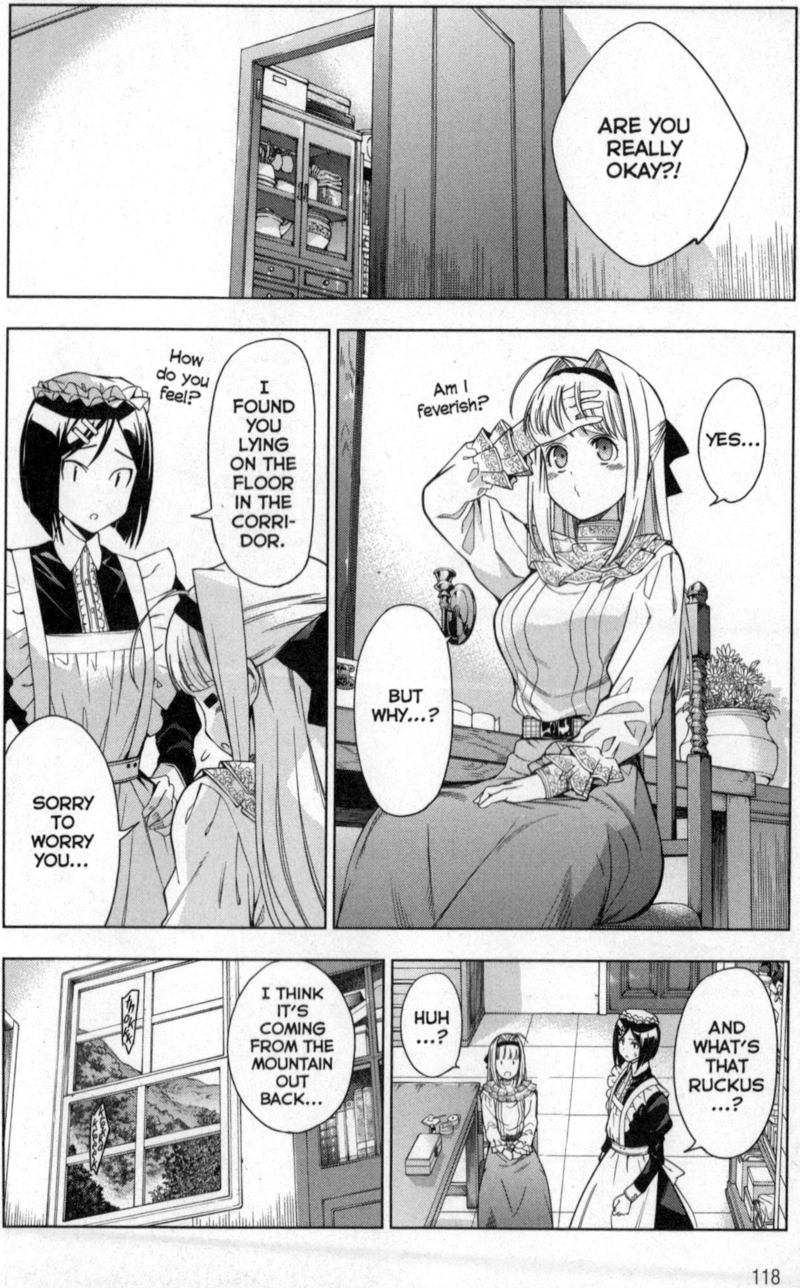
ARE YOU REALLY OKAY?!
YES...
Am I feverish?
BUT WHY...?
I FOUND YOU LYING ON THE FLOOR IN THE CORRIDOR.
How do you feel?
SORRY TO WORRY YOU...
AND WHAT'S THAT RUCKUS ...?
HUH ...?
I THINK IT'S COMING FROM THE MOUNTAIN OUT BACK...

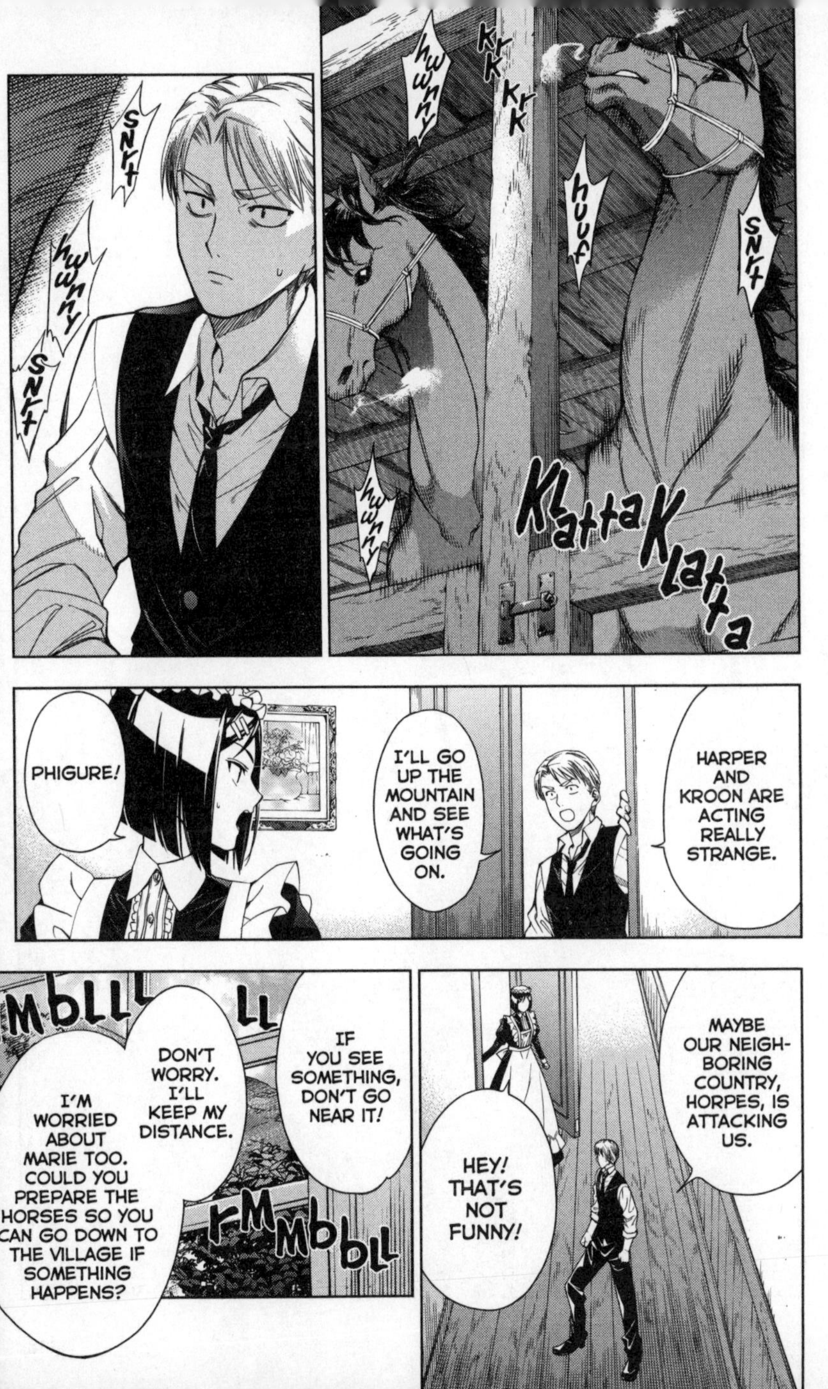
hwnny
Krk Krk
huuf
SNRT
hwnny
KlattaKlatta
SNRT
hwnny
SNRT
HARPER AND KROON ARE ACTING REALLY STRANGE.
I'LL GO UP THE MOUNTAIN AND SEE WHAT'S GOING ON.
PHIGURE!
MAYBE OUR NEIGH-BORING COUNTRY, HORPES, IS ATTACKING US.
HEY! THAT'S NOT FUNNY!
IF YOU SEE SOMETHING, DON'T GO NEAR IT!
MbLLL LL
DON'T WORRY. I'LL KEEP MY DISTANCE.
I'M WORRIED ABOUT MARIE TOO. COULD YOU PREPARE THE HORSES SO YOU CAN GO DOWN TO THE VILLAGE IF SOMETHING HAPPENS?
rMMbLL

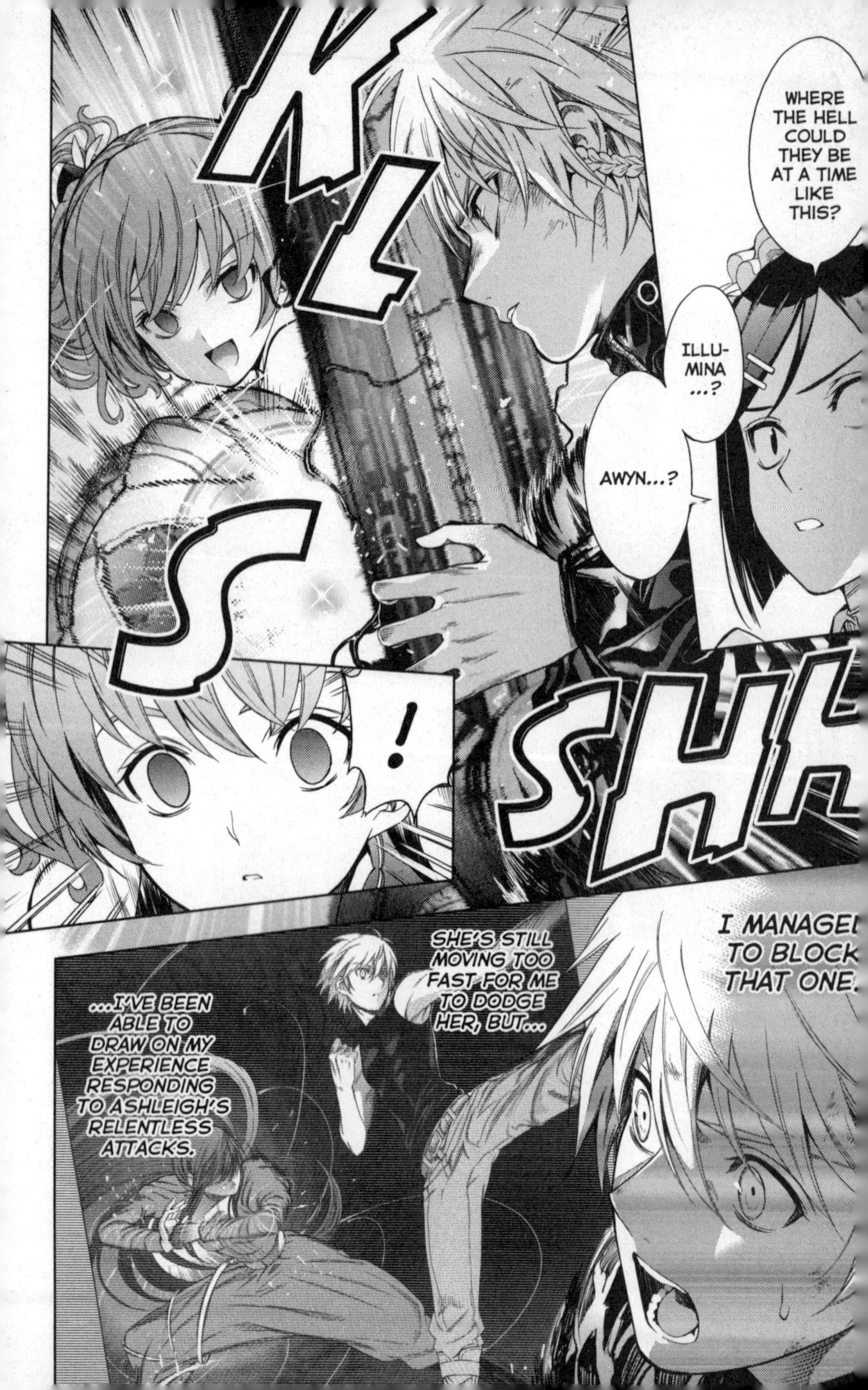
WHERE THE HELL COULD THEY BE AT A TIME LIKE THIS?
ILLUMINA...?
AWYN...?
KL
S
SH
!
I MANAGE TO BLOCK THAT ONE.
SHE'S STILL MOVING TOO FAST FOR ME TO DODGE HER, BUT...
...I'VE BEEN ABLE TO DRAW ON MY EXPERIENCE RESPONDING TO ASHLEIGH'S RELENTLESS ATTACKS.

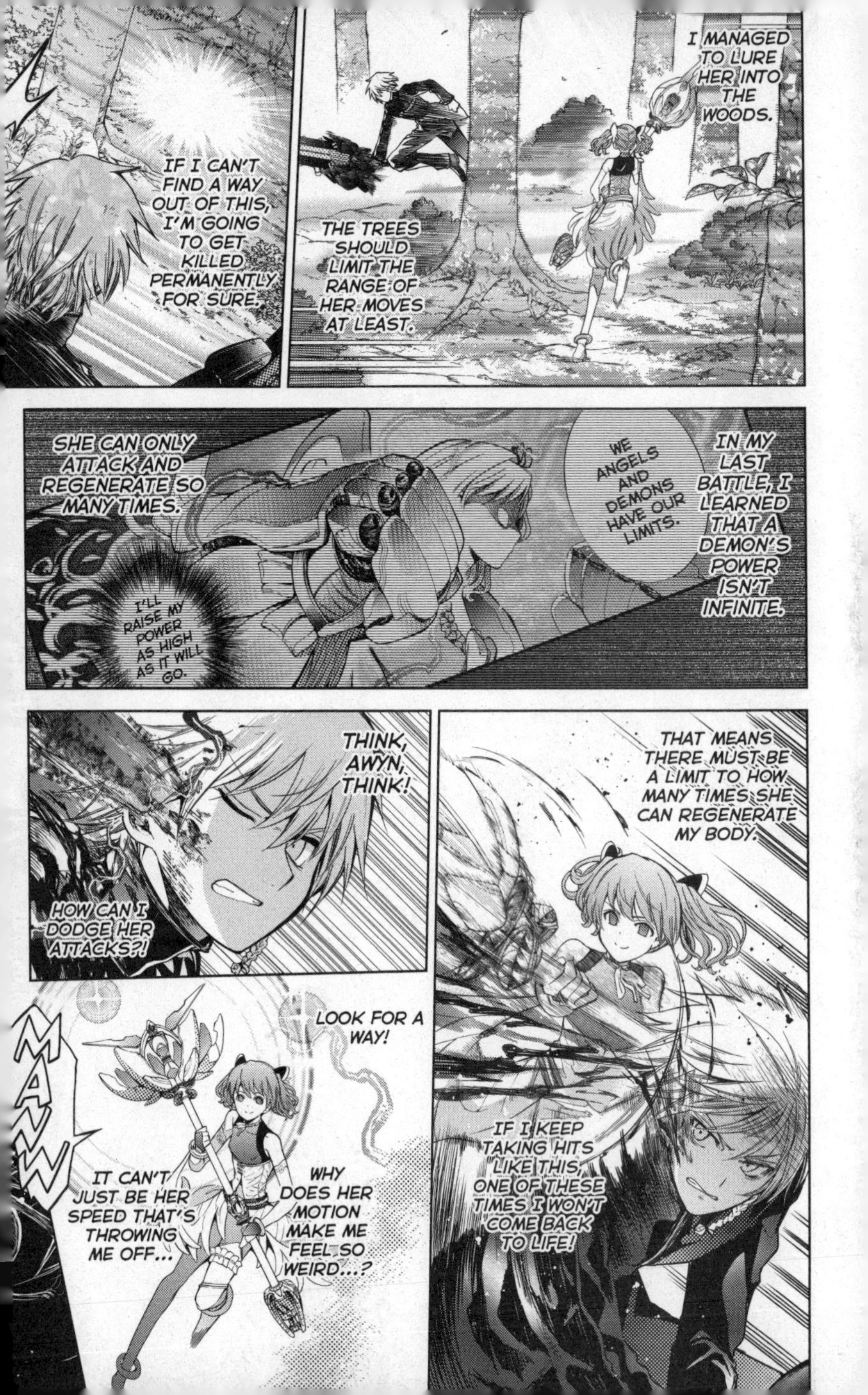
I MANAGED TO LURE HER INTO THE WOODS.
THE TREES SHOULD LIMIT THE RANGE OF HER MOVES AT LEAST.
IF I CAN'T FIND A WAY OUT OF THIS, I'M GOING TO GET KILLED PERMANENTLY FOR SURE.
IN MY LAST BATTLE, I LEARNED THAT A DEMON'S POWER ISN'T INFINITE.
WE ANGELS AND DEMONS HAVE OUR LIMITS.
SHE CAN ONLY ATTACK AND REGENERATE SO MANY TIMES.
I'LL RAISE MY POWER AS HIGH AS IT WILL GO.
THAT MEANS THERE MUST BE A LIMIT TO HOW MANY TIMES SHE CAN REGENERATE MY BODY.
IF I KEEP TAKING HITS LIKE THIS, ONE OF THESE TIMES I WON'T COME BACK TO LIFE!
THINK, AWYN, THINK!
HOW CAN I DODGE HER ATTACKS?!
LOOK FOR A WAY!
WHY DOES HER MOTION MAKE ME FEEL SO WEIRD...?
IT CAN'T JUST BE HER SPEED THAT'S THROWING ME OFF...
MANW

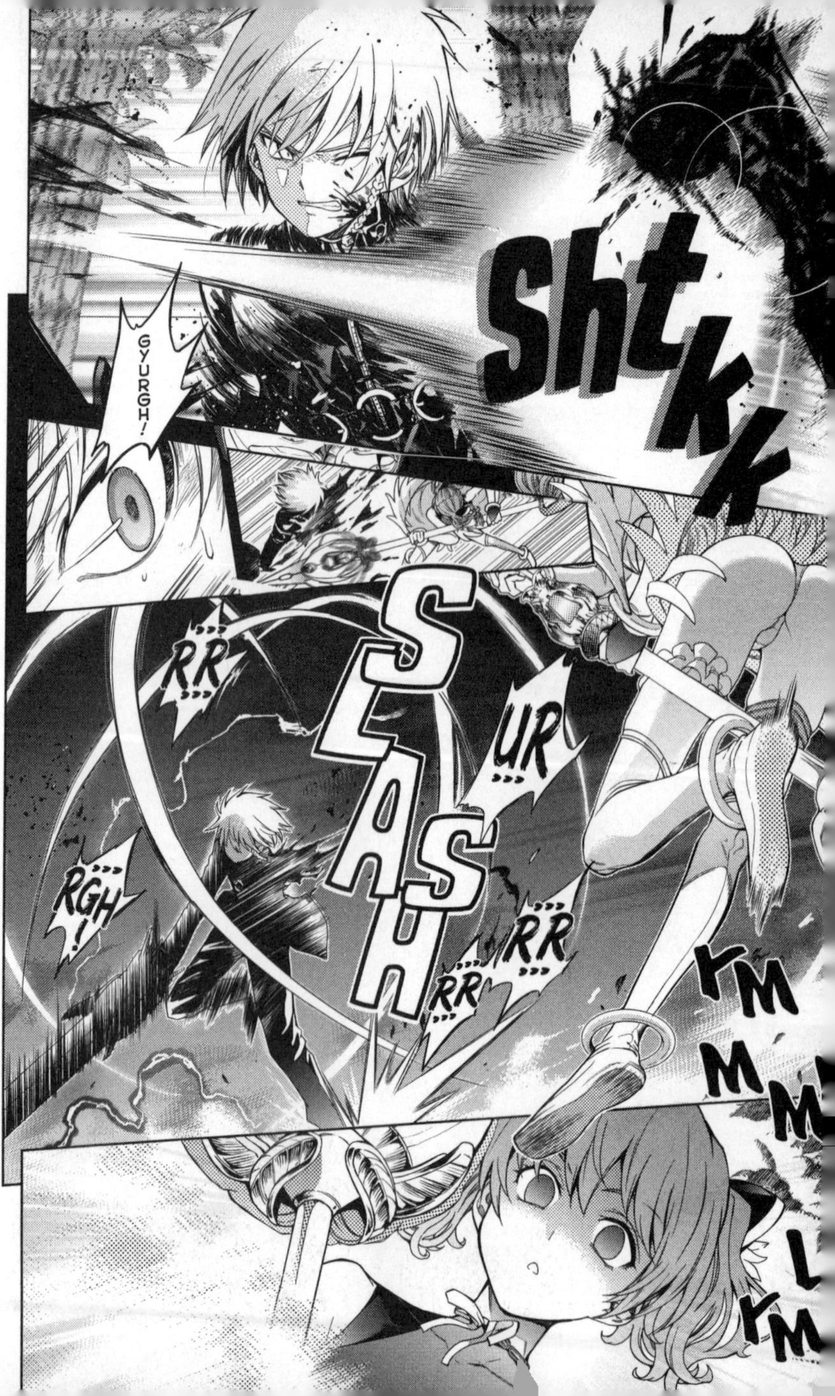
SHTKK
GYURGH!
SLASH
UR
RR
RR
RR
RGH!

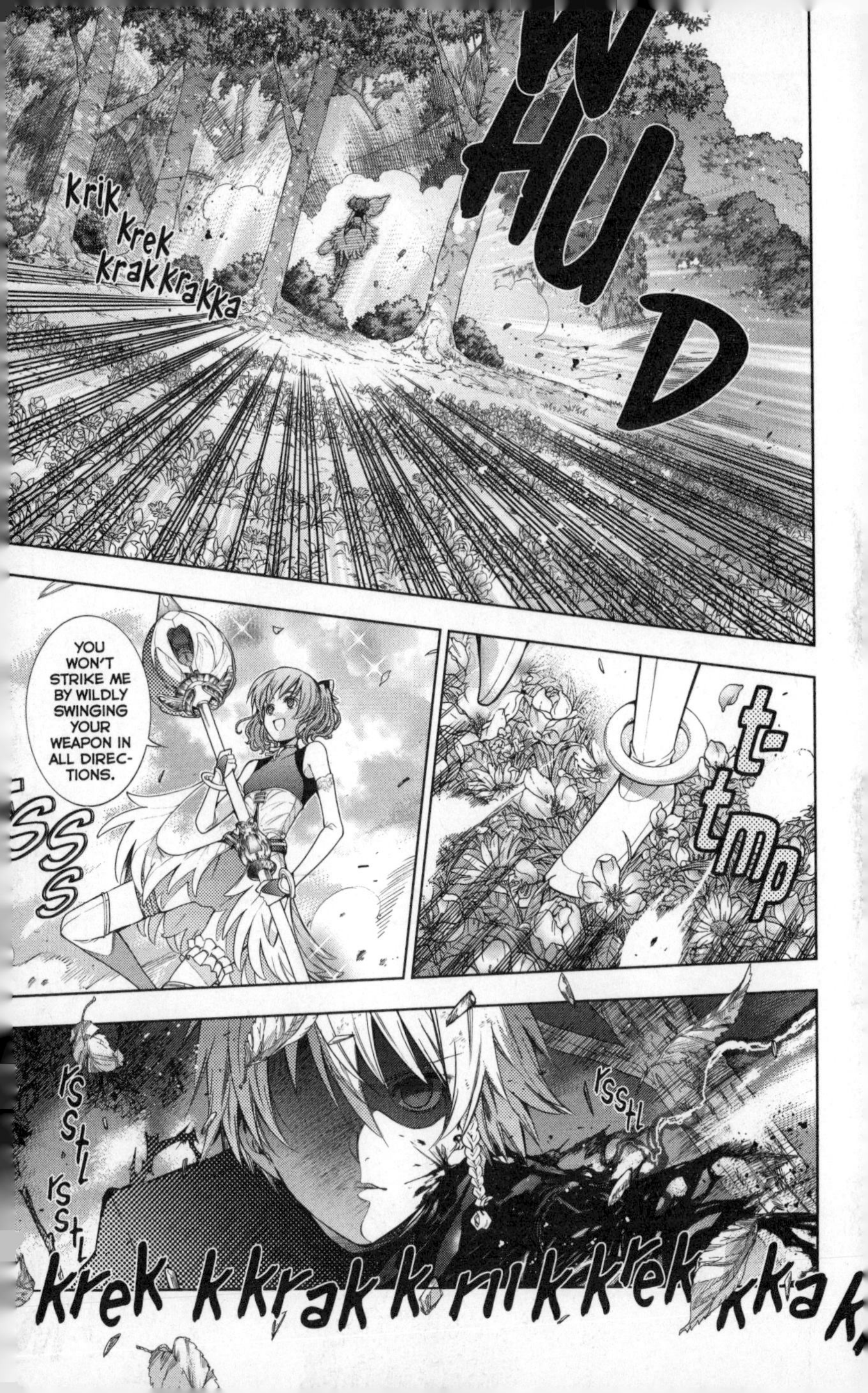
WHUD
krik krek krakkrakka
t-tmp
YOU WON'T STRIKE ME BY WILDLY SWINGING YOUR WEAPON IN ALL DIRECTIONS.
rsstl
rsstl rsstl
krek kkrak krikkrek kkak

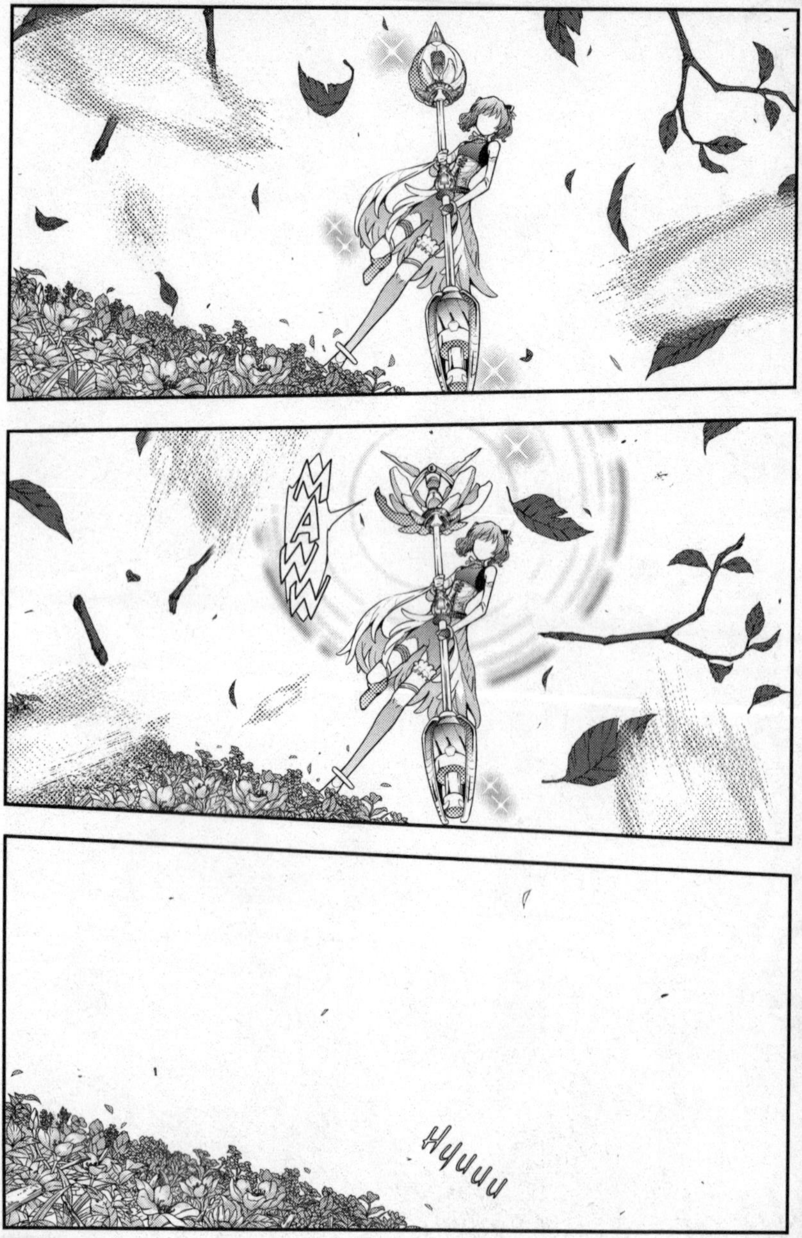
Hyuuu

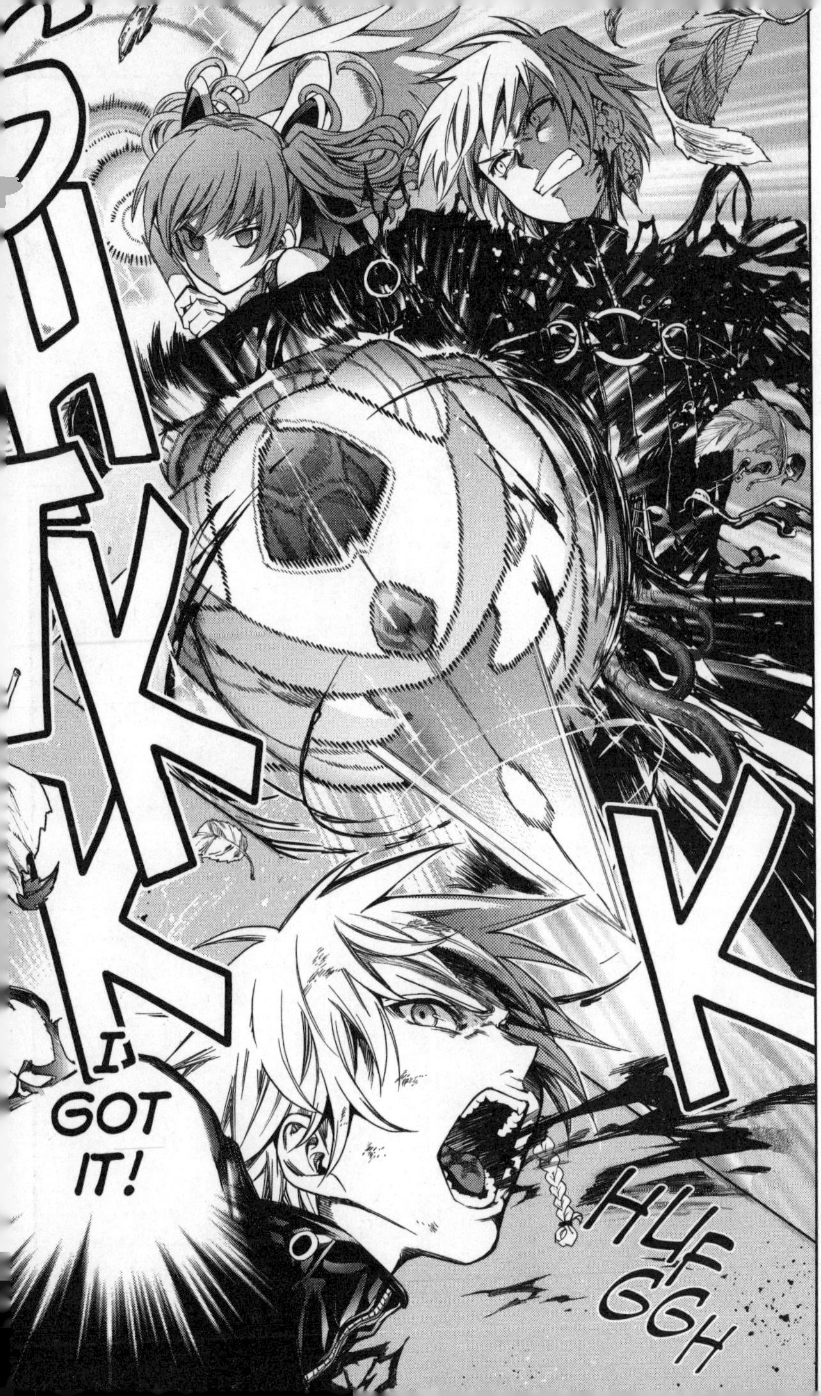
I GOT IT!
HUFGGH

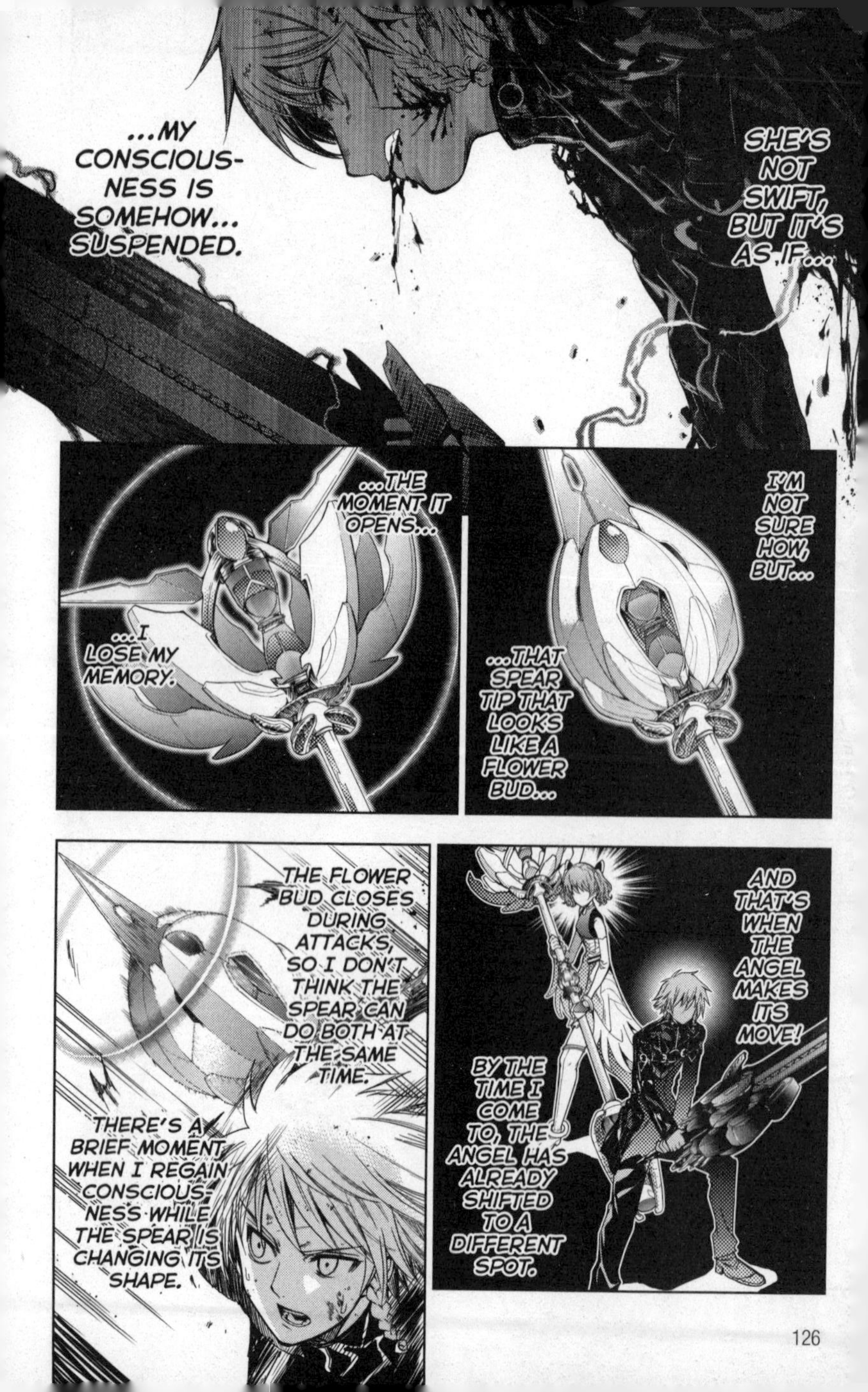
SHE'S NOT SWIFT, BUT IT'S AS IF...
...MY CONSCIOUS-NESS IS SOMEHOW... SUSPENDED.
I'M NOT SURE HOW, BUT...
...THAT SPEAR TIP THAT LOOKS LIKE A FLOWER BUD...
...THE MOMENT IT OPENS...
...I LOSE MY MEMORY.
AND THAT'S WHEN THE ANGEL MAKES ITS MOVE!
BY THE TIME I COME TO, THE ANGEL HAS ALREADY SHIFTED TO A DIFFERENT SPOT.
THE FLOWER BUD CLOSES DURING ATTACKS, SO I DON'T THINK THE SPEAR CAN DO BOTH AT THE SAME TIME.
THERE'S A BRIEF MOMENT WHEN I REGAIN CONSCIOUS-NESS WHILE THE SPEAR IS CHANGING ITS SHAPE.

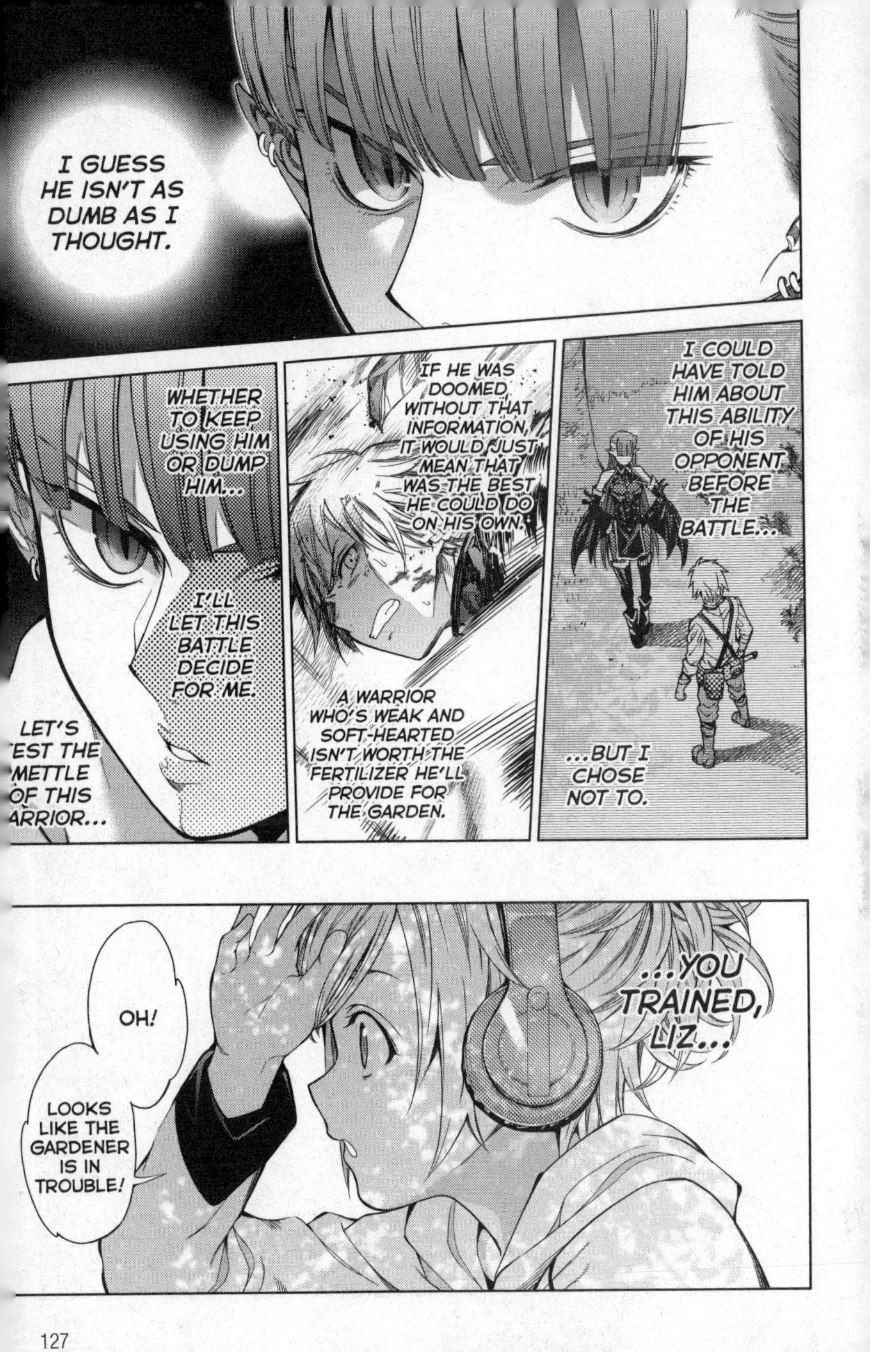
I GUESS HE ISN'T AS DUMB AS I THOUGHT.
I COULD HAVE TOLD HIM ABOUT THIS ABILITY OF HIS OPPONENT BEFORE THE BATTLE...
...BUT I CHOSE NOT TO.
IF HE WAS DOOMED WITHOUT THAT INFORMATION, IT WOULD JUST MEAN THAT WAS THE BEST HE COULD DO ON HIS OWN.
A WARRIOR WHO'S WEAK AND SOFT-HEARTED ISN'T WORTH THE FERTILIZER HE'LL PROVIDE FOR THE GARDEN.
WHETHER TO KEEP USING HIM OR DUMP HIM...
I'LL LET THIS BATTLE DECIDE FOR ME.
LET'S EST THE METTLE OF THIS ARRIOR...
...YOU TRAINED, LIZ...
OH!
LOOKS LIKE THE GARDENER IS IN TROUBLE!

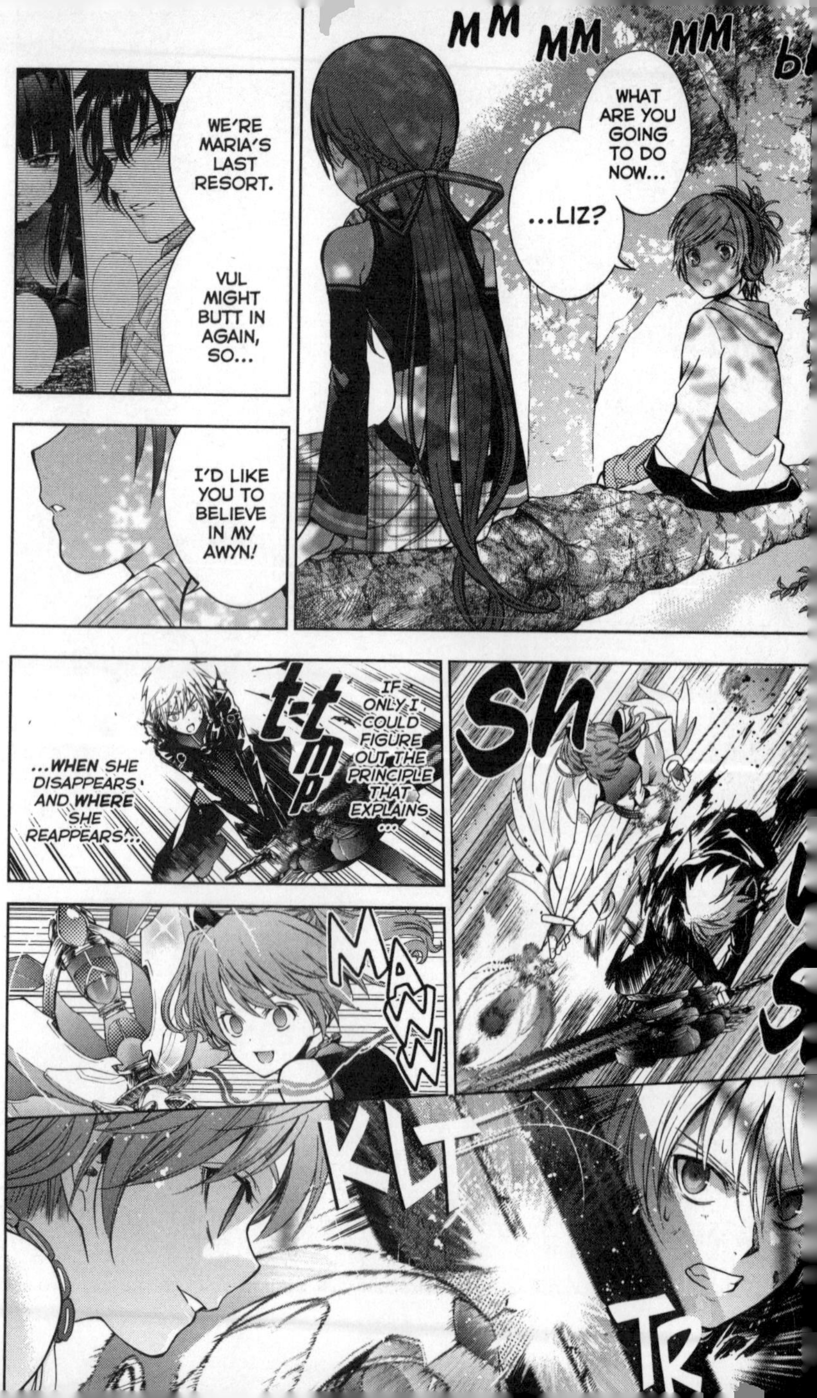
MM MM MM
WHAT ARE YOU GOING TO DO NOW...
...LIZ?
WE'RE MARIA'S LAST RESORT.
VUL MIGHT BUTT IN AGAIN, SO...
I'D LIKE YOU TO BELIEVE IN MY AWYN!
SH
IF ONLY I COULD FIGURE OUT THE PRINCIPLE THAT EXPLAINS...
T-T-MP
...WHEN SHE DISAPPEARS AND WHERE SHE REAPPEARS...
MAWWN
KLT
TR

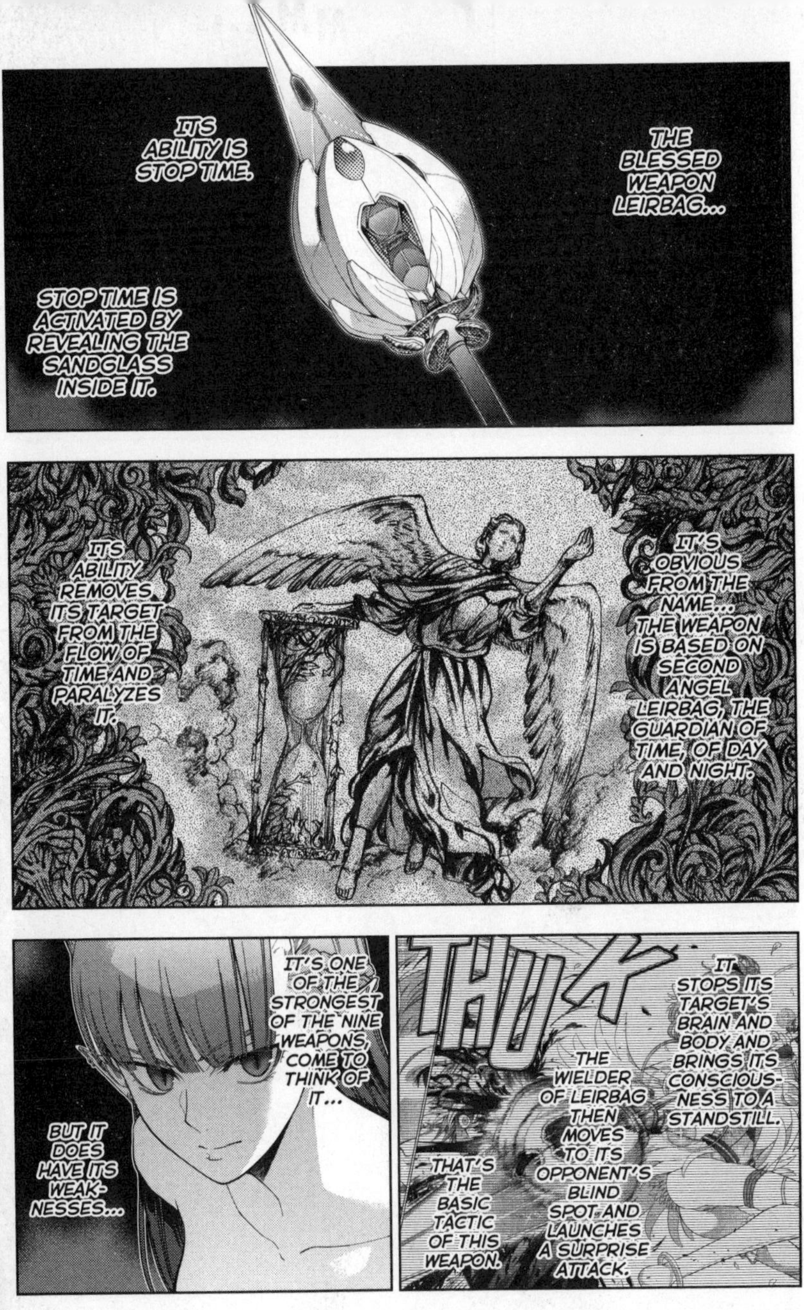
THE BLESSED WEAPON LEIRBAG...
ITS ABILITY IS STOP TIME.
STOP TIME IS ACTIVATED BY REVEALING THE SANDGLASS INSIDE IT.
IT'S OBVIOUS FROM THE NAME... THE WEAPON IS BASED ON SECOND ANGEL LEIRBAG, THE GUARDIAN OF TIME, OF DAY AND NIGHT.
ITS ABILITY REMOVES ITS TARGET FROM THE FLOW OF TIME AND PARALYZES IT.
THUK
IT STOPS ITS TARGET'S BRAIN AND BODY AND BRINGS ITS CONSCIOUS-NESS TO A STANDSTILL.
THE WIELDER OF LEIRBAG THEN MOVES TO ITS OPPONENT'S BLIND SPOT AND LAUNCHES A SURPRISE ATTACK.
THAT'S THE BASIC TACTIC OF THIS WEAPON.
IT'S ONE OF THE STRONGEST OF THE NINE WEAPONS, COME TO THINK OF IT...
BUT IT DOES HAVE ITS WEAK-NESSES...

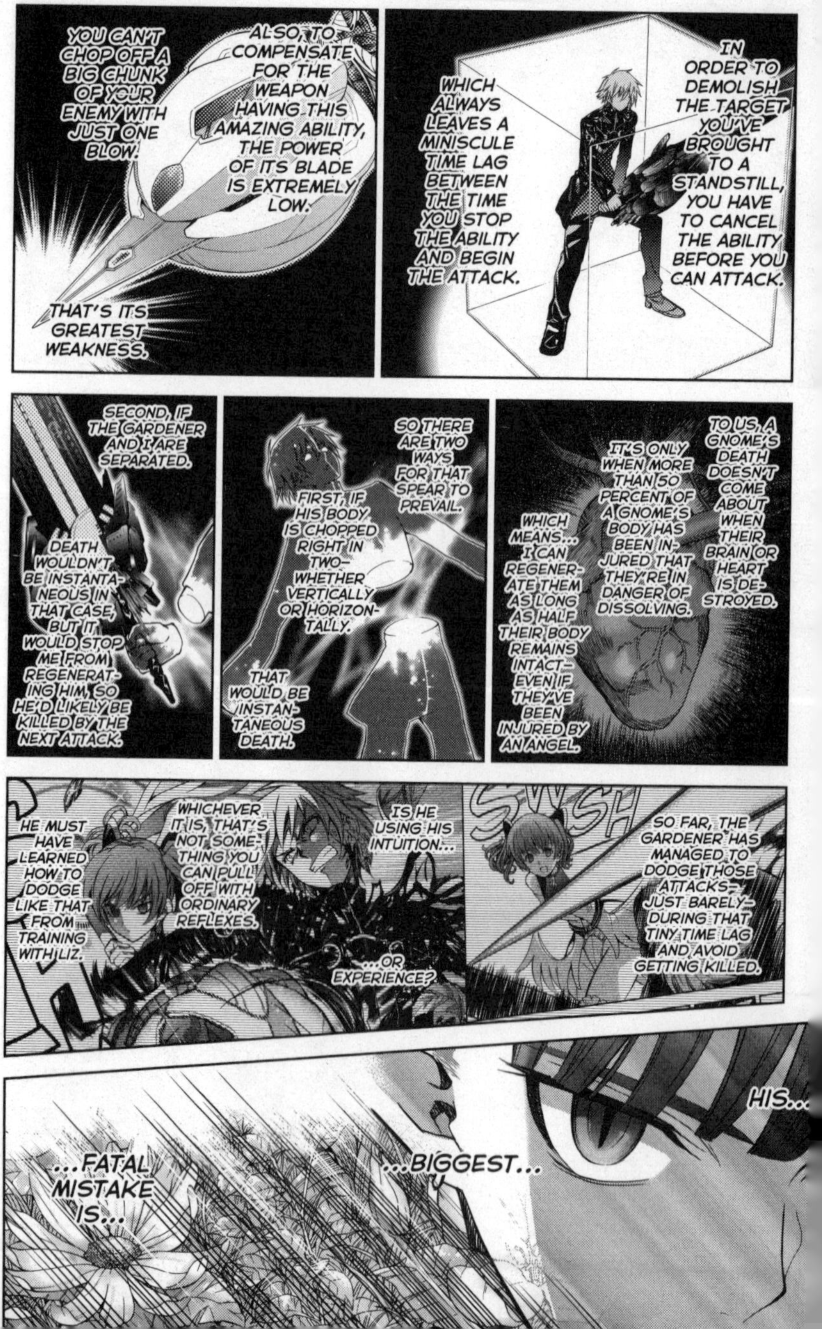
IN ORDER TO DEMOLISH THE TARGET YOU'VE BROUGHT TO A STANDSTILL, YOU HAVE TO CANCEL THE ABILITY BEFORE YOU CAN ATTACK.
WHICH ALWAYS LEAVES A MINISCULE TIME LAG BETWEEN THE TIME YOU STOP THE ABILITY AND BEGIN THE ATTACK.
ALSO, TO COMPENSATE FOR THE WEAPON HAVING THIS AMAZING ABILITY, THE POWER OF ITS BLADE IS EXTREMELY LOW.
YOU CAN'T CHOP OFF A BIG CHUNK OF YOUR ENEMY WITH JUST ONE BLOW.
THAT'S ITS GREATEST WEAKNESS.
TO US, A GNOME'S DEATH DOESN'T COME ABOUT WHEN THEIR BRAIN OR HEART IS DESTROYED.
IT'S ONLY WHEN MORE THAN 50 PERCENT OF A GNOME'S BODY HAS BEEN INJURED THAT THEY'RE IN DANGER OF DISSOLVING.
WHICH MEANS... I CAN REGENERATE THEM AS LONG AS HALF THEIR BODY REMAINS INTACT—EVEN IF THEY'VE BEEN INJURED BY AN ANGEL.
SO THERE ARE TWO WAYS FOR THAT SPEAR TO PREVAIL.
FIRST, IF HIS BODY IS CHOPPED RIGHT IN TWO—WHETHER VERTICALLY OR HORIZONTALLY.
THAT WOULD BE INSTANTANEOUS DEATH.
SECOND, IF THE GARDENER AND I ARE SEPARATED.
DEATH WOULDN'T BE INSTANTANEOUS IN THAT CASE, BUT IT WOULD STOP ME FROM REGENERATING HIM, SO HE'D LIKELY BE KILLED BY THE NEXT ATTACK.
SWISH
SO FAR, THE GARDENER HAS MANAGED TO DODGE THOSE ATTACKS—JUST BARELY—DURING THAT TINY TIME LAG AND AVOID GETTING KILLED.
IS HE USING HIS INTUITION...
...OR EXPERIENCE?
WHICHEVER IT IS, THAT'S NOT SOMETHING YOU CAN PULL OFF WITH ORDINARY REFLEXES.
HE MUST HAVE LEARNED HOW TO DODGE LIKE THAT FROM TRAINING WITH LIZ.
HIS...
...BIGGEST...
...FATAL MISTAKE IS...

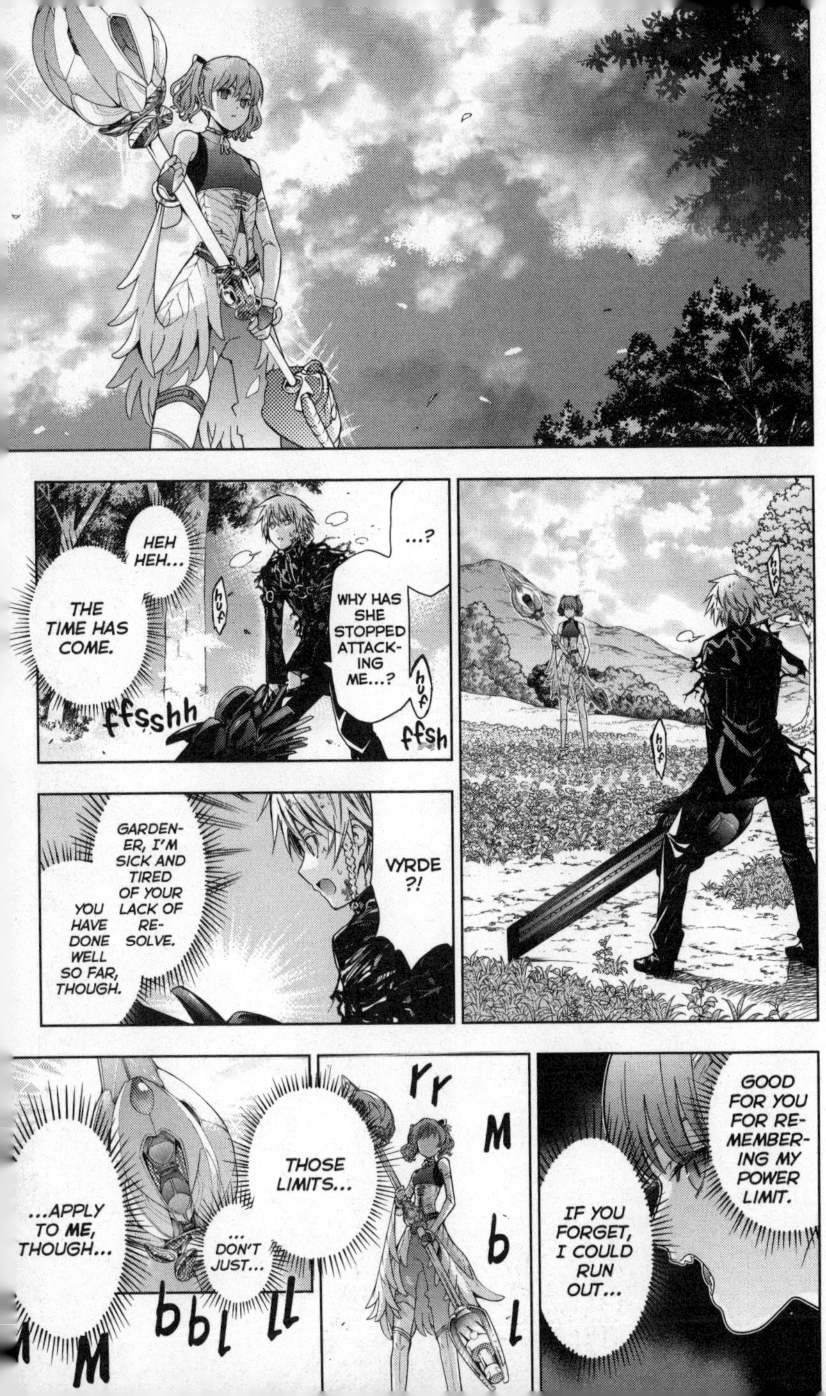
huf
huf
...?
WHY HAS SHE STOPPED ATTACKING ME...?
huf
ffsh
HEH HEH...
THE TIME HAS COME.
huf
ffsshh
VYRDE ?!
GARDENER, I'M SICK AND TIRED OF YOUR LACK OF RESOLVE.
YOU HAVE DONE WELL SO FAR, THOUGH.
GOOD FOR YOU FOR REMEMBERING MY POWER LIMIT.
IF YOU FORGET, I COULD RUN OUT...
rrMbl
THOSE LIMITS...
...DON'T JUST...
...APPLY TO ME, THOUGH...
bbl ll
M M

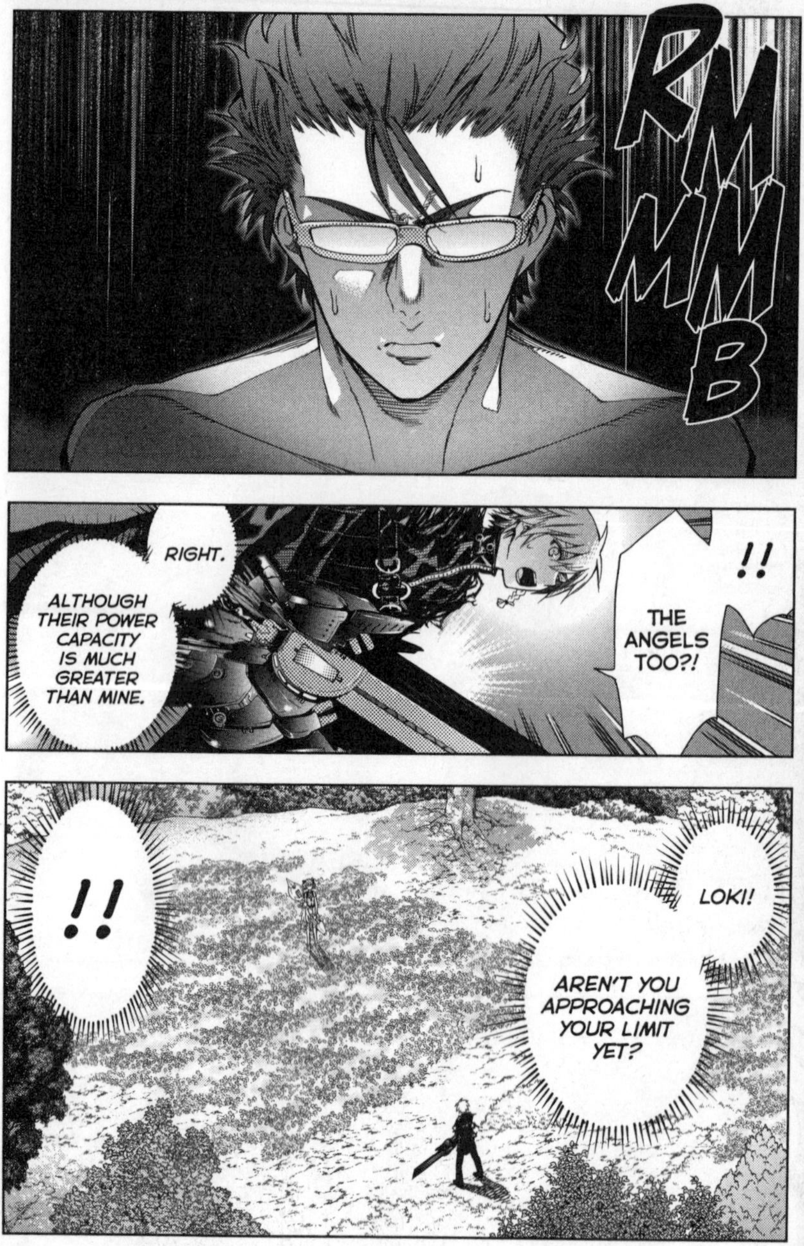
RMMMMMB
!!
THE ANGELS TOO?!
RIGHT.
ALTHOUGH THEIR POWER CAPACITY IS MUCH GREATER THAN MINE.
LOKI!
AREN'T YOU APPROACHING YOUR LIMIT YET?
!!

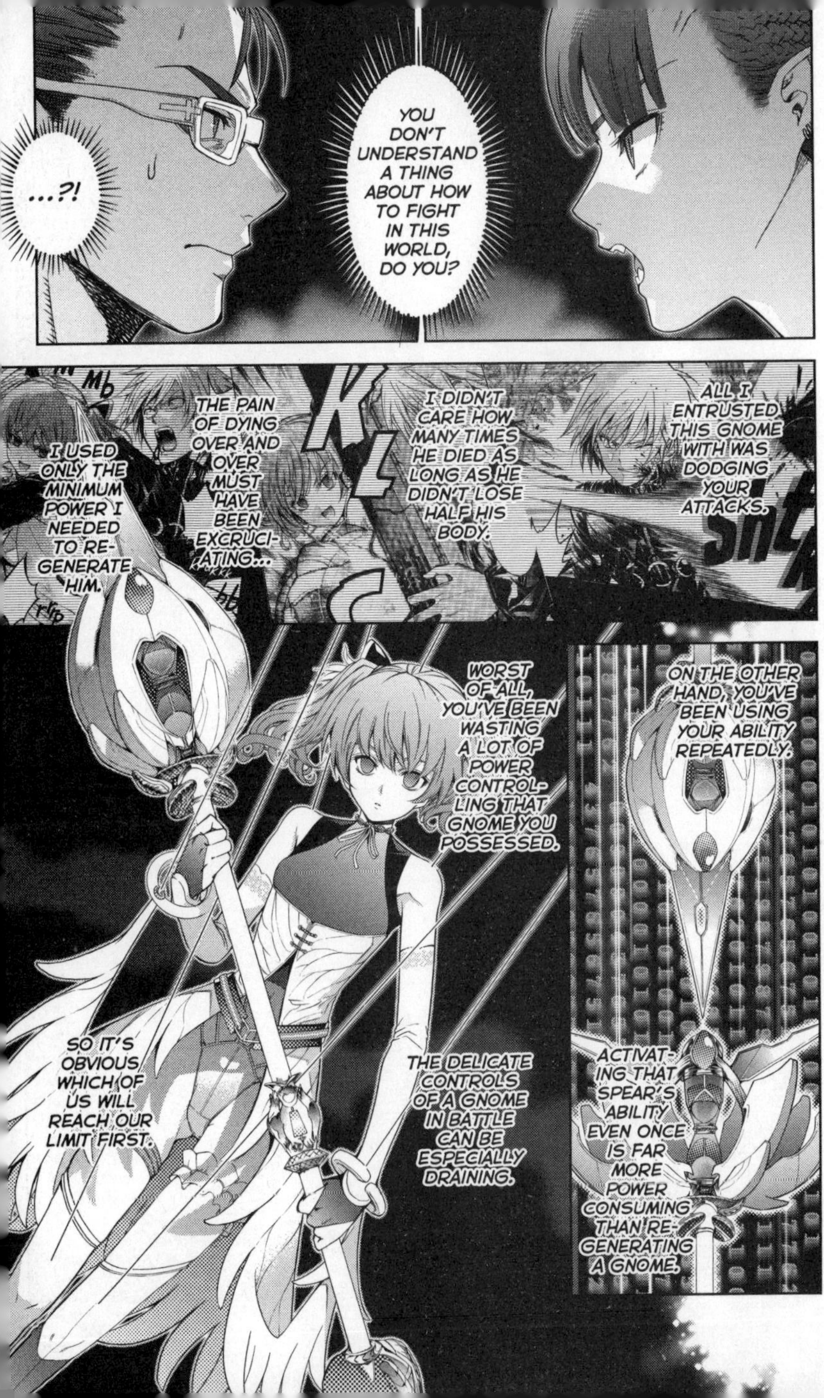
YOU DON'T UNDERSTAND A THING ABOUT HOW TO FIGHT IN THIS WORLD, DO YOU?
...?!
ALL I ENTRUSTED THIS GNOME WITH WAS DODGING YOUR ATTACKS.
I DIDN'T CARE HOW MANY TIMES HE DIED AS LONG AS HE DIDN'T LOSE HALF HIS BODY.
THE PAIN OF DYING OVER AND OVER MUST HAVE BEEN EXCRUCIATING...
I USED ONLY THE MINIMUM POWER I NEEDED TO REGENERATE HIM.
ON THE OTHER HAND, YOU'VE BEEN USING YOUR ABILITY REPEATEDLY.
ACTIVATING THAT SPEAR'S ABILITY EVEN ONCE IS FAR MORE POWER CONSUMING THAN REGENERATING A GNOME.
WORST OF ALL, YOU'VE BEEN WASTING A LOT OF POWER CONTROLLING THAT GNOME YOU POSSESSED.
THE DELICATE CONTROLS OF A GNOME IN BATTLE CAN BE ESPECIALLY DRAINING.
SO IT'S OBVIOUS WHICH OF US WILL REACH OUR LIMIT FIRST.

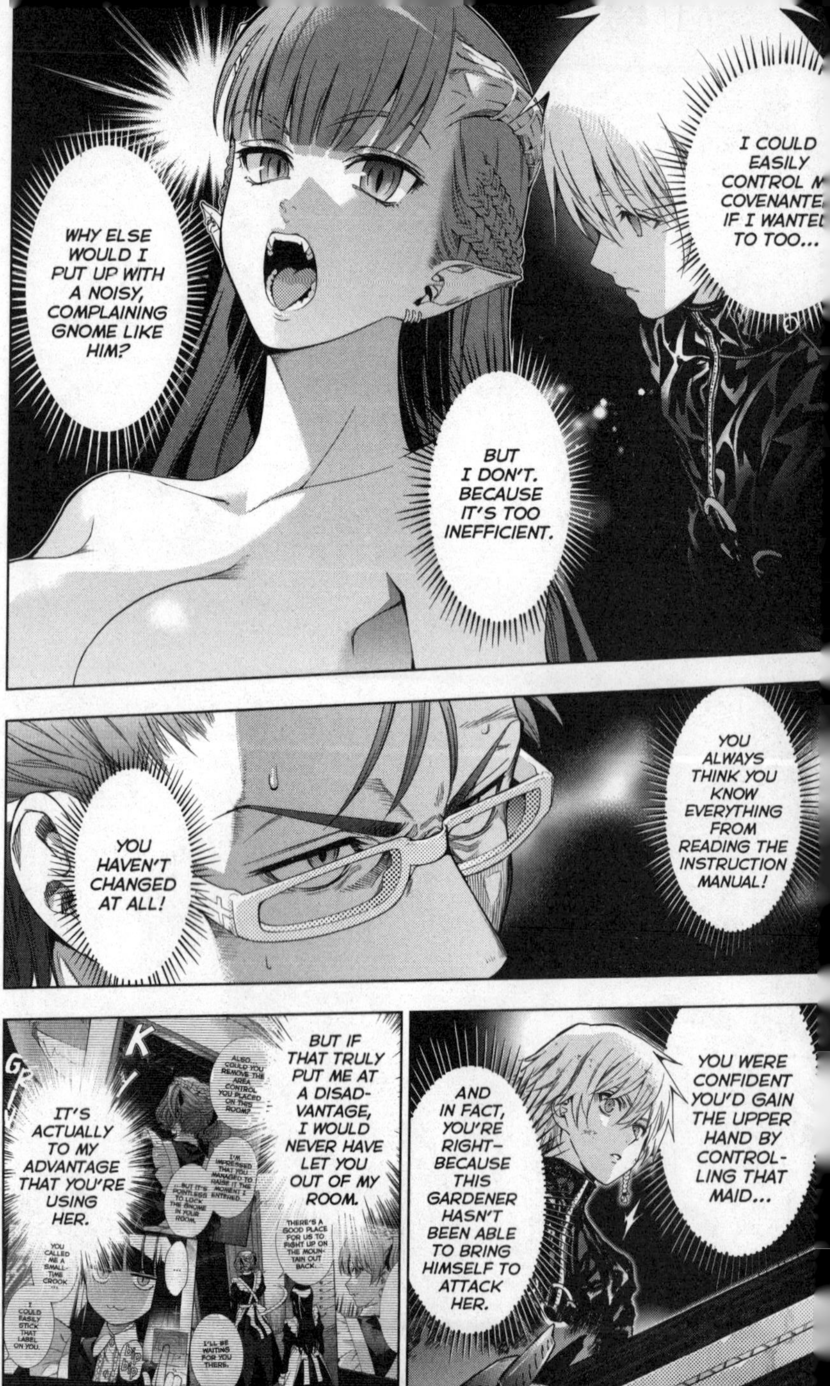
I COULD EASILY CONTROL M COVENANTE IF I WANTE TO TOO...
BUT I DON'T. BECAUSE IT'S TOO INEFFICIENT.
WHY ELSE WOULD I PUT UP WITH A NOISY, COMPLAINING GNOME LIKE HIM?
YOU ALWAYS THINK YOU KNOW EVERYTHING FROM READING THE INSTRUCTION MANUAL!
YOU HAVEN'T CHANGED AT ALL!
YOU WERE CONFIDENT YOU'D GAIN THE UPPER HAND BY CONTROL-LING THAT MAID...
AND IN FACT, YOU'RE RIGHT-BECAUSE THIS GARDENER HASN'T BEEN ABLE TO BRING HIMSELF TO ATTACK HER.
BUT IF THAT TRULY PUT ME AT A DISAD-VANTAGE, I WOULD NEVER HAVE LET YOU OUT OF MY ROOM.
K
ALSO... COULD YOU REMOVE THE AREA CONTROL YOU PLACED ON THIS ROOM?
I'M IMPRESSED THAT YOU MANAGED TO RAISE IT THE MOMENT I ENTERED...
...BUT IT'S POINTLESS TO LOCK THE GNOME IN YOUR ROOM.
GR
IT'S ACTUALLY TO MY ADVANTAGE THAT YOU'RE USING HER.
THERE'S A GOOD PLACE FOR US TO FIGHT UP ON THE MOUN-TAIN OUT BACK.
I'LL BE WAITING FOR YOU THERE.
...
YOU CALLED ME A SMALL-TIME CROOK...
I COULD EASILY STICK THAT LABEL ON YOU.
bip bip

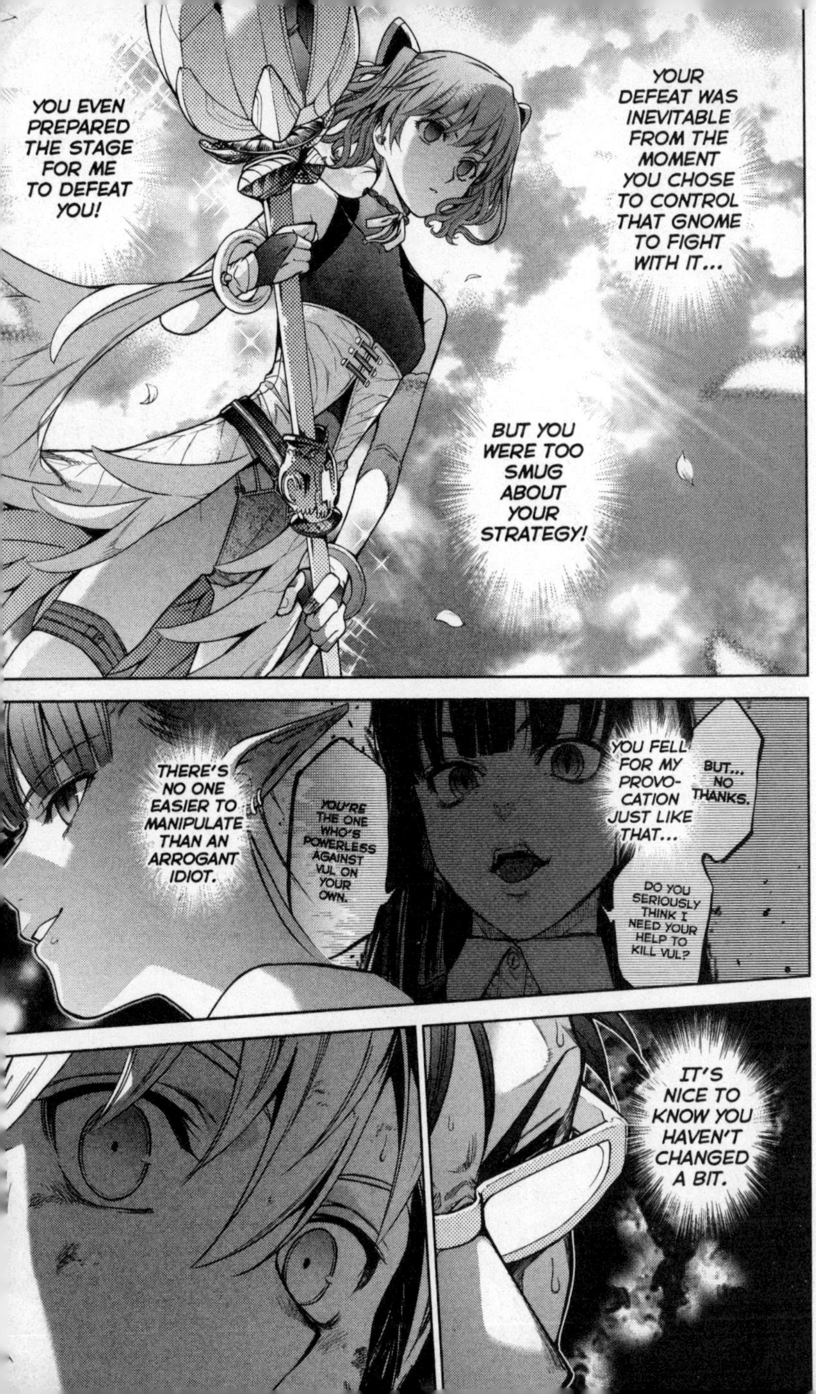
YOUR DEFEAT WAS INEVITABLE FROM THE MOMENT YOU CHOSE TO CONTROL THAT GNOME TO FIGHT WITH IT...
YOU EVEN PREPARED THE STAGE FOR ME TO DEFEAT YOU!
BUT YOU WERE TOO SMUG ABOUT YOUR STRATEGY!
BUT... NO THANKS.
DO YOU SERIOUSLY THINK I NEED YOUR HELP TO KILL VUL?
YOU'RE THE ONE WHO'S POWERLESS AGAINST VUL ON YOUR OWN.
YOU FELL FOR MY PROVOCATION JUST LIKE THAT...
THERE'S NO ONE EASIER TO MANIPULATE THAN AN ARROGANT IDIOT.
IT'S NICE TO KNOW YOU HAVEN'T CHANGED A BIT.

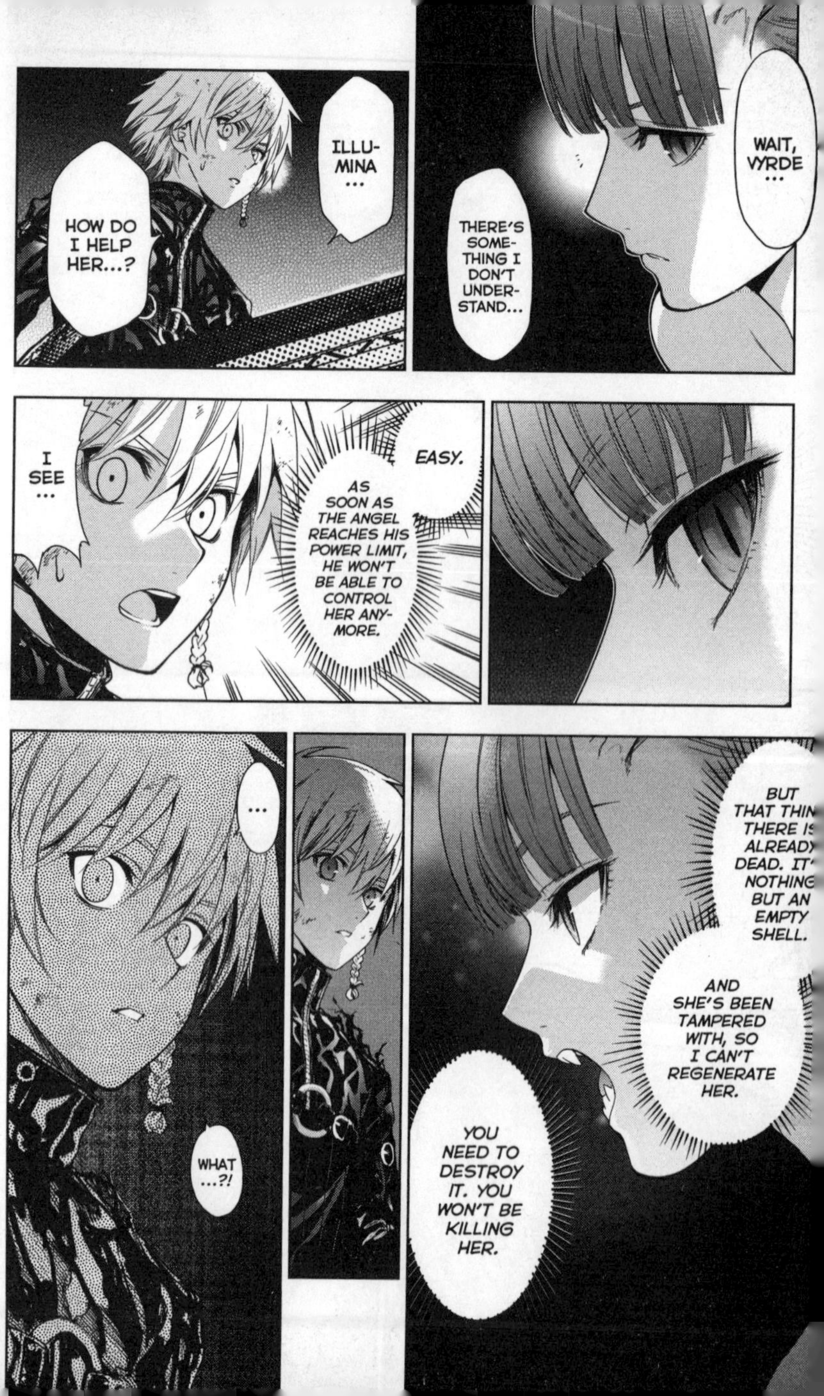
WAIT, VYRDE...
THERE'S SOMETHING I DON'T UNDERSTAND...
ILLUMINA...
HOW DO I HELP HER...?
EASY.
AS SOON AS THE ANGEL REACHES HIS POWER LIMIT, HE WON'T BE ABLE TO CONTROL HER ANYMORE.
I SEE...
BUT THAT THING THERE IS ALREADY DEAD. IT'S NOTHING BUT AN EMPTY SHELL.
AND SHE'S BEEN TAMPERED WITH, SO I CAN'T REGENERATE HER.
YOU NEED TO DESTROY IT. YOU WON'T BE KILLING HER.
...
WHAT...?!

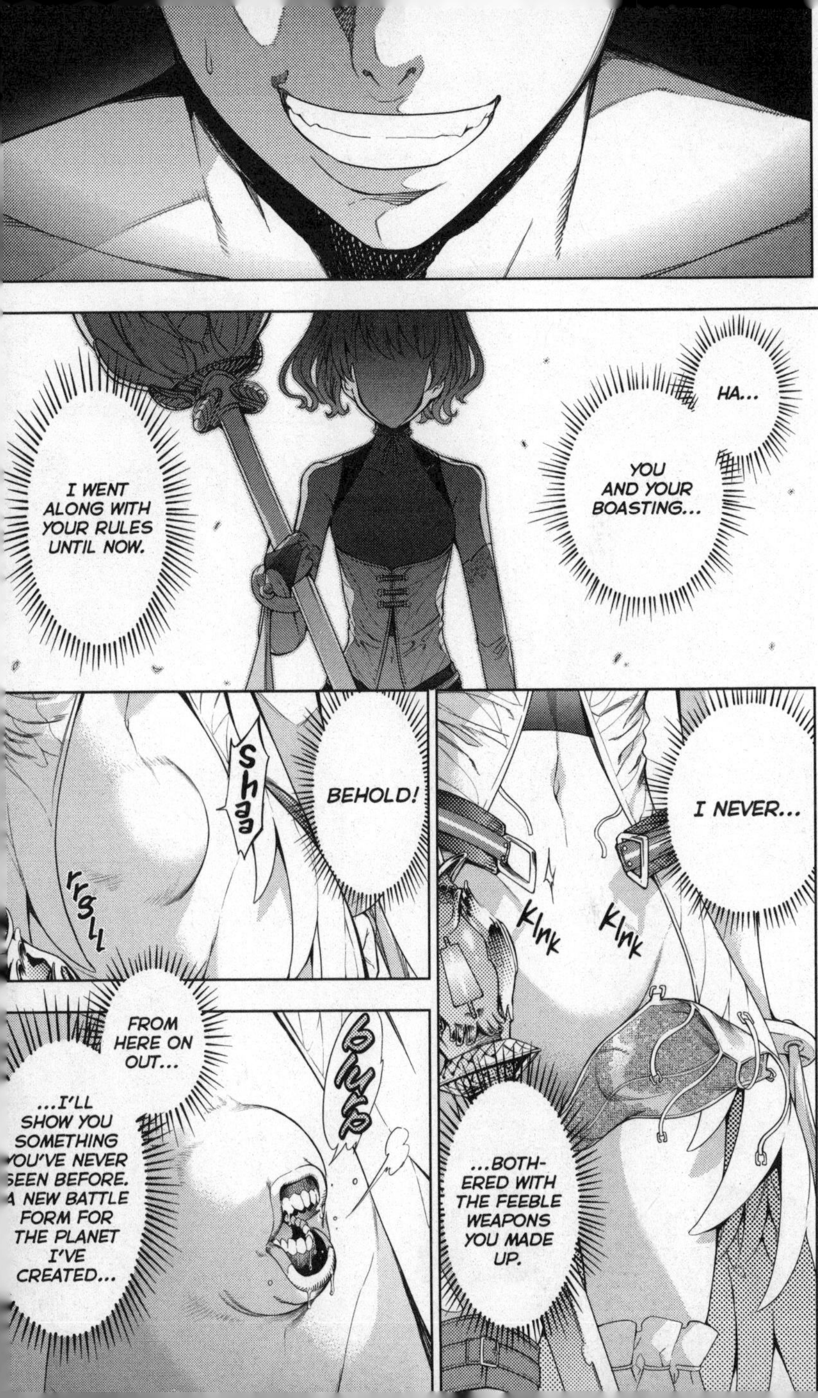
HA...
YOU AND YOUR BOASTING...
I WENT ALONG WITH YOUR RULES UNTIL NOW.
I NEVER...
Klink
Klink
...BOTHERED WITH THE FEEBLE WEAPONS YOU MADE UP.
BEHOLD!
Shaa
rrgll
FROM HERE ON OUT...
...I'LL SHOW YOU SOMETHING YOU'VE NEVER SEEN BEFORE. A NEW BATTLE FORM FOR THE PLANET I'VE CREATED...

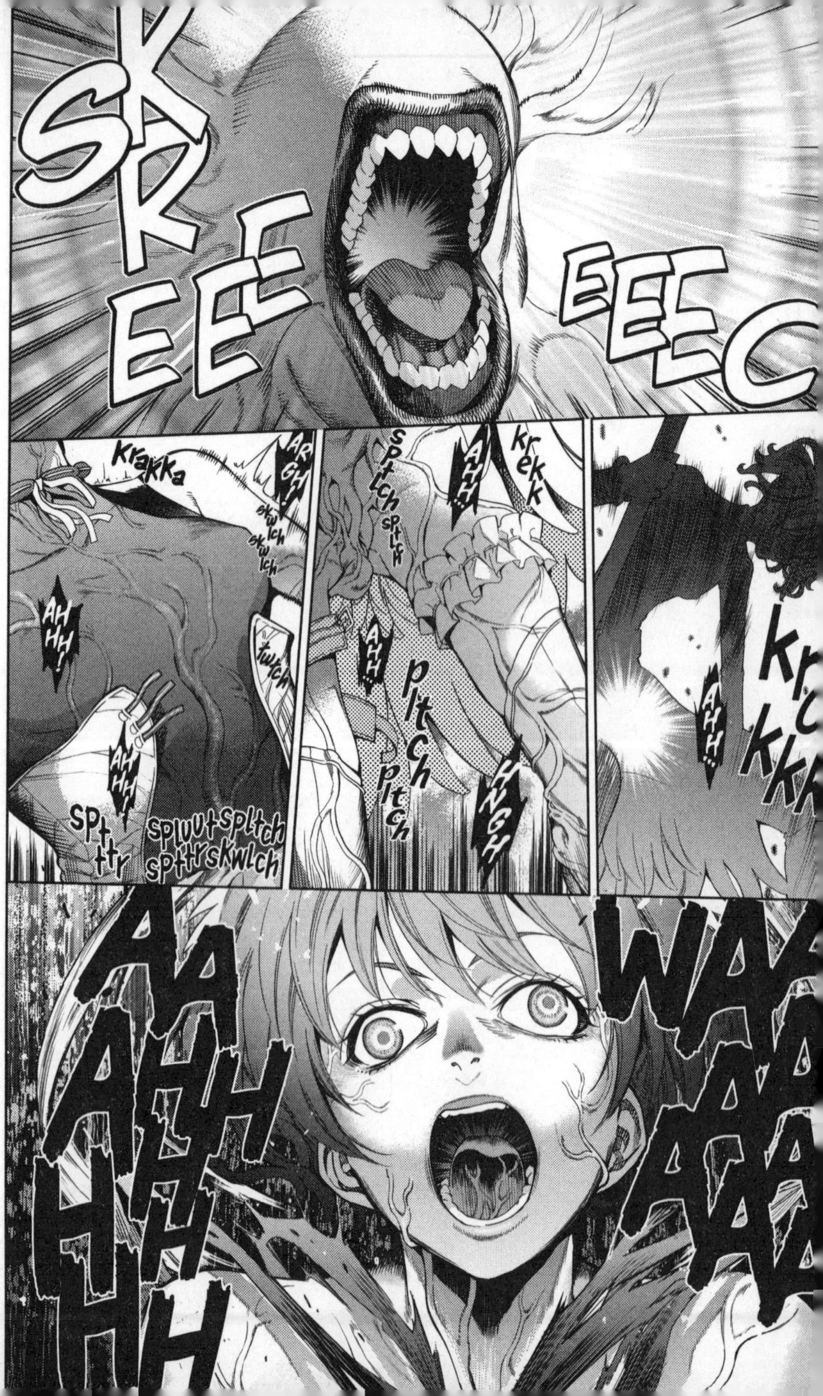
SKREEEE
EEEC
AHH...
krc
kkk
krekk
AHH...
spltch spltch
AHH...
pltch pltch
HNGH
ARGH!
krakka
skwlch skwlch
AHHH!
twitch
AHHHH
sptttr
spluutspltch spttrskwlch
WAAAAAA
AAHHHHHH

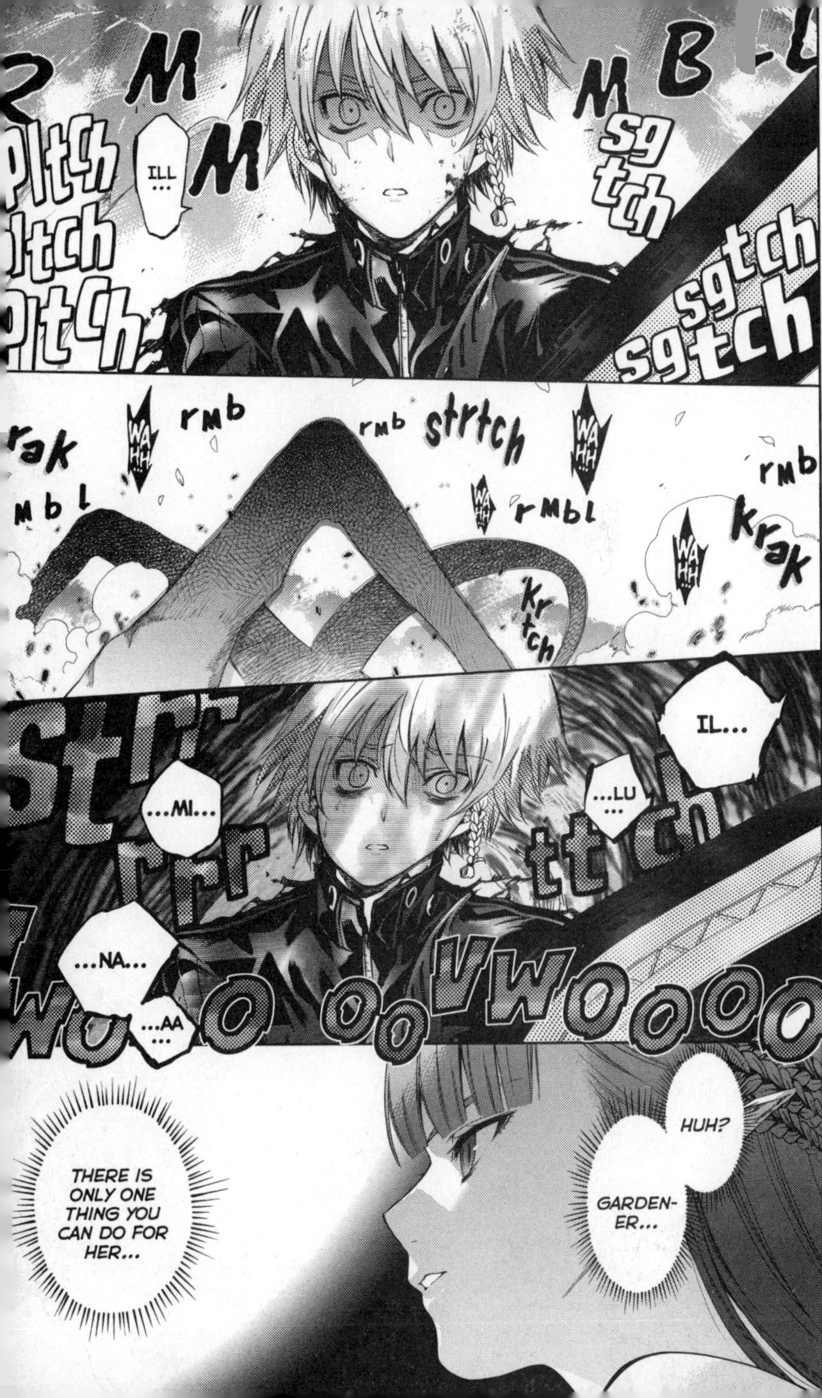

MBL
sg tch
sgtch sgtch
ILL...
M M
rmb krak
WAHH
rmbl
rmb strtch
WAHH
WAHH
rmb
krtch
IL...
...LU...
ttch
...MI...
VWOOOOO
...NA...
...AA...
HUH?
GARDEN-ER...
THERE IS ONLY ONE THING YOU CAN DO FOR HER...

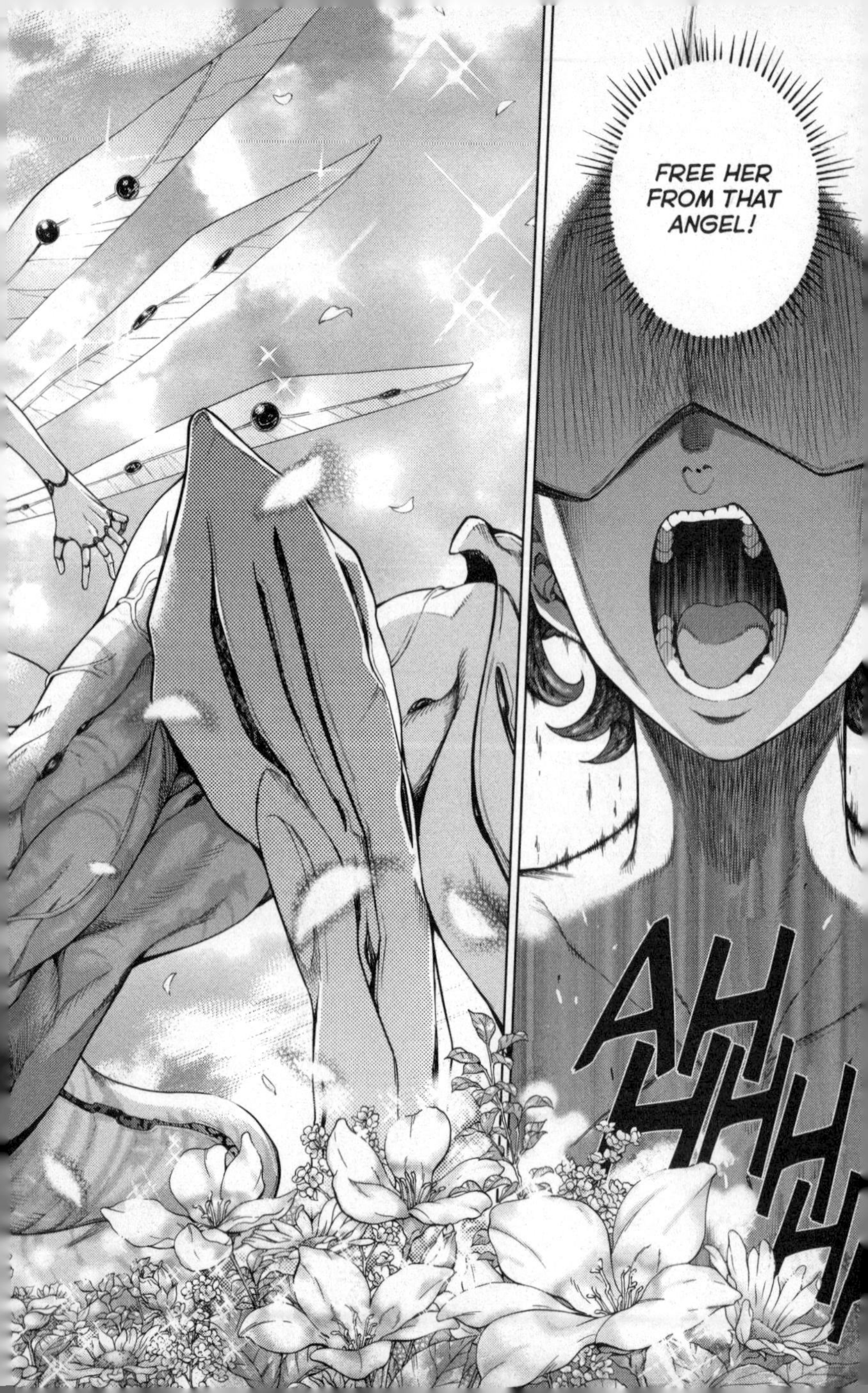
FREE HER FROM THAT ANGEL!
AHHHHH

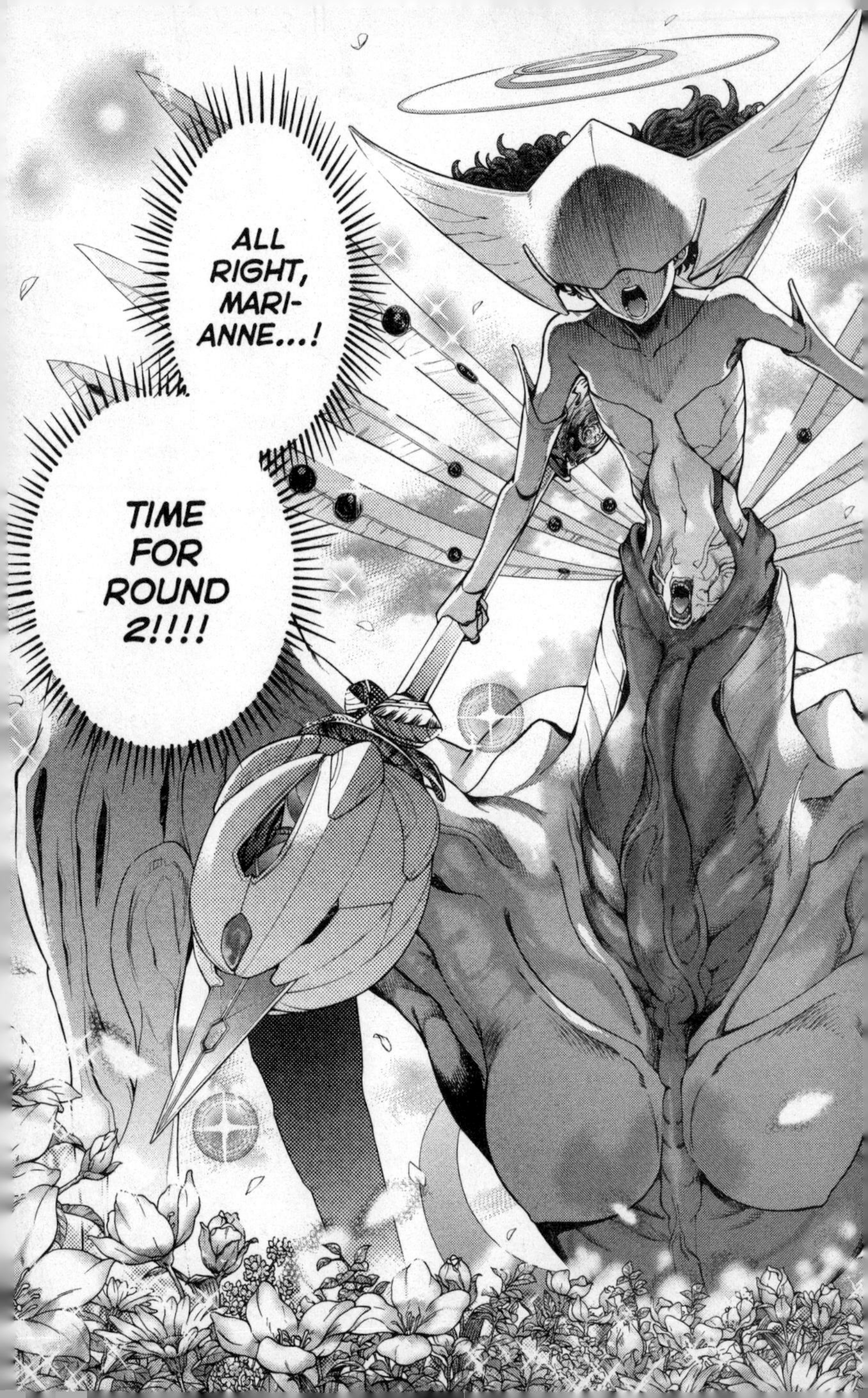
ALL RIGHT, MARIANNE...!
TIME FOR ROUND 2!!!!

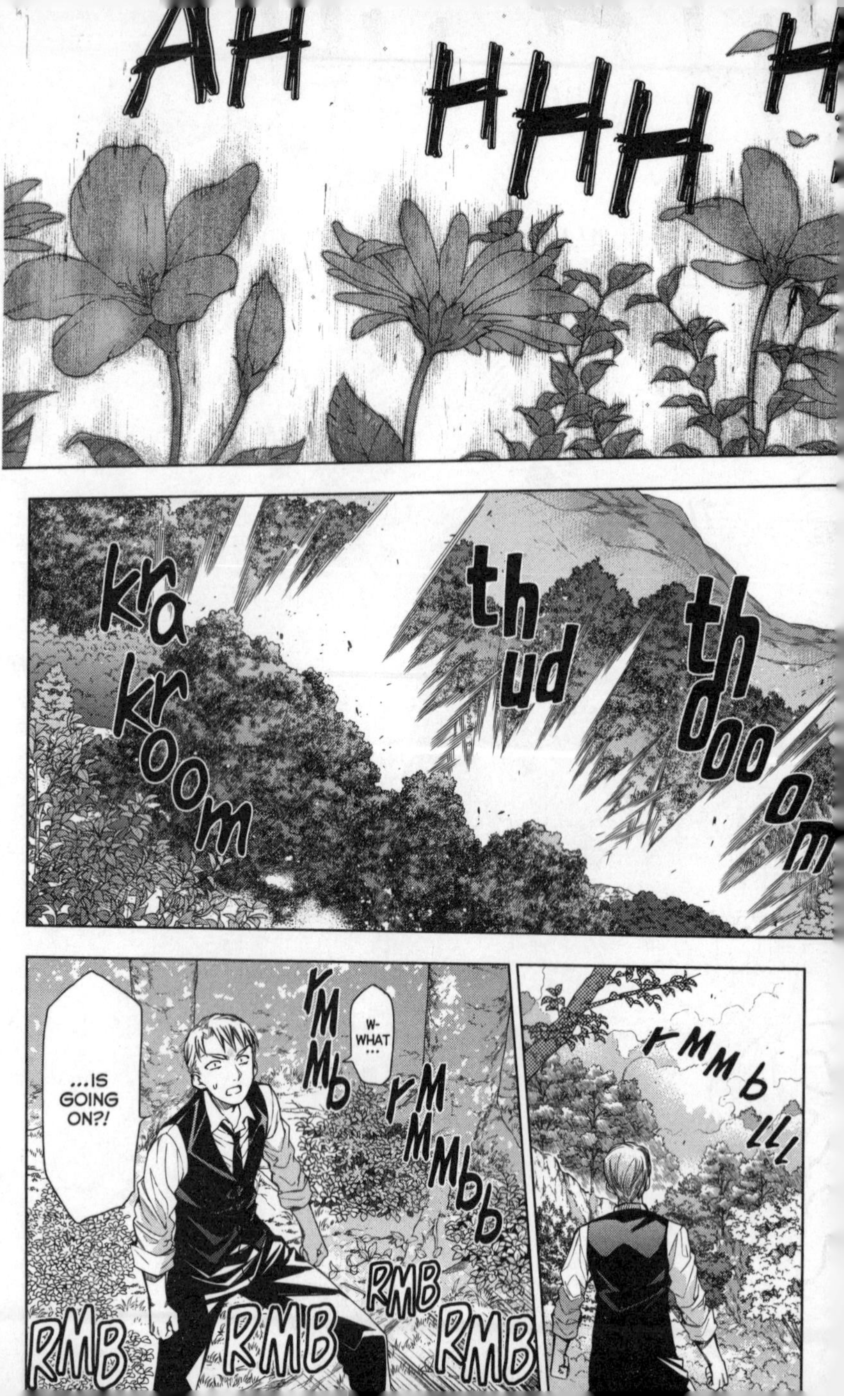
AH HHHHH
thdooom
thud
krakroom
rmmbll
rMMb
W-WHAT...
rMMMbb
...IS GOING ON?!
RMB
RMB
RMB
RMB

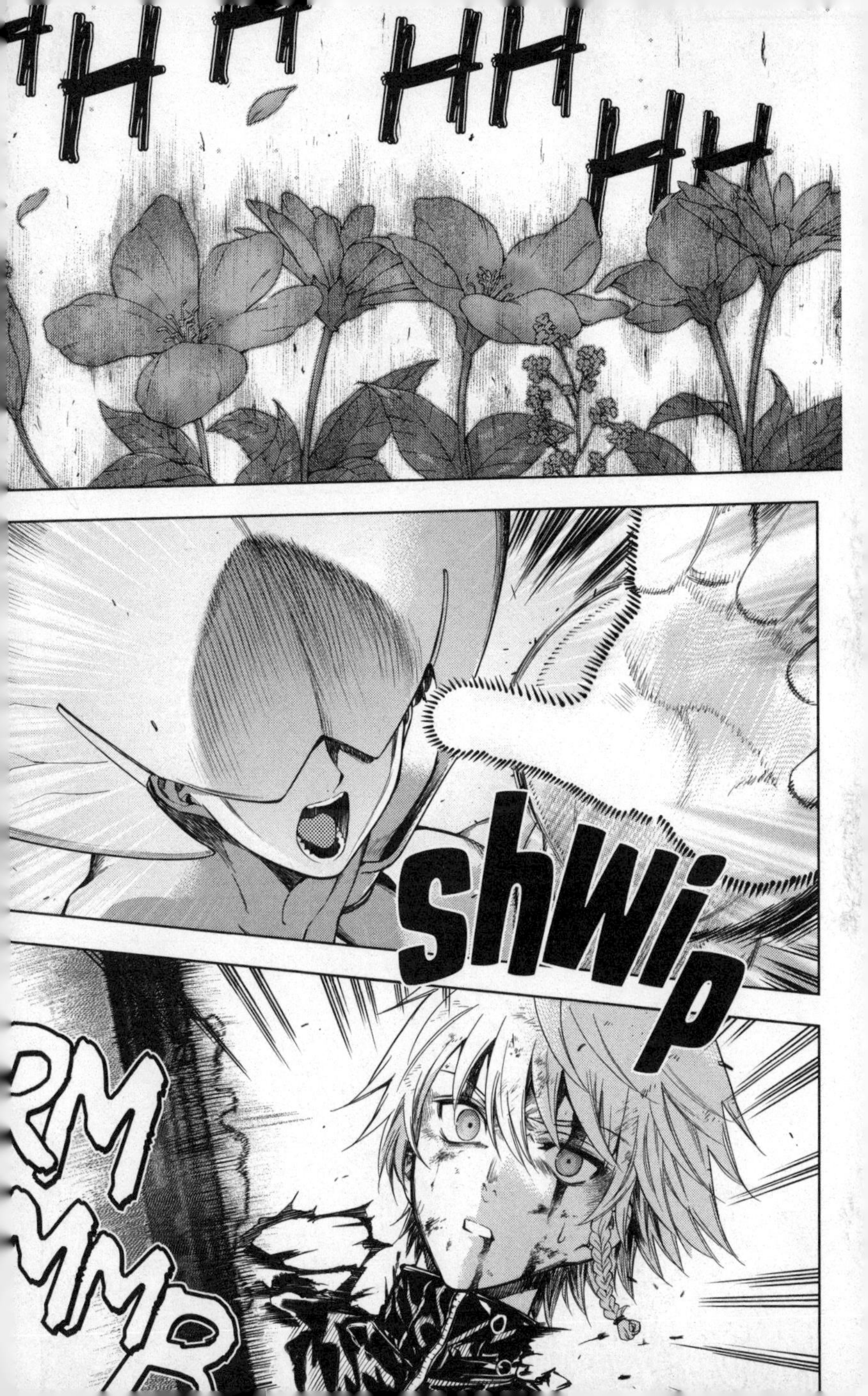
shwip

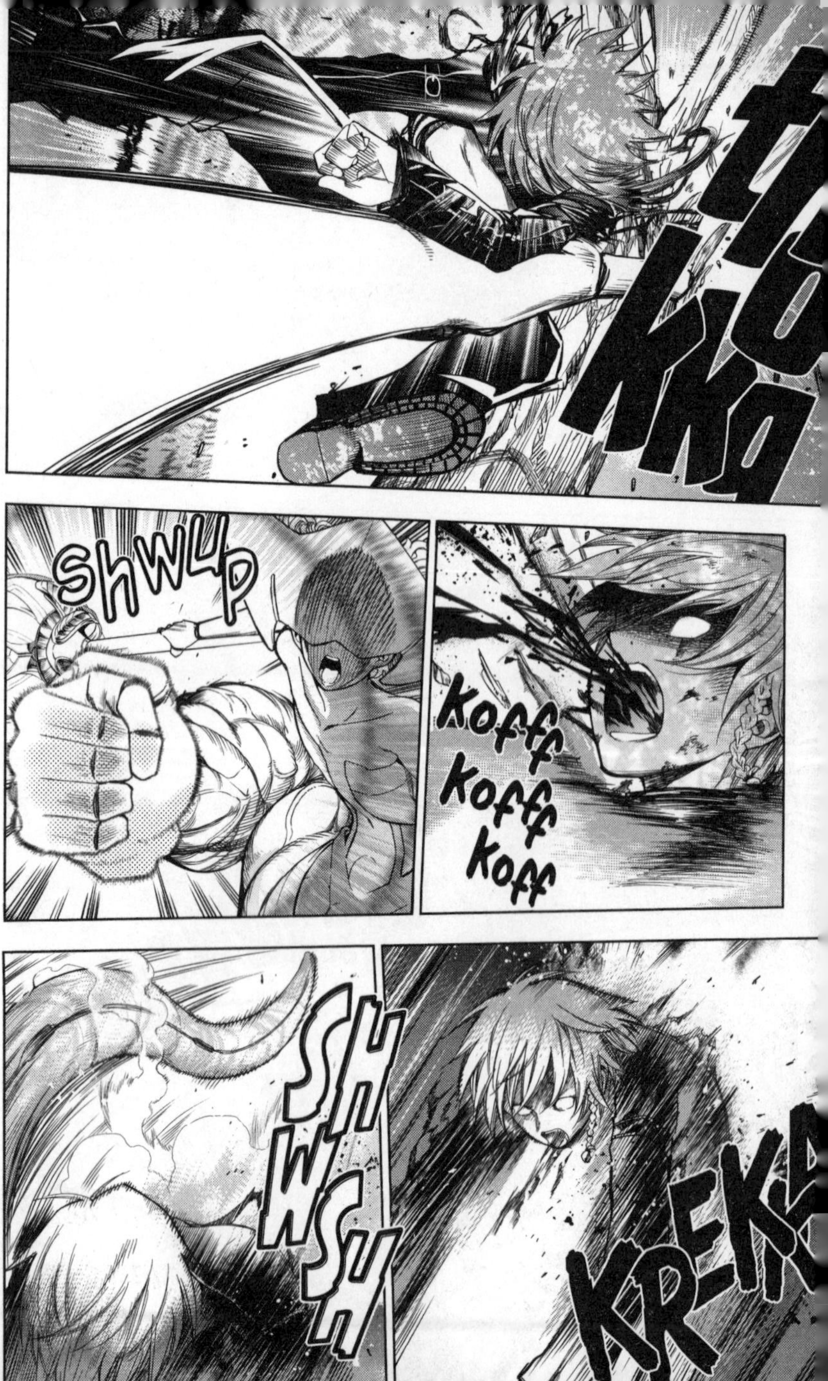
kofff kofff koff
shwup
SHWSH

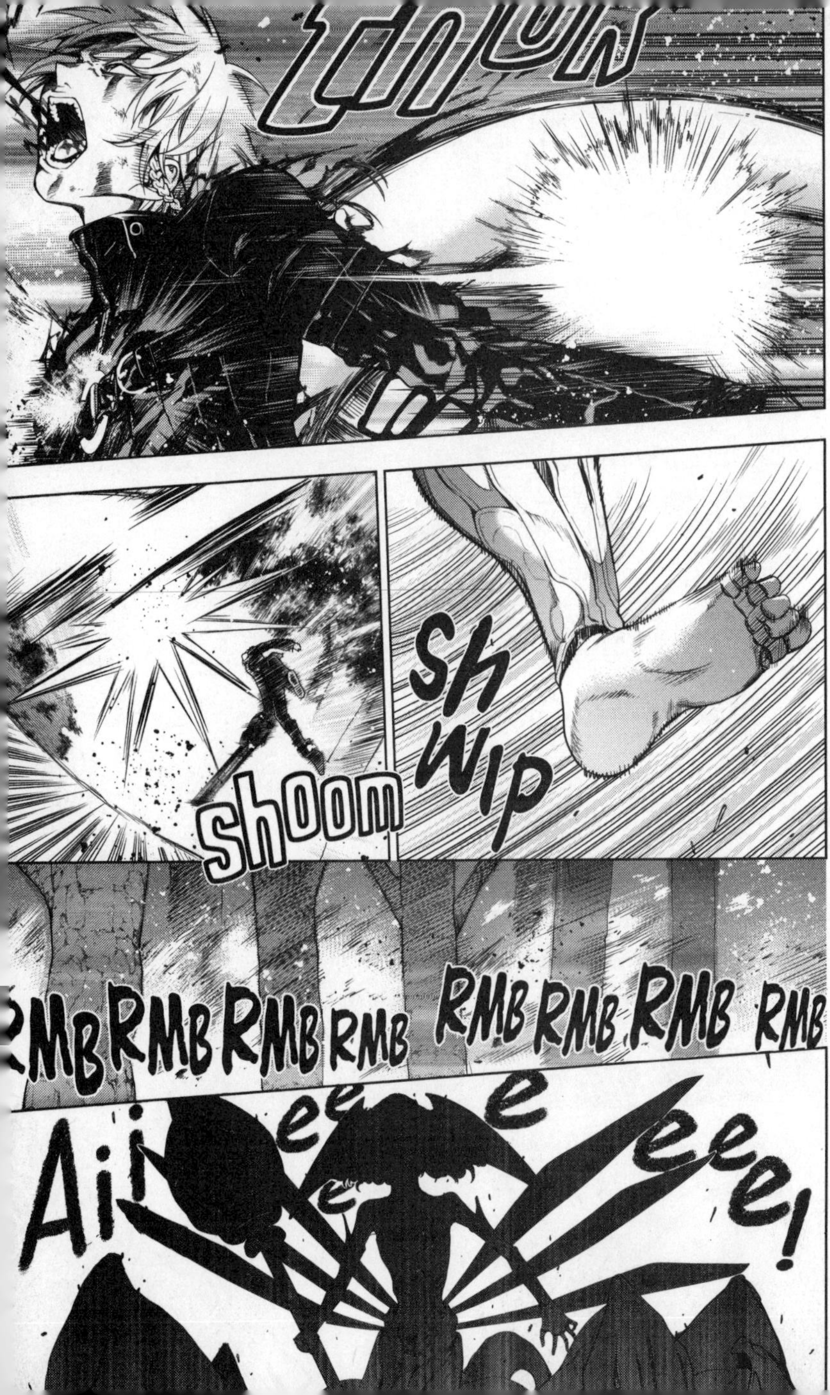
shwip
shoom
RMB RMB RMB RMB
RMB RMB RMB RMB
Aiieeeeeeeee!

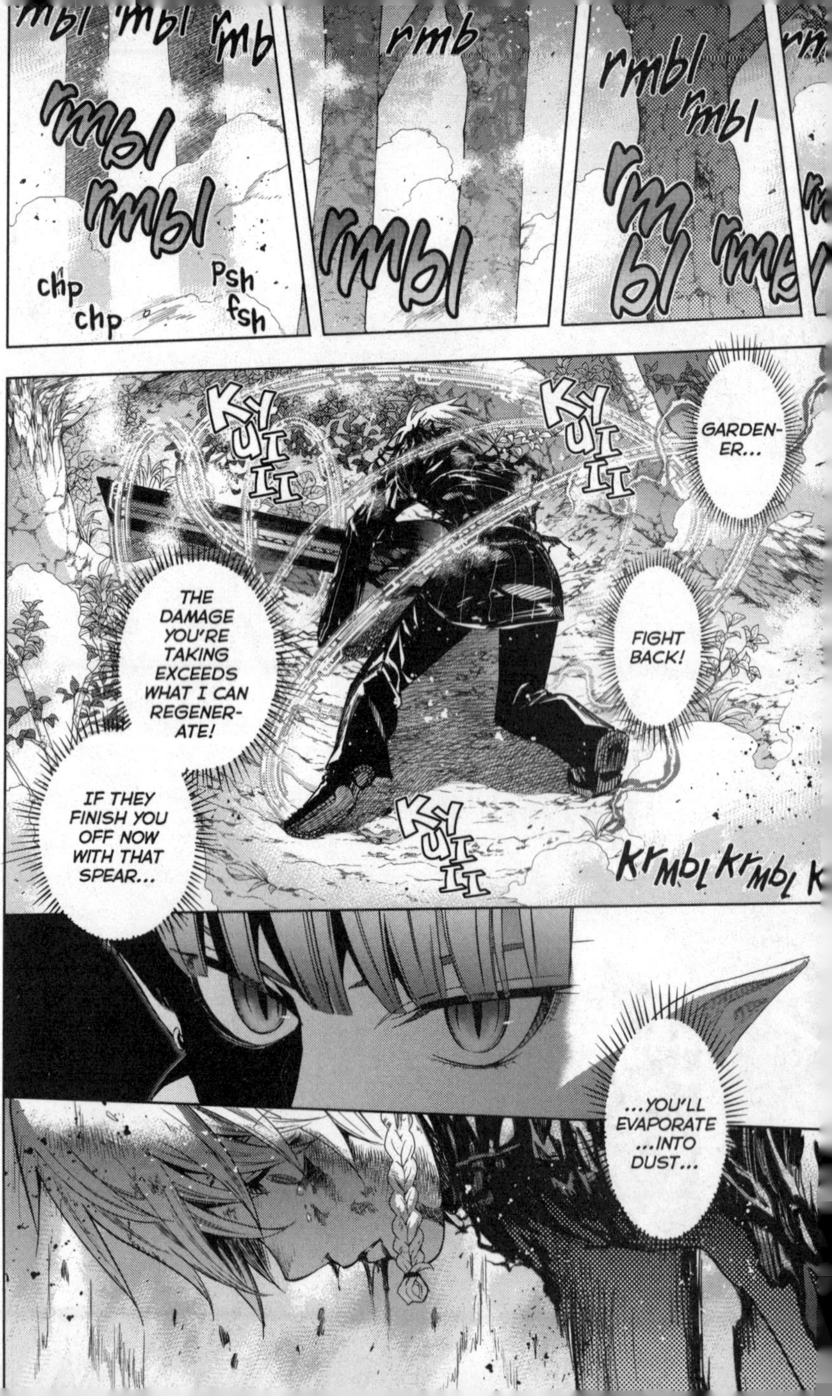
rmbl rmbl
rmbl rmbl rm bl
rmb
rmbl rmbl
mbl mbl rmb
rmbl rmbl
chp chp
psh fsh
GARDENER...
FIGHT BACK!
KYUIII
KYUIII
THE DAMAGE YOU'RE TAKING EXCEEDS WHAT I CAN REGENERATE!
KYUIII
KRMBL KRMBL
IF THEY FINISH YOU OFF NOW WITH THAT SPEAR...
...YOU'LL EVAPORATE ...INTO DUST...

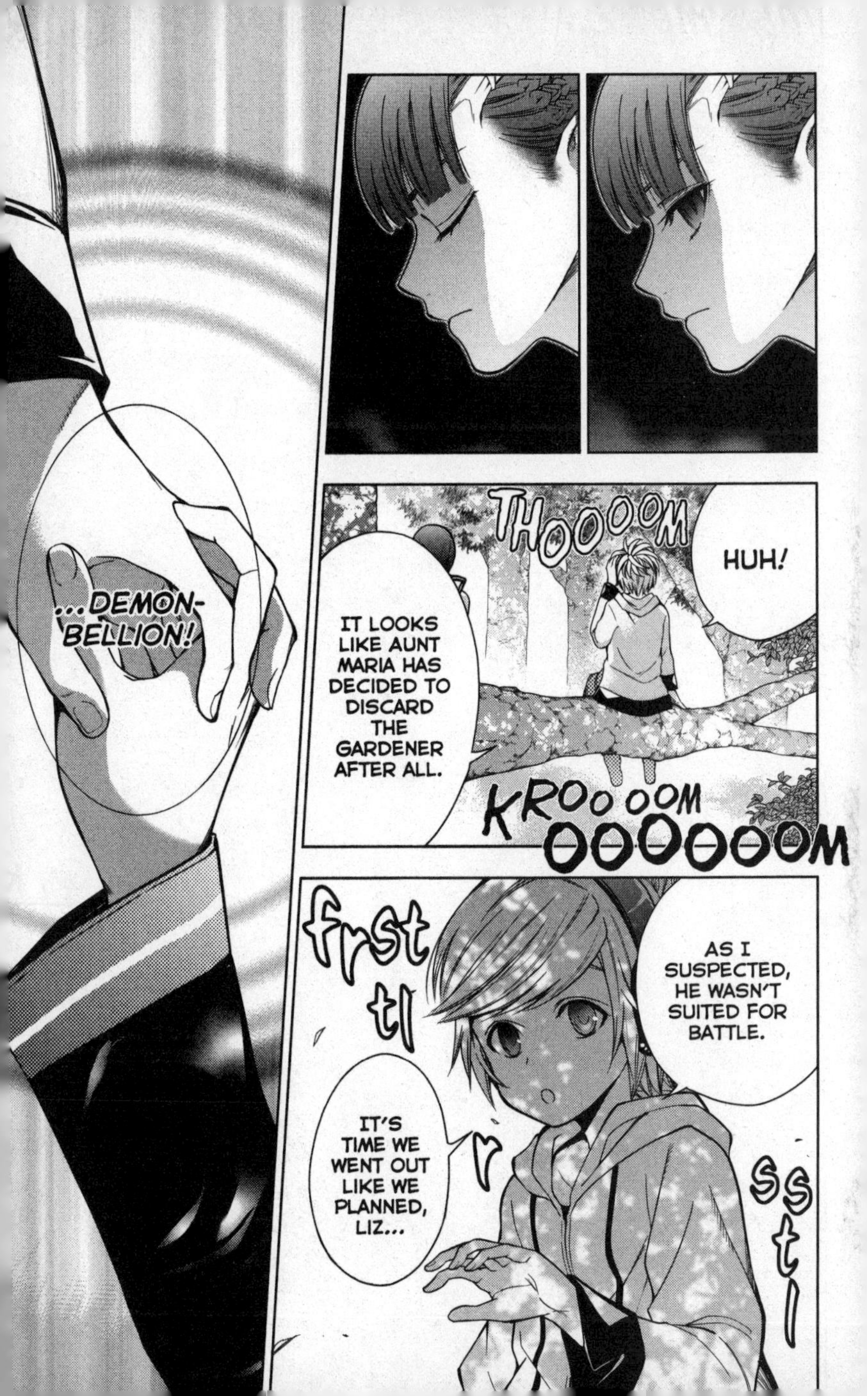
HUH!
THOOOOM
IT LOOKS LIKE AUNT MARIA HAS DECIDED TO DISCARD THE GARDENER AFTER ALL.
KROOOOM OOOOOOOM
AS I SUSPECTED, HE WASN'T SUITED FOR BATTLE.
frst tl
IT'S TIME WE WENT OUT LIKE WE PLANNED, LIZ...
sstl
...DEMON-BELLION!

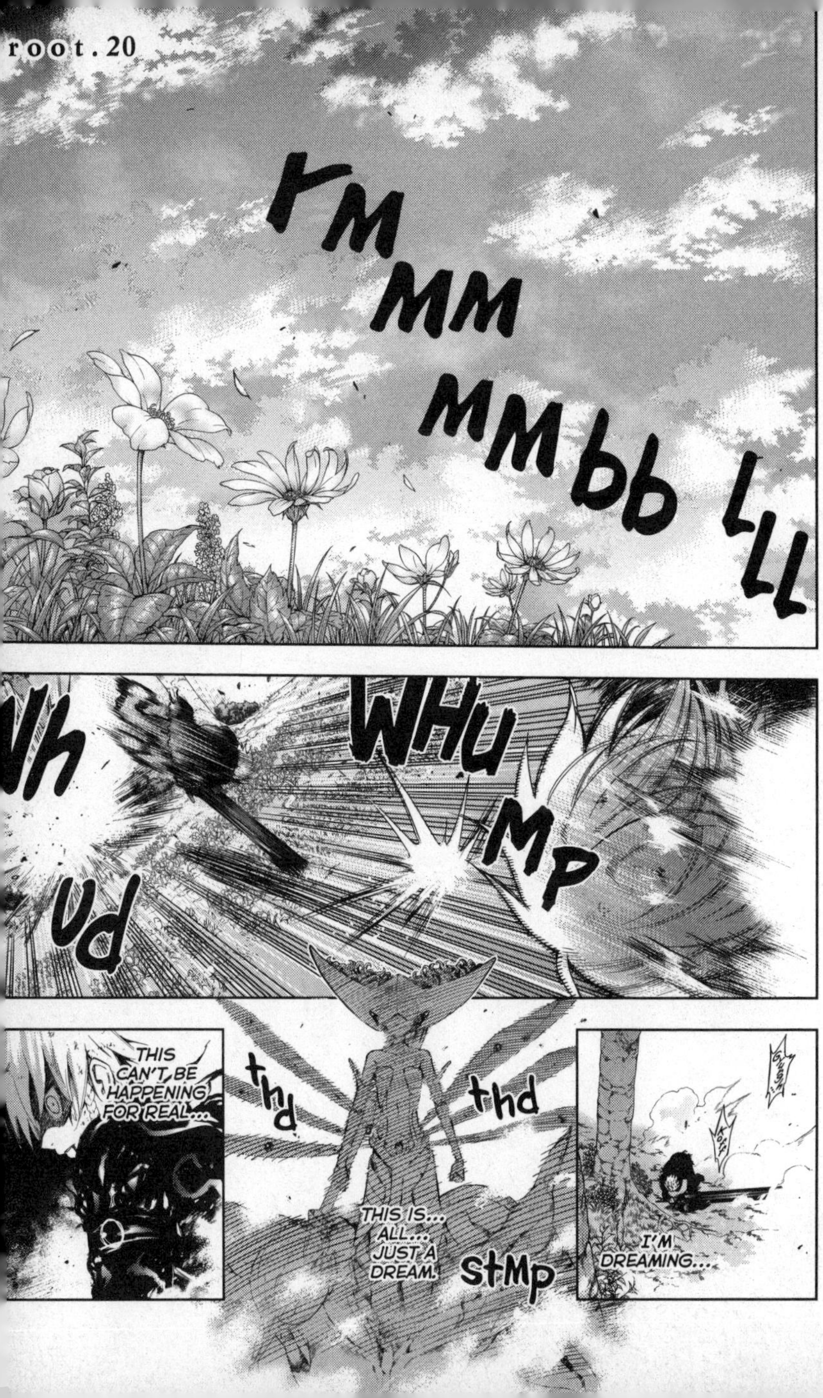
RMMMMMbbLLL
WHUMP
Wh
ud
I'M DREAMING...
GUHGH...
Koff
thd
thd
THIS IS... ALL... JUST A DREAM.
stMp
THIS CAN'T BE HAPPENING FOR REAL...

root.20 Choice, Conclusion, Withdrawal

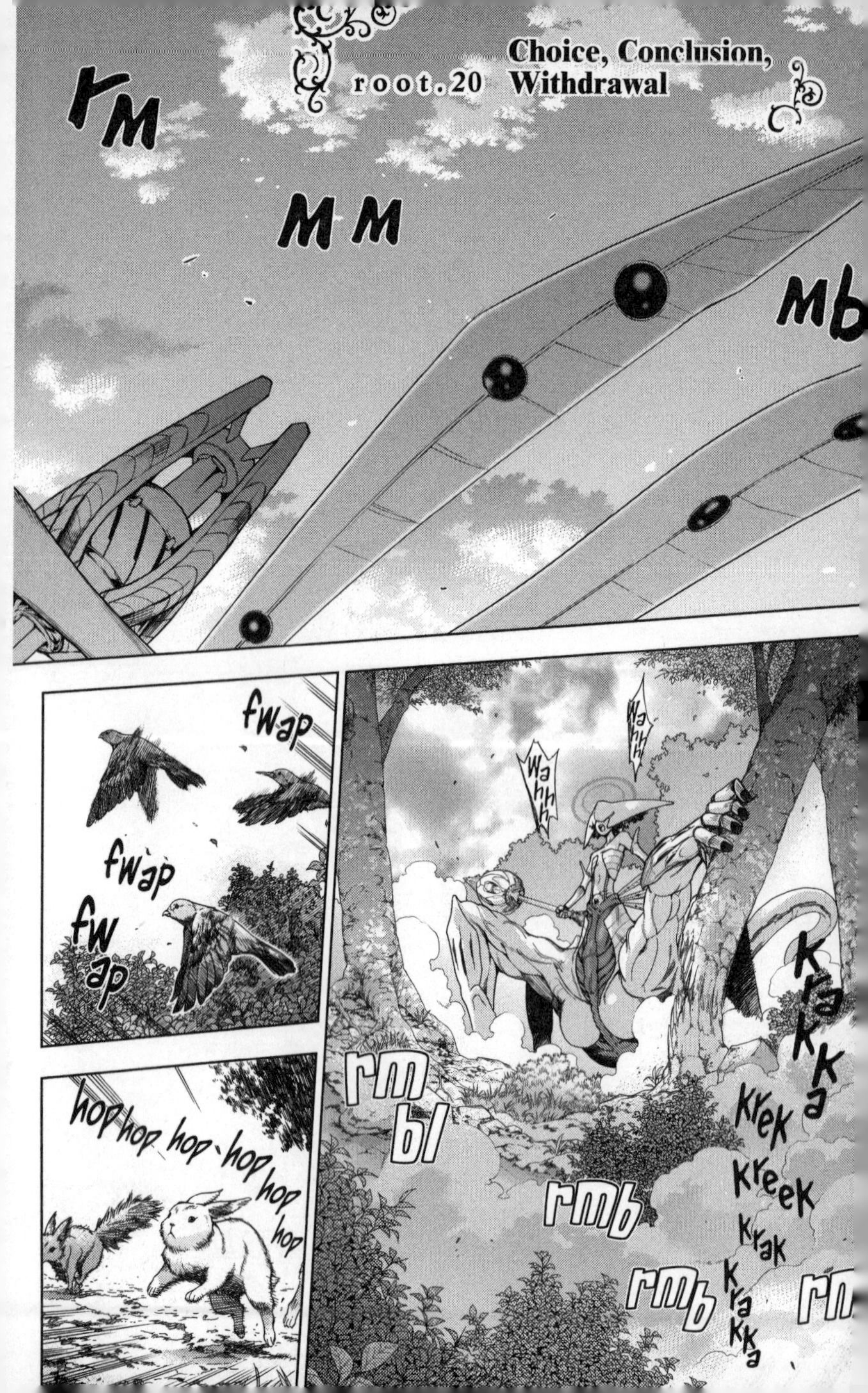
rM
MM
mb
Wahhh
Wahhh
Krakka
krek
kreek
krak
krakka
rm
rm bl
rmb
rmb
fwap
fwap
fwap
hop hop hop hop hop hop

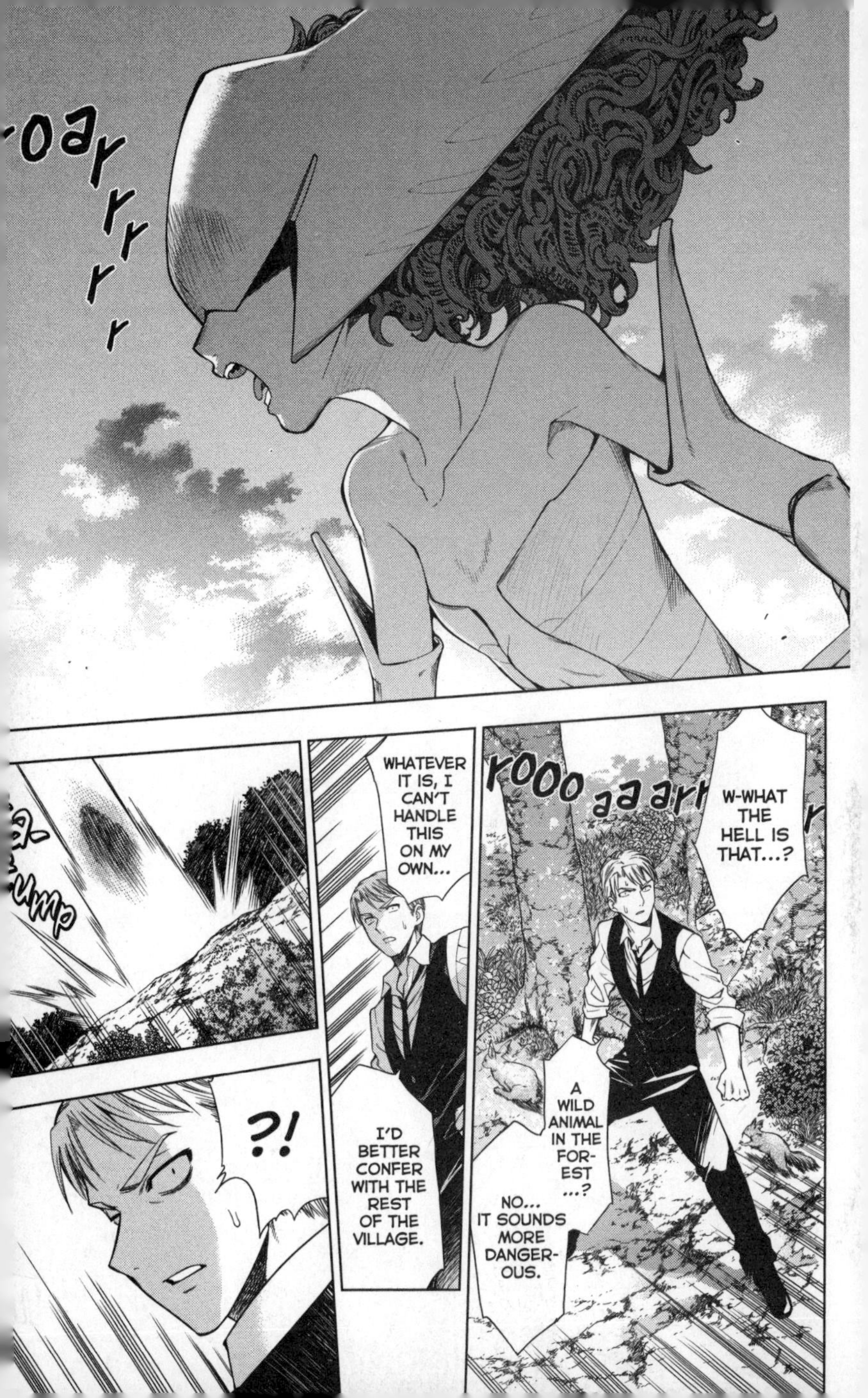
roarrrrr
roooaaarrr
W-WHAT THE HELL IS THAT...?
A WILD ANIMAL IN THE FOR-EST...?
NO... IT SOUNDS MORE DANGER-OUS.
WHATEVER IT IS, I CAN'T HANDLE THIS ON MY OWN...
I'D BETTER CONFER WITH THE REST OF THE VILLAGE.
?!

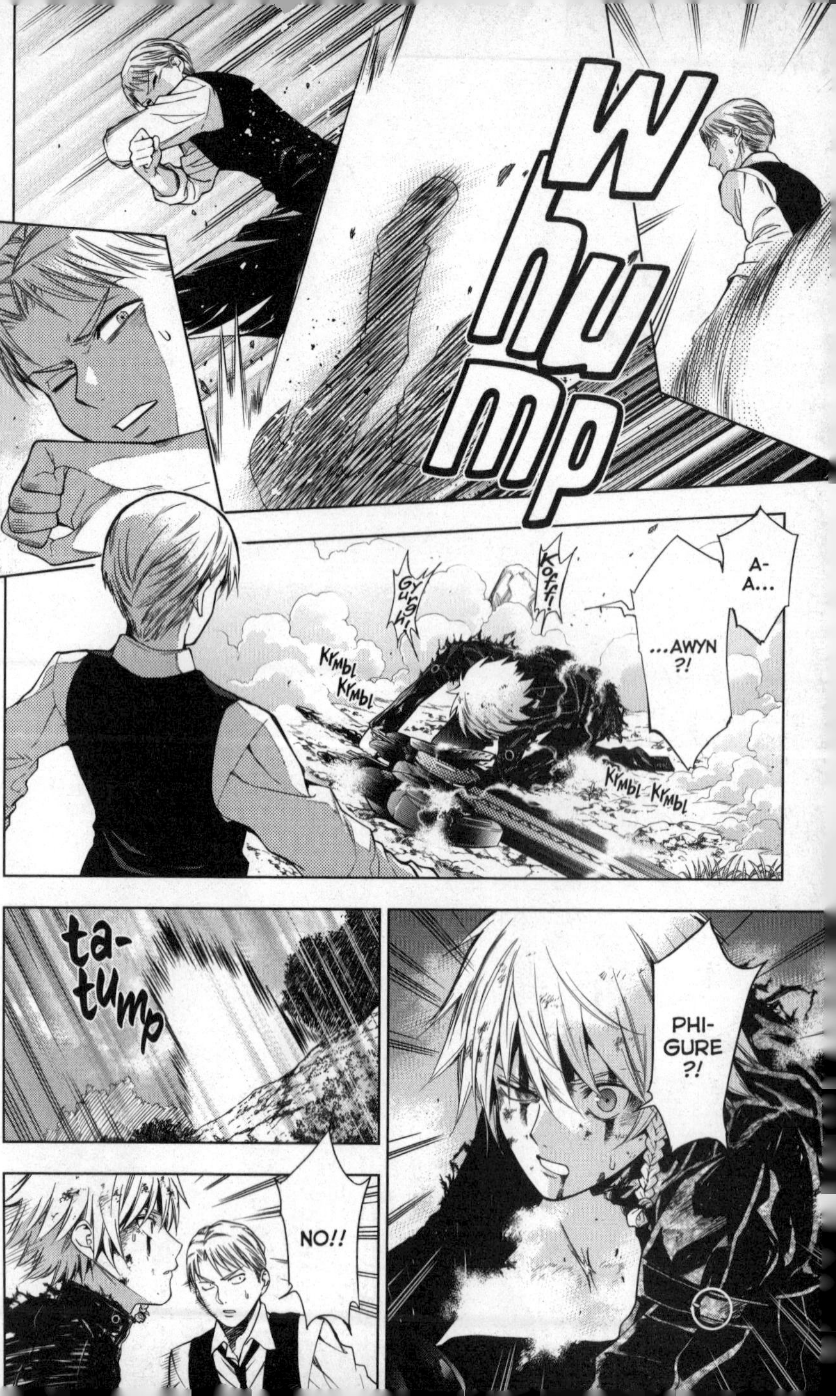
WHUMP
A-A...
...AWYN?!
Koff!
Gyurgh!
Krmbl Krmbl
Krmbl Krmbl
PHI-GURE?!
ta-tump
NO!!

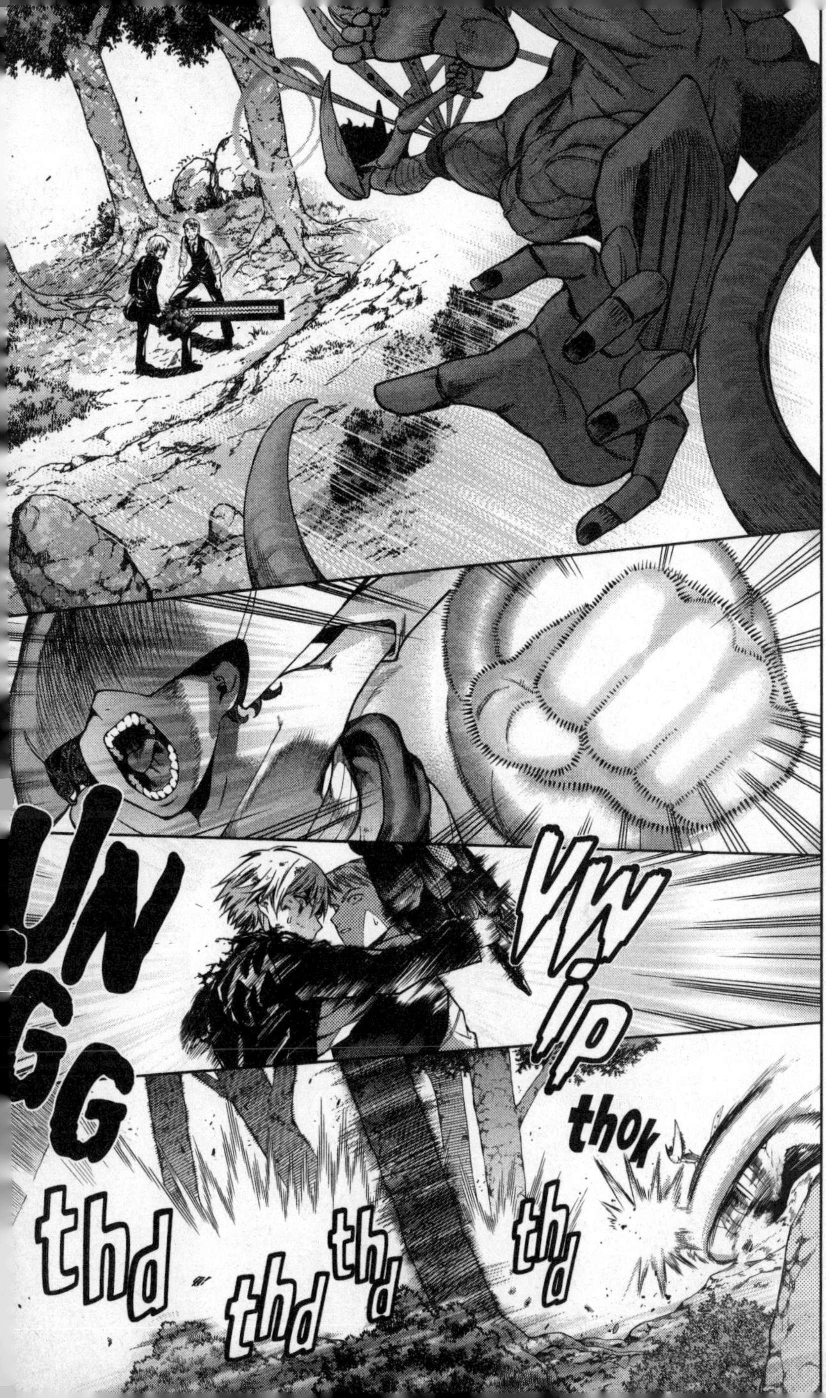
VWip
thok
thd
thd
thd
thd

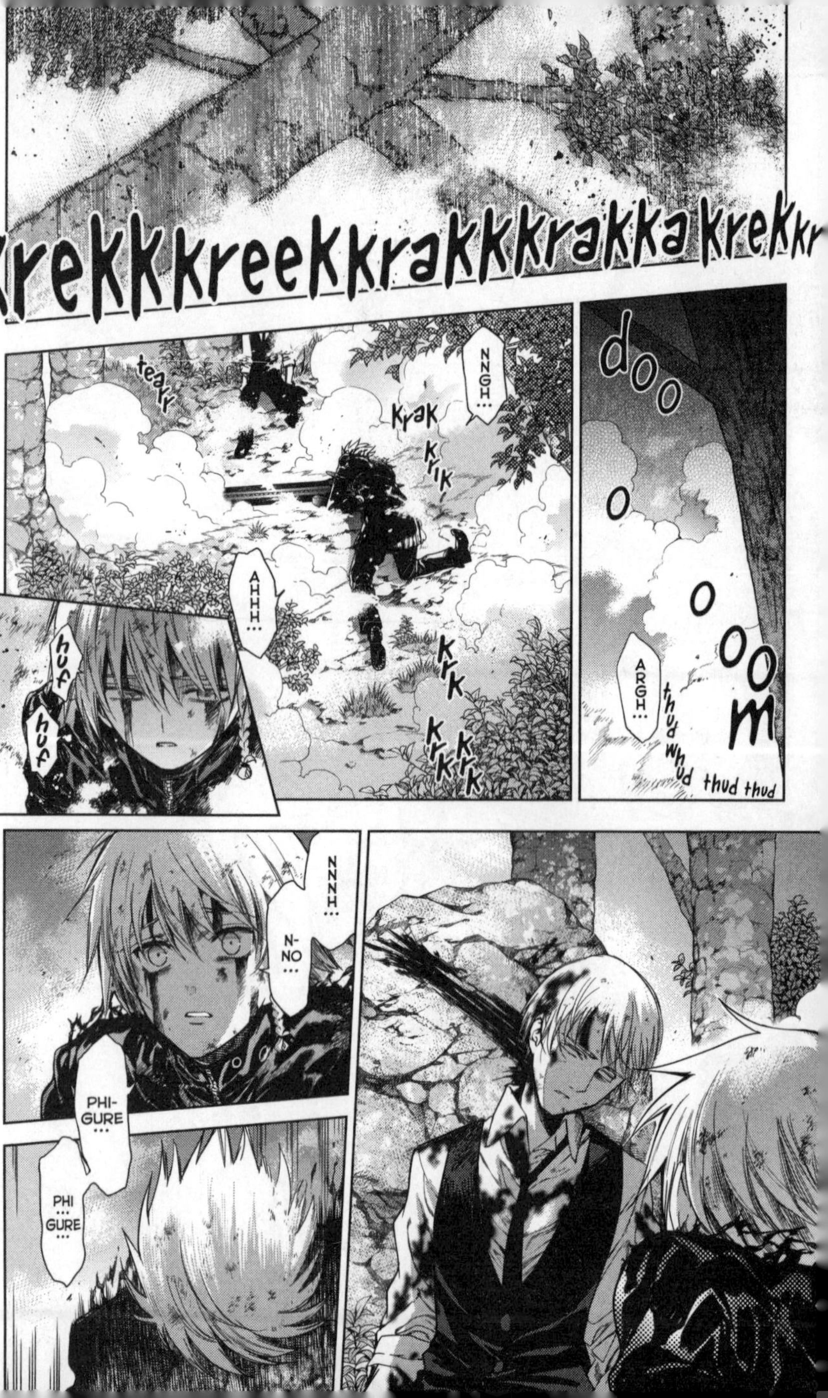
krekkkreekkrakkkrakka krekkr
doooooom
ARGH...
thud thud thud thud
NNGH...
tearr
krak
krik
krk krk krk
AHHH...
huf huf
NNNH...
N-NO...
PHI-GURE...
PHI... GURE...

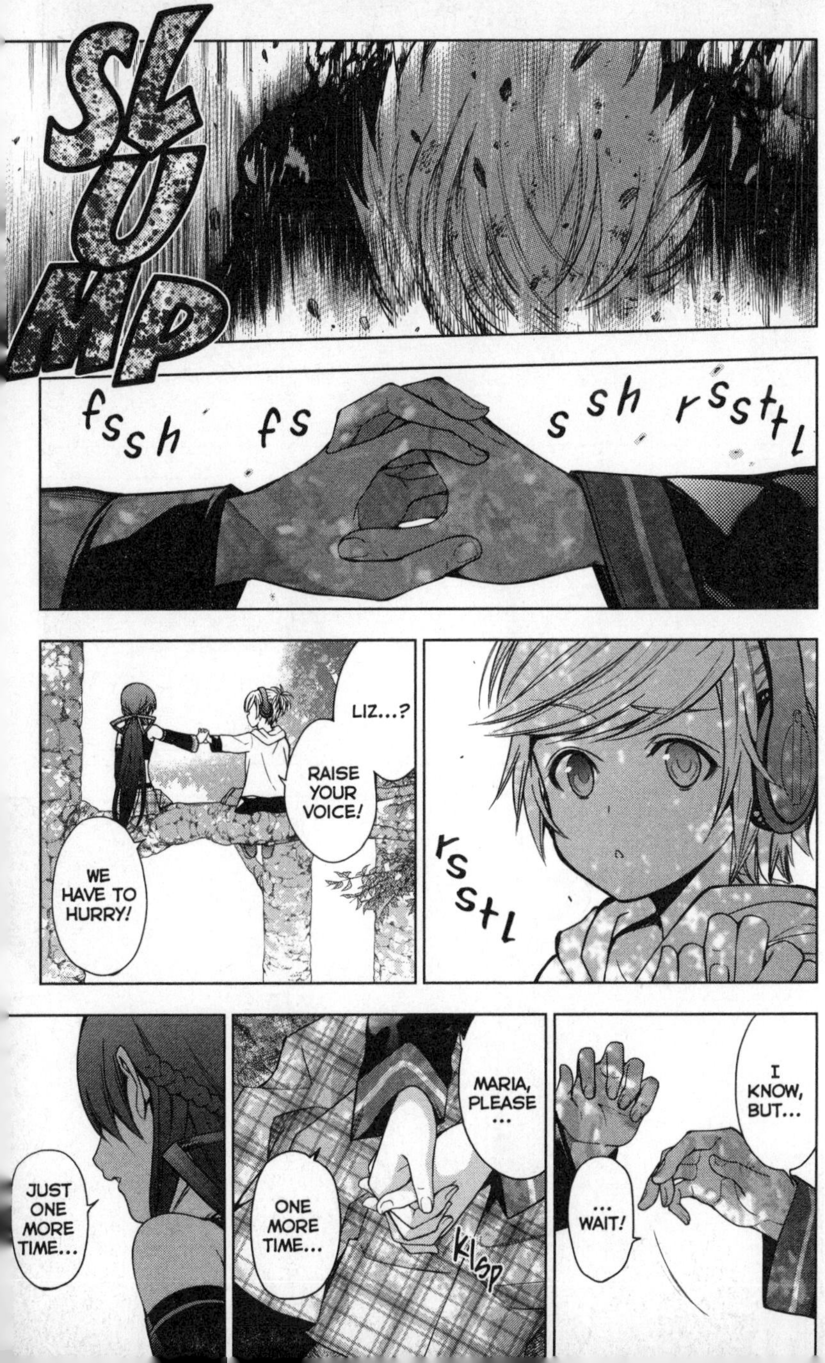
SLUMP
s sh rssttl
fssh fs
rsstl
LIZ...?
RAISE YOUR VOICE!
WE HAVE TO HURRY!
I KNOW, BUT...
...WAIT!
MARIA, PLEASE...
ONE MORE TIME...
klsp
JUST ONE MORE TIME...

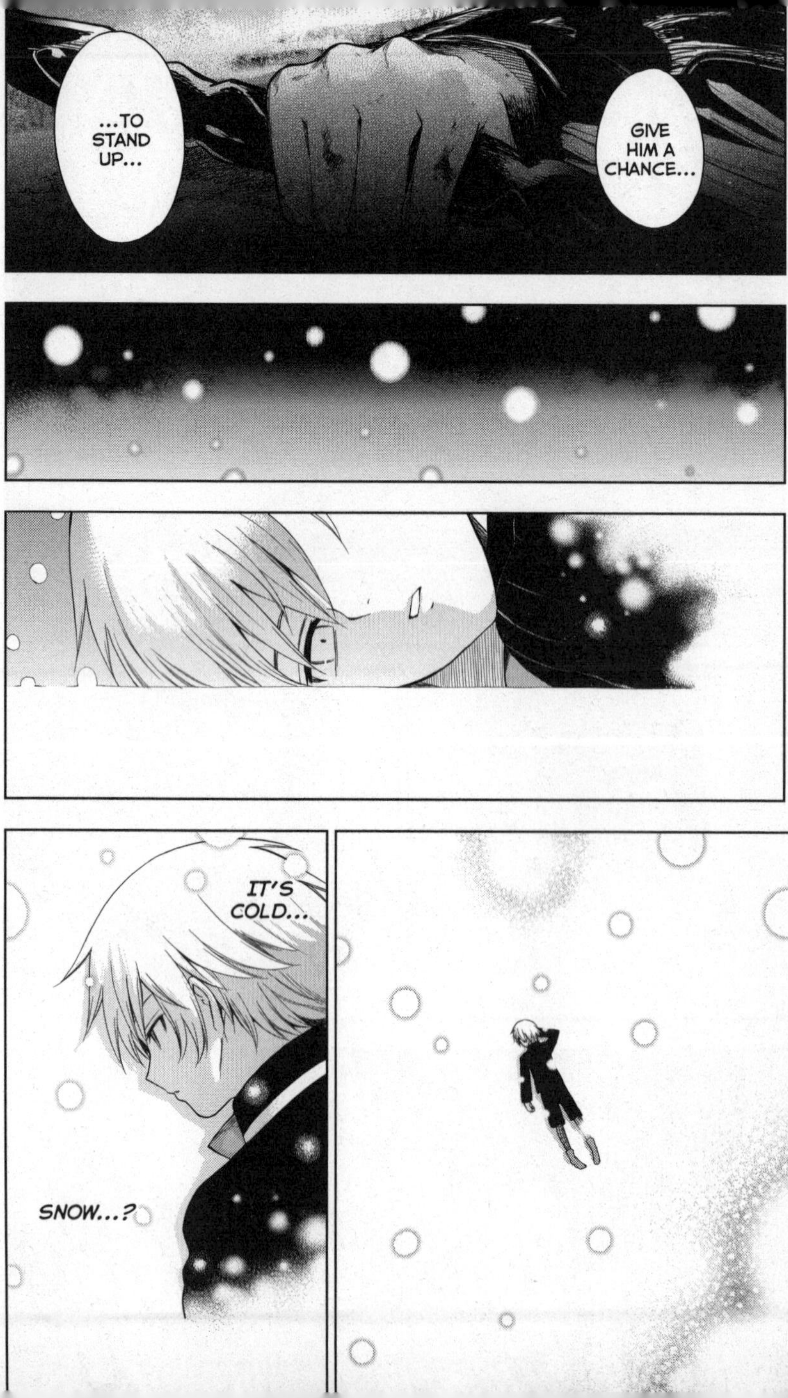
GIVE HIM A CHANCE...
...TO STAND UP...
IT'S COLD...
SNOW...?

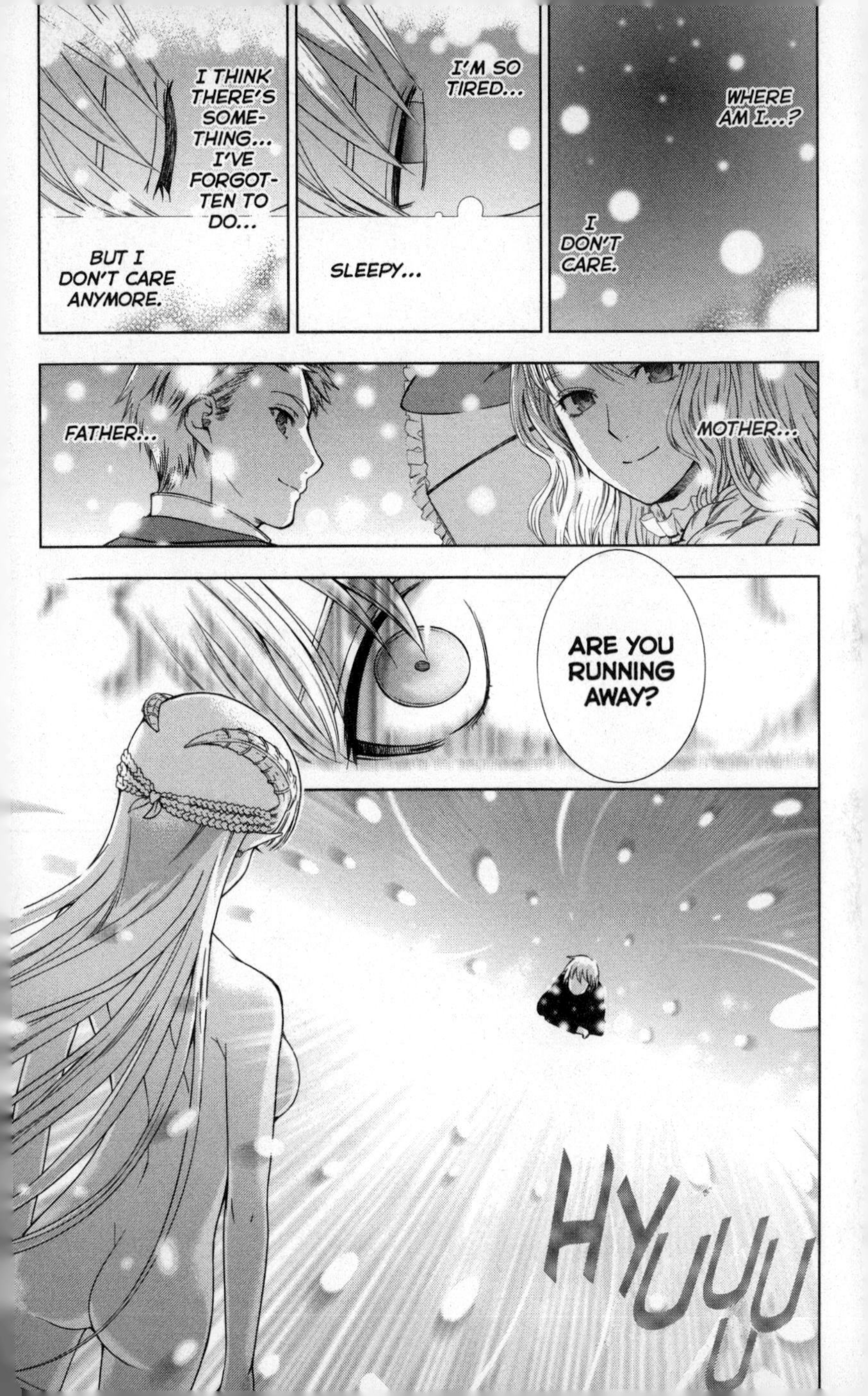
WHERE AM I...?
I DON'T CARE.
I'M SO TIRED...
SLEEPY...
I THINK THERE'S SOME-THING... I'VE FORGOT-TEN TO DO...
BUT I DON'T CARE ANYMORE.
MOTHER...
FATHER...
ARE YOU RUNNING AWAY?
HYUUU

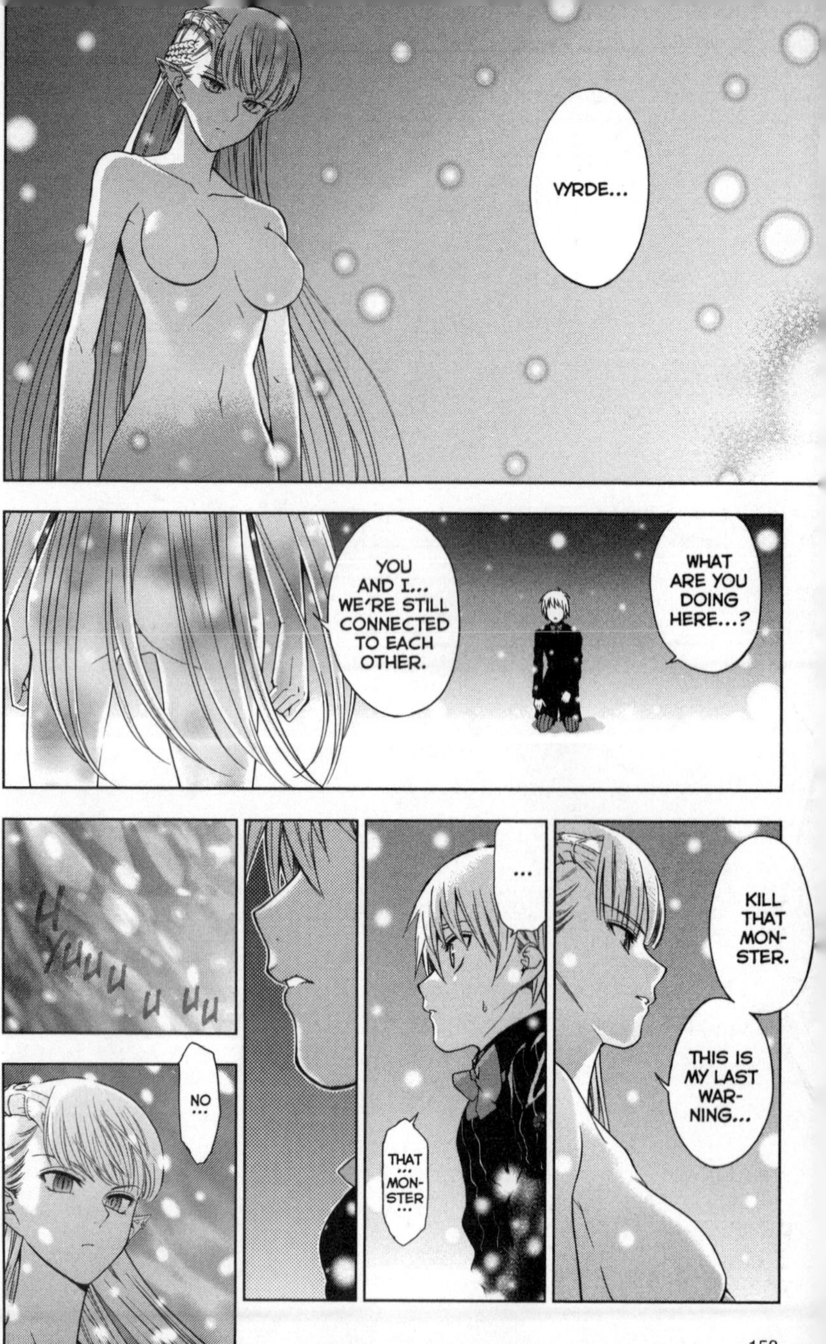
VYRDE...
WHAT ARE YOU DOING HERE...?
YOU AND I... WE'RE STILL CONNECTED TO EACH OTHER.
KILL THAT MON-STER.
THIS IS MY LAST WAR-NING...
...
THAT ... MON-STER ...
Hyuuu u uu
NO ...

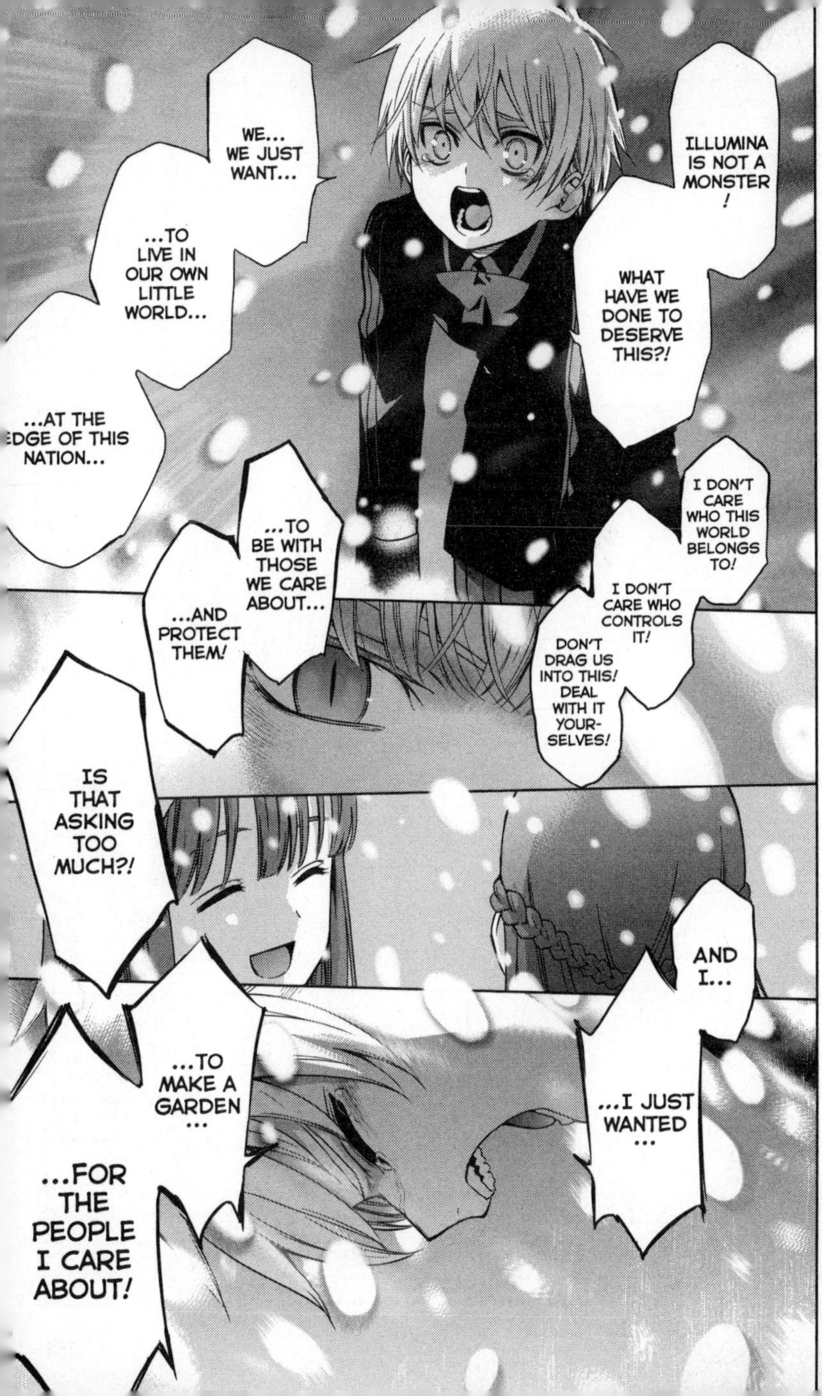
ILLUMINA IS NOT A MONSTER!
WHAT HAVE WE DONE TO DESERVE THIS?!
I DON'T CARE WHO THIS WORLD BELONGS TO!
I DON'T CARE WHO CONTROLS IT!
DON'T DRAG US INTO THIS! DEAL WITH IT YOURSELVES!
WE... WE JUST WANT...
...TO LIVE IN OUR OWN LITTLE WORLD...
...AT THE EDGE OF THIS NATION...
...TO BE WITH THOSE WE CARE ABOUT...
...AND PROTECT THEM!
IS THAT ASKING TOO MUCH?!
AND I...
...I JUST WANTED...
...TO MAKE A GARDEN...
...FOR THE PEOPLE I CARE ABOUT!

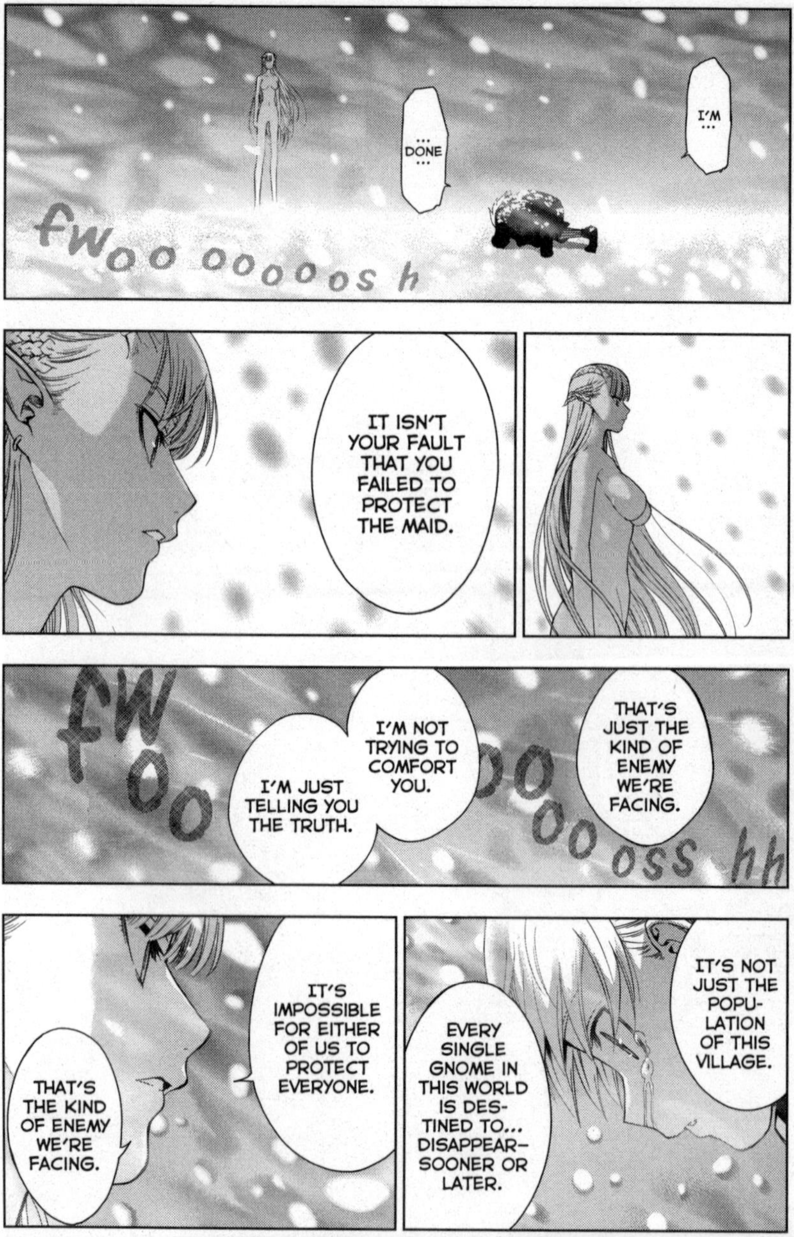

I'M ...
... DONE ...
fwoo oooooos h
IT ISN'T YOUR FAULT THAT YOU FAILED TO PROTECT THE MAID.
THAT'S JUST THE KIND OF ENEMY WE'RE FACING.
I'M NOT TRYING TO COMFORT YOU.
I'M JUST TELLING YOU THE TRUTH.
fwoooooooss hh
IT'S NOT JUST THE POPU-LATION OF THIS VILLAGE.
EVERY SINGLE GNOME IN THIS WORLD IS DES-TINED TO... DISAPPEAR– SOONER OR LATER.
IT'S IMPOSSIBLE FOR EITHER OF US TO PROTECT EVERYONE.
THAT'S THE KIND OF ENEMY WE'RE FACING.

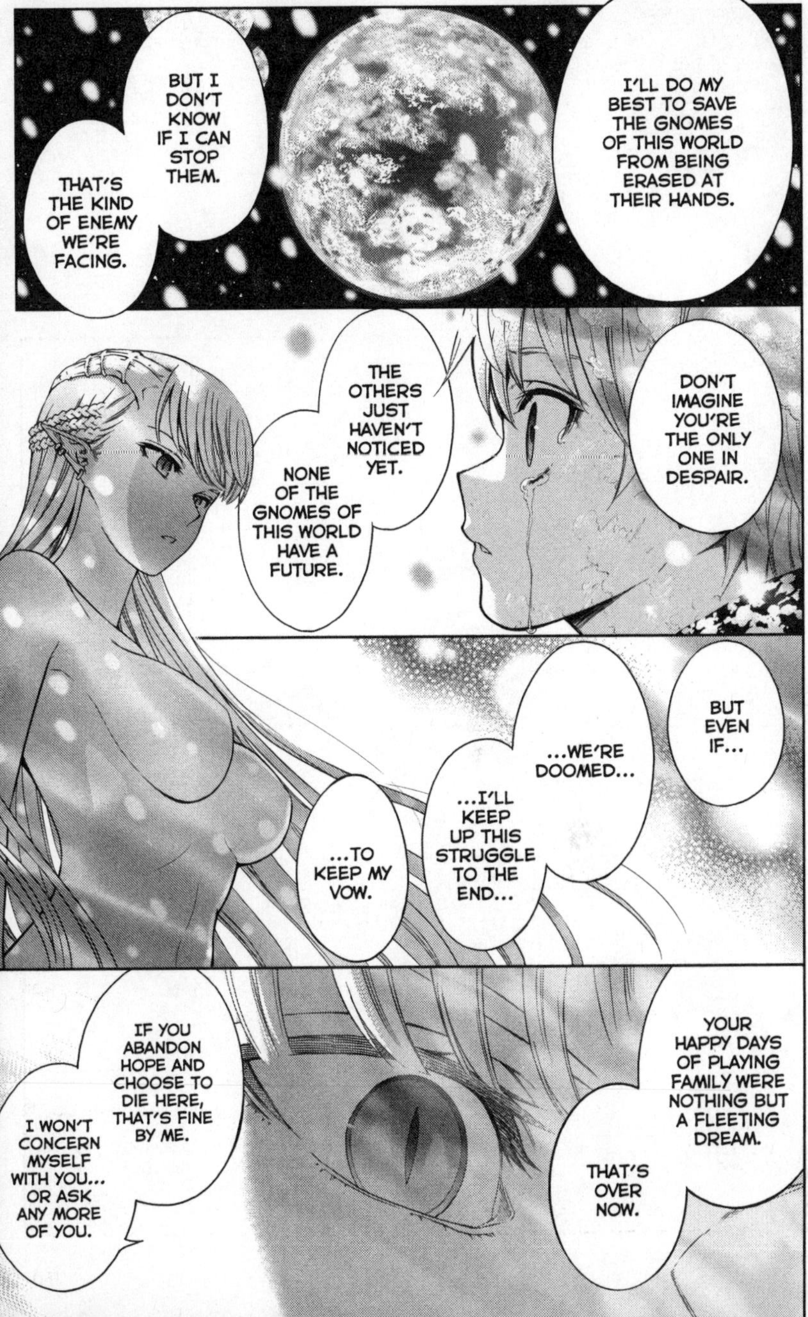
I'LL DO MY BEST TO SAVE THE GNOMES OF THIS WORLD FROM BEING ERASED AT THEIR HANDS.
BUT I DON'T KNOW IF I CAN STOP THEM.
THAT'S THE KIND OF ENEMY WE'RE FACING.
DON'T IMAGINE YOU'RE THE ONLY ONE IN DESPAIR.
THE OTHERS JUST HAVEN'T NOTICED YET.
NONE OF THE GNOMES OF THIS WORLD HAVE A FUTURE.
BUT EVEN IF...
...WE'RE DOOMED...
...I'LL KEEP UP THIS STRUGGLE TO THE END...
...TO KEEP MY VOW.
YOUR HAPPY DAYS OF PLAYING FAMILY WERE NOTHING BUT A FLEETING DREAM.
THAT'S OVER NOW.
IF YOU ABANDON HOPE AND CHOOSE TO DIE HERE, THAT'S FINE BY ME.
I WON'T CONCERN MYSELF WITH YOU... OR ASK ANY MORE OF YOU.

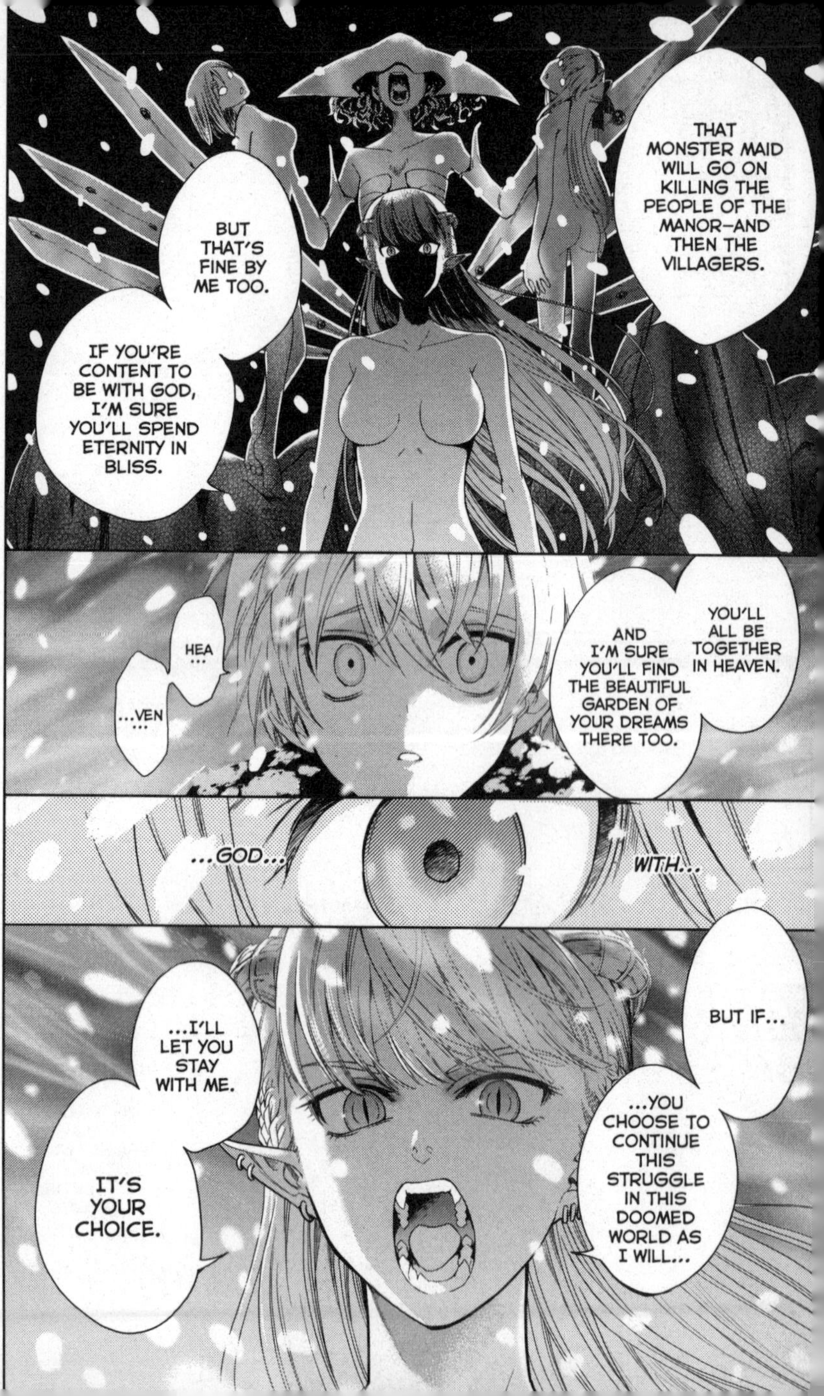
THAT MONSTER MAID WILL GO ON KILLING THE PEOPLE OF THE MANOR—AND THEN THE VILLAGERS.
BUT THAT'S FINE BY ME TOO.
IF YOU'RE CONTENT TO BE WITH GOD, I'M SURE YOU'LL SPEND ETERNITY IN BLISS.
YOU'LL ALL BE TOGETHER IN HEAVEN.
AND I'M SURE YOU'LL FIND THE BEAUTIFUL GARDEN OF YOUR DREAMS THERE TOO.
HEA...
...VEN...
WITH...
...GOD...
BUT IF...
...YOU CHOOSE TO CONTINUE THIS STRUGGLE IN THIS DOOMED WORLD AS I WILL...
...I'LL LET YOU STAY WITH ME.
IT'S YOUR CHOICE.

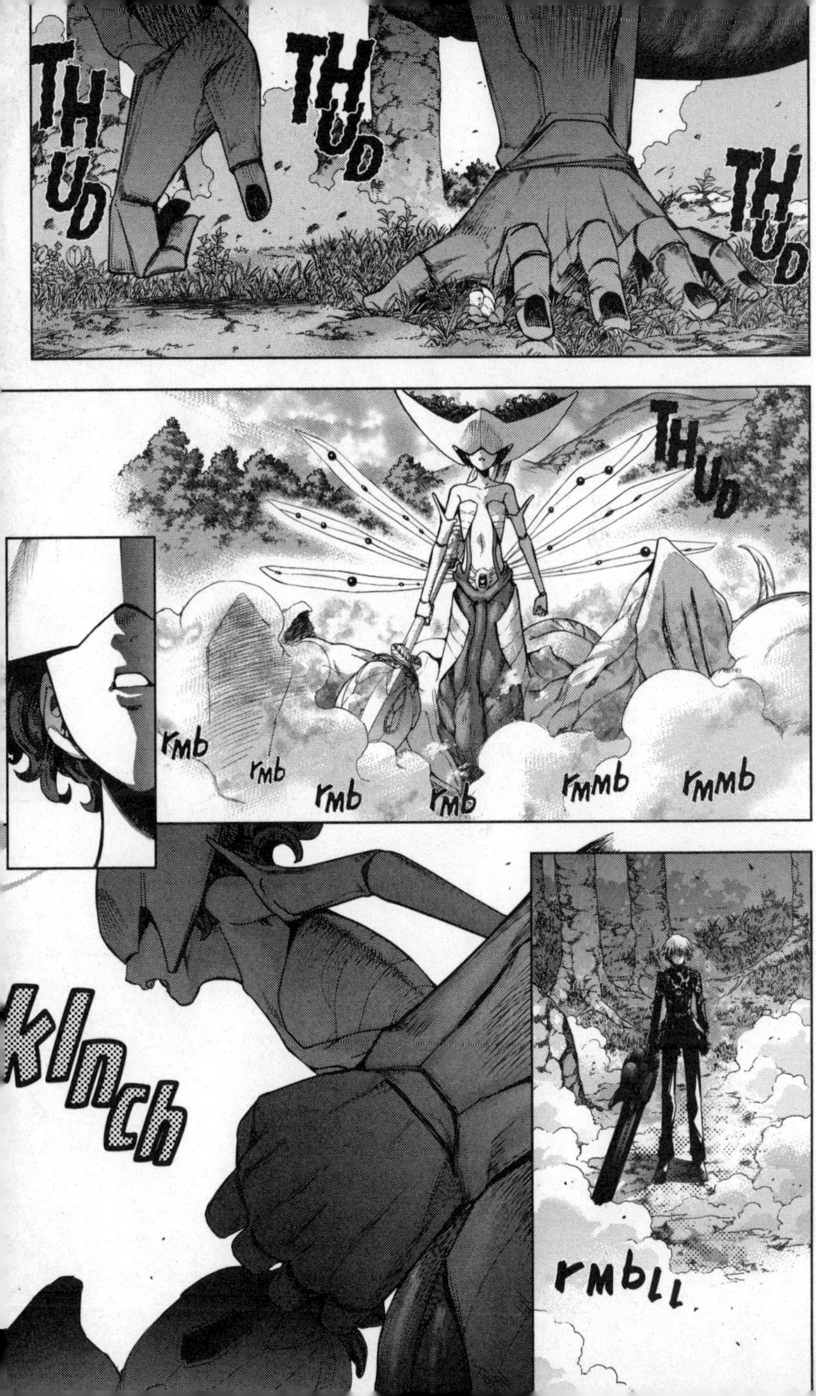
THUD
THUD
THUD
THUD
rmmb
rmmb
rmb
rmb
rmb
rmb
rmbll
klnch

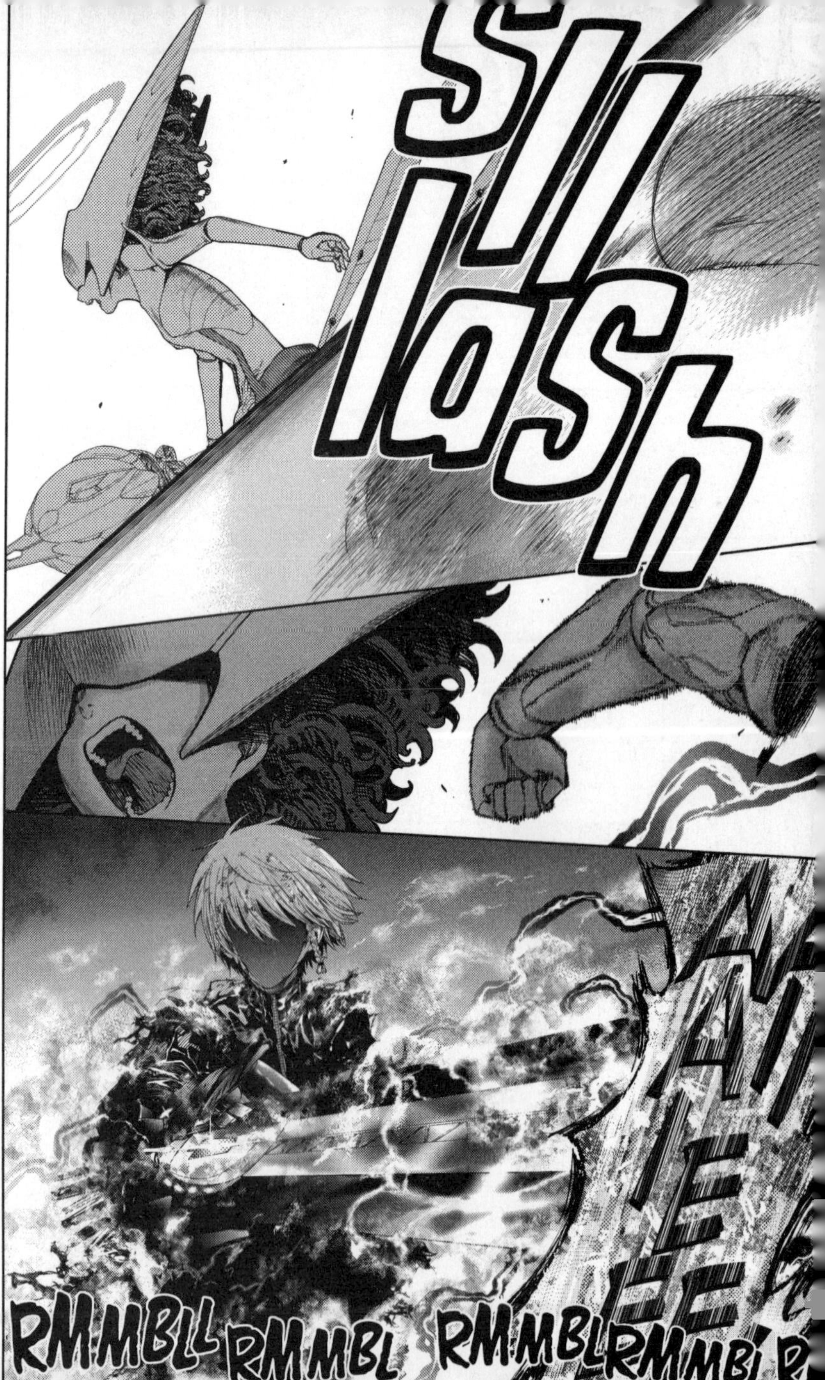
SHLASH
AAIIEEE
RMMBLL RMMBL RMMBLRMMMBL R

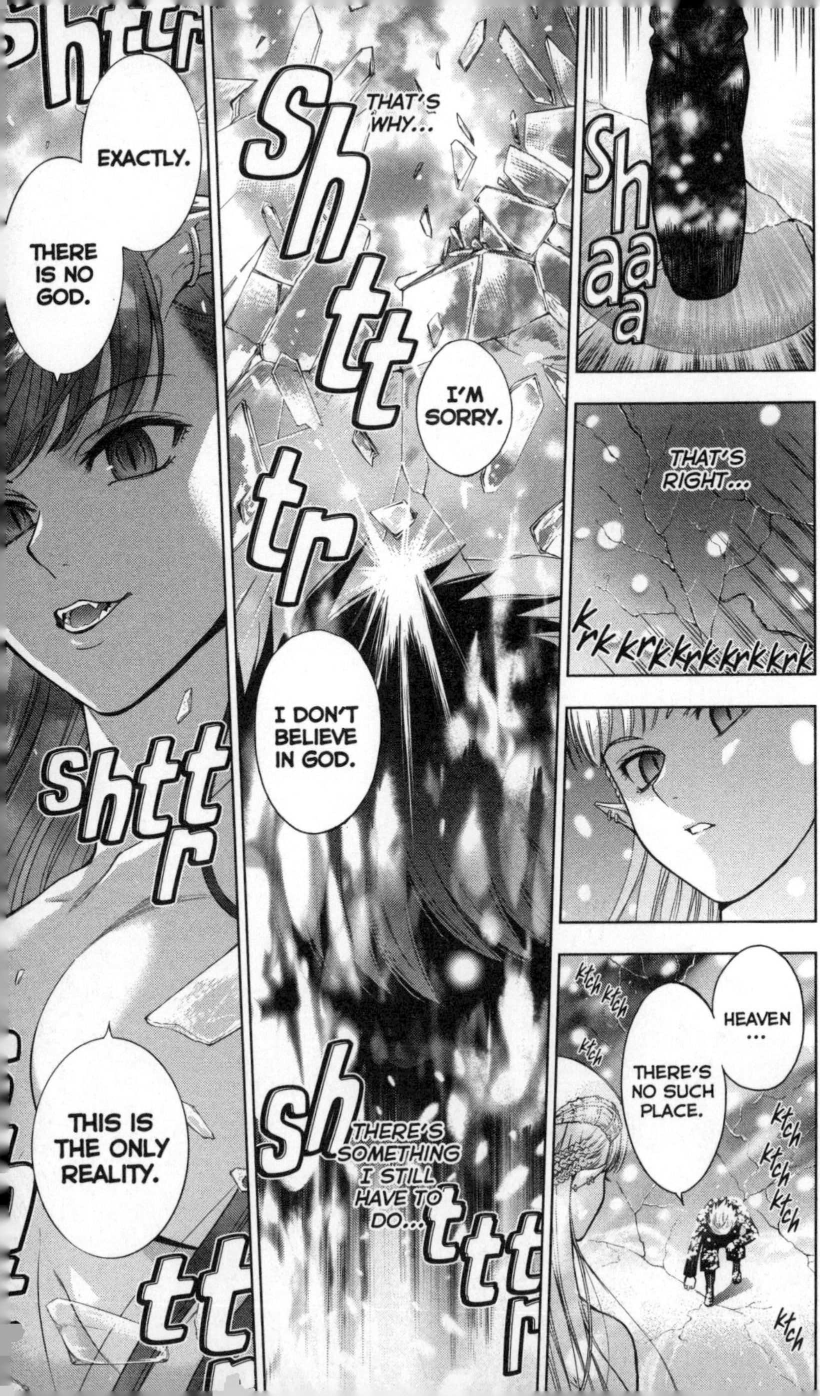
Shaaa
THAT'S RIGHT...
krk krk krk krk krk
ktch ktch
ktch
HEAVEN...
THERE'S NO SUCH PLACE.
ktch
ktch
ktch
ktch
Shtttr
THAT'S WHY...
I'M SORRY.
I DON'T BELIEVE IN GOD.
sh
THERE'S SOMETHING I STILL HAVE TO DO...
tttr
Shttr
EXACTLY.
THERE IS NO GOD.
shttr
THIS IS THE ONLY REALITY.
ttr

THIS REALITY...

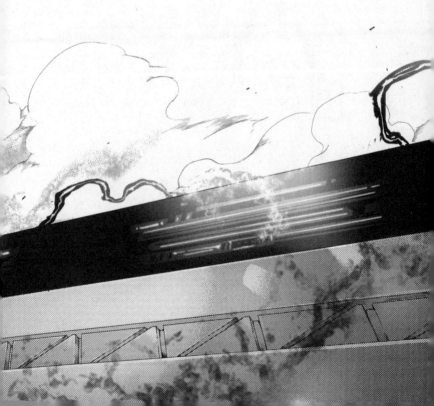

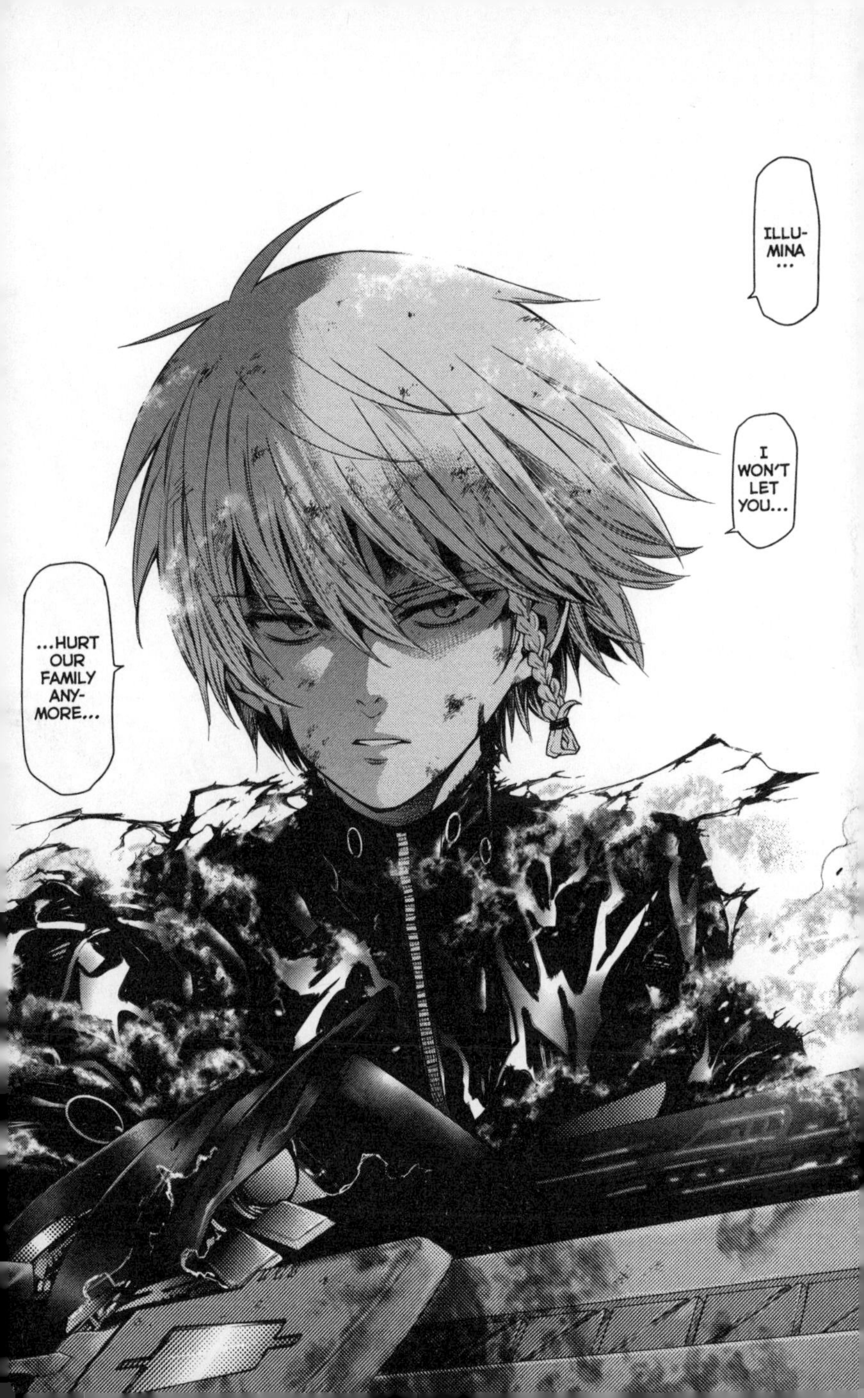
ILLU-MINA...
I WON'T LET YOU...
...HURT OUR FAMILY ANY-MORE...

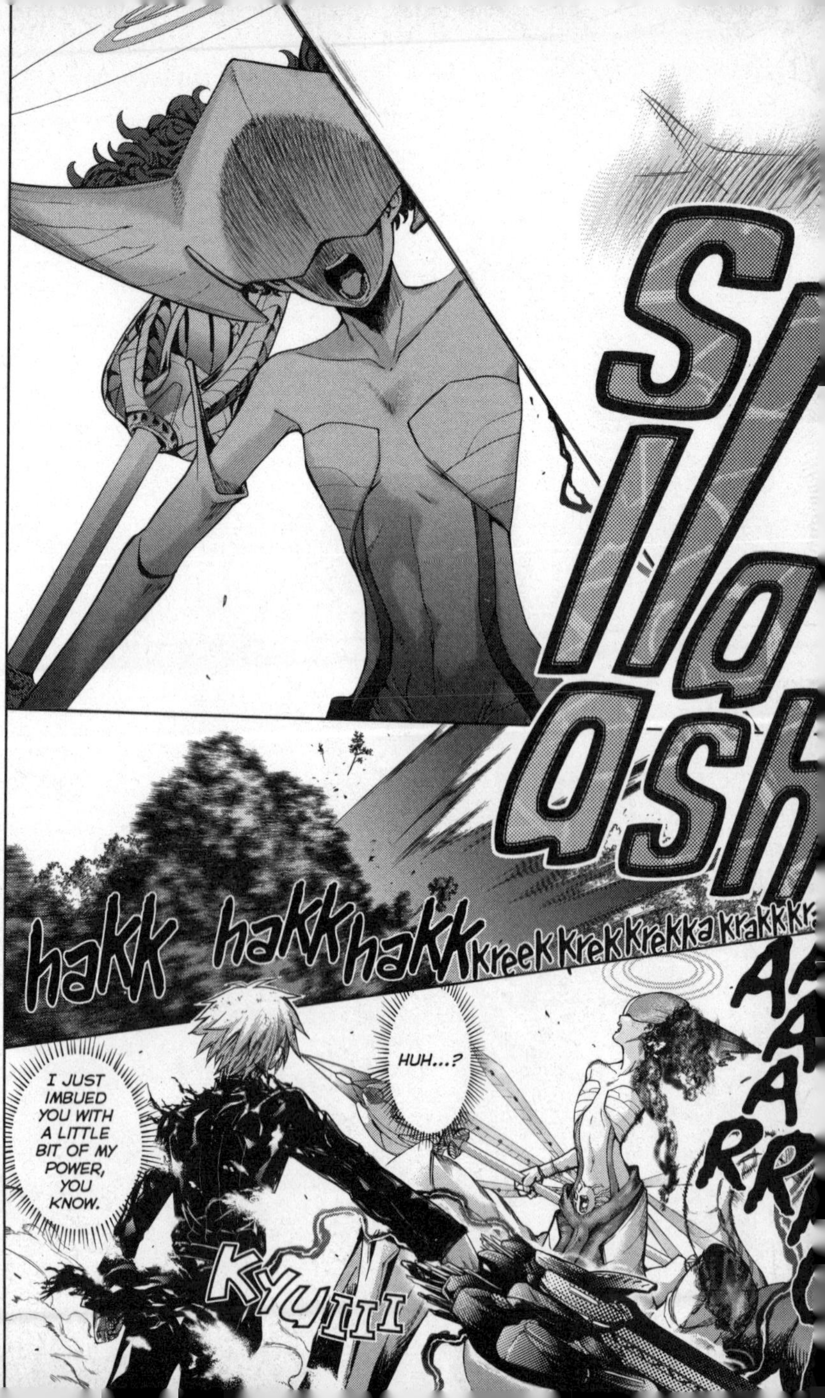
Sllaash
hakk hakk hakk kreek krek krekka krakkkra
AAAARR
HUH...?
I JUST IMBUED YOU WITH A LITTLE BIT OF MY POWER, YOU KNOW.
KYUIII

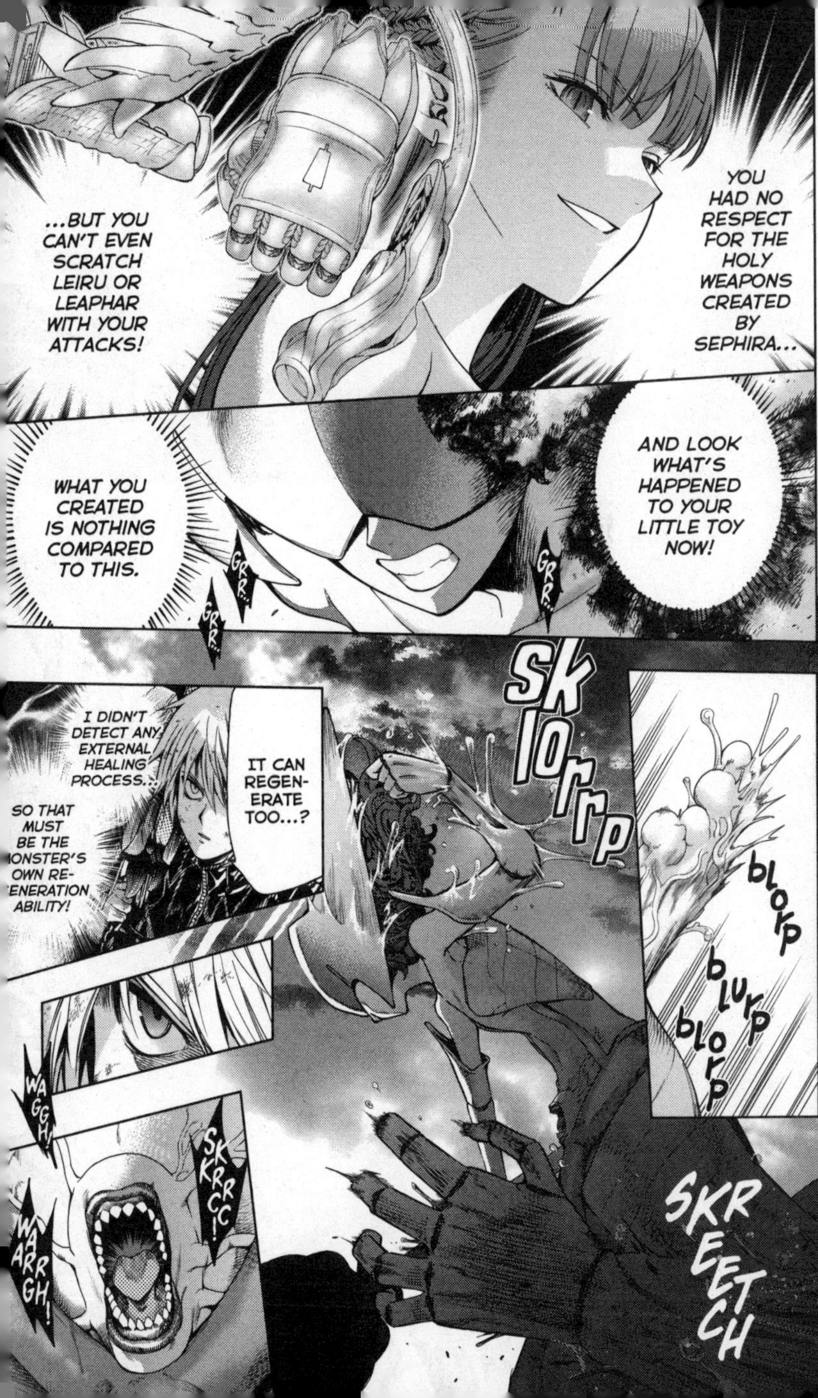
YOU HAD NO RESPECT FOR THE HOLY WEAPONS CREATED BY SEPHIRA...
...BUT YOU CAN'T EVEN SCRATCH LEIRU OR LEAPHAR WITH YOUR ATTACKS!
AND LOOK WHAT'S HAPPENED TO YOUR LITTLE TOY NOW!
GRR...
WHAT YOU CREATED IS NOTHING COMPARED TO THIS.
GRR...
GRR...
blorp blurp blorp
sklorrrp
IT CAN REGENERATE TOO...?
I DIDN'T DETECT ANY EXTERNAL HEALING PROCESS...
SO THAT MUST BE THE ONSTER'S OWN RE-ENERATION ABILITY!
SKREETCH
SKRRCC!
WAGGH!
WARRGH!

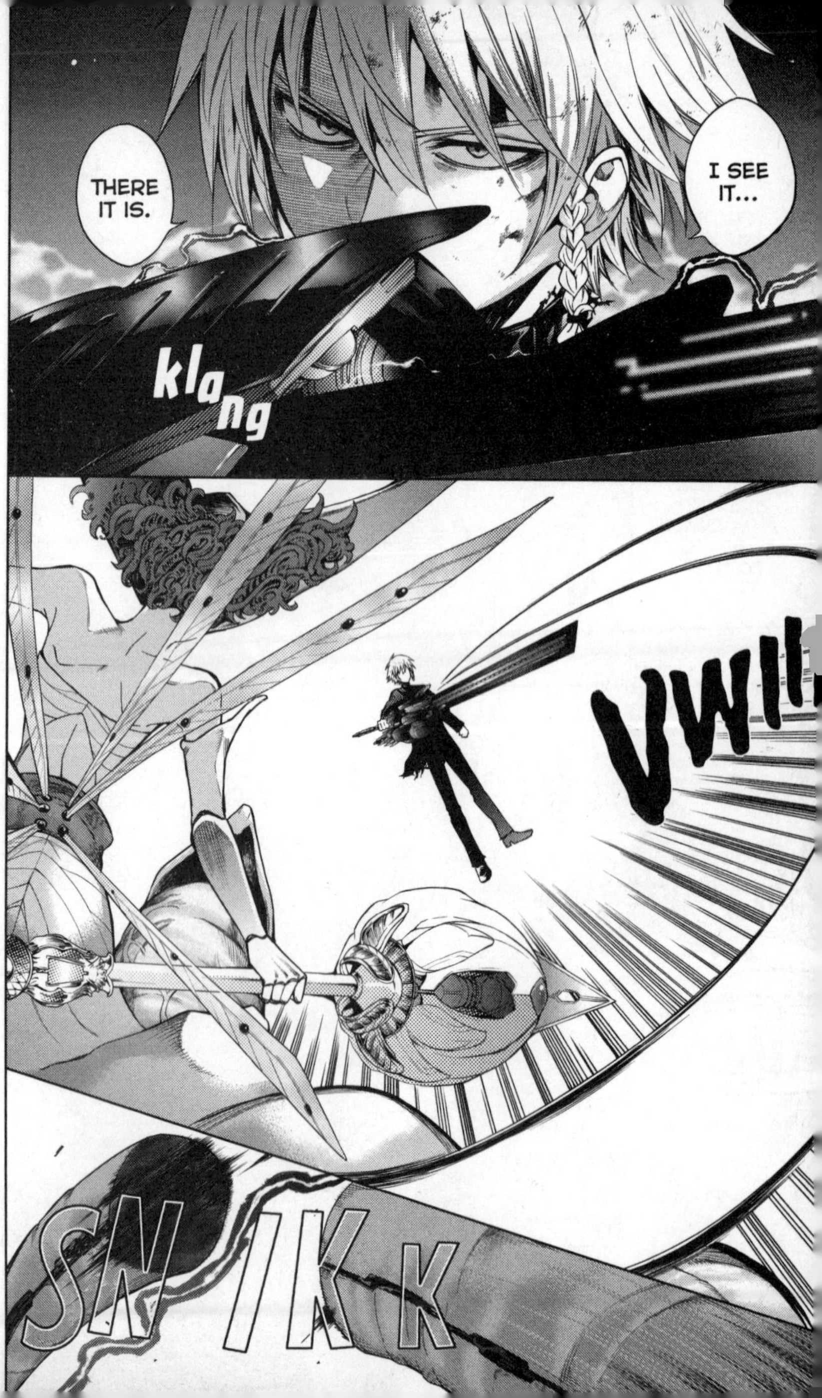
I SEE IT...
THERE IT IS.
klang
VWII
SNIKK

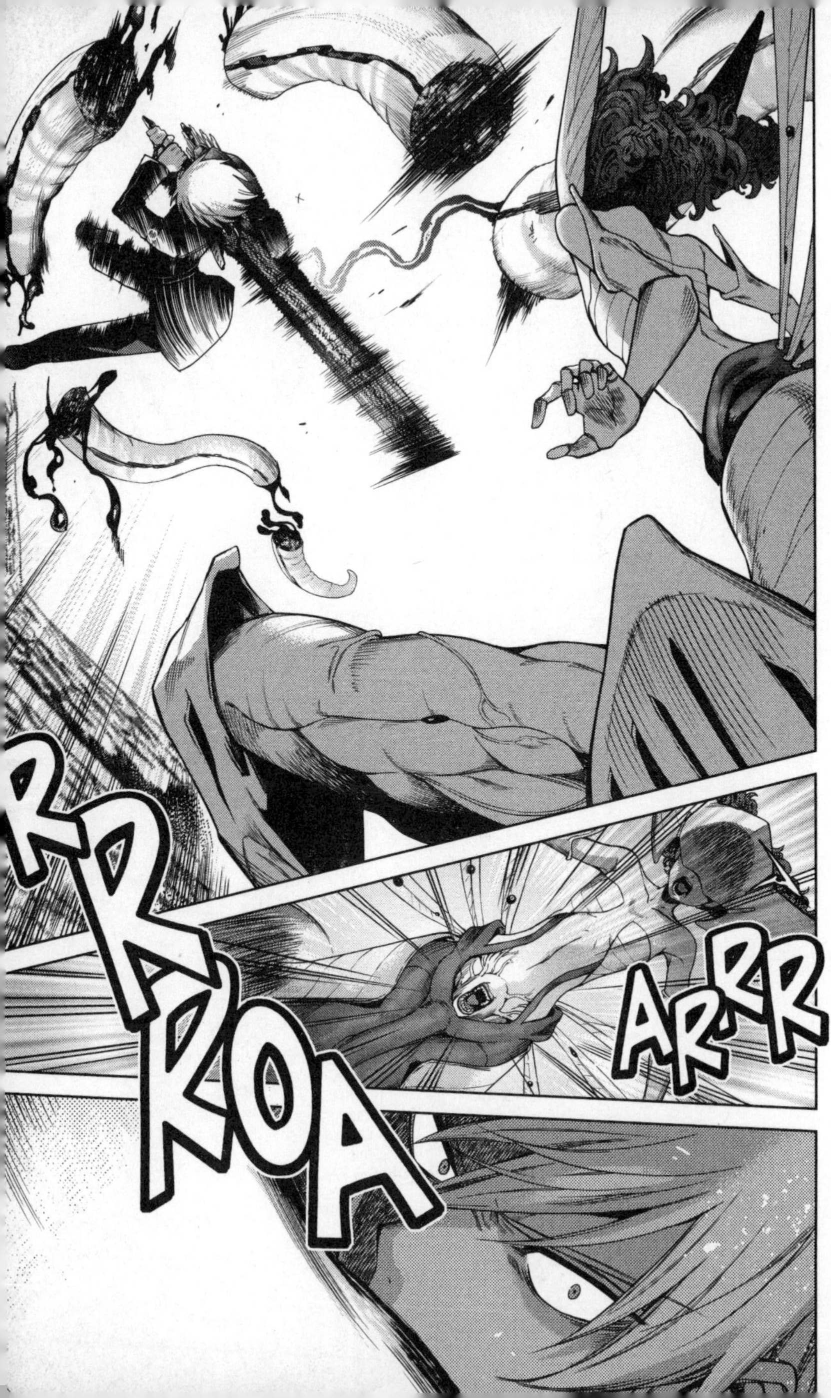
RRRROA
ARRR

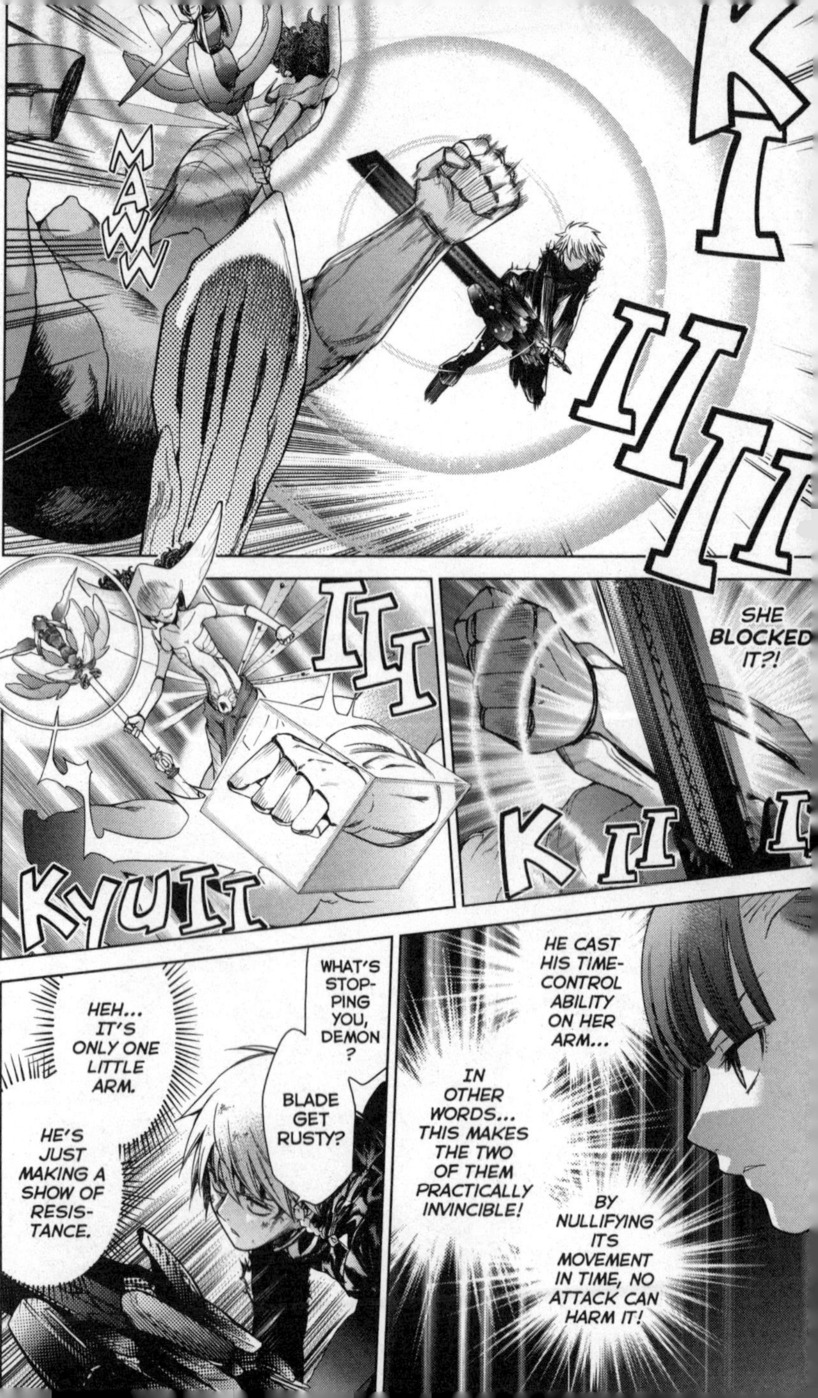
KIIIIII
MAWWW
SHE BLOCKED IT?!
KIII
III
KYUII
HE CAST HIS TIME-CONTROL ABILITY ON HER ARM...
IN OTHER WORDS... THIS MAKES THE TWO OF THEM PRACTICALLY INVINCIBLE!
BY NULLIFYING ITS MOVEMENT IN TIME, NO ATTACK CAN HARM IT!
WHAT'S STOP-PING YOU, DEMON?
BLADE GET RUSTY?
HEH... IT'S ONLY ONE LITTLE ARM.
HE'S JUST MAKING A SHOW OF RESIS-TANCE.

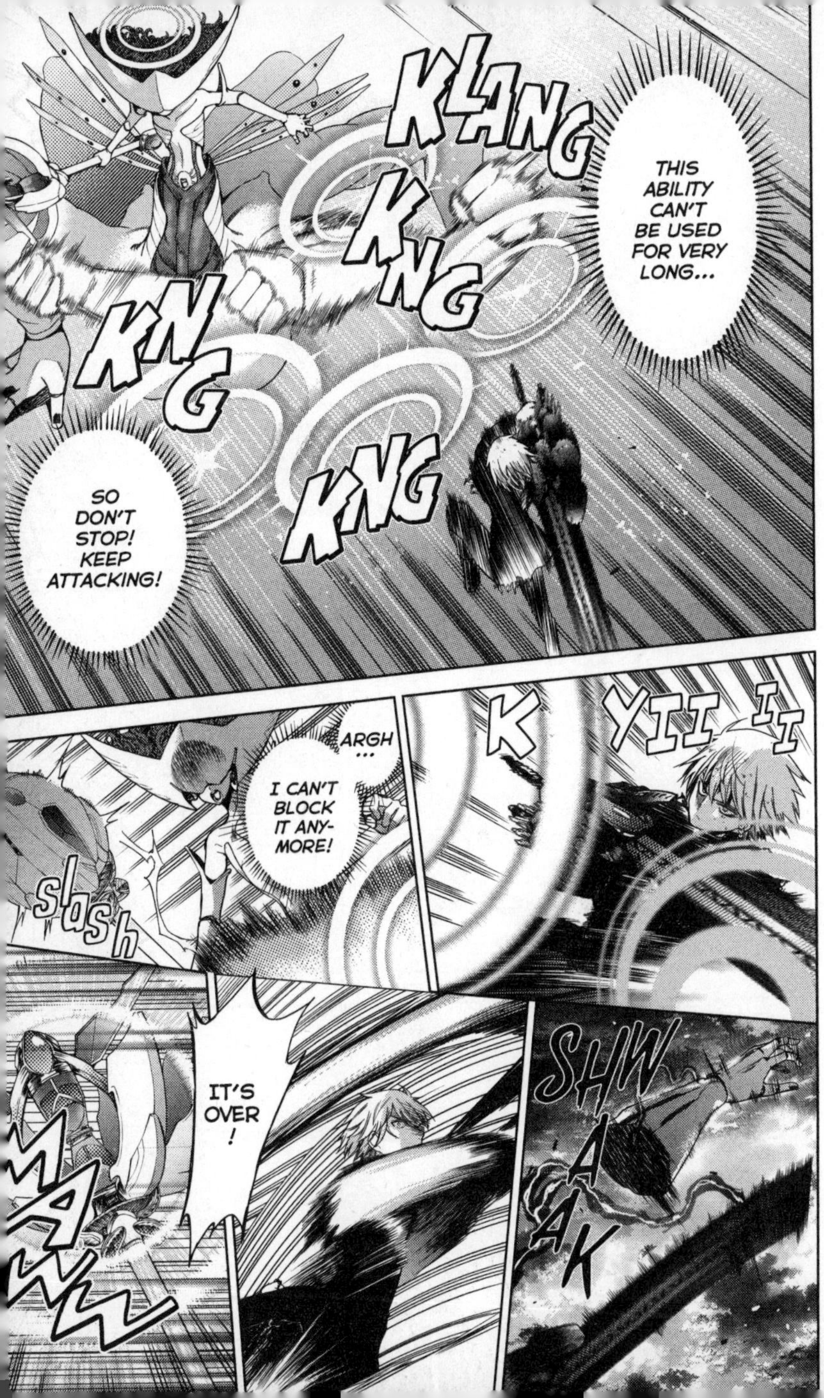
THIS ABILITY CAN'T BE USED FOR VERY LONG...
KLANG
KNG
KNG
KNG
SO DON'T STOP! KEEP ATTACKING!
K YIIII
ARGH...
I CAN'T BLOCK IT ANYMORE!
slash
SHWAAK
IT'S OVER!

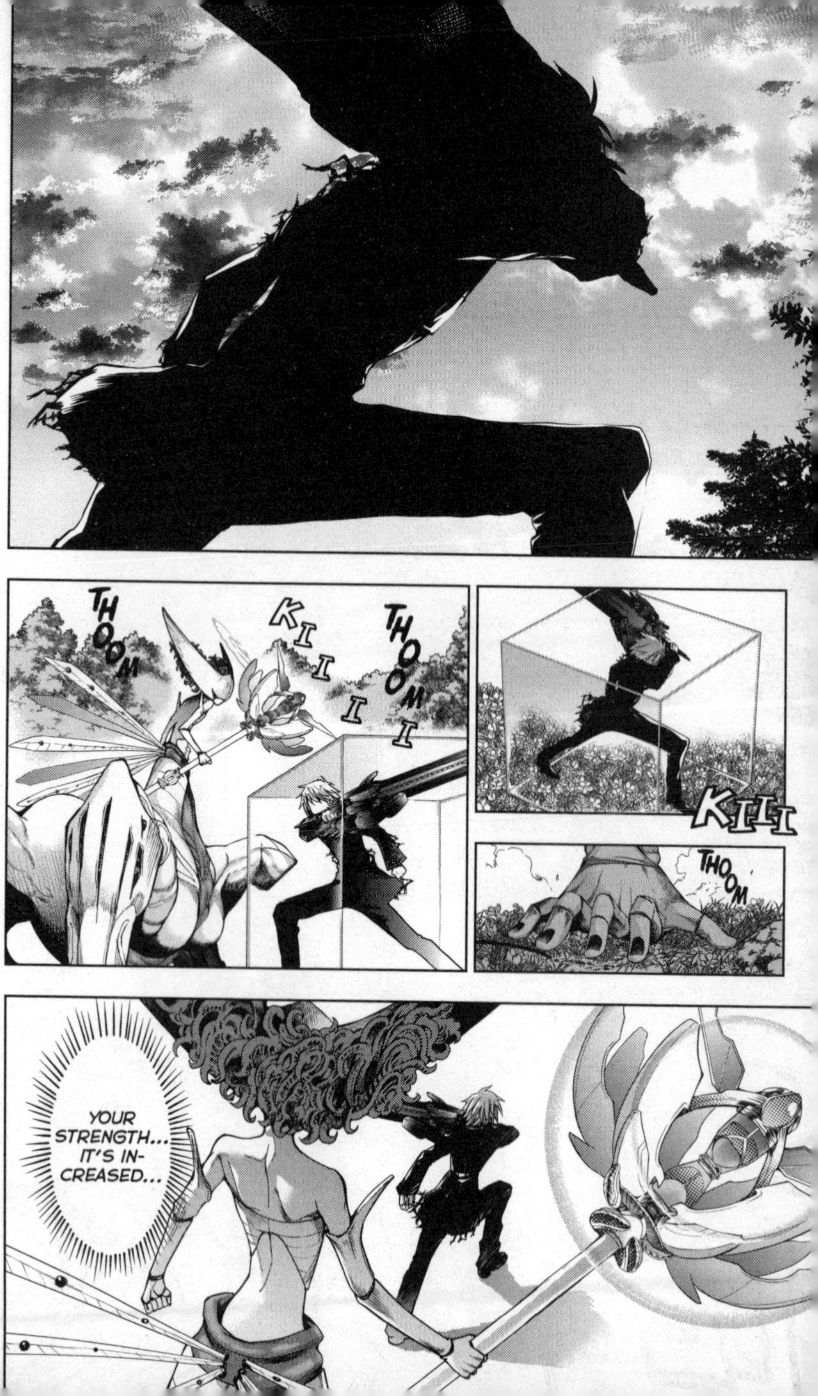
KIII
THOOM
THOOM
KIIIII
THOOM
YOUR STRENGTH... IT'S IN-CREASED...

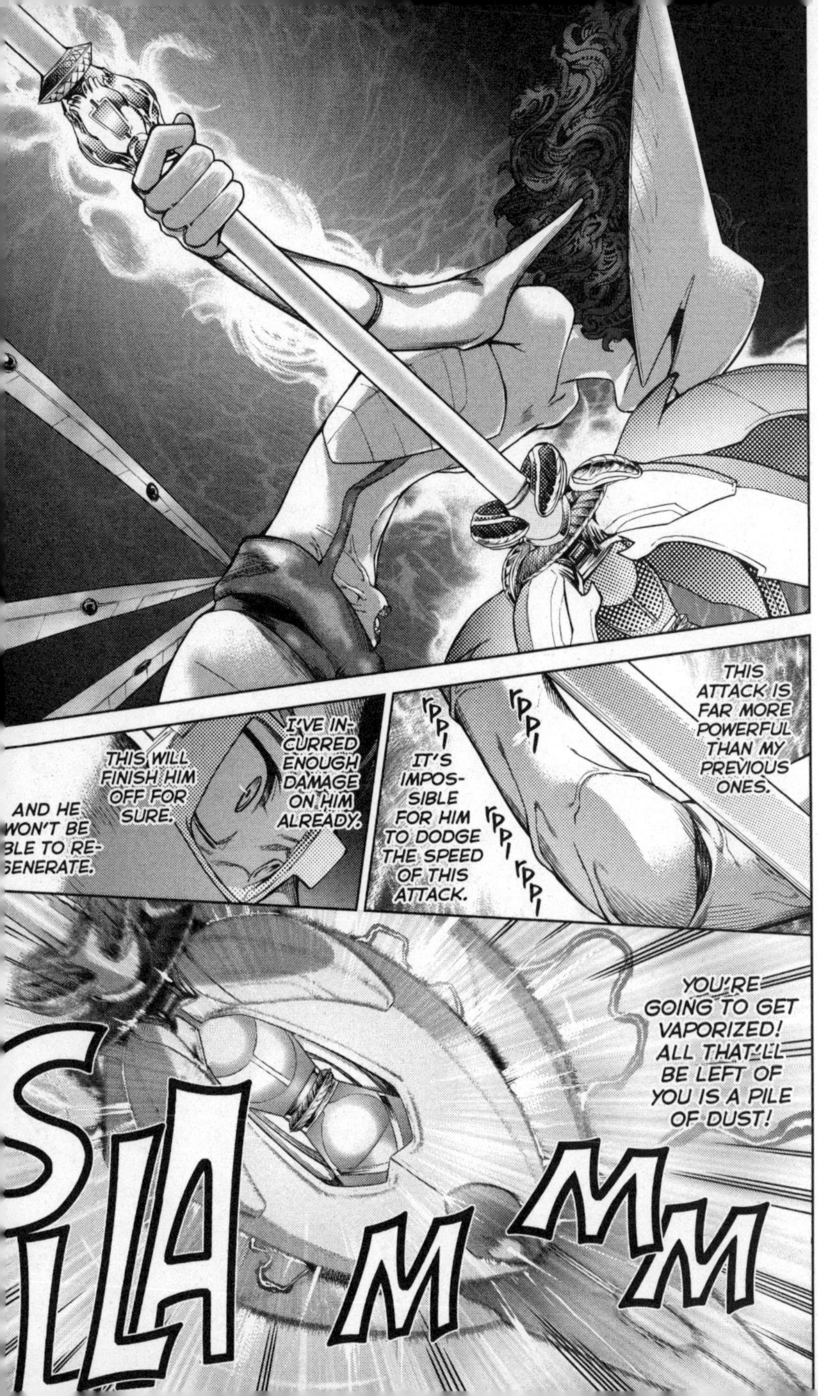
THIS ATTACK IS FAR MORE POWERFUL THAN MY PREVIOUS ONES.
rppi
rppi
rppi
rppi
rppi
IT'S IMPOSSIBLE FOR HIM TO DODGE THE SPEED OF THIS ATTACK.
I'VE INCURRED ENOUGH DAMAGE ON HIM ALREADY.
THIS WILL FINISH HIM OFF FOR SURE.
AND HE ON'T BE BLE TO RE-ENERATE.
YOU'RE GOING TO GET VAPORIZED! ALL THAT'LL BE LEFT OF YOU IS A PILE OF DUST!
SLAMMMM

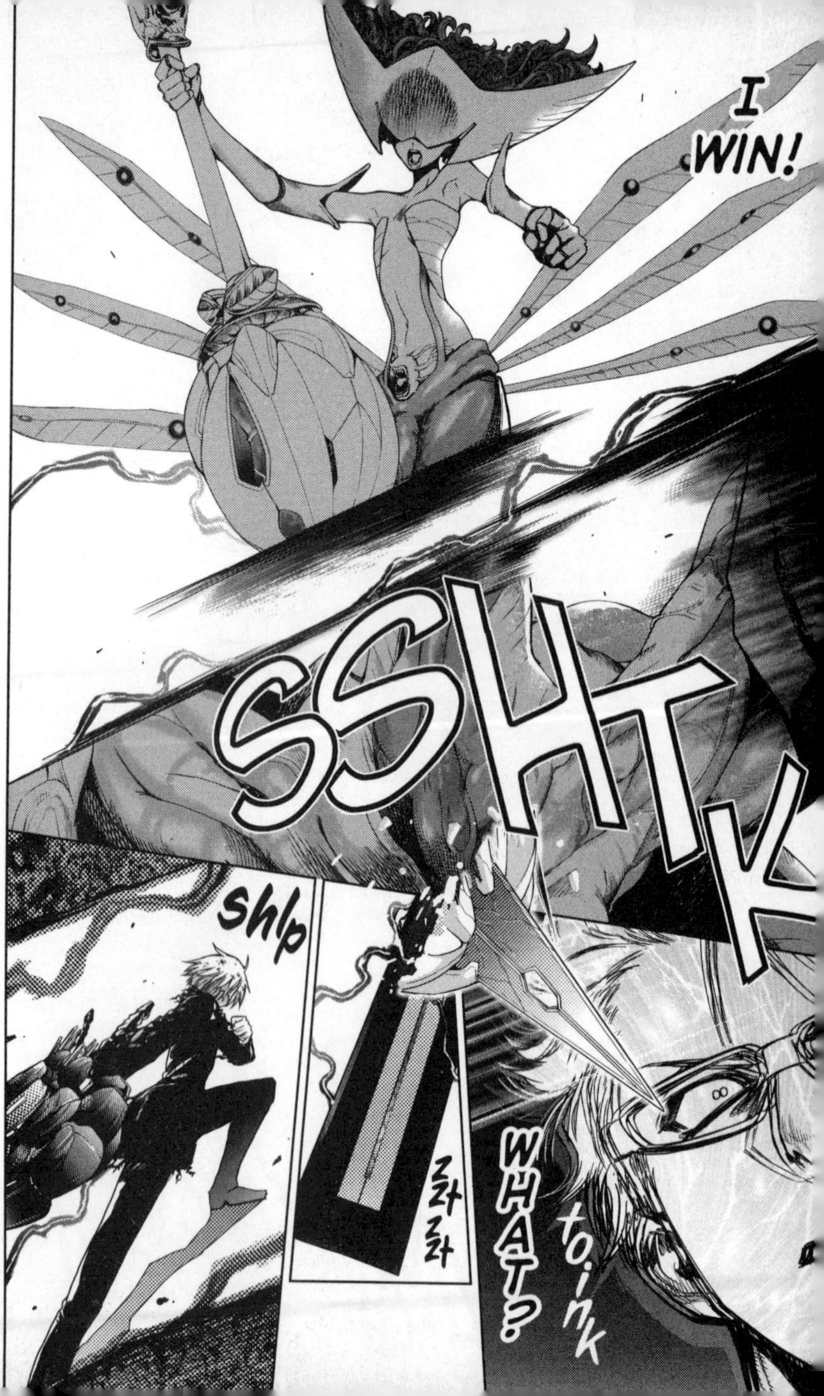
I WIN!
SSHTK
toink
WHAT?
zzt zzt
shlp

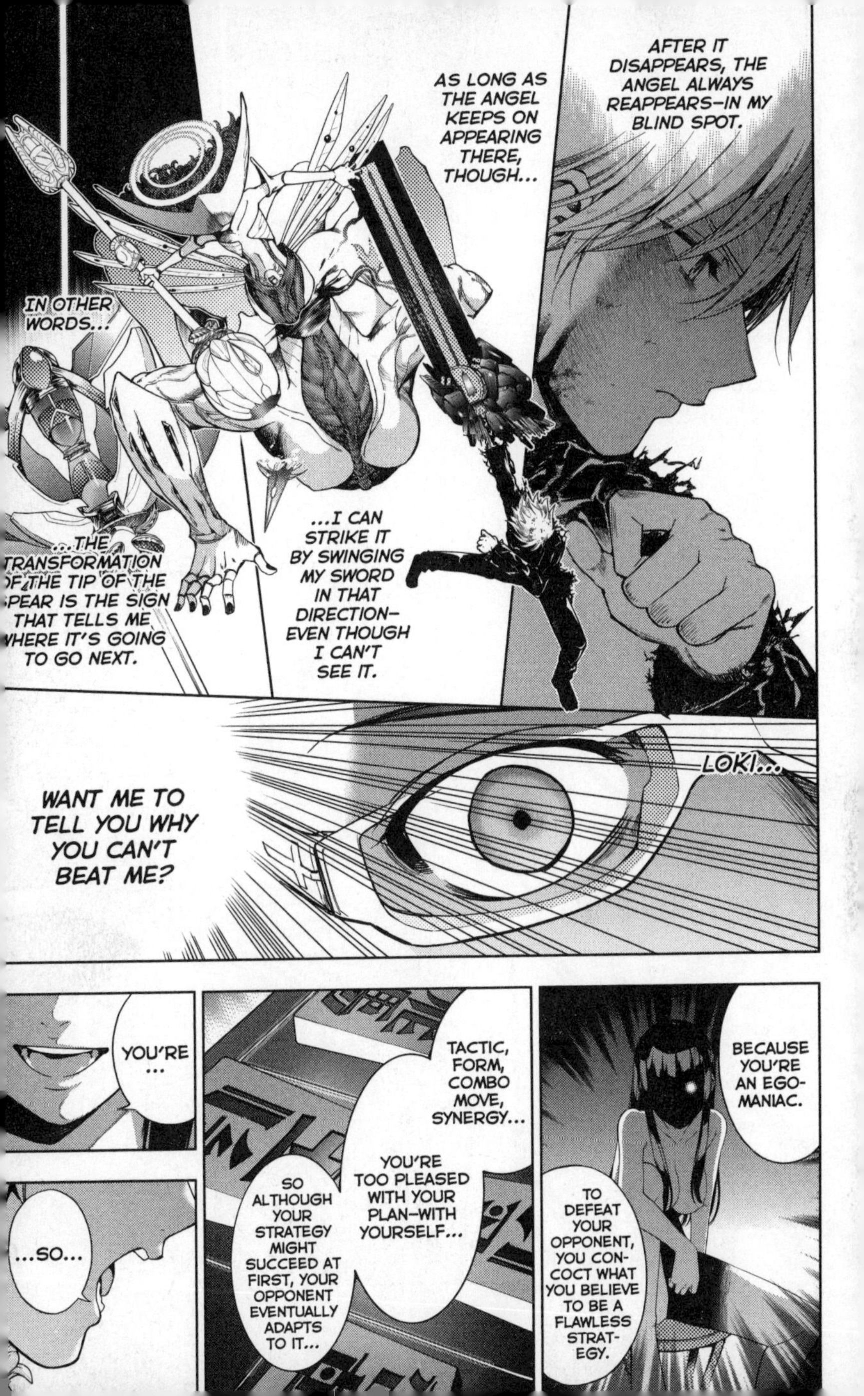
AFTER IT DISAPPEARS, THE ANGEL ALWAYS REAPPEARS—IN MY BLIND SPOT.
AS LONG AS THE ANGEL KEEPS ON APPEARING THERE, THOUGH...
...I CAN STRIKE IT BY SWINGING MY SWORD IN THAT DIRECTION—EVEN THOUGH I CAN'T SEE IT.
IN OTHER WORDS...
...THE TRANSFORMATION OF THE TIP OF THE SPEAR IS THE SIGN THAT TELLS ME WHERE IT'S GOING TO GO NEXT.
LOKI...
WANT ME TO TELL YOU WHY YOU CAN'T BEAT ME?
BECAUSE YOU'RE AN EGO-MANIAC.
TO DEFEAT YOUR OPPONENT, YOU CON-COCT WHAT YOU BELIEVE TO BE A FLAWLESS STRAT-EGY.
TACTIC, FORM, COMBO MOVE, SYNERGY...
YOU'RE TOO PLEASED WITH YOUR PLAN—WITH YOURSELF...
SO ALTHOUGH YOUR STRATEGY MIGHT SUCCEED AT FIRST, YOUR OPPONENT EVENTUALLY ADAPTS TO IT...
YOU'RE...
...SO...

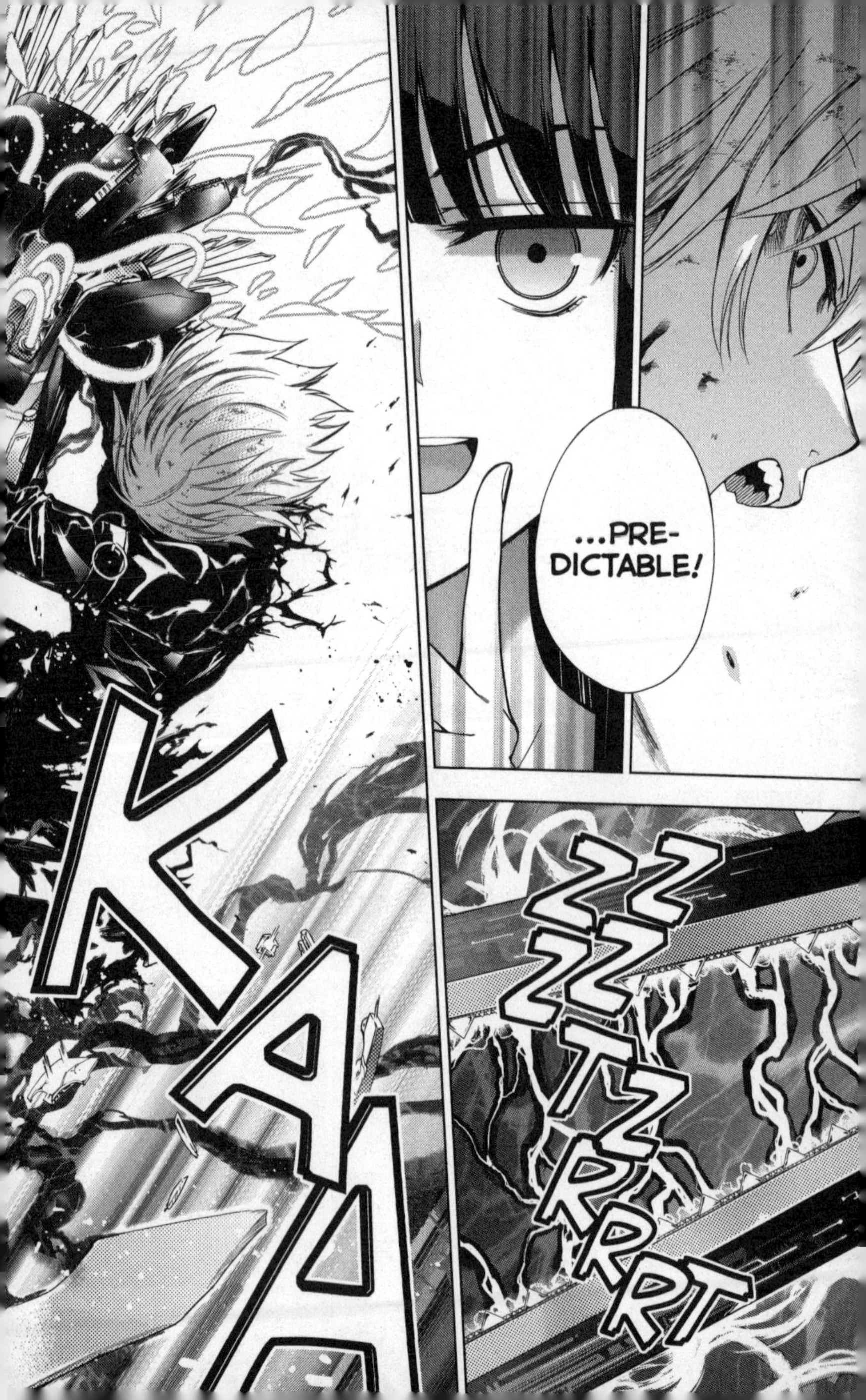
...PRE-
DICTABLE!
ZZZZTZZRRRRT
KA

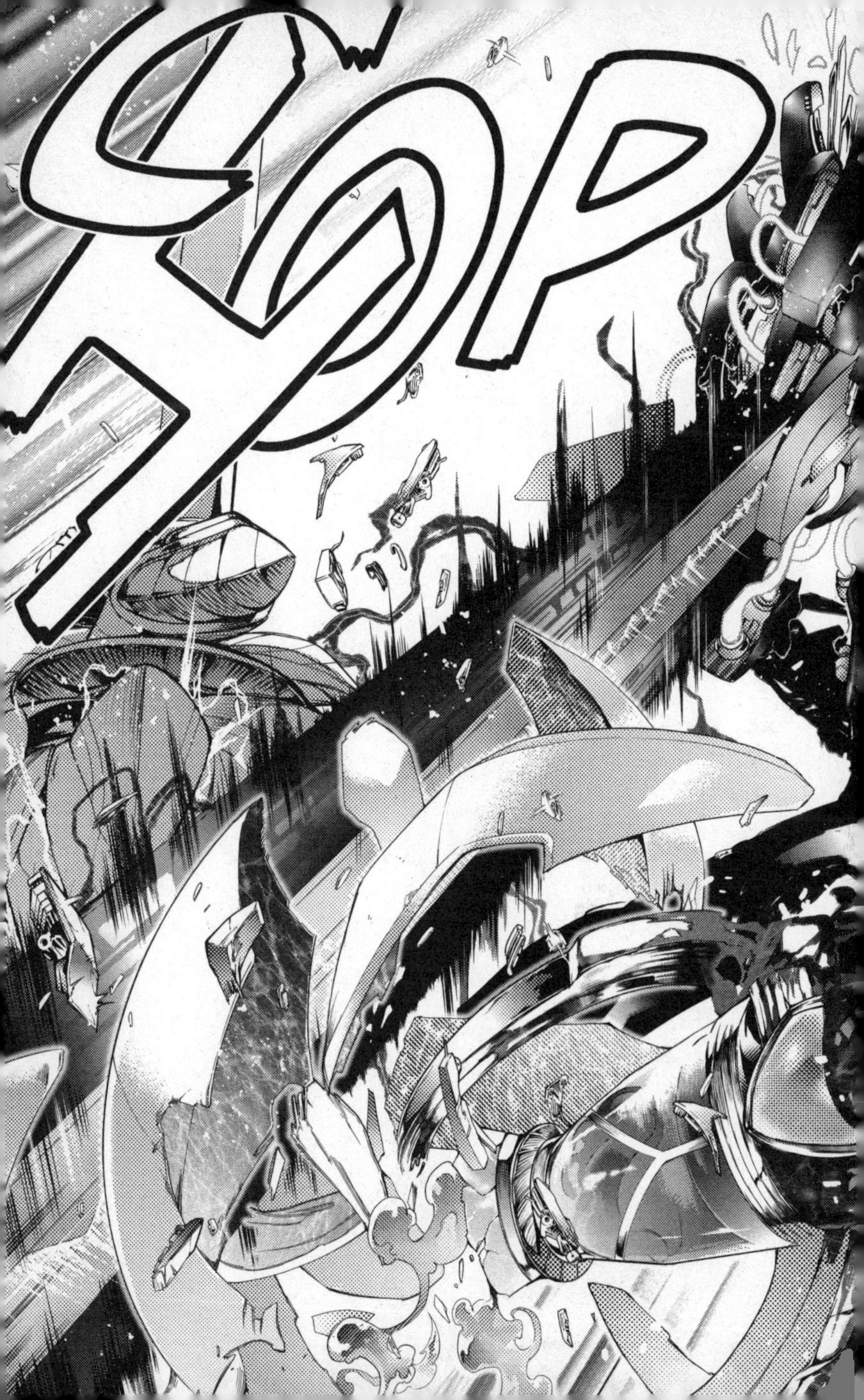

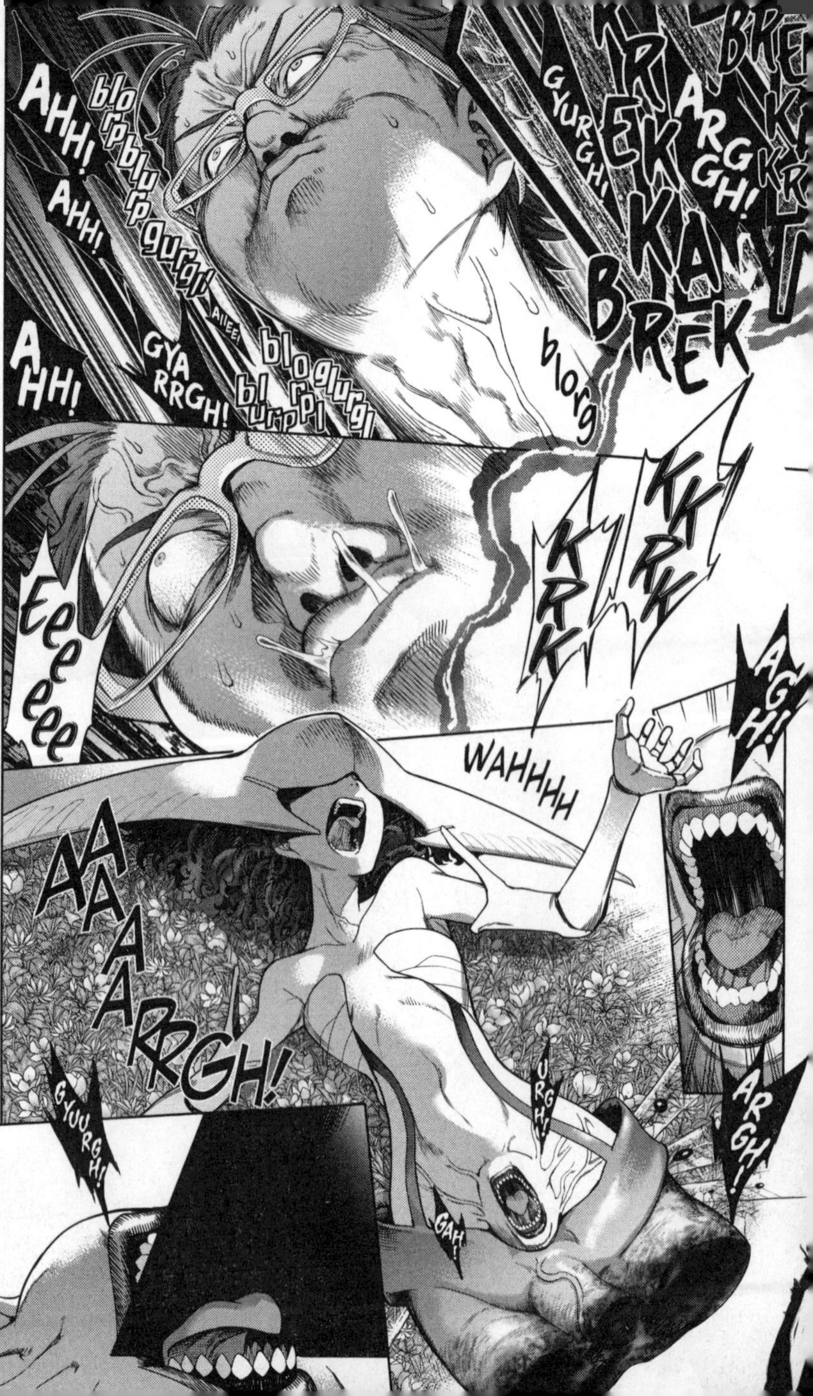

ARGGH!
GYURGH!
BREK
blorg
AHH!
blorpblurp
gurgl
AHH!
AIIEE!
GYARRGH!
AHH!
blogurgl
blurrpl
KRK
KKRK
eeeeeee
AGH!
WAHHHH
AAAARRGH!
ARGH!
URGH!
GAH!
GYUURGH!

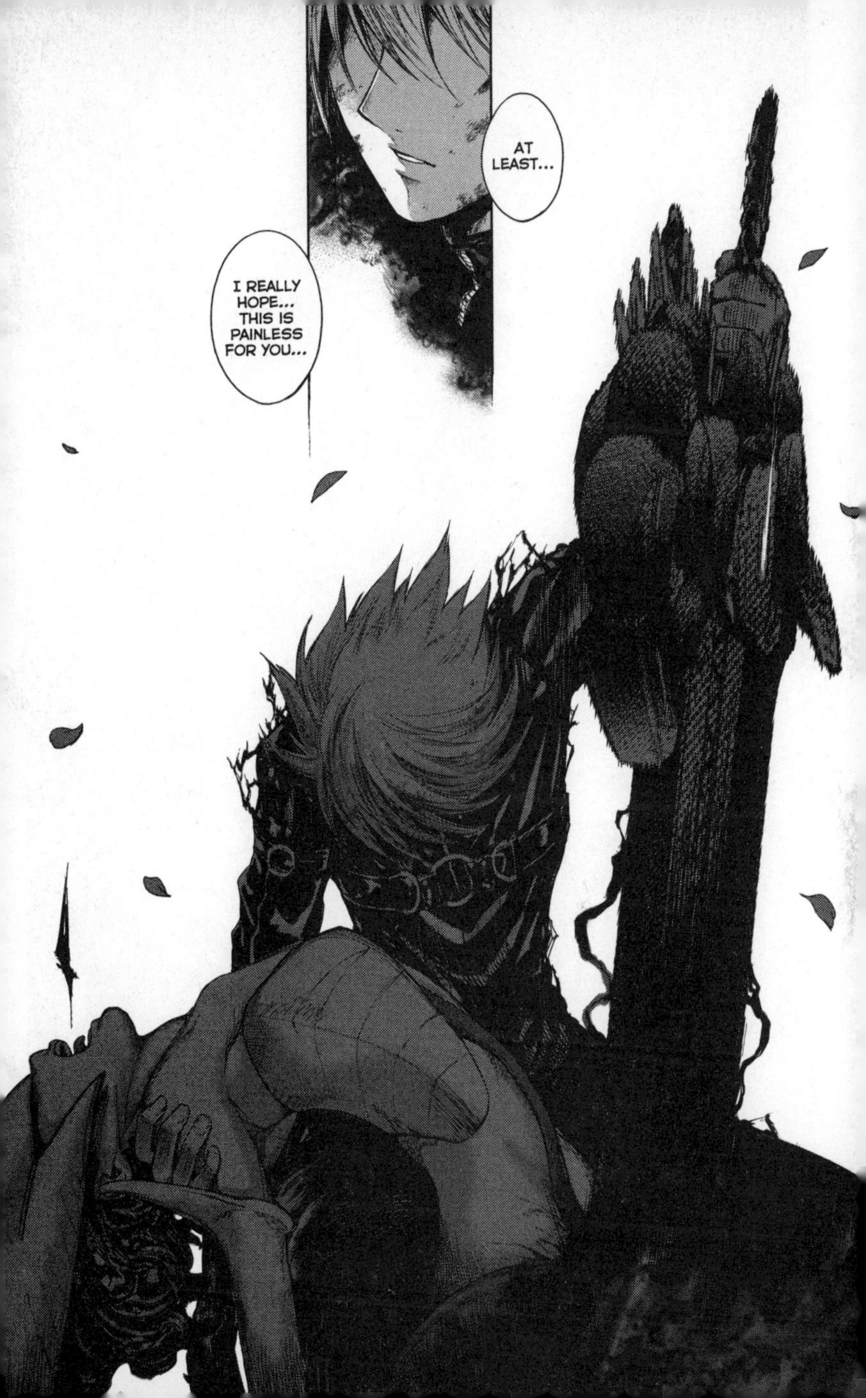
AT LEAST...
I REALLY HOPE... THIS IS PAINLESS FOR YOU...

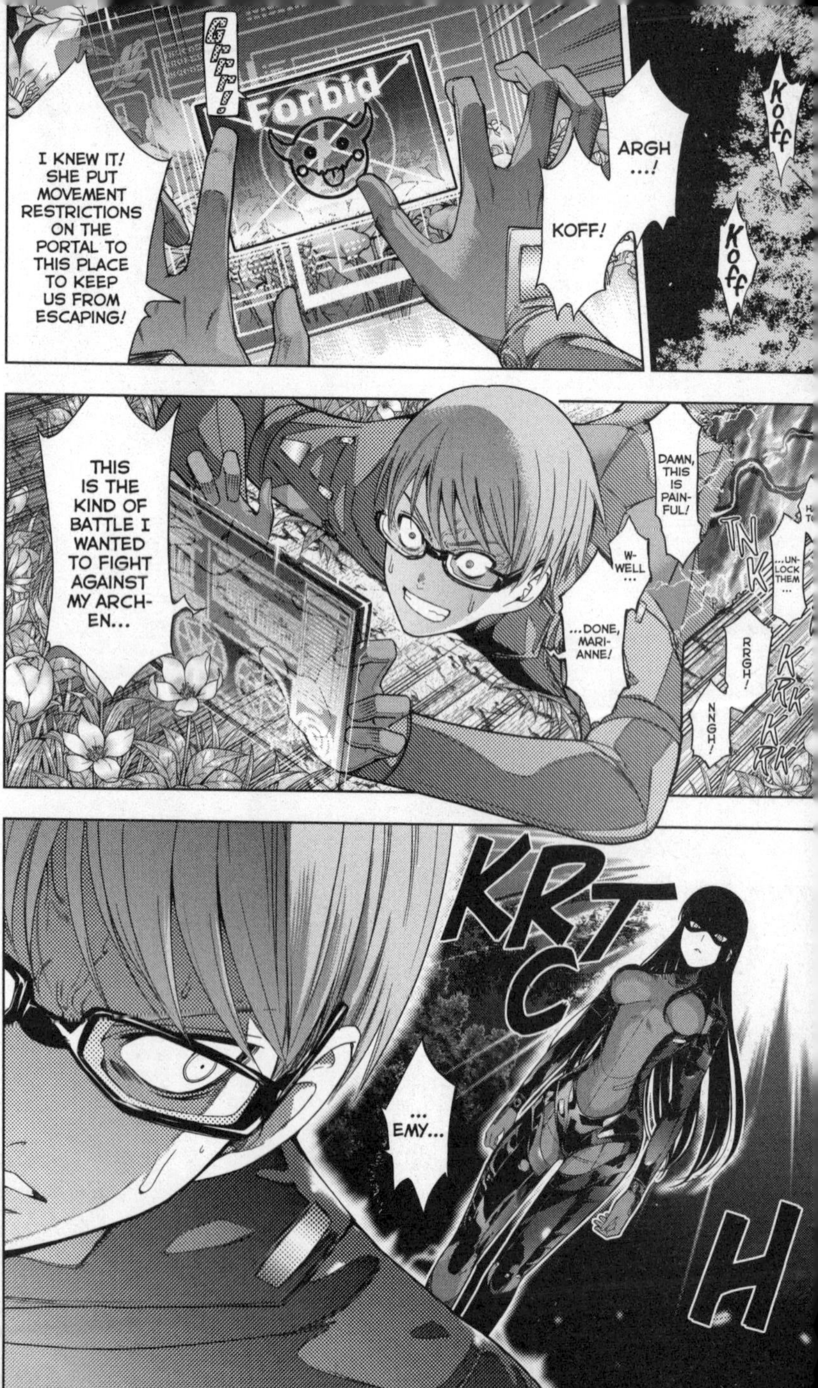
Koff
Koff
ARGH ...!
KOFF!
Grrr!
Forbid
I KNEW IT! SHE PUT MOVEMENT RESTRICTIONS ON THE PORTAL TO THIS PLACE TO KEEP US FROM ESCAPING!
...UN-LOCK THEM...
TNK
DAMN, THIS IS PAIN-FUL!
RRGH!
NNGH!
KRK KRK
W-WELL...
...DONE, MARI-ANNE!
THIS IS THE KIND OF BATTLE I WANTED TO FIGHT AGAINST MY ARCH-EN...
KRTCH
...EMY...

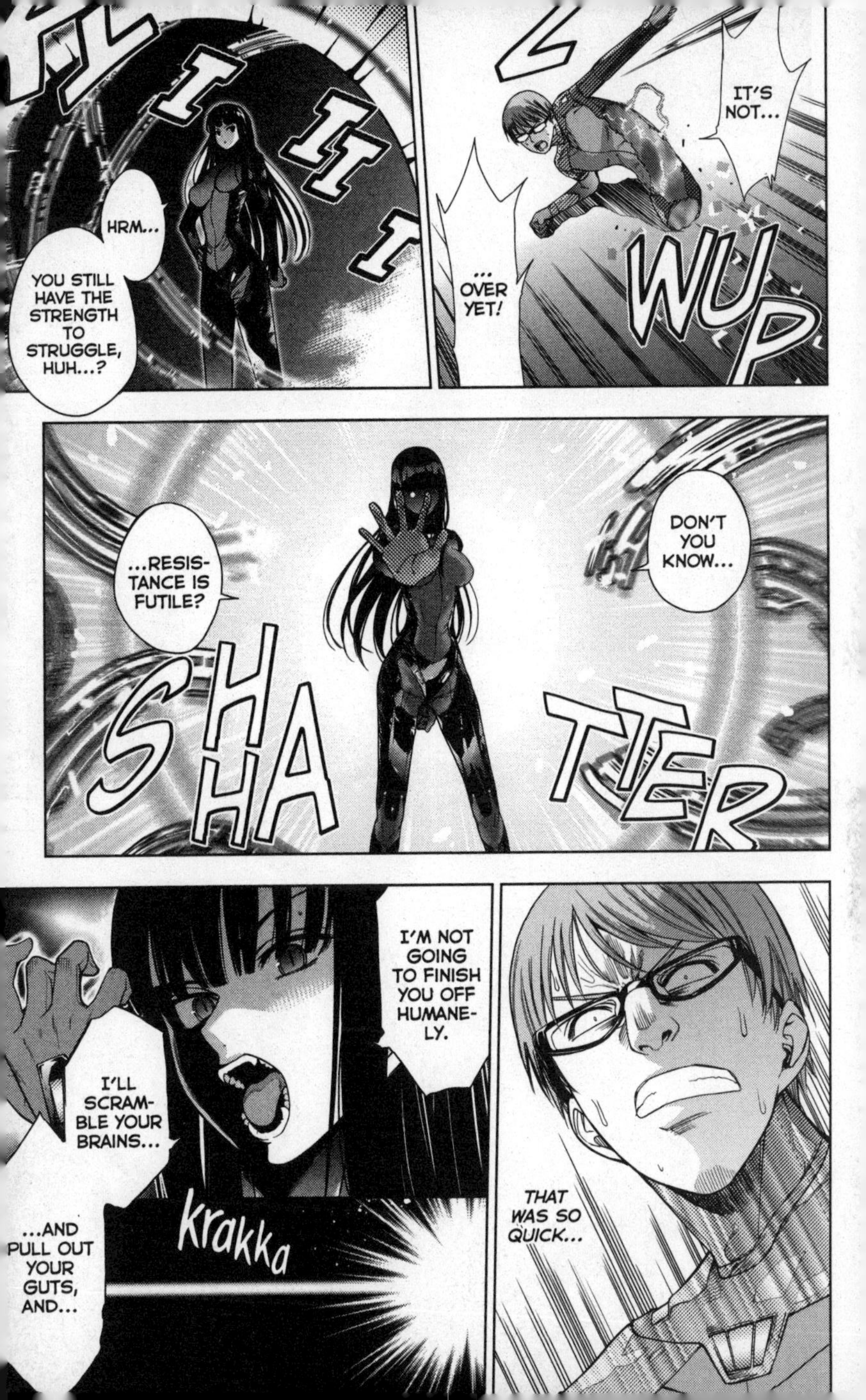
IT'S NOT...
...OVER YET!
WUP
HRM...
YOU STILL HAVE THE STRENGTH TO STRUGGLE, HUH...?
DON'T YOU KNOW...
...RESIS-TANCE IS FUTILE?
SHAHATTER
THAT WAS SO QUICK...
I'M NOT GOING TO FINISH YOU OFF HUMANE-LY.
I'LL SCRAM-BLE YOUR BRAINS...
...AND PULL OUT YOUR GUTS, AND...
krakka

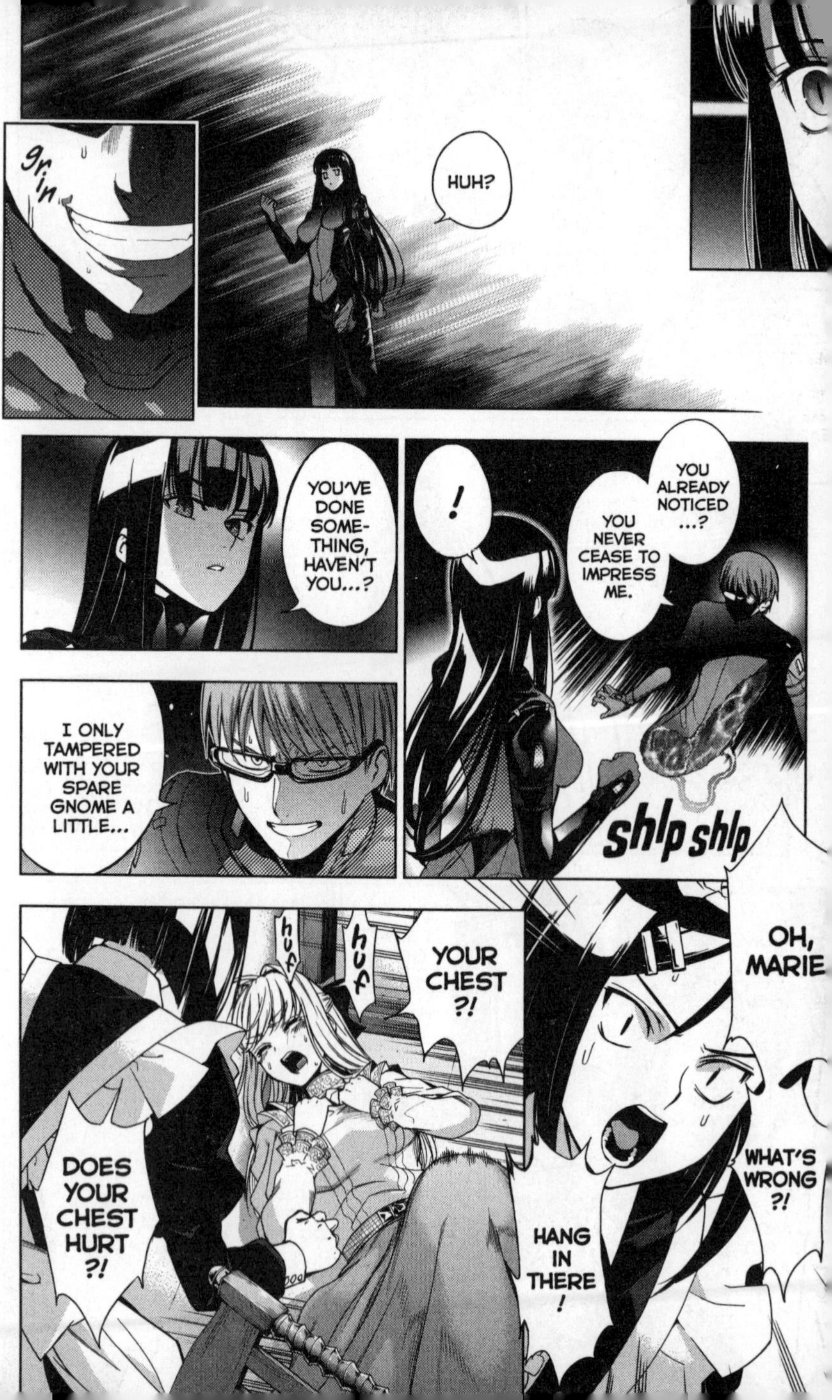
HUH?
grin
YOU ALREADY NOTICED...?
YOU NEVER CEASE TO IMPRESS ME.
!
shlp shlp
YOU'VE DONE SOME-THING, HAVEN'T YOU...?
I ONLY TAMPERED WITH YOUR SPARE GNOME A LITTLE...
OH, MARIE
WHAT'S WRONG?!
HANG IN THERE!
YOUR CHEST?!
huf huf
DOES YOUR CHEST HURT?!

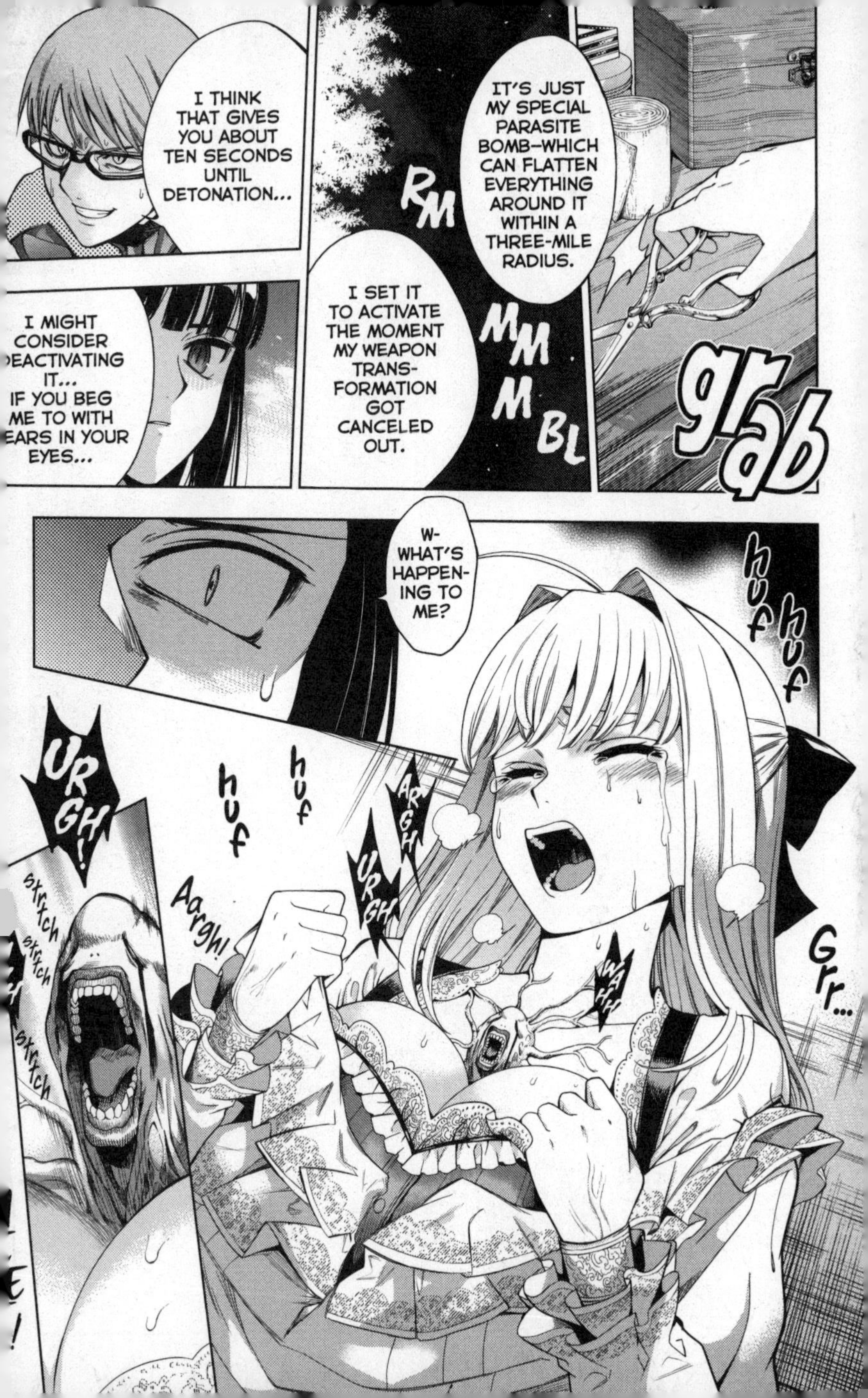
grab
IT'S JUST MY SPECIAL PARASITE BOMB—WHICH CAN FLATTEN EVERYTHING AROUND IT WITHIN A THREE-MILE RADIUS.
RMMMMBL
I SET IT TO ACTIVATE THE MOMENT MY WEAPON TRANS-FORMATION GOT CANCELED OUT.
I THINK THAT GIVES YOU ABOUT TEN SECONDS UNTIL DETONATION...
I MIGHT CONSIDER EACTIVATING IT... IF YOU BEG ME TO WITH EARS IN YOUR EYES...
huf huf huf
W-WHAT'S HAPPEN-ING TO ME?
Grr...
WAHH
ARGH
URGH
huf huf
Aargh!
URGH!
strtch strtch strtch

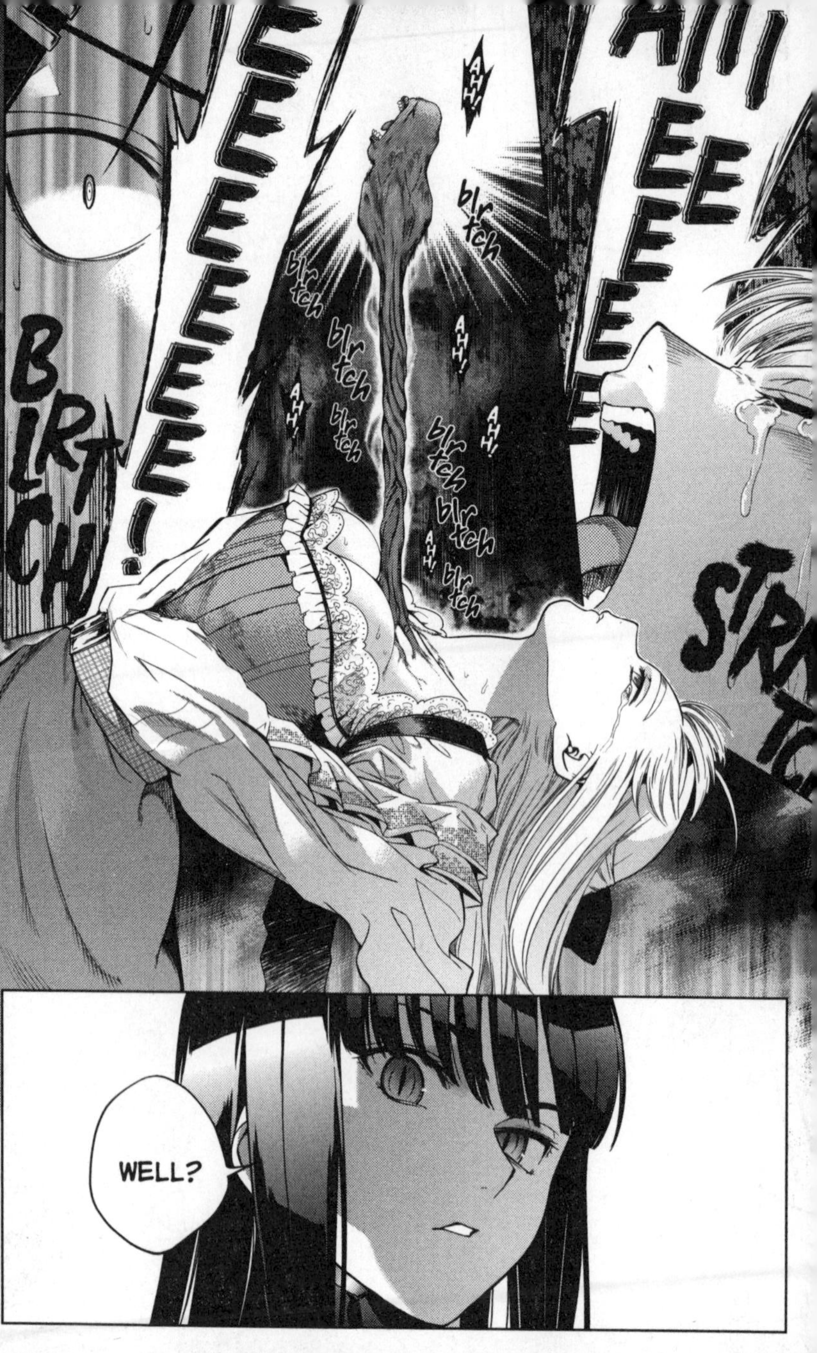

AIII EEEEEE
AHH!
blrtch
AHH!
blrtch
AHH!
blrtch
blrtch
AHH!
blrtch
blrtch
AHH!
blrtch
blrtch
EEEEEEEEEEE!
BLRTCH
WELL?

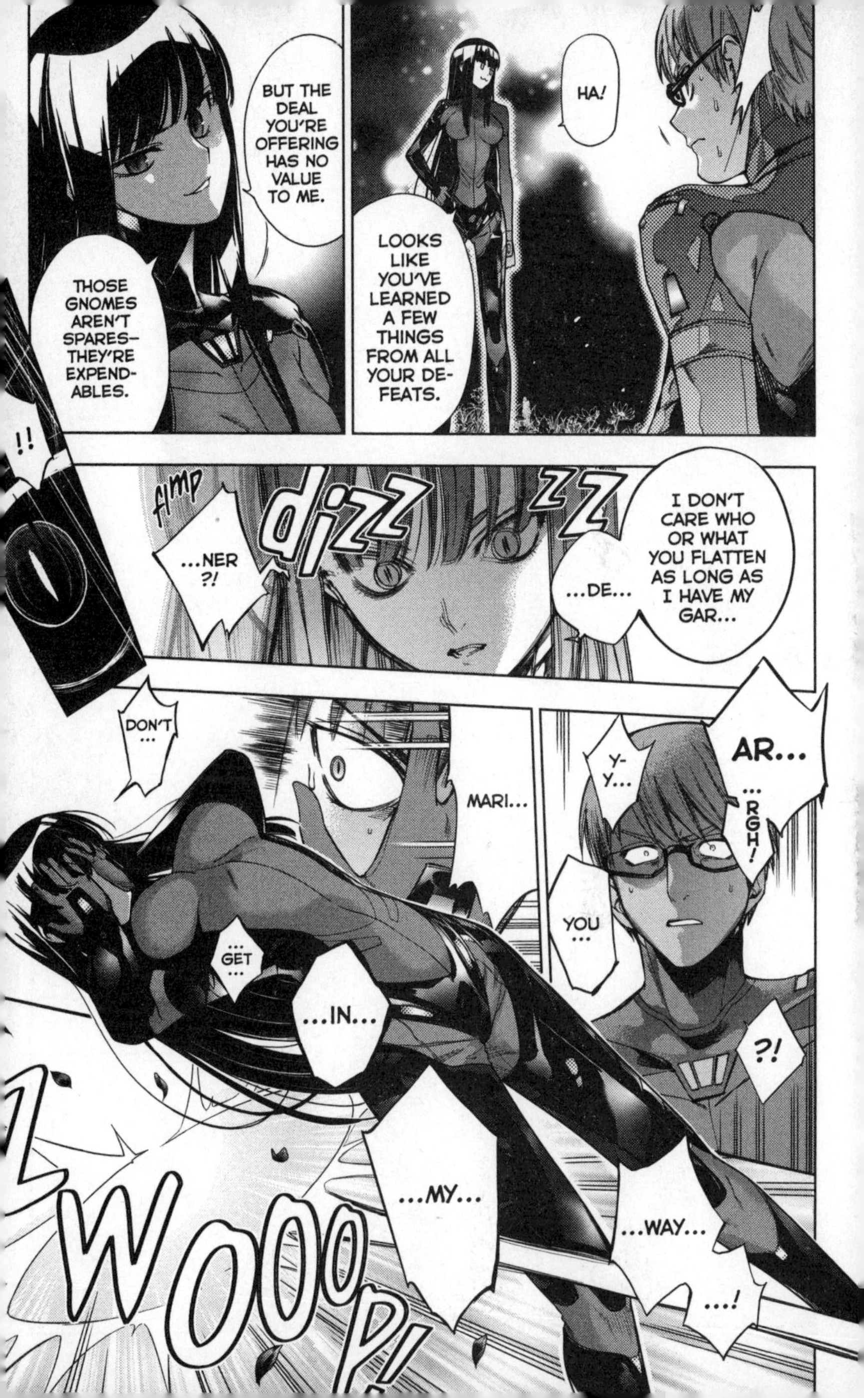
HA!
LOOKS LIKE YOU'VE LEARNED A FEW THINGS FROM ALL YOUR DE-FEATS.
BUT THE DEAL YOU'RE OFFERING HAS NO VALUE TO ME.
THOSE GNOMES AREN'T SPARES—THEY'RE EXPEND-ABLES.
I DON'T CARE WHO OR WHAT YOU FLATTEN AS LONG AS I HAVE MY GAR...
...DE...
dizzZZ
...NER ?!
flimp
!!
AR... ...RGH!
Y-Y...
YOU...
?!
...!
MARI...
DON'T...
...GET...
...IN...
...MY...
...WAY...
WOOOP!

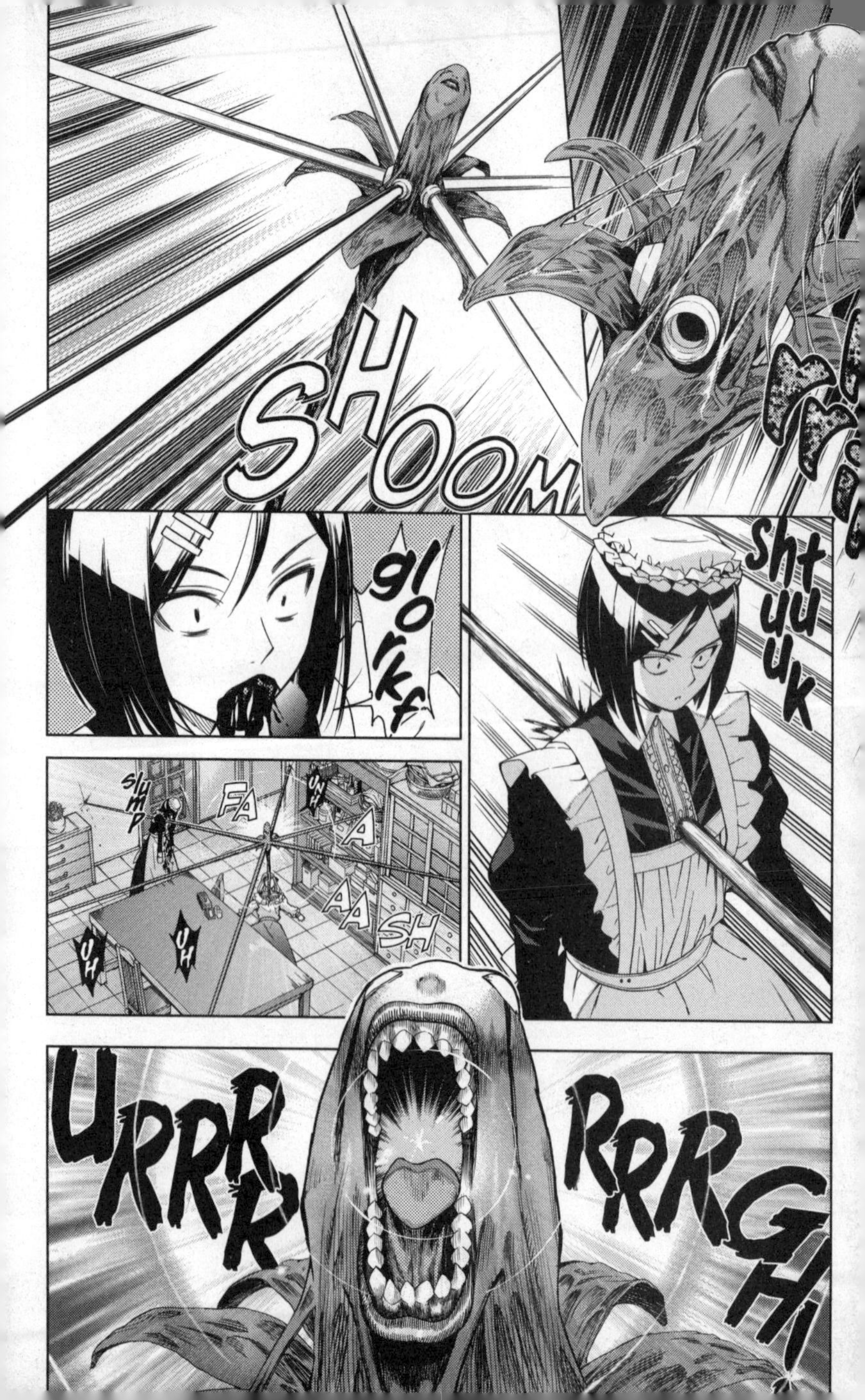
SHOOM
Shtuuuk
glorkf
UNH
FAAAASH
slump
UH
UH
URRRRRRRRRGH

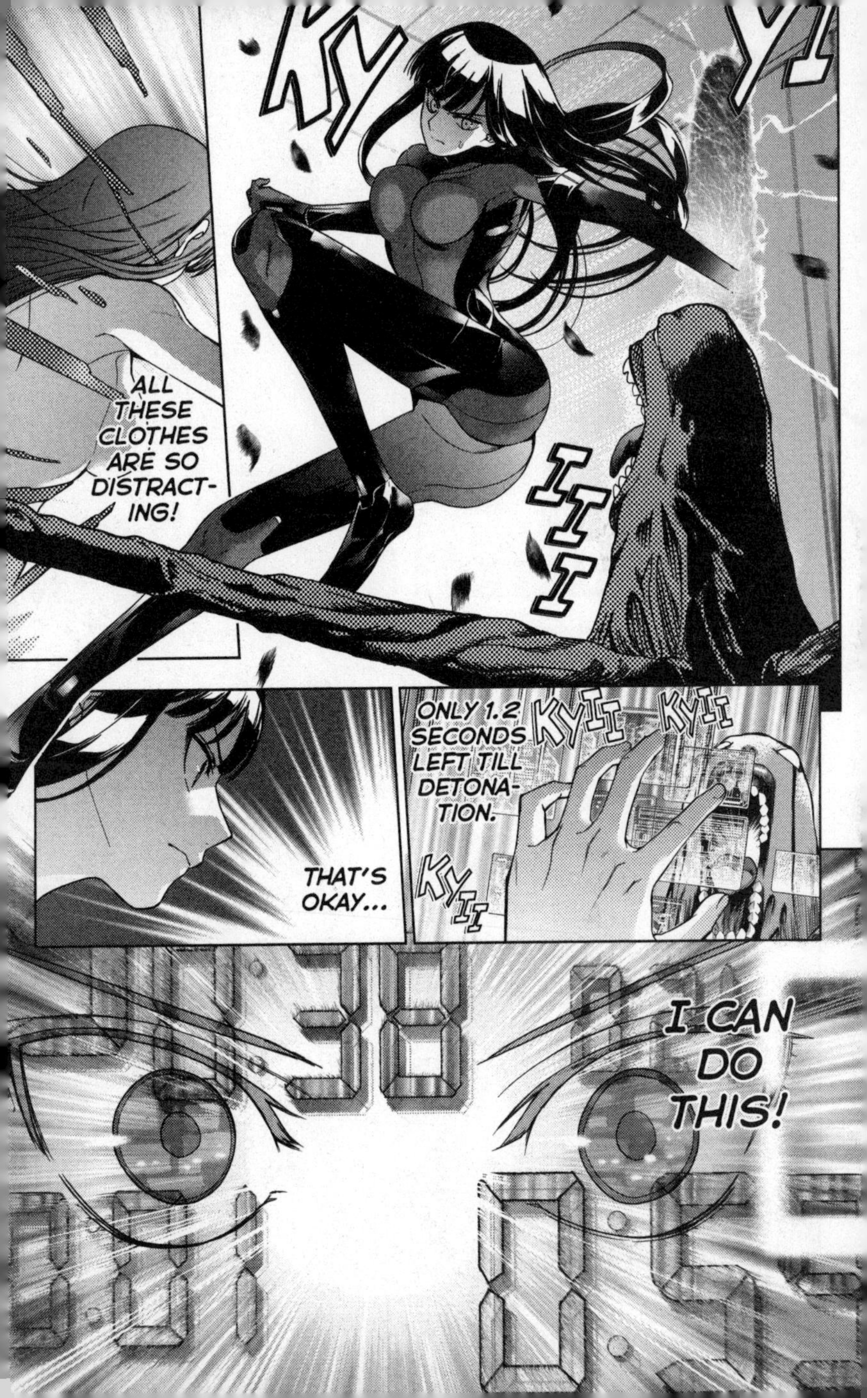
KY
YI
III
ALL THESE CLOTHES ARE SO DISTRACT-ING!
ONLY 1.2 SECONDS LEFT TILL DETONA-TION.
KYII
KYII
KYII
THAT'S OKAY...
I CAN DO THIS!

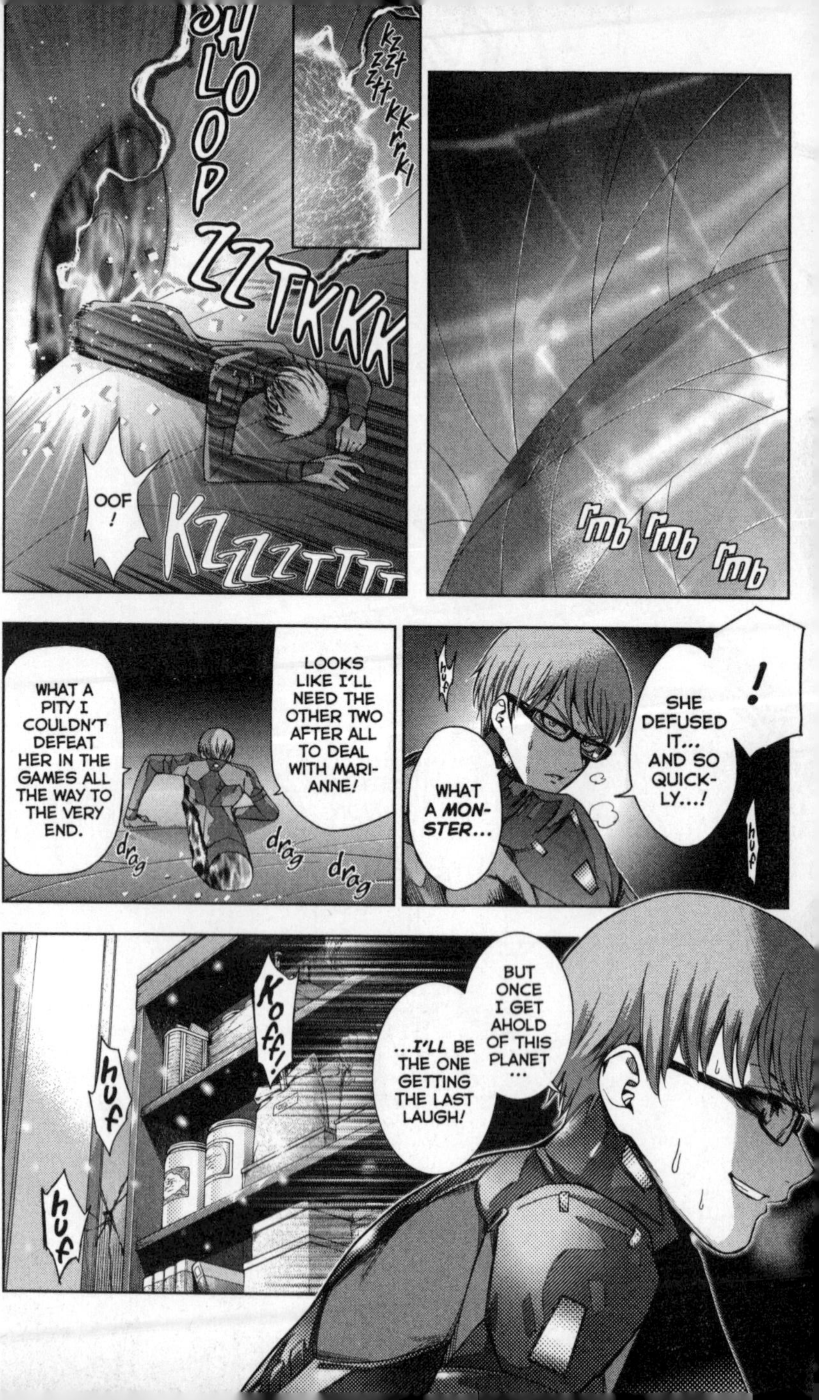
rmb rmb rmb
kzzt zzt zzt kkrrrkl
SHLOOP
ZZTKKK
KZZZZTTTTT
OOF!
!
huf
SHE DEFUSED IT... AND SO QUICKLY...!
huf
WHAT A *MONSTER*...
LOOKS LIKE I'LL NEED THE OTHER TWO AFTER ALL TO DEAL WITH MARIANNE!
WHAT A PITY I COULDN'T DEFEAT HER IN THE GAMES ALL THE WAY TO THE VERY END.
drag drag drag
BUT ONCE I GET AHOLD OF THIS PLANET...
...*I'LL* BE THE ONE GETTING THE LAST LAUGH!
Koff!
huf
huf

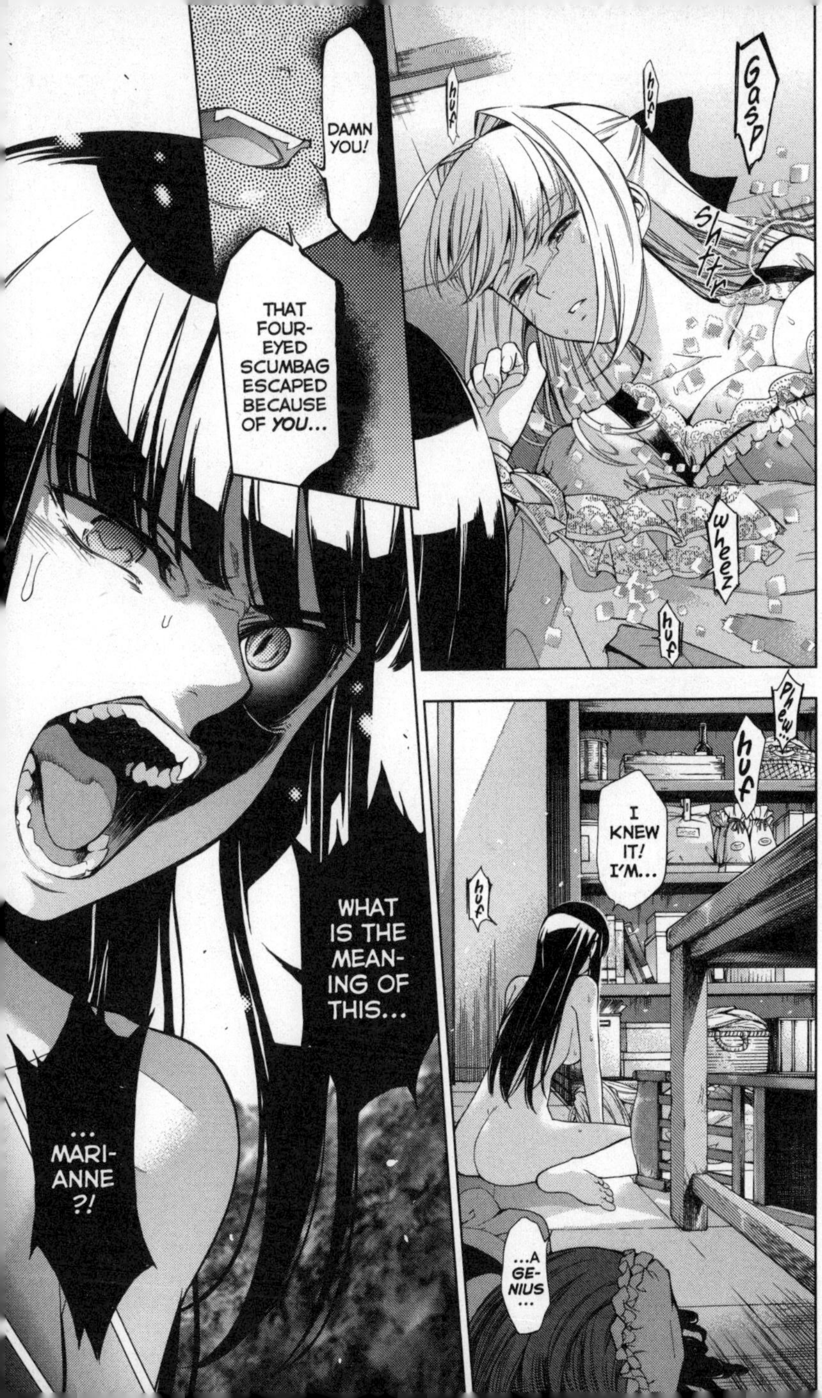
Gasp
huf
Shttr
wheez
huf
Phew...
huf
I KNEW IT! I'M...
huf
...A GENIUS...
DAMN YOU!
THAT FOUR-EYED SCUMBAG ESCAPED BECAUSE OF YOU...
WHAT IS THE MEANING OF THIS...
...MARIANNE?!

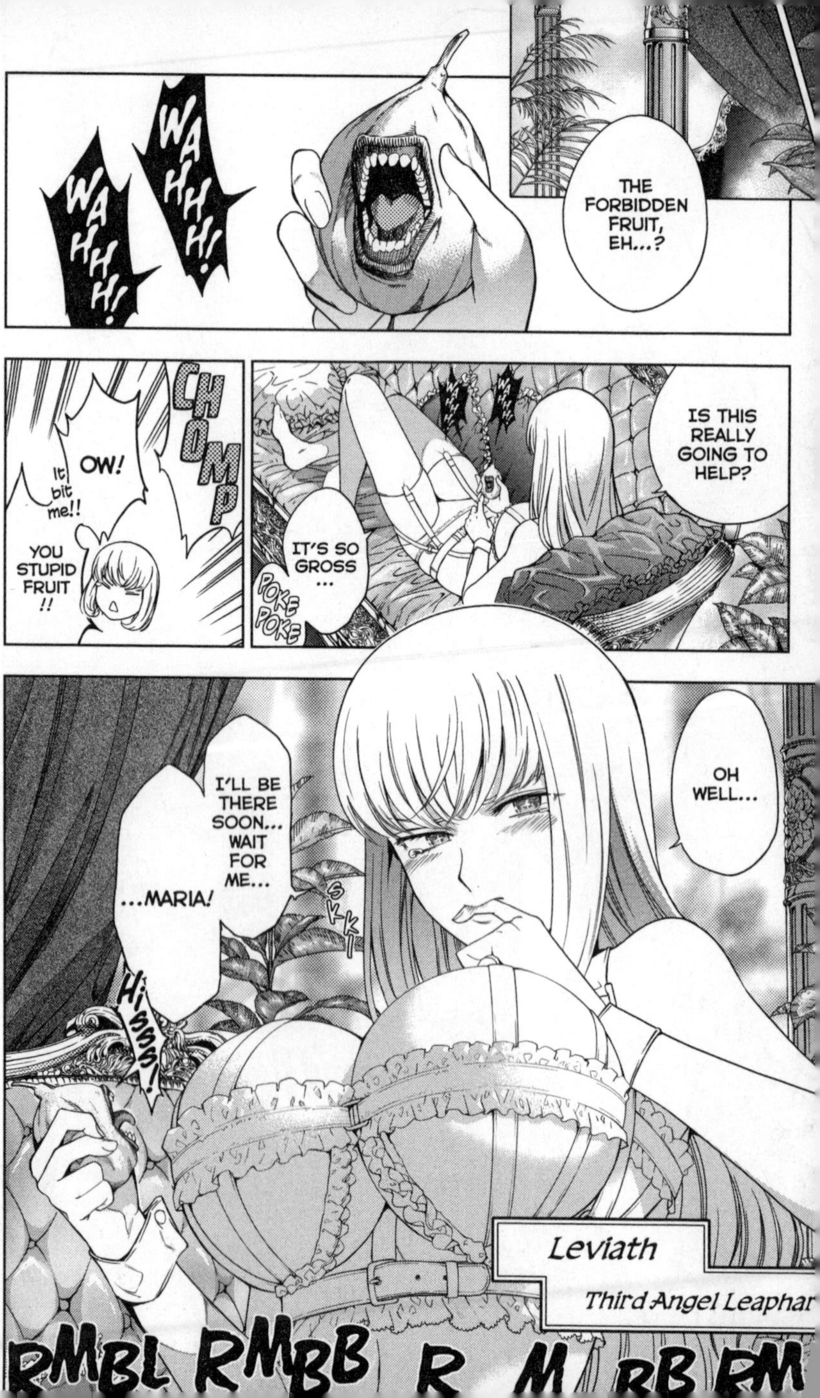
THE FORBIDDEN FRUIT, EH...?
WAHHH!
WAHHH!
IS THIS REALLY GOING TO HELP?
IT'S SO GROSS ...
POKE POKE
CHOMP
OW!
It bit me!!
YOU STUPID FRUIT !!
OH WELL...
I'LL BE THERE SOON... WAIT FOR ME...
...MARIA!
SKKI
HISSS!
Leviath
Third Angel Leaphar
RMBL RMBB R M RB RM

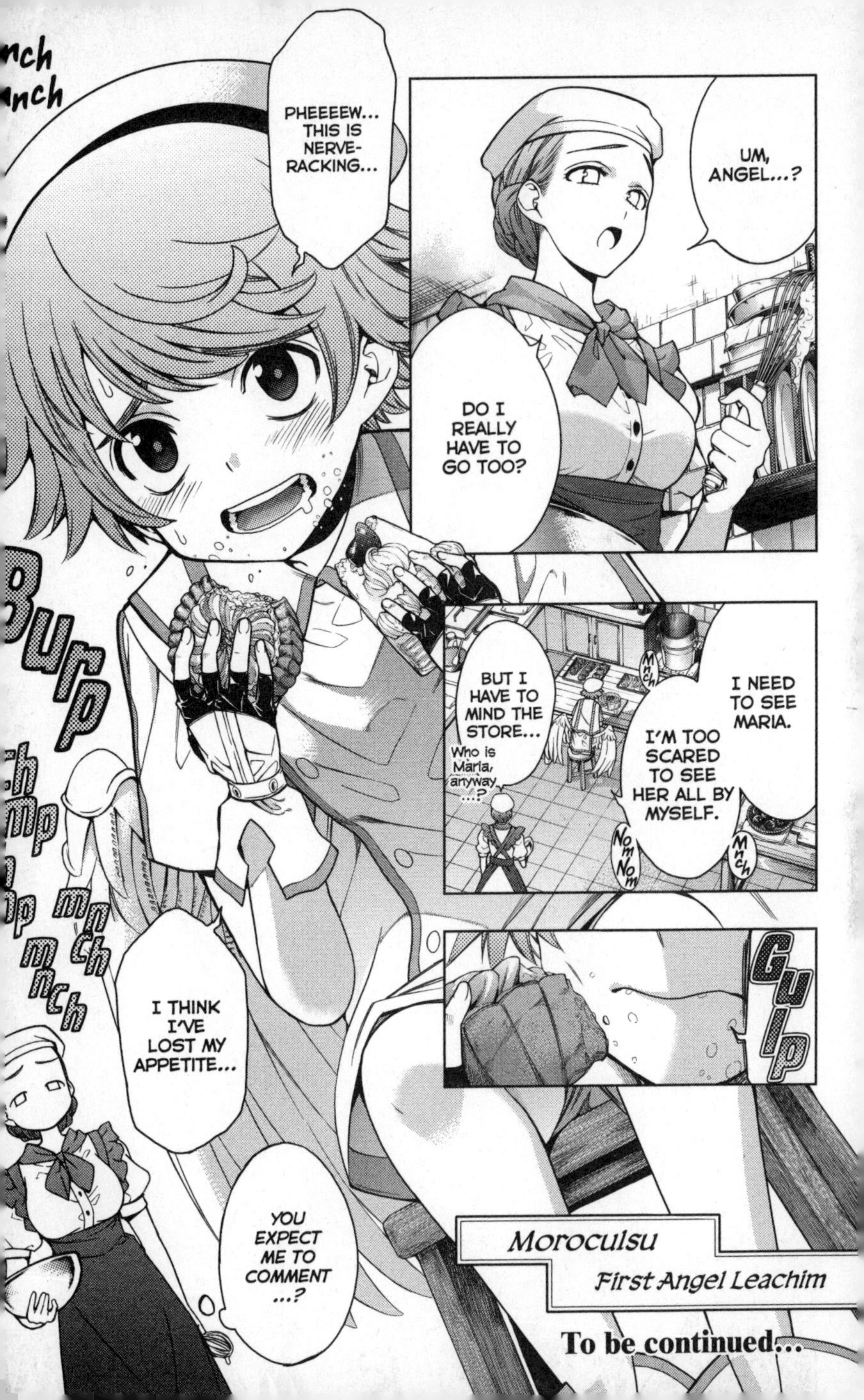
UM, ANGEL...?
DO I REALLY HAVE TO GO TOO?
I NEED TO SEE MARIA.
Mnch
I'M TOO SCARED TO SEE HER ALL BY MYSELF.
Mnch
Nom Nom
BUT I HAVE TO MIND THE STORE...
Who is Maria, anyway ...?
Gulp
Moroculsu
First Angel Leachim
To be continued...
nch
nch
PHEEEEW... THIS IS NERVE-RACKING...
Burp
mnch
mnch
I THINK I'VE LOST MY APPETITE...
YOU EXPECT ME TO COMMENT ...?

Mitsu Izumi

Mysterious manga creator Mitsu Izumi was born on February 7 in Kanagawa Prefecture and is the creator of the manga adaptation of *Anohana: The Flower We Saw That Day*, originally serialized in *Jump SQ*.

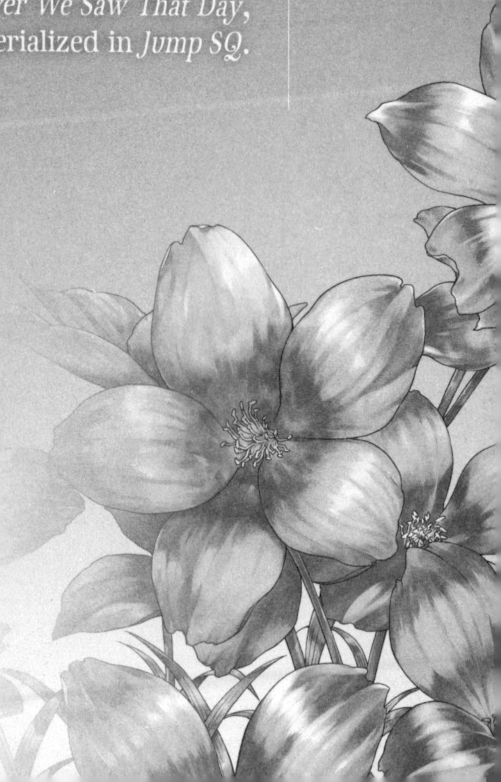

You choose.

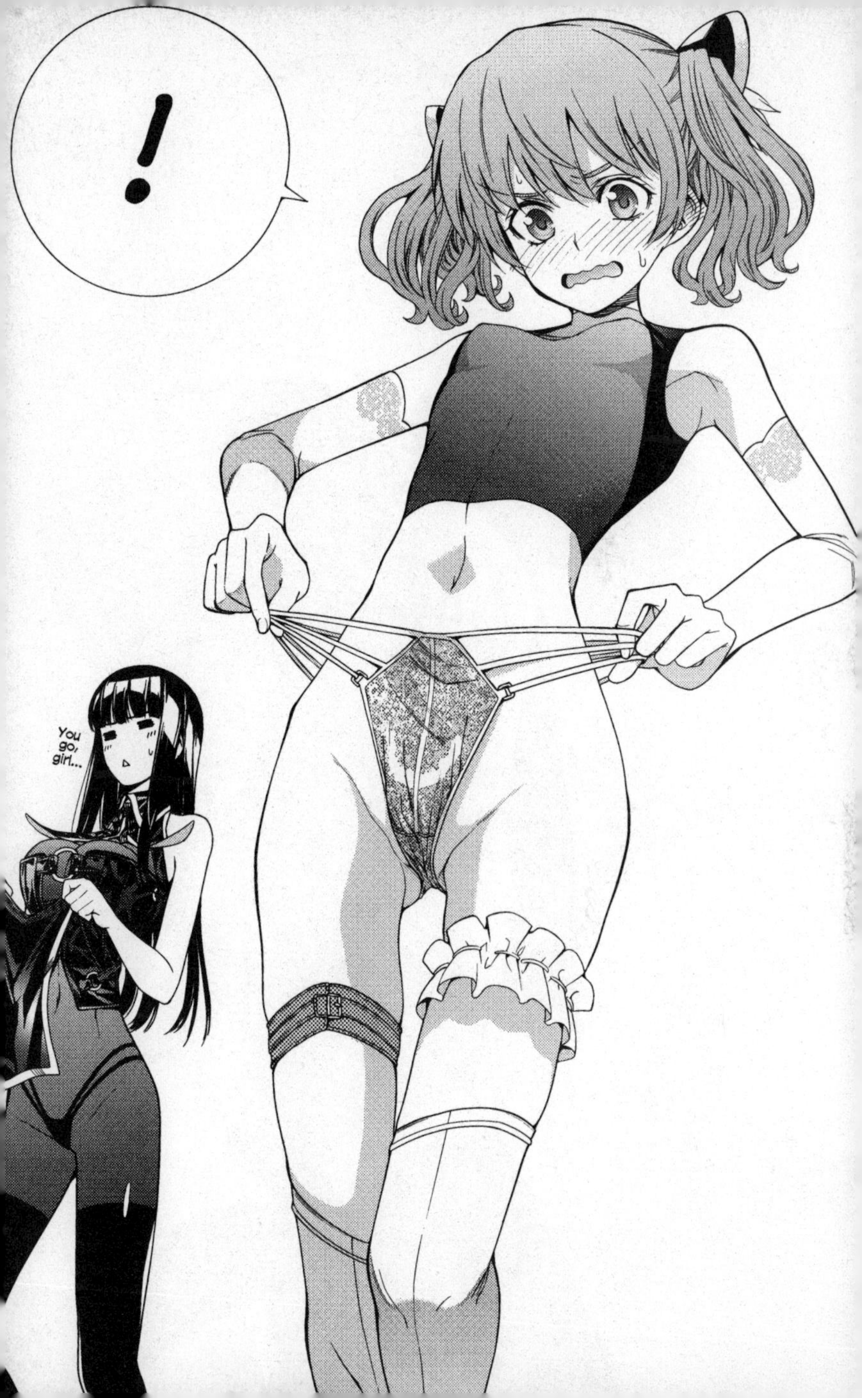
!
You go, girl...

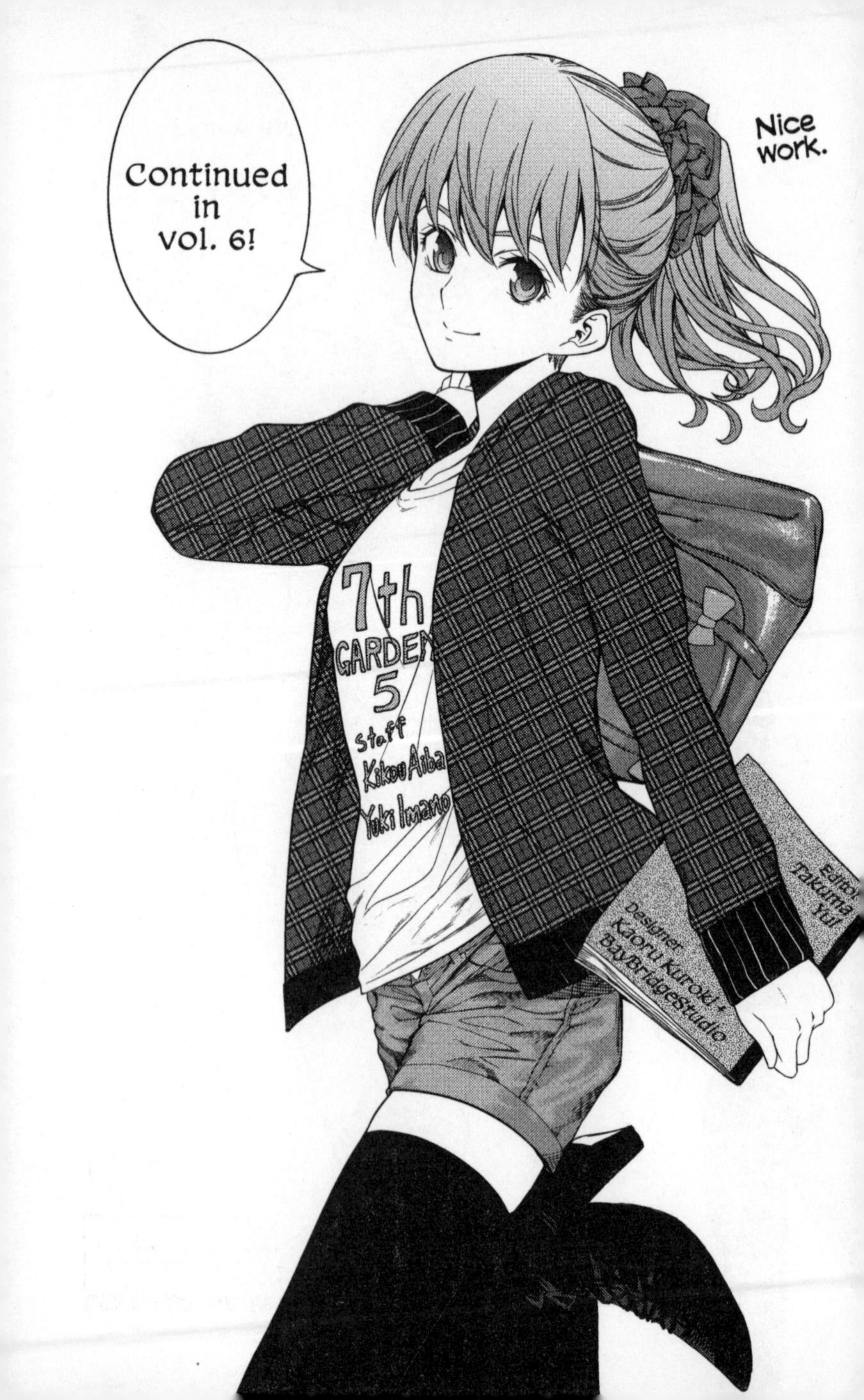
Nice work.
Continued in vol. 6!
7th GARDEN 5
staff
Kikou Aiba
Yuki Imano
Editor Takuma Yui
Designer Kaoru Kuroki + BayBridgeStudio

7thGARDEN
5

SHONEN JUMP Manga Edition

Story and Art by Mitsu Izumi

Translation/Tetsuichiro Miyaki
English Adaptation/Annette Roman
Touch-Up Art & Lettering/Susan Daigle-Leach
Cover & Interior Design/Izumi Evers
Editor/Annette Roman

Published by VIZ Media, LLC
P.O. Box 77010
San Francisco, CA 94107

10 9 8 7 6 5 4 3 2 1
First printing, July 2017

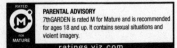

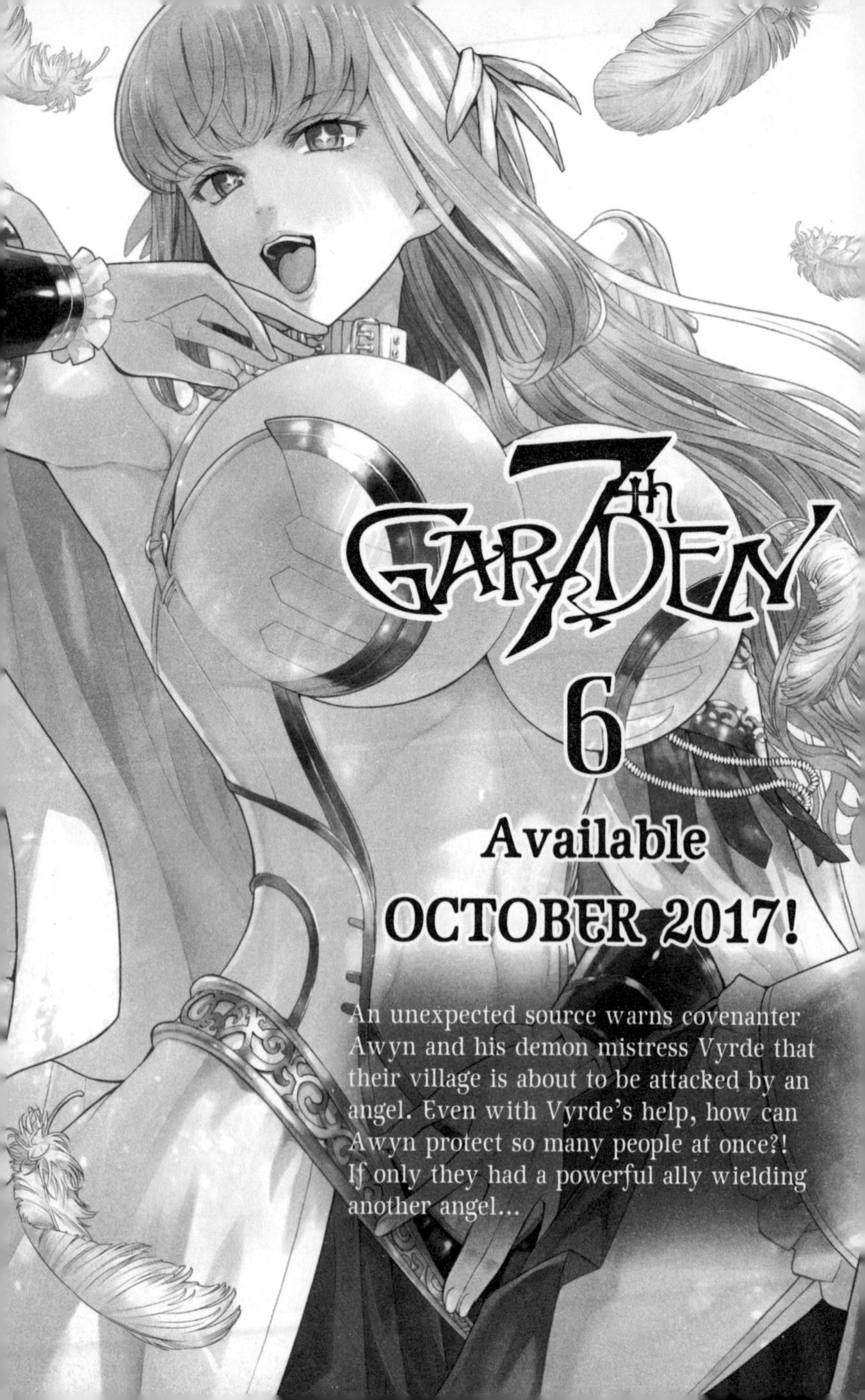
7th GARDEN
6
Available
OCTOBER 2017!
An unexpected source warns covenanter Awyn and his demon mistress Vyrde that their village is about to be attacked by an angel. Even with Vyrde's help, how can Awyn protect so many people at once?! If only they had a powerful ally wielding another angel...

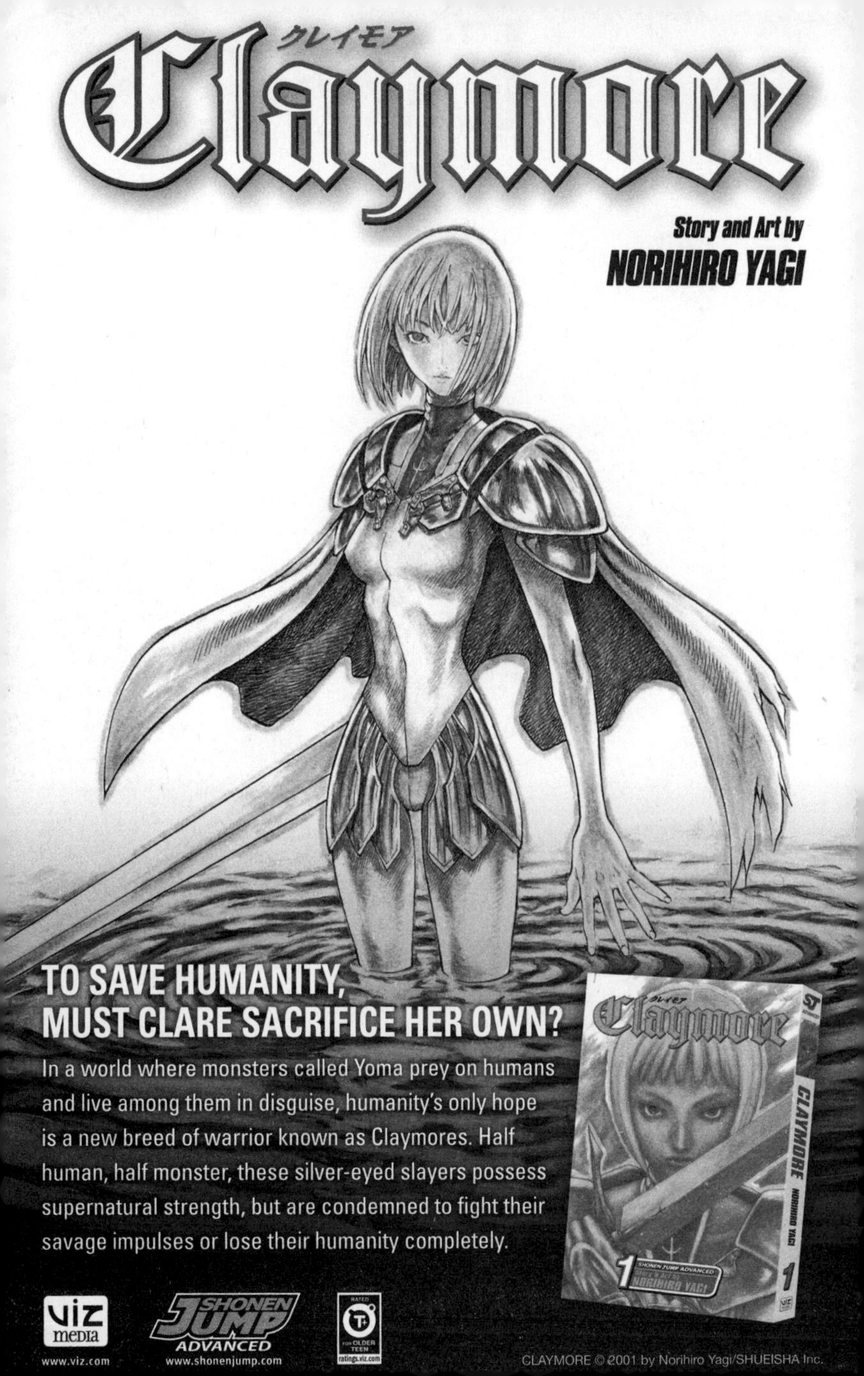
クレイモア
Claymore
Story and Art by
NORIHIRO YAGI
TO SAVE HUMANITY,
MUST CLARE SACRIFICE HER OWN?
In a world where monsters called Yoma prey on humans and live among them in disguise, humanity's only hope is a new breed of warrior known as Claymores. Half human, half monster, these silver-eyed slayers possess supernatural strength, but are condemned to fight their savage impulses or lose their humanity completely.
CLAYMORE
NORIHIRO YAGI
1
SHONEN JUMP ADVANCED
viz media
www.viz.com
SHONEN JUMP ADVANCED
www.shonenjump.com
RATED T+ FOR OLDER TEEN
ratings.viz.com
CLAYMORE © 2001 by Norihiro Yagi/SHUEISHA Inc.

You're Reading in the Wrong Direction!!

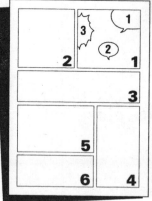

Whoops! Guess what? You're starting at the wrong end of the comic!

...It's true! In keeping with the original Japanese format, **7thGARDEN** is meant to be read from right to left, starting in the upper-right corner.

Unlike English, which is read from left to right, Japanese is read from right to left, meaning that action, sound effects and word-balloon order are completely reversed... something which can make readers unfamiliar with Japanese feel pretty backwards themselves. For this reason, manga or Japanese comics published in the U.S. in English have sometimes been published "flopped"—that is, printed in exact reverse order, as though seen from the other side of a mirror.

By flopping pages, U.S. publishers can avoid confusing readers, but the compromise is not without its downside. For one thing, a character in a flopped manga series who once wore in the original Japanese version a T-shirt emblazoned with "M A Y" (as in "the merry month of") now wears one which reads "Y A M"! Additionally, many manga creators in Japan are themselves unhappy with the process, as some feel the mirror-imaging of their art skews their original intentions.

We are proud to bring you Mitsu Izumi's **7thGARDEN** in the original unflopped format.

For now, though, turn to the other side of the book and let the adventure begin...!

—Editor